China's Township and Village Enterprises

Chief Editor: He Kang
Deputy Chief Editors: Guo Shutian Ma Jiesan

Foreign Languages Press

First Edition 2006

Home Page:
http://www.flp.com.cn
E-mail Addresses:
info@flp.com.cn
sales@flp.com.cn

ISBN 7-119-04184-3

Published by Foreign Languages Press
24 Baiwanzhuang Road, Beijing 100037, China
Distributed by China International Book Trading Corporation
35 Chegongzhuang Xilu, Beijing 100044, China
P.O. Box 399, Beijing, China
Printed in the People's Republic of China

The Huaxi Village Golden Tower houses a hotel and also shops.

One of the residential areas in booming Huaxi Village, Jiangsu Province

Minister of Agriculture He Kang chats with a villager who makes folk handicrafts at home.

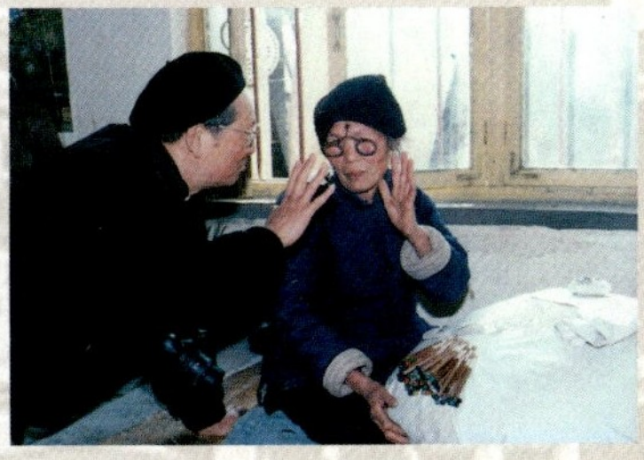

A local dishes restaurant run by villagers of the Li ethnic group at the foot of the Wuzhi Mountains, Hainan Province

Food packaging line of the Guangxi HAVLE Group, which produces five kinds of green fast food

The machinery workshop of Wanxiang System Co. Ltd, Zhejiang Province

The wire workshop of Shanxi Haixin Iron & Steel Group Co. Ltd

The textile workshop of Jiangsu Yangguang Group

The garment workshop of Beijing Gentleman Fashion Co. Ltd

The Business Town of the Fulin Group, Sichuan Province

Building constructed using a new type of steel structure produced by Panpan Security Industries Co. Ltd, Liaoning Province

The workshop of Henan Yalong Superhard Materials Co. Ltd

Conglin Group's 10,000-ton oil press went into operation on July 1, 2002 in Shandong Province.

The clothing workshop of Dalian Dayang Group Co. Ltd, Liaoning Province

Performance at the opening ceremony of the Chinese Countryside Tourism Festival held at the film and video production location of the Zhejiang Hengdian Group

The potato-processing line of Guangyou Tuber Crops Co. Ltd, Sichuan Province

Workers of the Guangxi Yuanantang Pharmaceuticals Co. Ltd checking medicines

Shop of Bajiahu Village's Cashmere Sweater Factory, Urumchi, Xinjiang

Foreword: China in General

Lying in East Asia on the west coast of the Pacific, China, with some 9.6 million sq km, has the third-largest territory in the world, next only to Russia and Canada, and is almost as large as Europe. It borders on Korea to the east, Russia to the northeast, Mongolia to the north, Kazakhstan, Kyrgyzstan, Uzbekistan and Tajikistan to the northwest, Afghanistan, Pakistan, Nepal, Sikkim, Bhutan and India to the west, and Myanmar, Laos and Viet Nam to the south. Its east coast is washed by the Bohai Sea, Yellow Sea, East China Sea and South China Sea, facing across the ocean the Republic of Korea, Japan, the Philippines, Indonesia, Malaysia and Brunei.

China stretches across the tropical, subtropical, temperate and frigid zones, with the terrain sloping down from west to east. Of its territory, mountains cover 33%, highlands 26%, rolling hills 10%, plains 12%, and basins 19%, and therefore its hilly land accounts for 69% of the total. The Himalayas, towering over the Qinghai-Tibet Plateau, with their highest point soaring over 8,844 m above sea level on the Chinese-Nepalese border, is known as the roof of the world, while Aiding Lake in the Turpan Basin of the Xinjiang Uygur Autonomous Region is 154 m below sea level.

China has a total coastline of more than 18,000 km, and its territorial waters are studded with more than 5,000 islands, the biggest of which is Taiwan, covering 35,760 sq km, Hainan coming next with 34,000 sq km and Chongming in the estuary of the Yangtze as third, covering more than 1,000 sq km. Its other lesser islands each with an area of upward of 200 sq km include Zhoushan, Donghai, Haitan, Changxing and Dongshan.

The vast territory of China is drained by thousands of rivers, of which 1,500 each drain at least an area of 1,000 sq km. The Yangtze,

China's longest river, runs 6,300 km along its main waterway, next only to the Nile and Amazon in length. The Yellow River, the second largest in China, is 5,464 km and the Yellow River valley was one of the cradles of Chinese civilization. The Tarim River in Xinjiang, running for 2,179 km, is China's longest inland river. In addition, China has the world's longest man-made waterway, the Grand Canal, running for 1,794 km from the capital Beijing to Hangzhou in east China. The Ertix River flows from Xinjiang and joins Russia's Arctic river system. The Yarlung Zangbo River originates in Tibet, runs through India and Bangladesh, and empties into the Indian Ocean. The Lancang River begins in China, runs through Myanmar, Laos, Thailand, Cambodia and Vietnam, and empties into the Gulf of Thailand. The Red River originates in China, runs through Vietnam and empties into the Pacific, too. In addition, there are the Nenjiang, the Songhua, the Heilongjiang, the Wusuli and the Liaohe rivers in northeast China, the Haihe and the Huaihe rivers in central China, and the Qiantang and the Pearl rivers in east and south China, respectively, all emptying into the Pacific. China abounds in lakes, notably Boyang, Dongting, Taihu, Hongze and Caohu lakes. Qinghai Lake in Qinghai Province is a very large salt lake.

As the largest gene bank in the world, China boasts more than 30,000 species of spermophytes, over 2,000 species of terrestrial animals, more than 2,000 species of birds, more than 2,000 species of fishes, and more than 400 species of beasts.

The country's political system has been based on counties and prefectures ever since the founding of the Qin Dynasty in 221 BC down through the Han, Tang, Song, Yuan, Ming and Qing dynasties. China today practices a five-level administrative jurisdiction of the central government — province (autonomous region or municipality directly under the central government) — prefecture (league) — county (banner) — township. There are 23 provinces, five autonomous regions (Xinjiang, Inner Mongolia, Ningxia, Tibet and Guangxi), four municipalities directly under the central government (Beijing, Tianjin, Shanghai and Chongqing), and two special administrative regions (Hong Kong and Macao). According to statistic figure made by the end of 2004, there are 333 prefectures and cities of that level, 2,862 counties and county-level cities, and finally 43,275 townships (and towns) at the grassroots level. China's legislation is based on people's congresses at all levels, and those exercising the state power at and above township level are people's congresses and their standing organs. There are some 740,000 administrative villages under township jurisdiction, and the administrative villages govern a total of more than four million natural villages. Each administrative village has a villagers' committee or villagers' team to exercise autonomy.

China is the most populous nation in the world today, with 56 ethnic groups totaling 1.3 billion people in 2004, accounting for almost 22% of the world's population. Among the Chinese people, 94% are majority Hans, and the rest are ethnic minorities. Where minorities live in compact communities, autonomous regions, autonomous prefectures (leagues), autonomous counties (banners) or autonomous townships (towns) exercise regional ethnic autonomy.

In terms of natural conditions and economic development, China falls into three regions: the eastern, the central and the western regions. The eastern region covers Beijing, Tianjin, Shanghai, Liaoning, Shandong, Jiangsu, Zhejiang, Fujian, Guangdong, Hainan and Taiwan (Taiwan remains to be reunified with the rest of China); the central region covers Heilongjiang, Jilin, Shanxi, Hebei, Henan, Anhui, Jiangxi, Hunan and Hubei; and the western region covers Shaanxi, Gansu, Ningxia, Qinghai, Xinjiang, Inner Mongolia, Yunnan, Guizhou, Sichuan, Chongqing, Tibet and Guangxi.

China is a traditionally agricultural country. Written records date China's agrarian history to more than 5,000 years ago. And as one of the cradles of Oriental agricultural civilization, China abounds with agricultural literature and has made world-renowned contributions in this field.

A feudal society arose in China during the Warring States Period (475-221 BC), which persisted for more than 2,000 years. Under feudalism the country had a self-sufficient natural agricultural economy. In such a large agricultural country, peasants comprised the absolute majority of the population, and were always held under feudal oppression. In the numerous changes of the feudal dynasties in Chinese history, peasant uprisings played a pivotal role. The country was reduced to the status of a semi-feudal, semi-colonial society after the Opium Wars of the mid-19th century, and the peasants, the most down-trodden sector of society, rose in repeated revolts against the feudal rulers. Dr. Sun Yat-sen, a great revolutionary, led the 1911 democratic revolution that toppled the Qing Dynasty, ending the country's feudal history and founding a republic. In 1921, the Communist Party of China (CPC) was born, and the great revolutionary Mao Zedong led the Chinese revolution by relying on the peasants to build rural revolutionary base areas to encircle and finally liberate the cities. Through the Northern Expedition, the Agrarian Revolution, the War of Resistance against Japanese Aggression and the Liberation War, the Chinese people finally succeeded in overthrowing imperialist, feudal and bureaucratic rule and founded the People's Republic of China in 1949, thereby ushering in a new era in Chinese history.

New China quickly recovered from the ravages of war, and soon restored the national economy to the level prior to the War of Resistance against Japanese Aggression. Then an agrarian reform was launched, realizing the dream of "land to the tillers" long cherished by Dr. Sun Yat-sen. In Old China, the landlords and rich peasants, who constituted less than 10% of the rural population, were in possession of 70-80 % of the farmland of the country, whereas the poor peasants, who comprised over 90% of the rural population, had only 20-30% of the land. The land reform placed 50 million ha of farmland and other means of production into the possession of some 300 million peasants, freeing them from the burden of working for or paying grain in rent to the landlords each year. The Chinese peasants thus won their liberation. After the land reform, Mao Zedong called on the peasants to organize themselves into mutual aid teams, then agricultural cooperatives (pooling land as shares), higher agricultural cooperatives (implementing collective ownership of the land) and the people's communes (based on a merger of the government and the commune). This practice dragged on until 1978. It was toward the end of that year that the prelude to the reform and opening-up policies was staged in rural China, following a resolution adopted at the Third Plenary Session of the 11th Central Committee of the CPC, based on the initiative of Deng Xiaoping, the chief architect of the reform and opening-up policies. In the rural reforms, a household-based land contracting system was introduced with the precondition that the land remained under collective ownership. The peasants obtained the right to contract the land for independent management and enjoyed the returns therefrom. That led to the disintegration of the people's communes, and the separation of the township governments from the management of the communes, thus the township governments were re-established. Indeed, the return of the right of land management to the hands of the peasants virtually meant a second emancipation for them. In the meantime, the peasants began to run industry and commerce, which led to the emergence of township and village enterprises (TVEs), an economic phenomenon that aroused the attention of the world. That was the beginning of a major economic and social change in rural China, a change which profoundly affected the dual economy of the Chinese urban and rural social structure. This book deals mainly with this historical change in rural China.

At its 16th Congress, held in November 2002, the CPC decided to propose to the Chinese nation the target of building a comprehensive well-off society. To realize this goal, it is necessary to place emphasis on the countryside, where the work is more difficult. Currently, China is undergoing the transition from a planned economy to a socialist market economy, and from an agrarian society to an industrial society, while confronted with a new situation that demands that China embrace the global economy in an all-round way. Rural China today has reached a new stage of development characterized by a readjustment of the industrial structure as the mainstream trend, and here the TVEs are shouldering an important historical mission to develop the rural economy comprehensively. Against this historical background, it is of tremendous significance, not only to the economy of China but also to that of the world at large, to sum up the experience of the TVEs in a comprehensive way, study the issues that have cropped up in the course of development, and assess the prospects for further development.

Contents

Chapter I

Historical Background of Township and Village Enterprises

Section 1 Industry in Old China

In order to investigate the rise of township and village enterprises (TVEs) in China, it is necessary to make a serious analysis of the specific situation of China and its historical process of industrialization.

According to archeological findings, human beings lived in China as long as two million years ago, and China was one of the cradles of world civilization. From about 457 BC, the traditional starting date of the Warring States Period, to the overthrow of the Qing Dynasty in the 1911 Revolution led by Dr. Sun Yat-sen , China was ruled by 16 dynasties, dominated by 182 emperors. The country was first unified in 221 BC, and made outstanding contributions to the world's development of education, culture, the arts, medicine, science and economy. Science and technology are important driving forces in the transition from an agrarian society into an industrial one. The study of the development of science and technology in China tells us that in history China was by no means backward in industry and technology.[1]

First, the development of science and technology in China prior to the Ming Dynasty (1368-1644) attained a marked characteristic of

---

[1] Li Shaobo: *A History of Science and Technology,* Central China College Press, 1986

creativeness. According to *A Chronology of Major Events in Natural Science* published in 1975 by the Shanghai People's Publishing House, some 300 major scientific discoveries and inventions had been made worldwide before the Ming Dynasty, of which 175, or 58.3% of the total, originated in China, and only some 20 items were made by Europeans on the basis of assimilating the major inventions and discoveries made by China. Dr. Joseph Needham in his *Science and Civilization in China* points out that China's discoveries and inventions far surpassed those of contemporary Europe, especially before the 15th century.

Second, the industrial revolution in the West began with the textile industry, which served as the cornerstone and "locomotive" of the industrial revolution. In China, however, the textile industry appeared much earlier than in Europe. The Chinese began rearing silkworms and weaving silk as a clothing fabric for the rich as early as in the Shang Dynasty, in the 16th century BC. In fact, China became known as "the country of silk." It was also in the Shang Dynasty that hemp was woven into clothing for the common people. Felt was made from wool for winter use during the Spring and Autumn Period (722-481 BC). The Chinese people began growing cotton first on Hainan Island, from where it spread to the Pearl River basin in the 11th century and to the Yangtze River valley in the 13th century, when cotton cultivation was introduced into the Weihe River basin from the western regions in the Yuan Dynasty (1206-1368).

Third, the industrial revolution stemmed from a revolution in tools (specifically, the loom) and motive power (specifically, the steam engine). In the field of textile tools, hand- and foot-propelled spinning wheels appeared before the Spring and Autumn Period in China. Around 100 BC, foot-pedaled single-spindle spinning wheels, foot-propelled looms capable of making patterns and shuttles were used extensively. By the year 220, during the period of the Three Kingdoms, foot-pedaled multiple-spindle looms were in use in China. By 960, during the Song Dynasty, 32-spindle looms driven by waterpower had appeared. During the Ming Dynasty, a great variety of specialized looms were in use for both cloth and silk fabrics.

Fourth, iron tools produced on a mass scale led to the formation of the industrial zone of the Eurasian continent. China discovered iron in the Shang Dynasty (1600-1046 BC), and iron smelting became a widespread occupation in the Spring and Autumn Period. Tools made of smelted iron appeared in China some 2,000 years earlier than anywhere else in the world.

Fifth, the capitalist mode of production appeared in China earlier than in other parts of the world. Karl Marx says: "That the majority of laborers work at the same time and at the same place (or in the same workshop) to produce the same category of commodities under the guidance of the same capitalist constitutes in both historical view and concept the point of departure for capitalist production."[1] During the Chenghua reign period (1465-1487) of the Ming Dynasty in China, the budding form of the capitalist mode of production was already obvious in some handicraft production departments in districts and cities with a more advanced commodity economy. In the mid-18th century — about the time the industrial revolution was taking off in Europe — this capitalist mode of production was gathering speed in China.

Sixth, historically China's industry accounted for a significant part of that of the whole world. In terms of total industrial output value, the ratio Chinese industry enjoyed was 32.8% in 1750 (in the reign of Emperor Qianlong of the Qing Dynasty), 33.3% in 1800 (in the reign of Emperor Jiaqing) and 29.8% in 1830 (in the reign of Emperor Daoguang), ranking first in the world. With the deepening of the industrial revolution in Europe, China's industrial production retrogressed in terms of its world ranking, accounting for 19.7% in 1860 (in the reign of Emperor Xianfeng), ranking second in the world; 12.5% in 1880 (in the reign of Emperor Guangxu), ranking third in the world; 6.2% in 1990, ranking sixth in the world, but still higher than Japan's, which was 2.4%. History shows that China's industry was quite developed and ranked first in the world before the European industrial revolution.

---

[1] Karl Mark: *Capital*, Vol. I, People's Publishing House, 1973

Figure 1-1 The Percentage of China's Industry in the World Total in History

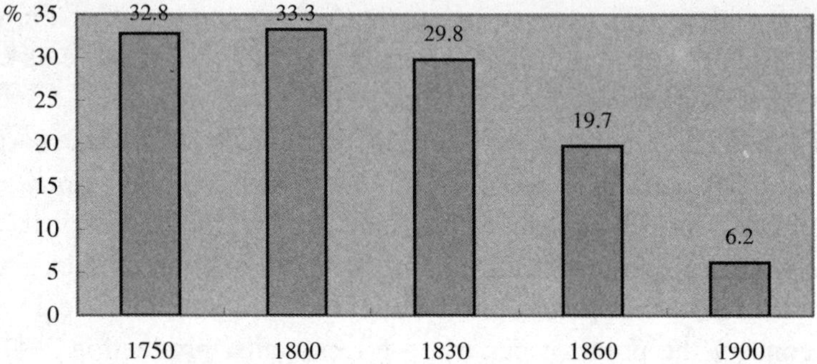

The facts cited above indicate that there were available conditions for an industrial revolution in China at that time, but unfortunately that revolution did not take place. This was because the feudal Qing regime was responsible for the following internal factors:

— Corruption and incompetence, that resulted in China becoming a weak country;

— The closed-door policy and arrogance that blocked the absorption of advanced technology and methods from abroad;

— Adherence to the outdated imperial examination system for choosing officials and the stifling anti-scientific ideology of Confucianism;

— The policy of emphasizing agriculture to the neglect of commerce, which put a brake on industrial development;

— The allowing of free trading in land, which led to capital being over-concentrated in land, thus hampering the growth of industry and commerce;

— Frequent wars and unrest, which also hampered the development of an industrial revolution.

China missed the opportunity of launching an industrial revolution. The industrial revolution has these five major features:

— A transition from manual production to mechanized production;

— The organizational form of production growing from that

of family and handicraft shops to large-scale social production in factories;

— Motive power for production changing man, animal, wind and water power to the steam engine;

— Transition from an agricultural economy to an industrial economy; and

— Movement of population from the countryside to the cities in a process of urbanization.

Those five features did not appear in China, and the Chinese economy remained a self-sufficient rural one. In the course of 100 years, China's world ranking in terms of industrial production dropped from first to sixth, in 1900, while that of Great Britain rose to first. In 1900, the per capita industrialization level of China was only 6%, the lowest among all the big nations, while that of Great Britain was 100%.

At the same time, the imperialist powers plundered China's resources and wealth, and unequal terms of trade were imposed on the country by imperialist gunboats. The British launched the first Opium War against China in 1840, and they, as well as other imperialist powers in their wake, swarmed into China to seize riches and land, and partitioned China into their spheres of influence. They also forced China to open trading ports, with extensive trafficking in opium, and to grant them extraterritoriality and special rights to run enterprises. The reparations they forced China to pay amounted to 85,000 tons of silver, more than 20 times the total investment by Chinese national industry at the time. Moreover, the opium trade deprived China of 7,500 tons of silver, and China's loss from unfavorable balance of trade was around 1,000 tons of silver every year. As Mao Zedong wrote, "The development of commodity economy in China's feudal society already bore the embryo of capitalism and without the influence of foreign capitalism, China would have grown slowly into a capitalist society."[1]

China became a semi-colony after the Opium War. Although the Qing regime launched a drive to build industry and the imperialists

[1] *Selected Works of Mao Zedong*, Vol. II, p. 589

with the protection of privileges set up factories on Chinese territory, industry remained rather weak up to the downfall of the Qing regime, in 1911, when Dr. Sun Yat-sen led the Chinese democratic revolution and founded the Republic of China. In the first year of the Republic, the total capital of modern Chinese industry was no more than 1.47 billion yuan, of which 1.22 billion yuan, or 83% of the total, was in the hands of foreign capitalists. That means foreign capital controlled the mainstay of China's modern industry. And of the 250 million yuan of Chinese capital, or 17% of the total industrial investment, Chinese bureaucrat capital controlled 88 million yuan, or 6% of the total, and national capital controlled 162 million yuan, or 11% of the total.

The position of the Chinese national bourgeoisie improved after the 1911 Revolution. In the belief that China's industrial revolution was just around the corner, Chinese national capitalists organized themselves into industrial bodies, and seized the opportunities offered by the new Republic to pave the way for such an economic advance. The Industrial Construction Society of the Republic of China was formed in Shanghai in 1912. The society set a goal of "building an industrial society with concerted efforts." The Chinese Industrial Group, founded in October 1912, advocated "developing industry in the interests of the well-being of the population throughout the country" and "aiming at the country's economic prosperity and the political progress of the Republic." Thanks to encouragement from the government and spurred by mass organizations, a wave of efforts to set up industrial enterprises swept the country. By 1913, the total industrial capital in China had risen to 1.54 billion yuan, including 1.24 billion yuan in foreign capital, or 80.5% of the total. Of the Chinese capital, the Chinese bureaucrat capital reached 147 million yuan, or 49%.

This coincided with the First World War (1914-1918) when the Western imperialist countries were too involved in the war to pursue their economic aggression against China, giving Chinese capitalists breathing space for development. Some 40 to 50 Chinese enterprises were founded every year. In 1920 (the ninth year of the Republic), the total industrial capital reached 2.37 billion yuan, up 53.9% as compared with 1913, with an average annual increase of 6.4%. Of this, foreign capital amounted to 1.67 billion yuan, or 70.4% of the total, averaging an annual increase of 4.3%, and the domestic capital amounted to 700 million yuan, or 29.6% of the total, averaging an annual growth of 12.9%. Of the domestic capital, the bureaucrat capital amounted to 270 million yuan, or 11.4% of the total of the domestic capital, averaging an annual growth of 8.9%, and the national capital amounted to 430 million yuan, or 18.2% of the total of the domestic capital, averaging an annual growth of 15.7%.

Figure 1-2 China's Industrial Composition 1912-1936

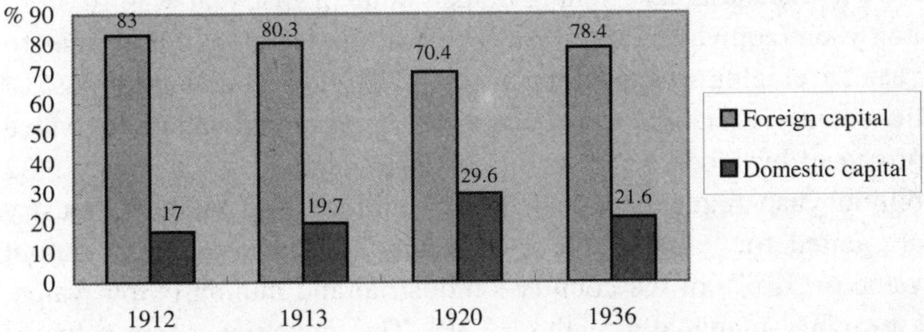

In the same year China's combined industrial and agricultural output value reached 21.9 billion yuan, including 16.52 billion yuan of agricultural output value, accounting for 75.4% of the total, and 5.38 billion yuan of industrial and mining output value, accounting for 24.6% of the total. The output value of modern industrial and mining enterprises reached about 1.066 billion yuan, making up 4.9% of the total industrial and agricultural output. But this situation did not last long. The imperialist powers headed by Japan and the US redoubled their economic aggression against China after World War I, while at the same time warlord strife, widespread unrest and exorbitant taxes and levies were devastating the domestic economy. By 1927 (the 16th year of the Republic), when the Chiang Kai-shek government was installed in Nanjing, the country had only 3,685,000 cotton spindles and 29,788 looms, and produced 437,000 tons of pig iron and 30,000 tons of steel. The bulk of industry in China was in the hands of the imperialists.

Although the Nanjing administration adopted some policies to revive the economy, the country's combined industrial and agricultural output value had reached only 30.6 billion yuan (or US$8.97 billion at the official rate of 3.41 yuan to US$1 at the time) in 1936, on the eve of the War of Resistance Against Japanese Aggression. This was an increase of a mere 39.7% in 16 years, averaging an annual growth of 2.1%.

The agricultural output value that year reached 19.9 billion yuan (equivalent to US$5.84 billion, an increase of 20.5% in 16 years, averaging an annual growth of 1.2% and accounting for 65% of the total industrial and agricultural output value.

The industrial and mining output value of that year was 10.5 billion yuan (equivalent to US$3.08 billion), an increase of 95.2% in 16 years, averaging an annual growth of 4.3% and accounting for 35% of the country's total industrial and agricultural output value. The value produced by modern industry (including mining) reached only 3.32 billion yuan (equivalent to US$970 million), and modern industry accounted for 9.2% of the total industrial and agricultural output value or 31.6% of the country's industrial and mining output value, averaging an annual growth of 7.3%. The industrial output value of the handicrafts industry was 7.18 billion yuan (about US$2.1 billion), accounting for 25.8% of the combined industrial and agricultural output value, or 68.4% of the total industrial output value.

Figure 1-3 The Ratio between Agriculture and Industry in China 1920 c.f. 1936

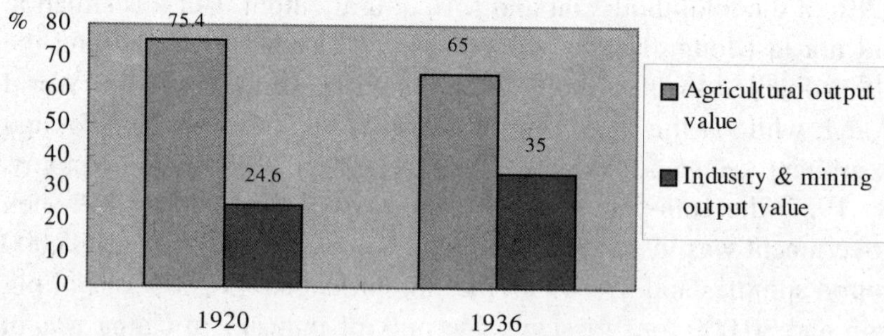

Despite the progress of the country's industry, it remained in the primary phase of light industry, with heavy industrial enterprises accounting for only 16% of the total industrial enterprises. Heavy industrial capital accounted for only 4.4% of the total industrial capital, and the number of workers employed by heavy industry was only 7.3% of the total industrial work force.

Of the total industrial capital of US$2.41 billion, US$1.89 billion was in the form of foreign capital, accounting for 78.4% of the total, and US$520 million was in the form of domestic capital, accounting for 21.6% of the total. Of the domestic capital, US$390 million was owned by the national bourgeoisie, accounting for 76% of the total domestic capital, and US$130 million was in the hands of the bureaucrat capitalist class, accounting for 24% of the total. China's annual output of cotton cloth was 3.46 billion m, ranking fourth in the world; that of pig iron, 810,000 tons, 12th in the world; that of steel, 410,000 tons, 18th in the world; that of raw coal, 39.56 million tons, seventh in the world; and that of electricity, 5.8 billion kwh. In per capita terms, China's electricity output was only 7.9 kwh; coal, 83 kg; pig iron, 1.7 kg; steel, 0.9 kg; and cotton cloth, 7.3 m — all far from the targets set in Dr. Sun Yat-sen‘s "Industrial Program."

At that time, China's economic lifeline was in the hands of the imperial powers, who controlled 73.9% of China's machine-mined coal, 96.5% of its pig iron output, 46.2% of its cotton spindles and 56.4% of its looms. If we make a comparison between China in 1936 and the Western powers in economic strength in 1939 before World War II, the GNP of the US was 7.4 times that of China, and the percentage of the labor force employed in agriculture in the US was 19%, as opposed to 80% in China. The combined feudal, bureaucrat capitalist and imperialist rule reduced China to a large semi-colonial, semi-feudal agricultural society.

The country's combined industrial and agricultural output value per capita in 1936 among the population of 469 million people at that time came to only US$19, and that of the output value of modern industry was US$2.1.

In 1937, Japan invaded China, and soon gobbled up a huge part of Chinese territory. The Japanese imperialists committed horrible crimes against the Chinese people, notably:

— Widespread destruction. In Shanghai alone, the Japanese aggressors destroyed more than 2,270 factories, causing a loss of more than 800 million yuan. Half of the industrial equipment in the Yangtze River Delta was destroyed or seriously damaged. The textile industry there suffered a loss of 20% of its equipment and 290,000 cotton spindles. In the eight years of the War of Resistance against Japan up to the Japanese surrender in 1945, China lost 36% of its pre-war industrial assets.

— Wanton plundering. For coal, Japan relied totally on supplies stolen from China under its occupation, and 70% of its pig iron supply came from China. In addition, it stole all the 13.08 million tons of steel China produced between 1935 and 1944.

— Massacres of Chinese people. More than 21 million Chinese people were killed or injured during the Japanese invasion.

— Heavy losses. China lost property worth some US$60 billion in the Japanese war of aggression.

According to the information published by the Ministry of the Economy of the KMT Government at the end of 1945, after the Japanese surrender, there were 1,382 industrial enterprises in China, with a combined capital of 7.41 billion KMT yuan. Among them, 411 were registered State-owned enterprises, accounting for 29.7% of the total, with actual capital invested totaling 1.91 billion yuan, or 25.8% of the total; and 971 were private enterprises, 70.3% of the total, with the actual capital investment totaling 5.5 billion yuan, or 74.2% of the total. However the ministry, in a statement published in July 1947, announced that the assets confiscated from the enemy and traitors' enterprises — worth a total of 4,000 billion yuan — all went into the pockets of the bureaucrat bourgeoisie. In May 1946, the capital controlled by the bureaucrat bourgeoisie constituted more than 80% of all industrial capital in the area under KMT rule. According to data issued in 1947, the enterprises owned by bureaucrat capitalists in the area under KMT rule accounted for 98% in the iron and steel industry, 78% in the power industry, 80% in coal mining, 100% in the oil industry, 67% in cement production, 60% in cotton spinning, and 90% in machine-refined sugar production. The KMT government failed to bring the national industry back to the level of 1936 before 1949, when it fled from the mainland of China to Taiwan.

Table 1-1 Major Industrial Products in China in 1949 and 1936

(Unit: 1,000 tons)

Product	1949	1936	Year with highest output	
Coal	32,000	39,560	1942	61,880
Pig iron	250	810	1943	1,800
Steel	158	414	1943	923
Electricity (billion kwh)	4.3	3.79	1941	5.96
Cotton cloth (billion m.)	1.9	2.8	1936	2.8

Source: Wang Haibo: *History of the Industrial Economy in New China* (Oct.1949-1957), Economic Management Press

That was the historical background against which the People's Republic of China was founded in 1949. Left behind by the fleeing KMT was a dilapidated and poverty-stricken country. Big in terms of population (549 million), it was small and poor economically. The country's gross national product (GNP) in 1949 was worth 55.7 billion yuan, averaging only 101.5 yuan per person; its industrial output value was 14 billion yuan, averaging 25.5 yuan per person and accounting for only 30% of the industrial and agricultural output value of 48.6 billion yuan; 89.9% of its people lived in the countryside, with the number of industrial workers accounting for only 1.6% of the population. China was thus a typical agricultural country at that time. Light industry accounted for 73.6%, and heavy industry for only 26.4%. The types of ownership of the country's industry are shown in the table below:

Table 1-2 Industrial Output Value and Work Force of Enterprises of Different Ownerships in China in 1949

Item	Output value		Fixed asset	Workforce	
Unit	billion yuan	(%)	billion yuan	1,000 men	(%)
Total	14			8,024	
State-owned	3.68	26.3	80.7	283	14.2
Cooperative	0.07	0.5		89	1.0
Joint public and private	0.22	1.6	1.5	106	1.2
Private	6.83	48.8	17.8	1,644	18.2
Foreign			12.1	126	1.4
Individual handicraftsmen	3.2	22.8		5,776	64.0

Source: *National Economic Construction and People's Living Conditions in China*, Statistics Press, 1958

A comparison between China and the US, the most industrially advanced country, and India, another developing country, in the output of major industrial products in 1949 is shown in the table below:

Table 1-3 Major Industrial Products in China, the US and India in 1949

Item	Electricity	Coal	Iron	Steel
Unit	billion kwh	billion tons	1,000 tons	1,000 tons
China	4.3	0.032	250	158
USA	345.1 billion	0.44 billion tons	49,820	70,740
India	4.9 billion kwh	0.032 billion tons	1,640	1,374

Source: Paul Kennedy: *The Rise and Fall of the Great Powers*, China Economy Press, 1989

From the above table we can see that it was on a very low level that China began its industrialization construction.

Section 2 The Industrialization Drive of New China

After its inauguration, the People's Republic of China set out to rehabilitate the national economy, improve the living conditions of the people and strengthen the national power, despite extreme difficulties. New China succeeded in restoring the national economy to the highest pre-war level by 1952, at an average annual GNP increase of 18%. In the same period, Japan's annual GNP increase was 9.7%, Britain's was 8%, that of the US was 5%, that of West Germany was 5%, France's was 5% and Italy's 4%. (See Table 1-4)

Table 1-4 Industrial and Agricultural Production 1949 c.f. 1952 and Pre-1949 Highest

Item	Unit	Highest year before 1949	Record before 1949	1949	1952
Industrial output value	100 million yuan	1936	286	140	343
Electricity	100 million kwh	1941	60	42	73
Coal	10,000 tons	1942	6,188	3,243	6,649
Steel	10,000 tons	1943	92	16	135
Cement	10,000 tons	1942	229	66	286
Cotton cloth	100 million m	1936	28	19	38
Agricultural output value	100 million yuan	1936	408	326	484
Grain	1 million tons	1936	138.7	108.1	154.4
Cotton	1,000 tons	1936	849	444.5	1,303.5
Large domestic animals	10,000 head	1935	7,151	6,002	7,646
Pigs	10,000 head	1934	3,853	5,775	8,977

Source: Liu Suinian: *The National Economy in the Rehabilitation Period*, Heilongjiang People's Publishing House, 1984

China launched its First Five-Year Plan in 1953, and set out to reform its agriculture, handicrafts industry, and capitalist industry and commerce. The Chinese people displayed unprecedented patriotic fervor and zeal for work. All this, plus the start of the building of a series of construction projects with aid from the Soviet Union and Eastern European countries, and good agricultural harvests in consecutive years, caused the country's GDP to grow at the high annual rate of 11.3%. Between 1952 and 1957 China gradually narrowed the GNP gap with other major countries. For example, the gap between China and the US narrowed from 13.3 times to 11.9 times, and that between China and Great Britain from 1.71 times to 1.66 times.

Table 1-5 GDP of China and Other Major Countries in 1952 & 1957

Year	1952		1957	
Item	Billion US dollars	Times more than China	Billion US dollars	Times over China
China	23.9		36.9	
US	317.6	13.3	440.5	11.9
Britain	41	1.71	61.4	1.66
France	37.4	1.56	57.8	1.57
W. Germany	29.4	1.23	51.5	1.39
Japan	16.2	0.68	30.7	0.83

Source: Paul Kennedy: *The Rise and Fall of the Great Powers,* China Economy Press, 1989

Based on the exchange rate between the Chinese yuan and the US dollar at the time, China's per capita national income in 1949 was US$18, rising to US$58 in 1957 — a 3.2-fold increase. But in comparison with the US, the gap narrowed from 56.3 times to 45.7 times. (See Table 1-6)

Table 1-6 Per Capita GDP of China and the US 1949-1957

(Unit: US$1)

Year	China	US	Times over China
1949	18		
1950	31	1,746	56.3
1951	35	1,964	56.1
1952	42	1,789	42.6
1957	58	2,561	45.7

Source: Liu Guoping: *A Comparison of Economic Growth Between China and the Rest of the World*, Hunan Publishing House, 1991

Beginning in the late 1950s, the world entered the period of the third technological revolution and overall economic restructuring. Some countries made rapid growth in the period. China, however, suffered serious setbacks in its economy owing to the raging of one political movement after another under the influence of the thinking of taking class struggle as the guiding principle. Despite occasional economic recoveries in between, China's national economy, as a whole, developed very slowly and the people's income did not increase much. China remained a poor and weak country.

Table 1-7 Major Economic Indices of China in 1965 and 1957

Year	Unit	1957	1965	Increase rate (%)	Average annual increase %
GDP	billion yuan	106.8	171.6	60.7	6.1
Per capita GDP	yuan	165	236.7	43.3	4.6
Industrial output value	billion yuan	70.4	140.2	99.1	9.0
Ratio to GDP	%	43.8	52.0		
Agricultural output value	billion yuan	55.7	83.3	49.6	5.1
Ratio to GDP	%	33.5	30.9		
Total population	million	646	725	12.2	1.45
Urban population	million	106	121	14.2	1.67
Urbanization rate	%	16.4	16.6		
Rural population	million	540	604	11.9	1.4
Ratio to total	%	83.6	83.4		
Work force	million	238	287	20.6	2.37
Rural workforce	million	193	234	21.2	2.44
Ratio to total	%	81.1	81.5		
Per capita urban income	yuan	205	237	15.6	1.8
Per capita rural income	yuan	79	100	26.6	2.99
Ratio between urban and rural income	:	1:2.6	1:2.4		

Source: *China Statistical Yearbook*

The above table shows:

(1) Although its GDP grew at an average annual rate of 6.1%, and its per capita income increased from US$58 to US$84.9, China remained an underdeveloped nation as compared with the US, where the per capita income was US$3,517. China's per capita income was only 2.4% of that of the US.

(2) The fact that industry accounted for only 52% of the total social product in 1965, that the rate of urbanization was as low as 16.6%, and that the per capita industrial output value was only 193 yuan (the equivalent of US$45), shows that China was in the initial stage of its industrialization drive, starting from the position of an agricultural country.

(3) China's rural population accounted for 83.4% of the total and the rural workforce accounted for 81.5% of the total in 1965. Yet the peasants had only 0.17 ha of land per person, and agricultural production remained at the level of manual labor plus draft animals. Therefore, the peasants, agriculture and the countryside constituted the fundamental issues of Chinese society.

(4) The Chinese peasants were constantly struggling to feed and clothe their families. The average peasant's income from the collective distribution, household sideline undertakings and other sources came to 100 yuan in 1965 (the equivalent of US36), 93% of which went on basic living expenses. The average peasant had only 226 kg a year of raw food grains. Meanwhile, the average urban resident's income was 237 yuan (equal to US$85), almost 2.4 times of that of a peasant's.

(5) The glaring difference between "advanced" industry and "backward" agriculture, the "advanced" cities and "backward" countryside, between the workers and the peasants, and between mental work and manual labor indicates that the economy of China was characterized by a marked duality[1]. Deepening this disparity was the rigid household registration policy[2] China implemented at that time, which restricted peasants' migration into cities.

---

[1] The theory of "dual economy" was first advanced by W. A. Lewis in an article "Economic Development with Unlimited Supplies of Labor," published on *The Manchester School* in 1954. For greater detail, please look up in Chapter 12 of this book.

[2] The policy of "unified purchase and marketing (of food grains)" was adopted by the Chinese government in 1953 to centralize the purchase and marketing of food grains as a means of stabilizing the grain price and ensuring the food supply to the urban residents. As a complementary policy, the Chinese government enforced the policy of dividing residence registration into urban residence registration and rural residence registration as a means to check the free movement of the rural population into cities.

(6) The prevailing policy at the time not only prevented the peasants working in cities, it did not allow them to engage in industry, commerce, construction or even catering. The peasants were tied to the land and to the villages they lived in, and that land was 0.17 ha per person on the average. That was the root cause of the backwardness of China's economy. Barred from going to cities to become workers, the Chinese peasants were forced to find a way out and blaze a new trail in their pursuit of a better life. That was the basic spur to the rise of township and village enterprises, the unavoidable choice for the industrialization of China's countryside.

Section 3 Historical Background of the Rise of TVEs

In the 1980s there arose in the vast countryside of China a new economic mode — the township and village enterprise (TVE). For some time, they eluded people's attention and were met the cold, doubtful eyes of those bound by traditional ideas. However, the Chinese peasants nurtured TVEs in the course of rural economic restructuring and economic development, and rural industry played a leading role in China's market economy after overcoming numerous difficulties and setbacks. Rural industry is now a mainstay of China's rural economy, and an important component of the national economy, producing half of the country's industrial added value, employing half of all Chinese workers and becoming a major foreign exchange earner and tax payer. For this, they have aroused the attention of the whole country and the rest of the world as well. Some people call TVEs "China's secret weapon for developing its economy." They are not only bringing a gradual change to the poor and backward countryside but also playing a pivotal role in the country's economic and social development. They are contributing a great deal to making the whole of China become well-off, changing the dual economic structure and blazing a new trail in industrialization with unique Chinese characteristics. This new type of economy has no precedent in the history of economic development anywhere in the world. This is hardly comprehensible, not only to outside observers but also to many Chinese scholars themselves. Actually it is a great creation accomplished by the Chinese rural dwellers in the light of the realities of China.

Before the emergence of TVEs, i.e. during the agricultural cooperation period in the 1950s, many agricultural cooperatives had already set up their own side-line teams to meet their specific needs in production and daily life.[1] In order to speed up the pace of industrialization, in 1958 the Central Committee of the Communist Party of China (CPC) urged the development of local industry, allowing township government — the grassroots political power, and the agricultural cooperatives — the grassroots economic organizations, to run industry. Such industry was called township industry or cooperative-run industry.

In order to boost the development of agricultural cooperatives with the aim of realizing the "transition from collective ownership to ownership by the whole people" and the "transition from socialism, to communism" in 1958 the CPC Central Committee decided to set up people's communes throughout the country, a major economic foundation of which was commune-run industry. The output of such industry in 1959 reached 10 billion yuan, accounting for 20.7% of the national total. However, owing to the miscalculation of the reality of China, neglect of the objective laws governing industrial development and blind reliance on government directives and mass movements to push economic growth, the country sustained tremendous waste and losses in human, material and financial resources. This, coupled with serious natural adversities and crop failures forced the CPC Central Committee to apply an abrupt brake to the development of industries run by communes and their production brigades. Industry run by communes and production brigades virtually came to a halt.

After the "cultural revolution" was unleashed in 1966, anarchism for a time was the order of the day. Chaos wrecked the country. Ex-

[1] By sideline production, it was actually the production activities other than farming in the agricultural cooperatives. Those non-farming activities were called sideline production as a contrast to farming.

cept for farming, which continued, all economic activities were paralyzed, and the national economy of the country was on the verge of total bankruptcy. But people must live and their need for daily necessities couldn't disappear just for the sake of the "revolution." Governments at all levels at the time had too many troubles themselves to intervene in the peasants' activities of running their own industries.[1] So some production brigades of communes in the coastal regions, where the commodity economy used to be relatively more developed, made use of their idle labor power and local material resources and professionals to run light industry and make small farm tools to increase their incomes. Later, some people's communes also ran their own industries. Such ventures set up by peasants spontaneously were called commune- or brigade-run enterprises.

The guideline for the development of commune- and brigade-run industry was to "run industries that are associated with and support farming." Under socialist public ownership and the planned economy, there were two taboos for peasants when running industry: One was that no individual or group of people were allowed to run industry privately or collectively, and only the communes and production brigades were allowed to run collectively-owned industry; and the other was that it was forbidden to engage in commerce, transportation or service industry. Moreover, such industrial endeavors were not covered by the State plan. The government material supply departments did not allocate or sell raw materials to communes or production brigades; the government commercial departments did not market their products; the banks (all owned by the State) did not grant them loans; power plants did not supply them with electricity; the administrative authorities for industry and commerce refused to grant them registration and business licenses. Enterprises run by communes and production brigades were "orphans," and they had to rely entirely on the market in the entire process from the purchase of raw materials through the marketing of their products. It was not until 1976 that the State Council gave approval to the Ministry of Agriculture and Forestry to set up the Bureau for Enterprises of

[1] The government at the time believed that the peasants' task was to grow crops and it was up to the government to run other economic undertakings in a planned way.

People's Communes to administer the affairs of enterprises run by communes and production brigades.[1]

The "cultural revolution" came to an end in 1976, and after that industries run by communes and production brigades began to grow again. At the end of 1978, a resolution was adopted at the Third Plenary Session of the 11th CPC Central Committee, declaring the start of economic reforms and opening to the outside, from the rural areas. This resolution was in fact based on the experience of the peasants of a small village called Xiao'gang in Fengyang County, in East China's Anhui Province. The villagers, with the approval of the village cadres, defied all risks to contract their collective land to individual households. Their venture won the support of Wan Li, then the first secretary of the Anhui Provincial CPC Committee. The contracting system fired the enthusiasm of local peasants for production because they could get returns from their labor. That autumn the village reaped a bumper crop, and that served as a prelude to rural reform across China. Based on the aspirations of the peasants, in 1980 the Chinese Government summed up the peasants' experience, and officially introduced the responsibility system of contracting land-use right to peasant households to replace the old commune system of collective labor and unified management and distribution. The Xiangyang Commune in Guanghan County, Sichuan Province took the lead in switching over to a township government. Soon the communes had been disbanded, and township governments had been set up all over the country, with the management of enterprises separated from government functions. The government administrative system in the countryside consists of the township (town) governments, administrative villages and peasant teams. The initiative and creativeness of the Chinese peasants were emancipated, and productivity shot up. As a result, the Chinese countryside produced a

[1] The name of this ministry under the State Council underwent many changes. It was called the Ministry of Agriculture between October 1949 and April 1970, the Ministry of Agriculture and Forestry between May 1970 and January 1979, the Ministry of Agriculture between February 1979 and April 1982, the Ministry of Agriculture, Animal Husbandry and Fisheries between May 1982 and April 1988 and the Ministry of Agriculture since.

tremendous surplus of labor power. In their efforts to find new jobs and increase their income, some peasants began to run private or partnership enterprises. As the enterprises run by peasants were mostly concentrated at the seats of township or town governments and in villages, the central government in 1984 decided to give such enterprises the name township and village enterprises (TVEs).

The Eighth Standing Committee of the National People's Congress (NPC) of the People's Republic of China at its 22nd session in 1996 adopted the "Law of the People's Republic of China on Township and Village Enterprises," which defines the TVE as follows: "It refers to various types of enterprises set up with investment mainly from rural collective economic organizations or peasants at townships and towns (including villages) and is responsible for supporting agriculture." More than half of the investment comes from rural collective economic organizations or peasants, and even if the investment made by the rural collective economic organizations or peasants does not exceed 50%, these organizations or groups of peasants still exercise control over the enterprises. The law also says, "The subsidiaries which TVEs set up in cities or the enterprises which rural collective economic organizations set up in cities responsible for supporting agriculture shall be treated as TVEs." In addition, "A TVE which is qualified as a body corporate shall be entitled to the status of a body corporate in accordance with the law." That means that a township enterprise should be qualified in three aspects: namely, first, the investment comes mainly from peasants; second, it is under the control of peasants; and third, it has the obligation to support agriculture. Qualified in those three aspects, an enterprise is considered a TVE, no matter whether it is in the countryside or in a city. A TVE differs markedly both from State-owned enterprises and the old commune-run enterprises in the following aspects:

(1) Ownership. TVEs have broken through the limitation of collective ownership. They have mushroomed into diverse types of ownership which have developed simultaneously, including publicly owned collective enterprises, such as those run by township and village collective economic organizations, joint-stock cooperative enterprises, liability limited companies, joint stock companies with

limited liability, associated enterprises with mixed ownership, Sino-foreign joint ventures, industrial and commercial undertakings run by individuals, and private enterprises.

(2) Lines of business. Instead of being confined to agriculture-related industry, TVEs may engage in manufacturing, transportation, construction, commerce, catering, tourism and other tertiary industries, and any type of industry other than those explicitly prohibited by the State.

(3) Geographical distribution. Nowadays, TVEs can be found both in the countryside and in cities, and even overseas, although they are mainly located in townships and villages.

(4) Area limit for peasants to run businesses. Although most rural people who have turned from farming to industry remain in their native villages or towns, there are a large number who have left their native places to work or run enterprises in cities. The employees of TVEs are all rural people, including local peasants and those from other parts of the country. The TVEs have become a major absorbent of surplus rural labor and have created millions of jobs.

(5) Internal management. Instead of following the model of State-owned enterprises, TVEs have the right to appoint and remove their executives, hire and fire workers, and raise and reduce wages. They have generally introduced the piecework system and distributed income based on labor contribution. In addition, they have introduced the dividend system paid on shares held by workers.

(6) Relations between industry and agriculture. Doing away with the traditional barrier between industry and agriculture, TVEs make industry support agriculture by allocating a portion of their profits to "aid and strengthen" agriculture.[1] At the same time, TVEs assume the duty of financing rural infrastructure and public undertakings, such as country roads, water and power supply facilities, schools, homes for the elderly, public libraries, etc.

[1] In the countryside, the collective enterprises run by townships and towns earmark part of their profits to support agriculture and finance agricultural capital construction. This includes price support to farm products, construction of small water conservancy projects, purchase of farm machines, the building of agro-technical setups and wages of agro-technicians.

(7) Mode of operation. TVEs, from the very beginning, have been excluded from the planned economy in production, raw material supply and marketing. They operate entirely in compliance with the law of the market economy.

(8) Ways of raising funds. TVEs do not have recourse to State allocations. They have to raise funds mainly on their own, with only a small amount borrowed from banks.

(9) Decision-making power. TVEs have independent decision-making power. With little intervention from the government, TVEs are entirely independent in operation and management, and profit and loss, and enforce their own discipline. They appoint their own managerial personnel and hire employees using the contract system on their own initiative. They therefore display great creative power and quick response to market changes.

(10) Pattern of growth. TVEs are growing gradually in size, from simple to complex, from crude to sophisticated, and from scattered to concentrated. Some of them have grown into powerful enterprise groups capable of competing on the international market.

Benefiting from the reform and opening-up policy and support from the government, TVEs have been developing vigorously. Deng Xiaoping called them a "shock brigade."[1] The noted sociologist Fei Xiaotong described them as "grassroots industry." Their organizational form and operation mode constitute a great creation by Chinese peasants. They have contributed their share to the sustained growth of China's economy over the past two decades and more, and provided economists with an important subject for theoretical research.

Section 4 Economic Basis for the Growth of TVEs

TVEs have grown on the basis of the rural handicraft and commune-run industry.

[1] *Selected Works of Deng Xiaoping*, People's Publishing House, 1993, Vol. 3, p. 251

In the early days of feudal society, the Chinese countryside comprised production units based on individual farm households engaged not only in farming, but also in spinning and weaving, silk reeling, farm produce processing, handicrafts, small tool making, paper making, mining, woodworking, construction and other household-based manual labor for a self-sufficient living. This way of life and mode of production persisted up to the time of the founding of the People's Republic of China. The year 1953 saw the launching of the socialist transformation of agriculture and the handicrafts industry, and the organization of agricultural cooperatives and handicraft production cooperatives in the Chinese countryside.

The output value of rural handicraft industry was 1.16 billion yuan in 1949, 1.36 billion yuan in 1950, 1.49 billion yuan in 1951, 1.83 billion yuan in 1952 and 1.96 billion yuan in 1953.

The socialist transformation drive began in 1953, when the rural handicrafts industry was organized into a large number of cooperatives where handicraftsmen lived in relatively compact communities, and into sideline production brigades or teams in agricultural cooperatives where they lived in scattered groups. Sideline production was attached to agriculture, and members of the sideline brigades or teams joined in farming during the busy farming season, and took up handicrafts and other sideline production during the slack season. Members of the handicraft production brigades or teams within the agricultural cooperatives joined the other members of the cooperatives in the appraisal of their work contribution on the basis of work-points and obtained their shares of the distribution accordingly. The output value of rural handicraft production was 1.97 billion yuan in 1954; 2.11 billion yuan in 1955; 2.26 billion yuan in 1956; and 2.29 billion yuan in 1957.

In 1953, the CPC laid down a general line for the transition from new democracy to socialism through the industrialization of the country and the socialist transformation of agriculture, handicraft industry, and capitalist industry and commerce (the "Three Transformations"). Meanwhile, the First Five-Year Plan was launched. By 1956, the "Three Transformations" had been completed, and industrialization unfolded with assistance from the Soviet Union and patterned after the Soviet model. Agriculture made some progress at the time, but the life of the Chinese peasants remained very difficult. Visiting Moscow in November 1957 as head of the CPC delegation to the World Conference of Communist and Workers Parties there, Mao Zedong, with the idea of speeding up China's economic development and pace of industrialization, proposed to Soviet Premier Nikita Khrushchev that the Soviet Union should catch up with the US in 10 years and China should catch up with Britain in 15 years.

The CPC Central Committee held a working meeting on January 11, 1958 in Nanning, in the Guangxi Zhuang Autonomous Region. It was attended by some of the leaders of the CPC Central Committee and CPC secretaries from nine provinces and two municipalities. At that meeting, known as the Nanning Conference, summing up the experience in revolution and construction during the First Five-Year Plan period was put at the top of the agenda, and the plan for 1958, the Second Five-Year Plan and a long-range State plan were discussed. At this meeting, Mao Zedong put forth the general line of "going all out, aiming high and building socialism with greater, faster, better and more economic results." Many local leaders urged that local governments should be allowed to develop local industry. Mao agreed to this proposal, saying, "How long will it take for local industry to exceed agriculture (in output value)? Five years? Ten Years? We need a plan."

Based on the essence of Mao's speech at the meeting, the State Economic Commission drew up a document titled, "Views of the Chinese Communist Party Central Committee on the Question of Developing Local Industry." The draft was approved by the CPC Central Committee on March 23, 1958. With the approval of the CPC Central Committee Political Bureau at its April 5 meeting held in Chengdu, the document was distributed throughout the country for implementation.

The document pointed out in the first place the great importance of developing local industry: "On the question of developing industry, the Chengdu Conference explicitly puts forth the principle of developing central and local industry simultaneously. In view of the more direct and closer relationship between local industry and agriculture, implementation of this principle shall enhance the simultaneous development and mutual support of industry and agriculture more effectively and bring into full play the enthusiasm of the local governments and people in running industry ever more extensively and amply, hence accelerating the industrialization and agricultural technical transformation of our country."

The document, for the first time in history, affirmed that cooperatives and townships should run industry. It pointed out, "Generally, local industrial enterprises at present are run by counties, townships and cooperatives (agricultural cooperatives and handicraft cooperatives) or run by a county and some cooperatives or by a township and some cooperatives. Small industry run by agricultural cooperatives should primarily meet the needs of the cooperatives themselves, such as farm tool repair, the making and processing of farm fertilizer and the processing of farm produce on a very limited scale."[1]

A new situation appeared following the circulation of this document at the grassroots level across the country.

Many localities were overzealous, and lost no time building local industry on a large scale in total disregard of the actual conditions. Industrially backward Gansu Province, for example, set up more than 1,000 factories in February and March 1958. The number of new factories and mines increased to 3,500 between March and May and the number of mines further shot up to 220,000 by June, of which 185,000 were set up by rural cooperatives. Each township in the province had an average of 110 factories and mines and each agricultural cooperative had an average of 12 factories and mines. Dingxian County in Hebei Province built as many as 1,530 factories in a little more than one month, with 35 new factories going into operation each day. Butha Banner in Hulun Buir League, Inner Mongolia, a tiny county with a population of a little over 130,000,

---

[1] *Selected Important Archives since the Founding of the People's Republic of China*, compiled by the Archive Research Center of the CPC Central Committee, Central Archives Press, 1995, Vol. 11, pp. 223-227

had 307 factories and mines by the end of May, 1958.[1]

Deng Zihui, former vice-premier of the State Council in charge of rural work, wrote an article titled, *The Great Significance of Township-Run Industry* in the May 1958 issue of the *Newsletter of Rural Work.* In the article, Deng wrote, "Since Chairman Mao and the CPC Central Committee have given the directive to develop industry and agriculture simultaneously and called on the 'whole Party and the entire people to run industry,' and 'all the townships and cooperatives to run industry,' the local governments have displayed tremendous enthusiasm in developing local industry," adding, "According to information published by the State Statistics Bureau, more than 800,000 small and medium-sized enterprises are under construction across the country." He believed that the township-run industry was of profound importance in that:

First, "it has rejected the old dogma that the development of the economy should be controlled in lineal administration by different government departments according to different industries, thus affecting those industries' close cooperation with agriculture. Now it is time to unify the many divisions of industry into a whole system so that it will play a great role in promoting the great leap forward of agriculture."

Second, "industry run by townships and agricultural cooperatives will also play a big role in regulating the income of the agricultural cooperatives."

Third, "industry run by townships and agricultural cooperatives will play an even greater role in helping bring about a great leap forward of industry as a whole."

And finally, "industry run by townships and agricultural cooperatives will create the material conditions for the future communist society."

On the issue of how to run industry, Deng Zihui pointed out, "Industry run by townships and cooperatives should follow the prin-

---

[1] Figures cited in this passage are quoted from the book *The Surging Tides of the Great Leap Forward*, by Xie Xiangtao, Henan People's Publishing House, 1986, p. 57

ciple of relying on local resources and starting with simple facilities. It should give full play to the 'indigenous masters,' 'local methods' and 'locally available materials,' and develop gradually in scope and technical level. They should make whatever is possible with whatever is available locally, and start production while building to achieve quick results with as little investment as possible. It is impractical to start on a large scale and in a showy way, and then wait for the purchase of big machines." [1]

In the latter half of 1958, a craze for setting up people's communes swept across the vast areas of rural China. Mao Zedong and some other leaders at the time hoped to realize the transition from collective ownership to ownership by the whole people and the transition from socialism to communism through the people's communes. They imagined that agricultural modernization and rural industrialization could be realized through the people's communes. A popular ballad of the time contained the following line: "Communism is Heaven, and the commune is the bridge to Heaven." On the question of the relations between rural industrialization and the people's communes, the decision-makers of the country at the time believed the commune to be the parent of rural industrialization, and rural industrialization to be the economic basis for the people's commune.

The CPC Central Committee, at a meeting at Beidaihe on August 29, 1958, adopted "A Resolution of the Central Committee of the Communist Party of China on the Question of Setting Up People's Communes in the Countryside," which pointed out: "Large and comprehensive people's communes have not only appeared but are developing extensively in many localities and very rapidly in some localities. A possible high tide of the development of people's communes may emerge across the country with an irresistible force. Building fully developed people's communes in agriculture, forestry, animal husbandry, fisheries and sideline production, and with an integration of industry, agriculture, commerce, education and military affairs is a fundamental guiding policy necessary for guiding

[1] *Deng Zihui's Works*, People's Publishing House, 1996, pp. 518-521

socialist construction at an accelerated pace and realizing ahead of schedule the gradual transition from socialism to communism." [1]

The CPC Central Committee held a meeting at Mount Lushan in July 1959 after the Beidaihe Meeting. At the Lushan Meeting, Mao Zedong said that he did not invent the people's commune but he had the right to advocate it. The idea of the people's commune is said to have been first mentioned by Chen Boda in the winter of 1956. Chen, at the time an alternate member of the Political Bureau of the CPC Central Committee and political secretary to Mao Zedong, carried out an investigation of rural work in Liantang Township, Fujian Province. He wrote a report early in 1957 on his findings, and presented it to the Party Central Committee. In the report, he proposed that township governments be merged with agricultural cooperatives to become the grassroots institutions, and the local supply and marketing cooperatives and credit cooperatives might also be merged with this basic unit.

In 1958, Chen went to Hubei Province on an investigation tour. There, he found that some agricultural cooperatives ran both agriculture and industry. That reminded him of an opinion of Engels to the effect that in the future the same people will run both agriculture and industry, instead of two different classes doing so. Chen thought that it would be unrealistic if an agricultural cooperative running both agriculture and industry continued to be called an "agricultural production cooperative."

In February and March that year, Chen Boda mentioned his idea to Mao Zedong, and they discussed the question of integrating township administration with the agricultural production cooperatives, and integrating industry, agriculture, commerce, education and military affairs into one institution as an embryo of communism. According to Bo Yibo's reminiscences, Mao Zedong described his ideal picture of the future society to President Liu Shaoqi, Premier Zhou Enlai, CPC propaganda chief Lu Dingyi and others in Guang-

---

[1] Archive Research Center of the CPC Central Committee: *Selected Important Archives since the Founding of the People's Republic of China*, Central Archives Press, 1996, Vol. 11, pp. 446-447

zhou in 1958. At the second session of the Eighth CPC Congress, held in May that year, Lu Dingyi said: "When speaking of the future of our country decades later, Chairman Mao and Comrade Liu Shaoqi said that by then there would be many communist communes, each with its own agriculture, industries, universities, middle schools and primary schools, hospital, scientific research institutions, shops, service industry, transportation facilities, kindergartens and public canteens, clubs and police, and many other things. A number of rural communes clustered around a city would form a bigger communist commune. The Utopia dreamed of by some people in the past will become a reality, and shall be surpassed." [1]

Chen Boda in his article *"New Society, New People"* published in July 1958, in the third issue of the magazine *Red Flag*, mentioned the term "people's commune" for the first time." He wrote: "In fact, this is a people's commune that integrates industry with agriculture."

In August 1958, in the fourth issue of *Red Flag*, Chen Boda published the text of a speech he had made at Peking University. In that article, titled "Under the Banner of Mao Zedong," he wrote that early in 1958 "Chairman Mao was thinking of merging industry, agriculture, commerce, education and culture, and the militia into big communes in an orderly and progressive way, to make them into the basic units of our society. In the commune, industry, agriculture and exchange would constitute the people's material life, and the entire people in arms would defend this material and spiritual life. Before the system of exploitation of man by man is completely extirpated from the globe, it will be necessary for the entire people to be in arms. Comrade Mao Zedong's thinking about this type of commune is based on the experience of actual life." [2]

Mao Zedong first used the term "people's commune" on August 9, 1958, on a visit to the Xiaotun Agricultural Production Coopera-

[1] Bo Yibo: *A Review of Several Important Policy Decisions and Major Events*, CPC Central Party School Press, 1993, p. 731

[2] *Mao Zedong's Scripts since the Founding of the People's Republic of China*, Central Archives Press, 1992, Vol. 7, p.317

tive in Licheng County, Shandong Province. When local officials told him that a number of agricultural cooperatives intended to merge into a big farm, Mao said, "Better set up a people's commune. It has the advantage of integrating industry, agriculture, commerce, education and military affairs into one for the convenience of leadership." This news was released by Xinhua News Agency across the country on August 12, which touched off a nationwide high tide of building people's communes. In the short span of one month, virtually all people in rural China were in people's communes. People at the time believed that the people's commune was in fact the creation of a fairly complete and concrete model of socialism put into practice, thus making an unprecedented, world-famous social experiment among the 600 million people on the mainland of China. This experiment was going on at a time when the system of exploitation had been eliminated and a socialist system had been established. It was aimed at addressing the problem of how to advance from socialism to communism. In promoting the general line of "going all out, aiming high and building socialism with greater, faster, better and more economic results," the CPC Central Committee in 1958 cited the general line, the Great Leap Forward and the people's commune as the "Three Red Banners."

The CPC Central Committee and Mao Zedong believed that the development of the rural people's communes would open the road to the gradual industrialization of rural China. The people's communes followed the principle of developing industry and agriculture simultaneously, and integrating them, which would lead to closing the disparity between the cities and the countryside and between workers and peasants, help realize the industrialization of the country, and help build China into a socialist country with highly advanced industry, modern agriculture, and modern science and culture. In the people's commune, the land, manpower and products were nominally the public property of the commune, but actually in the possession of the production teams. In other words, there was ownership at the three levels of the commune, the production brigade and the production team, with the production team as the basis. The land, labor power, draft animals, and farm machines and tools were fixed to the production team, and known as the "four things fixed to the team."

Mao believed that it would take a fairly long period of time for a poor team to become rich. The first phase would be a process of mechanization and electrification of agriculture, industrialization of the commune and industrialization of the country, a process of the rise of the socialist and communist awakening and the rise of the ethical quality of the people's communes, and a process of raising the people's educational, cultural and scientific levels. And there would be second and third phases before the accomplishment of socialist construction. It was necessary to make the incomplete socialist system become complete socialism through commune ownership, that is, a transition from ownership by the production team to ownership by the production brigade and then to ownership by the commune, from collective ownership to ownership by the whole people, and finally from ownership by the whole people under socialism to that under communism. At the time, the few things owned by the communes such as the commune-run industry, commune-run undertakings, and the public accumulation fund and public welfare fund in the control of the commune, did not amount to much. Still, Mao believed that "here lies our greatest and brightest hope."

Guided by such thinking, commune-run industry was born at the time of the inception of the commune itself. In the early days of the communes, this comprised the following:

First, industry originally run by the agricultural cooperatives was turned totally into the property of the commune and commune-run industry without any compensation. For example, the 185,000 industrial enterprises set up by the higher form of agricultural production cooperatives under the slogan of energetically developing local industry in Gansu Province were turned into commune-run industrial institutions.

Second, all the former handicraft cooperatives in the countryside were placed under the guidance of the communes, and became commune-run industry. By June 1959, a total of 35,300 handicraft cooperatives had become commune-run handicraft institutions.

Third, a mass movement was launched to build industry. In this nationwide drive, rural people built more than 600,000 crude blast furnaces, more than 9,000 small coal mines, more than 4,000 small hydroelectric power stations, more than 9,000 small cement plants, and more than 80,000 farm tool repair shops. And that did not include numerous crude chemical fertilizer plants, crude pesticide plants, crude machine plants and food-processing mills.

Fourth, some small and medium-sized State-run enterprises were handed over to people's communes to manage, but they remained responsible for handing their profits to the State.

Fifth, the communes seized fund, equipment, factory buildings, raw materials from the commune members in the name of "communization" to organize new commune-run industrial institutions. An investigation conducted by a rural work team of Heilongjiang Province in the Taiping People's Commune in Shuangcheng County, Heilongjiang Province disclosed that the commune found it lacking in funds, equipment, buildings, technicians and raw materials when it set out to build industry. In order to raise funds, the commune mobilized its members to deposit money in the local credit cooperative voluntarily, and in just three days it raised 91,000 yuan. At the same time, the commune organized sideline production on a large scale, and raised another 93,000 yuan. By the end of 1958, it had succeeded in building 302 factories of varying sizes and types.

Under the dominant "Left" thinking at the time, all the local industries were owned and run by people's communes for the sake of making the transition from collective ownership to ownership by the whole people. In just four months toward the end of 1958, the commune-run industrial enterprises numbered 6.02 million, with a combined output value of 6.25 billion yuan, accounting for 5.8% of the national total of industrial output value. However, the commune-run industrial enterprises all suffered from a shortage of funds, machinery and equipment and technical personnel. They were called "small, indigenous and mass" industrial enterprises because they had only crude (indigenous) machines, crude machine tools, crude blast furnaces and crude ball bearings, and operating the equipment were indigenous "specialists" who used to be peasant blacksmiths, carpenters and other indigenous "specialists." What they produced was crude steel, crude iron, crude chemical fertilizer and crude pesticides. They were not modern factories, but just small and very simple workshops, each with only a few workers.

Commenting in 1958 on this "small, indigenous and mass" fashion of commune-run industry, an article in the 13th issue of the Communist Party organ *Red Flag* wrote in glowing terms: "Generally speaking, commune-run industry built in the mass movement is small and indigenous. But that is by no means unexpected. This 'small' and 'indigenous' feature is bound to change in the course of development. Within what is 'indigenous' there are not only crude things, but also sophisticated things. We expect that the majority will become sophisticated gradually. The 'small, indigenous and mass' feature is a product of the great mass movement that has been sweeping across our country, and this new product has tremendous vitality." In an attempt to help commune-run industry develop, Mao proposed that the State invest in them. He said: "I propose that the State invest in the communes hundreds of millions or dozen billions of yuan in the coming decade to help them develop industry, and help the worse-off production brigades develop production."[1]

Unfortunately, it turned out to be just the opposite of what people desired. The result of the steel-making drive with mass participation by the people's communes in an effort to develop industry in 1958 was a massive destruction of forests, untold waste of resources, serious damage to the natural environment, mass production of useless products, great waste of labor, and ultimately a grave injury to the zeal of the people for socialism.

After the people's communes were set up, Mao Zedong was elated that his "ideal socialism" was about to come true, but on the other hand, he was not sure what to do next. So within less than half a year following the Beidaihe Meeting, he made two investigation tours of the country. On his first inspection tour, of Hubei, Anhui, Jiangsu and Shanghai September 10-29, 1958, what he heard everywhere was applause, and he discovered nothing. But on the next

---

[1] *Mao Zedong's Scripts since the Founding of the People's Republic of China*, Central Archives Press, 1993, Vol. 8, p. 69

trip, to Shijiazhuang Prefecture and Handan Prefecture in Hebei Province and Xinxiang Prefecture in Henan Province, he found that the "wind of communism" was blowing fiercely on the issues of ownership and distribution in the people's communes and that the distinction between collective ownership and ownership by the whole people and between socialism and communism was seriously blurred. That greatly hurt the enthusiasm of the peasants, and was disruptive of production. He was shaken by the fact that his original "ideal socialism" was refuted by facts and the practice of the people. That made him stop to think and to take into consideration the actual situation of China to find solutions.

The CPC Central Committee convened its Zhengzhou Meeting, Wuchang Meeting, second Zhengzhou Meeting and then the Shanghai Meeting between November 1958 and November 1959. Those meetings were meant to solve the problem of "the wind of communism" (requisition of the property of agricultural cooperatives and commune members without compensation), the problem of egalitarianism and reallocation of materials and labor without remuneration between communes, between production brigades and between commune members, the problem of banks demanding repayment of loans ahead of schedule, blind guidance by commune leaders, exaggerated statistics in accounting statements and the problem of making a quick transition from fixing the basic accounting unit on production teams to production brigades, and then from production brigades to communes, and the transition from collective ownership of the communes to ownership by the whole people. Those were known at the time as the "five evil winds." And making things worse were the extensive practice of setting up public canteens in the communes where food was provided free of charge, resulting in untold waste.

The crops growing in the fields promised a good harvest in 1958, but no significant harvest was brought home. Then the country was hit by bad weather for three consecutive years — 1959-1961. In normal years, about 20 million ha of farmland may be hit by bad weather and half of it may suffer crop failures. But more than 41 million ha of farmland was hit by drought or flood, and 13.33 million ha suffered losses in 1959. The areas of farmland hit by natural disasters and those actually suffering losses were 53 ha million and 22.7 million ha, respectively, in 1960, and 53 million ha and 26.7 million ha in 1961. The crop losses grew year by year, reducing the total food output (including that of tubers) to 200 million tons in 1958, to 170 million tons in 1959, to 143.5 million tons in 1960 and to 147.5 million tons in 1961. Coupled with a shortage of non-staple foodstuffs, the supply of food grain averaged 198 kg per person in 1958, and the figure dropped to 187 kg in 1959, to 164 kg in 1960 and 159 kg in 1961. Despite their heavy manual work, Chinese peasants got a food grain supply of only 183 kg per person in 1959, 156 kg in 1960 and 154 kg in 1961, averaging only 0.42 kg per person per day. Thousands upon thousands of people died, and nearly a hundred million suffered from dropsy as a result of malnutrition. The specter of hunger loomed over China.

At the critical moment, the CPC Central Committee summed up this experience, and lost no time readjusting its policies. In order to tide over the food shortage, the central government took emergency measures with the guiding principle of "readjustment, consolidation, filling out and raising the standard." It was decided to make redoubled efforts to boost grain production by strengthening the agricultural front and curtail the input in other fields. The mass-scale steel-making drive was halted. Agricultural capital construction was suspended. The labor power originally deployed on the industrial front was moved back to farming. More than 50 million urban residents and workers were resettled in the countryside. In order to stabilize the countryside and agricultural production, the CPC Central Committee worked out the "Working Regulations for Rural People's Communes" ("the 60 articles") between March and May 1961. The document from its first draft to the final version all emphasized the fixing of the basic accounting unit on the production team, fixing the land, labor power, draft animals and farm implements on the production team, reintroducing the system of distribution on the basis of labor contributed and the basic policies of allowing once more freedom of household sideline production, private plots assigned to individual households as vegetable gardens, rural farm produce markets and other relevant basic policies.

Commune-run industry also underwent readjustment in the following four phases:

Phase 1: The steel-making drive with mass participation was called off. The State-owned enterprises originally handed over to the custody of the communes and the handicraft cooperatives originally merged with the communes were returned to the charge of the original authorities. The commune-run industrial enterprises were changed from independent undertakings to ones closely connected with agricultural production and to be operated with the surplus labor during slack farming seasons, with the exception of those that required year-round operation. Thus commune-run industry was reduced to a position subordinate to agriculture, and made to shrink in business scope. The tasks of commune-run industry were defined as:

(1) Primarily to make and repair farm implements;

(2) Simple processing of local farm produce and sideline products;

(3) Producing traditional local products; and

(4) Mining small pits, making bricks and tiles, lime, and other crude building materials. Commune-run industry which competed with State-run industry for raw materials should make way for State-run industry.

After the readjustment and consolidation, the number of commune-run industrial enterprises was reduced from 6.02 million with a combined output value of 6.25 billion yuan at the end of 1958 to 870,000 with a combined output value of 7.34 billion yuan in May 1959, and further down to 700,000 with a combined output value of 10 billion yuan at the end of 1959.

Phase 2: The CPC Central Committee determined that the production brigades of people's communes should not run enterprises. In its "Express Directive Regarding the Current Policies Concerning Rural People's Communes" released on November 3, 1960, the CPC Central Committee pointed out: "All district administrations (production brigades), as representative organs of the communes, should focus on supervising the work of the production teams, and should not directly run production enterprises. Those already running production enterprises should hand them over to production teams or to communes, so that the brigades do not compete with the production teams for labor power and production materials, in order to overcome the practice of egalitarian acquisition." [1]

Phase 3: The people's communes should not run enterprises. The CPC Central Committee, in its "Revised Draft Regulations on the Work of Rural People's Communes" released on September 27, 1962, pointed out: "The management committee of a people's commune generally should not run enterprises in the coming few years. Those which have set up enterprises should stop running them if the enterprises lack the necessary conditions for production or are disliked by the people. As for those required to remain, they should be determined through discussion at the congresses of the commune members, and handed to handicraft cooperatives or production teams or to become individual handicraft shops or household sideline undertakings in light of the actual conditions. Only a limited number of enterprises should be allowed to be run by communes with the approval of the congresses of the commune members and the official approval of the county people's government."[2]

Phase 4: The communes and production brigades stopped running enterprises. The CPC Central Committee and the State Council jointly issued the "Resolution Regarding the Development of Rural Sideline Production" on November 22, 1962, which stipulates: "The communes and production brigades in principle shall not run enterprises, nor set up specialized sideline production teams. Enterprises originally run by communes or production bridges on the basis of acquisition of sideline operations from production teams should be handed back to production teams. If a production team is unable to operate any enterprise, the enterprise may be run jointly by a number of production teams or in the form of a joint venture with profits

---

[1] Archive Research Center of the CPC Central Committee: *Selected Important Archives since the Founding of the People's Republic of China*, Central Archives Press, 1996, Vol. 13, p. 664

[2] Archive Research Center of the CPC Central Committee: *Selected Important Archives since the Founding of the People's Republic of China*, Central Archives Press, 1997, Vol. 15, p. 621.

distributed on the basis of shares, or commonly owned by all the production teams of a brigade which can adopt unified management. For the few communes and brigades which used to be basic accounting units and their sideline enterprises are well run, the enterprises may continue to be operated by communes or brigades."

The Resolution also points out: "Farming and sideline production in our country have always gone hand in hand, and promoted one another. Farming is the main occupation, while sideline production is an important component. Farming provides sideline production with food grains and raw materials whereas sideline production accumulates funds for farming and produces part of the material for reproduction in farming as a way to help increase the income of the peasants. Meanwhile, sideline production also supplies part of the industrial raw materials and export materials, increases the number of small commodities needed on the market and is useful for the enlivening of both the urban and the rural economy." With regard to enterprises and sideline projects run by production teams, the Resolution stipulates: "Priority should be given in general to the revival of the production of those traditional products urgently needed by the people in their daily life or in production. New projects shall not be added unless the necessary conditions are available. Positive efforts should be made to run those sidelines that serve farming. Other sidelines should be run so long as they do not interfere with farm production. Projects with sufficient supply of raw materials, small investment and quick returns should be given free rein to develop. If the raw materials are needed by State-run industry, priority should be given to State-run industry. A few enterprises unfit for State-run industry to operate may be transferred to production teams to run."[1]

After the 1962 decision of the CPC Central Committee and the State Council that the people's communes and their production brigades in general should not run industry, commune and production brigade-run enterprises were closed down by the government. Those

---

[1] Archive Research Center of the CPC Central Committee: *Selected Important Archives since the Founding of the People's Republic of China*, Central Archives Press, 1997, Vol. 15, p. 700.

peasants who had been drawn into the enterprises thus divorced from farming returned to their original production teams. Thanks to the resolute measures taken, commune-run industries were reduced in number from 700,000 with a combined output value of 10 billion yuan in 1959 to 117,000 with a combined output value of five billion yuan in 1960, further to 45,000 with a combined output value of 1.98 billion yuan in 1961, to a combined output value of 790 million yuan in 1962 and to a combined output value of 420 million yuan in 1963. The combined output value of industry run by the production brigades and teams was 3.2 billion yuan in 1961, which increased to 3.3 billion yuan in 1962 and further to 3.6 billion yuan in 1963. The industrial output value of the communes and production brigades and teams put together reached 5.18 billion yuan in 1961, 4.09 billion yuan in 1962, and 4.02 billion yuan in 1963.

This big change in State policy virtually meant the total failure of the commune-run industry that had been built by government mandate. That failure inflicted a heavy loss on the country's rural economy. The total rural social output value of China in 1961 was 55.9 billion yuan, a drop of 8.4% as compared with the 61 billion yuan in 1956. In this period, the peasants' average per capita annual income rose from 76 yuan to 82 yuan, with an actual annual increase of just 1.2 yuan. As a result, the disparity between the rural residents and the urban population was widened from 1:1.26 to 1:1.39. The food grain for an average rural resident in a year was 154 kg, 26 kg less than that for an urban resident. Furthermore, 18.87 million urban workers lost their jobs in cities, and they, together with their families, totaling 26 million people were resettled in the countryside from January 1961 to June 1963. In addition, some other urban residents also went to live in the countryside. In all, about 50 million urban residents were resettled in the countryside. The government did not give any financial subsidies to the new settlers. Production teams had to accommodate them, and give them work to do. That large-scale resettlement of urbanites further aggravated the rural situation.

In 1964 a great controversy raged in the international communist movement. Mao Zedong warned that China should guard against revisionism at home. At his proposal, the CPC Central Committee decided to launch the "Four Clean-ups" movement [1] (cleaning up accounts, cleaning up warehouses, cleaning up financial affairs and cleaning up work points) in the countryside and the "Five Oppositions" movement (opposing corruption and embezzlement, speculation and profiteering, extravagancy and waste, decentralization and bureaucracy) which were deemed as major strategic measures for the prevention and eradication of revisionism in China. The main targets of these movements were "those in power within the Communist Party taking the capitalist road."

When "Four Clean-ups" work teams arrived in the villages, they found the production teams had no other source of income apart from the production of grain and a very limited amount of industrial crops, and that the peasants had tremendous difficulties in both production and life. When a production team needed to hold a meeting in the evening, the team had no money to buy oil for its oil lamp. When a work team wanted to check accounts, there was no money to buy paper. And the production team had no funds to continue production. This situation worried the work teams. They tried to help the production teams start some sideline production so as to raise funds. Some production brigades and teams in the more economically developed areas found that some urban workers and residents who had now settled in the countryside had special skills. In order to help them tide over difficulties in their new lives, the production brigades and teams restarted some of the closed-down industrial enterprises by relying on the skills of the new settlers. They started a number of labor-intensive handicraft industrial workshops as sideline production of the production brigades and teams while they continued to stress farming as their main line of production.

On April 28, 1964, Lin Hujia, Huo Shilian, Jiang Hua and some other leading members of the CPC Zhejiang Provincial Committee briefed Mao Zedong on the situation mentioned in the previous passage. When they touched on the influence of the "60-Articles" document regarding commune-run enterprises, Mao said, "What if

[1] The "Four Clean-ups" movement started from China's rural areas and then spread to urban areas by extending its scope of "cleaning up" to the fields of politics, ideology, organization and economy.

we keep the '60-Articles' document as it is for the time being. When the majority of the communes and production brigades have their commune and production brigade-run enterprises and public accumulation funds, the '60-Articles' may recognize the established facts. Law is recognition of facts. If the relations of production fetter the productive forces, the productive forces will ultimately break the fetters."[1] The output value of commune-run industry rose from 460 million yuan in 1964 to 580 million yuan in 1965. Many rural enterprises were forced to close down in the "Four Clean-ups" movement, which directed its spearhead of struggle against leaders of the production brigades and enterprises and the output value of production brigade-run industry dropped to 2.4 billion yuan in 1965 from the previous year's four billion yuan, a fall of 40%. The combined output value of industry run by communes and production brigades was 4.46 billion yuan in 1964, 10.9% more than in the previous year, but the figure in 1965 again dropped to 2.98 billion yuan, down by 33% as compared with the previous year. (See Table 1-8)

Table 1-8 Industrial Output Value of Communes and Production Brigades 1958-1965

Year	Output value of commune-run industry	Output value of brigade-run industry	Output value of commune and brigade-run industry	Annual increase or decrease
Unit	100 million yuan	100 million yuan	100 million yuan	%
1958	62.5		62.5	
1959	100		100	60.0
1960	50		50	-50.0
1961	19.8	32	51.8	3.8
1962	7.9	33	40.9	-21.0
1963	4.2	36	40.2	-1.0
1964	4.6	40	44.6	10.9
1965	5.8	24	29.8	-33.0

Source: *Township Enterprises in Contemporary China*, Contemporary China Press, 1991

[1] Gu Longsheng: *A Chronology of Mao Zedong's Economic Works*, CPC Central Party School Press, 1993, p. 594

References

1. Chihkeski (Soviet Union): *A Modern History of China*, Joint Publishing Company, 1974

2. Department of Politics and Economy of Renmin University of China: *A Modern Chinese Economic History*, People's Publishing House, 1979

3. *Economic Management in Contemporary China*, China Social Science Press, 1987

4. Fan Wenlan/Cai Meibiao: *A General History of China*, People's Publishing House, 1996

5. Fang Weizhong: *An Economic Chronology of the People's Republic of China*, China Social Science Press, 1984

6. Ji Long: *Collective Industry in Contemporary China*, Contemporary China Press, 1991

7. Kennedy, Paul (USA): *The Rise and Fall of the Great Powers*, China Economy Press, 1989

8. Li Shaobai: *A History of Science and Technology*, Central China Engineering Institute Press, 1986

9. Mao Lei et al.: *A Comparison between China and the Western Countries over 500 Years*, Chinese Workers Publishing House, 1991

10. Modern Chinese History Compilation Group: *A Modern Chinese History*, Zhonghua Book Company

11. People's Commune Study Group of the Institute of Law under the Chinese Academy of Sciences: *March Forward Victoriously with the Red Banner of the People's Commune Held High*, Law Press, 1960, Book 1

12. Stavrianos, L. S. (USA): *A Global History*, Shanghai Academy of Sciences Press, 1995

13. Wang Fangzhong: *A Draft History of the Economy of Modern China*, Beijing Publishing House, 1982

14. Xie Chuntao: *The Surging Tide of the Great Leap Forward*, Henan People's Publishing House, 1986

15. Xu Qingquan: *A Secret History of How Unequal Treaties Betraying China's Interests Were Signed*, Guangming Daily Press, 1996

16. Yang Ting: *A History of Science and Technology*, Zhejiang Education Press, 1986

17. Zhang Wenru: *Mao Zedong and China's Modernization*, Contemporary China Press, 1993

18. Zhu Cishou: *Industrial History of Modern China*, Chongqing Publishing House, 1989

Chapter II

How Township Enterprises Have Developed

Section 1 TVEs During the "Cultural Revolution" (1966-1976)

The year 1966 was an unusual one. That year, Mao Zedong launched the world-shaking "cultural revolution." Students stopped classes; workers put down their tools and left their workshops; and government functionaries stopped their office work. A revolutionary fever engulfed the whole of urban China. Leaders of the Party and government were given all sorts of labels and forced to leave their posts, subjected to mass criticism and denunciation. The power of the Party and government institutions was seized by the "revolutionary masses," and China was in the grip of anarchy. The normal economic order was disrupted, and the original channels of material distribution and circulation were blocked. The shortage of commodities, which had been serious, became even worse. However, the Chinese peasants had to live and carry on with production. The need for daily necessities and means of production did not disappear due to the "cultural revolution." Government functionaries and workers could afford to stop working and continue to receive their wages, and students were provided with food while making revolution. But the peasants would have starved if they had stopped production.

Under these extraordinary circumstances, peasants saw that the market demand for commodities was great and urgent, and commodities were in short supply. They felt that there was a golden opportunity for them to make money. Peasants in those areas with a more developed commodity economy restarted the industrial enterprises built in the high tide of the Great Leap Forward period by using the available factory buildings, equipment and technical personnel to produce what was needed in the market without neglecting farming. The social order of the countryside remained virtually without disruption, and the peasants continued undisturbed in their farming while at the same time beginning to run industrial enterprises again. That phenomenon was rather queer, but it played a role not to be underrated in helping stabilize the State power of the country during the 10 years of the "cultural revolution."

Enterprises run by communes and production brigades, which had been closed down during the Great Leap Forward period, were revived and grew in the "cultural revolution." That was convincing proof of the vitality of rural industry. The peasants of Huiguo Town, Gongyi City, Henan Province, built a number of industrial enterprises during the People's Commune Movement in 1958, and all of them were closed down later. Seven local peasants set up a farm machinery repair shop with just a crude oven and a hand-propelled grinding wheel in an abandoned temple, which served as workshop during the day and a bedroom at night. They used scrap iron and steel they collected to make crude lathes, transformers and assorted farm machines. Soon afterwards, a small nitrogen fertilizer plant, a phosphate fertilizer plant, a cement plant, a foundry, a cotton mill, a chemical works, a machine-made brick kiln, and an electrical appliances plant were built in the same commune, which helped the development of a batch of small enterprises run by production brigades. By 1970, the industry run by communes and production brigades in this commune had provided more than three million yuan of production funds and 1,100 pieces of farm machines for agriculture. Mao Zedong believed that enterprises run by communes and production brigades "promise a bright future" when he saw the enterprises at Huiguo Town.

The agricultural machinery plant of the Xitang Production Brigade of Qianzhou Commune in Wuxi County, Jiangsu Province, is another vivid example. When the members of the brigade set out to build the plant in 1970, they had neither factory building nor equipment, and they had only 160 yuan as start-up capital. They produced small farm tools to raise funds bit by bit, built a crude factory building, and made or bought pieces of equipment. Also in this county, the industrial enterprise of the Minzhu Brigade of the Yuqi Commune began as a blacksmith shop with 500 yuan it had borrowed. The shop started with a few skilled workers who had returned from cities. They did blacksmithing first, and then borrowed three belt lathes from the commune to produce farm machines. A group of carpenters belonging to the Chunlei Brigade of the Dongting Commune in the same county built a woodworking shop. Later, the brigade set up a service center offering hairdressing, sewing and shoemaking services. During the People's Commune period, it set up a construction squad, a painting team, a feed-processing shop, a shipyard and an agricultural machinery plant. By 1970, the brigade-run industry and sidelines had created a total output value of over 410,000 yuan.

The enterprises built by people's communes and production brigades during the "cultural revolution" served as a foundation for the future TVEs. Today, the production brigades have changed into administrative villages, and rural industry has become a leading force of the rural economy at the village level.

More opportunities turned up later, and the Chinese peasants did not miss them. Enterprises run by communes and production brigades benefited from these opportunities, and continued to grow.

The first opportunity was a large-scale drive to send urban educated youth to the countryside during the "cultural revolution." The leading Chinese newspaper, *People's Daily*, on December 22, 1968 published Mao Zedong's instruction: "It is absolutely necessary for educated youth to go to the countryside to receive re-education from the poor and lower-middle peasants. We should persuade our cadres and other people in cities to send their sons and daughters to the countryside after they graduate from junior and senior secondary schools and colleges. We should make a general mobilization. Comrades in the countryside everywhere should welcome them." [1]

---

[1] *Mao Zedong's Scripts since the Founding of the People's Republic of China*, Vol. 12, Central Archives Press, 1998, p. 615

Accompanying this speech of Mao's was a news report about some urban residents of Huining County, Gansu Province, re-settling in the countryside. Mao's instruction touched off a high tide of educated youth going to the countryside across the country. In this nationwide drive, 16 million young students went to the countryside, two million went to State farms and production and construction corps. The government, public institutions and State enterprises spent more than 10 billion yuan financing the re-settlement project. A small part of this fund was spent on enterprises run by the educated youth. Some communes and production brigades capitalized on the social connections of educated youth to win help from urban factories in building industrial enterprises in rural areas.

The second opportunity was one of accelerating the pace of agricultural mechanization. In his report "On the Cooperative Transformation of Agriculture," delivered in July 1955, Mao Zedong pointed out that "the social and economic features of China will not be completely changed until the socialist transformation of the social and economic system is completely accomplished and, in the technical field, machinery is used in all possible branches and places. The country's economic conditions being what they are, the technical transformation will take longer than the social one. It is estimated that the basic completion of the nationwide technical transformation of agriculture will take roughly four or five five-year plans, that is, 20-25 years. The whole Party must fight for the fulfillment of this great task." [1]

But the pace of agricultural mechanization was extremely slow. In August 1970, Zhou Enlai called a meeting on agricultural work in the northern parts of China in the name of the State Council under the extremely difficult conditions during the "cultural revolution." The meeting pointed out that "the fundamental way out for agriculture is mechanization. It is impossible to rely only on manual labor without developing farm machinery to raise agricultural productivity quickly and to change the State of affairs in which all

---

[1] *Selected Works of Mao Zedong*, Vol. V, p. 203, First Edition, Foreign Languages Press, translated from the first Chinese edition published by People's Publishing House, 1977, pp. 188-189

the 600 million peasants are occupied with the task of growing food, nor is it possible to have surplus labor power to speed up industrial construction. Chairman Mao instructed us to 'use 25 years to realize the basic mechanization of agriculture,' but 15 years have already elapsed. We must have a firm grasp of this work in the coming decade."

In order to implement the spirit of this meeting, in September 1971 the State Council called the National Conference on Agricultural Mechanization. The meeting set the target for the following 10 years: to bring the level of mechanization to 70% in all major productive activities in farming, forestry, animal husbandry and fisheries by the year 1980. To achieve this goal, the meeting called for:

(1) The building of a repair network at the three levels of the county, commune and brigade;

(2) The development of the "five small" industries (referring to small blast furnaces, small coal mines, small machine-building factories, small cement plants and small chemical fertilizer plants) as the material foundation for agricultural mechanization;

(3) The mechanization of the processing of farm produce and sideline products, cold storage and transportation; and

(4) Priority given to the supply of small farm tools and improved farm tools.

The meeting recommended the experience of a number of units in the work of agricultural mechanization. The Dazhai Production Brigade in Xiyang County, Shanxi Province, realized almost complete mechanization of grain grinding, flour milling, corn threshing, hay cutting and feed crushing, and partial mechanization of field leveling, soil improvement, plowing and field transportation. The Liuji Commune in Xinzhou County, Hubei Province, relied on mechanization not only to achieve intensive cultivation but also to deploy one quarter of its labor power to run sideline production and commune-run industry, The income from industry and sideline production covered one third of the commune's total revenue in 1970. The Jianming Commune, known as the "Paupers' Commune" for its original poverty, in Zunhua County, Hebei Province, succeeded in developing commune industry from scratch, and achieved simultaneous development of both agriculture and industry. After the CPC Central Committee and the central government called on the nation to speed up the pace of agricultural mechanization and build the "five small" industries, communes across the country did so. Data shows that commune and brigade industry produced a combined output of 4.4 billion yuan in 1967, five billion yuan in 1968 and 5.6 billion yuan in 1969. Enterprises run by communes and brigades grew at an annual rate of 24%. (See Table 2-1)

Table 2-1 Output Value of Industry Run by Communes and Production Brigades 1970-1974

Content	Unit	1970	1971	1972	1973	1974
Output value of commune-run industry	100 million yuan	27.6	39.1	46.0	54.8	66.8
Output valuc of brigade-run industry	100 million yuan	40.0	52.9	64.6	71.6	84.5
Output value of industry of both	100 million yuan	67.6	92.0	110.6	126.4	151.3
Increase over the previous year	%	20.7	36.1	20.2	14.3	19.7

Source: *Township Enterprises in Contemporary China*, Contemporary China Press, 1991

The third opportunity presented itself when Deng Xiaoping pointed out that urban industry should help the countryside develop small-scale industry. When Premier Zhou Enlai was seriously ill, Deng Xiaoping once more came to preside over the work of the central government. At the August 18, 1975 State Council meeting to ponder on the overall concept of economic planning which he convened, Deng Xiaoping pointed out: "We must uphold firmly the principle of taking agriculture as the foundation of the national economy, and all departments should serve agriculture. It is important for industry to support agriculture and promote agricultural modernization. Industrial districts and industrial cities should lead the neighboring rural areas, and help them build small industrial enterprises and do agricultural production well. This must be included in their plans. In the Northwest and Southwest, we built a number of factories as a measure of preparedness against war. Factories scattered in the remote rural areas, far from the coastal regions may also help the neighboring communes and production brigades. One big factory there can help a vast area around it. This has the advantage of winning the confidence of the peasants in the neighborhood, who will stop stealing the property of the factories. If industry aids agriculture, then agriculture in turn will support industry. This is a way to strengthen the worker-peasant alliance."[1] With the help of the State-run factories, industry run by communes and production brigades developed further. Jiangsu Province which was more advanced in this respect, reported an average annual increase of 26.5% in output value between 1970 and 1975, namely, 690 million yuan in 1970; 930 million yuan in 1971; 1.14 billion yuan in 1972; 1.36 billion yuan in 1973; 1.67 billion yuan in 1974; and 2.24 billion yuan in 1975.

When "Left" thinking ran rampant during the "cultural revolution," however, peasants were criticized for running industry. In order to avoid being caught running industry, peasants resorted to "guerilla tactics." When the authorities sent inspectors, they suspended industrial production. As soon as the inspection teams left, they immediately resumed operations. By 1975, the total output value of industry run by communes and production brigades had reached 19.78 billion yuan, of which 8.68 billion yuan was from commune-run industry and 11.1 billion yuan was from industry run by production brigades, increases of 30.7%, 29.9% and 13.1%, respectively. Their combined output value accounted for 3.3% of the country's total industrial output value in 1970, rising to 9.3% in 1975.

An important event happened in 1975 after Deng Xiaoping was

---

[1] *Selected Works of Deng Xiaoping*, People's Publishing House, Vol. II, pp. 28- 29

reinstated. On September 5, some financial workers of Zhejiang Province wrote a letter to Mao Zedong and the Party Central Committee saying, "We recently read Comrade Hua Guofeng's letter to the Hunan Provincial Committee, and we were greatly enlightened and inspired. The letter says that now enterprises run by communes and production brigades are like wild flowers on the mountains which have blossomed brilliantly despite all sorts of adversities... But at present some leading comrades in our province show a lukewarm attitude toward this new thing — enterprises run by communes and brigades. They refuse to take a clear stand, and dare not support them. This problem is still being kicked around like a football among relevant departments of the provincial government." The writers of the letter requested the CPC Central Committee to give new instructions. Attached to this letter were the letter Hua Guofeng wrote to the Hunan Provincial Party Committee on December 28, 1974 and a news report carried by the *Henan Daily* on December 15, 1974, based on an investigation of the Huiguo Town Commune in Gongxian County, Henan Province. The report praised the commune for running industry related to agriculture and having its agriculture promoted by industry. The report was titled "Bright Hopes."

Hua Guofeng, then Vice Premier of the State Council, in his December 28, 1974 letter to Zhang Pinghua, Secretary of the Hunan Provincial Party Committee, and members of its Standing Committee, wrote, "Under the leadership of Party organizations at all levels and supported by the broad masses of the poor and lower-middle peasants, enterprises run by communes and production brigades are blossoming like mountain flowers and have made heartening progress. It is an ample proof of the great vitality of this new socialist phenomenon. It is just as the article says: 'Enterprises run by communes and production brigades are products of the people's communes, and they grow along with the communes.' This is of great significance for the consolidation and development of the commune collective economy, the realization of agricultural mechanization at an accelerated pace and the elimination of the 'Three Major Distinctions' [between workers and peasants, cities and countryside, and manual and mental labor]. It represents the great hope and future of the people's commune. Unfortunately, some comrades among us are just like those Chairman Mao criticized: 'Although going by the name of Communists, they show little interest in the current socialist cause. They refuse to support the enthusiastic masses; instead, they pour cold water on their efforts.' They despise the tender buds of enterprises run by communes and production brigades, and refuse to believe that the buds will grow into beautiful flowers. They are blind to the numerous tremendous superior elements. They pick holes, and criticize this as indecent or that as abnormal. They resort to all pretexts to eliminate or restrict enterprises run by communes and production brigades. They are happy when there is nothing to be done, and they think that is 'normal.' We advise those comrades not to follow the example of Duke Ye who took a fancy to dragons in paintings but was scared to death when a real dragon appeared. We have been talking about socialism for many years. But now that socialism is appearing before our eyes, they are scared. They should resolutely discard such erroneous thinking, support this new phenomenon with effervescent enthusiasm, take an active part in the actual struggles, and, together with those steadfast comrades, persist in the basic line of our Party. It is necessary to strengthen the Party leadership, with the secretaries taking a personal role, mobilize the whole party, trust and rely on the masses, make a comprehensive plan, go all out to make revolution, use one year, or two years if one year is not enough, or three years if two years are not enough, or five years if three years are not enough, or 10 years if five years are not enough. We should display the unswerving spirit of the 'Foolish Old Man' in removing big mountains, persevere in our endeavors, make redoubled efforts, and constantly sum up both positive and negative experiences so as to propagate what is good and guard against what has been proved to be wrong. Only in this way is it possible for enterprises run by communes and production brigades to grow from scratch, and from a low level to a high level, and make continuous progress. A new socialist countryside will ultimately emerge before us. 'Socialism is making victorious advances everywhere.' We must fight with redoubled efforts and make a greater contribution to mankind."

After receiving the letter, Mao Zedong wrote an instruction on it on September 27, 1975: "Comrade Xiaoping, please consider whether to reprint these three pieces (the two letters and the news report), and distribute them among the comrades of the Central Committee now in Beijing." Deng Xiaoping immediately acted on the instruction, replying, "I have acted on your instruction, and distributed them to the comrades on the Party Central Committee." He also distributed the documents among leading comrades from the provinces attending the National Conference on Learning from Dazhai in Agriculture.

Hua Guofeng gave a summary report to the National Conference on Learning from Dazhai in Agriculture on October 15, 1975, on behalf of the CPC Central Committee and the State Council. He said: "The development of enterprises run by communes and production brigades has strengthened the economy at the commune and brigade levels, effectively helped the poor brigades, enhanced agricultural production, supported national construction, and accelerated the pace of agricultural mechanization...To develop enterprises run by communes and production brigades, it is necessary to persist in the socialist orientation, primarily to serve agricultural production, serve the people's life, and serve State-run industry and exports as well. It is necessary to make full use of local resources, and develop crop farming, animal raising, aquaculture, processing and mining. But attention should be paid to avoiding fighting for resources with State-run industry or disrupting national resources... Party committees at all levels should take an active attitude and effective measures to speed up the development of enterprises run by communes and production brigades...The leadership of the communes and production brigades should be strengthened. Once problems are found, positive measures should be taken to solve them." This report was distributed to the Party committees at all levels in the form of a document of the CPC Central Committee. The development of the industry run by communes and production brigades began to gather speed after the conference. (See Table 2-2)

Table 2-2 Output Value of Industry Run by Communes and Production Brigades 1975-1978

Item	Unit	1975	1976	1977	1978
Output value of commune-run industry	100 million yuan	86.8	123.9	192.0	224.0
Output value of brigade run industry	100 million yuan	111.0	119.6	140.0	161.0
Combined total	100 million yuan	197.8	243.5	332.0	385.0
Increase over the previous year	%	30.7	23.1	36.3	16.0

Source: *Township Enterprises in Contemporary China*, Contemporary China Press, 1991

The political situation deteriorated in 1976. With the approval of Mao Zedong, a movement to "criticize Deng Xiaoping's 'Right' tendency and reverse the verdict" was launched across the country, which opened the sluice gate for extreme 'Left' thinking. As a result, many things which had been rectified were negated again. Enterprises run by communes and production brigades once more ran into difficulties.

First, they could find no government department to be in charge of them. China was practicing a highly centralized planned economy and the State-run enterprises monopolized the home market. Now these enterprises run by communes and production brigades which practiced the market economy had to fight for "space" with the State-run enterprises, but they could not find a government department to take charge of them. The government department in charge of industry said that it took care of only State-run industry. The Second Light Industry Department said that it was in charge only of collective enterprises in cities. The agricultural department said that it was in charge of agricultural production only, and had no business with industry. Enterprises run by communes and production brigades complained that they were "like orphans with no one to take care of them."

Second, since the country practiced a planned economy, funds, equipment, and raw and other materials were all supplied "first to the State-run enterprises and second to collective enterprises (in cities)," without any consideration given to enterprises run by communes and production brigades. Therefore, when the communes and production brigades needed funds to build industry, they could get neither government allocations nor bank loans. So enterprises run by communes and production brigades could not get State allocations or supplies. They could not even buy the equipment they needed. The raw and other materials were supplied in the same manner. The products of State-run and urban collective enterprises were all purchased by the government material supply department. Enterprises run by communes and production brigades could not find a department to purchase their products. Leaders of some enterprises run by communes and production brigades grumbled: "We are stepmothers' sons."

Third, China at the time practiced socialist public ownership, and forbade individuals to run enterprises. All enterprises nominally were the assets of the whole of society or of all the members of a commune brigade. In reality, however, the peasants had no decision-making power over enterprises run by communes and production brigades, or the right to elect or to stand for election, let alone the right of supervision and distribution. Everything was decided by the leaders of the commune or brigade. Even an enterprise run by an individual had to be affiliated to a commune or production brigade. The concept of ownership was thus blurred, as all enterprises seemed to be run "officially." The No. 1 Garment Factory in Pikou Town in Xinjin County (now Pulandian City), Liaoning Province, was actually built by five housewives, with Sun Juhua as their leader. They moved their own sewing machines into a shack of no more than 20 sq m to start making shoe pads and over-sleeves for the market. Later, their sewing team grew into a garment factory working on orders placed by big State-run garment factories for export. Because the factory enjoyed a good reputation for the quality of its products and its high creditability, it grew rapidly, and became a mainstay enterprise of the town.

Fourth, Chinese peasants at that time were not allowed to engage in commerce or transportation or other businesses in the sphere of commodity circulation; nor were they allowed to run hotels or restaurants. The "Directive on Combating Corruption, Embezzlement, Speculation and Profiteering" promulgated by the CPC Central Committee on February 5, 1970 stipulated: "Except for State- and collective-run and certified commerce, no unit or individual is allowed to engage in commercial activities." And, "The administration of marketplaces should be strengthened. No commodities barred from sale are allowed to enter the market. Unless otherwise approved by the local relevant authorities, no organization is allowed to make purchases at the rural marketplaces or directly from communes and production brigades or teams. It is forbidden to conduct barter trade under the pretext of mutual cooperation. It is forbidden to 'take the backdoor.' All underground workshops, underground shops, underground building squads, underground transportation brigades and underground clubs must be banned resolutely." That was a heavy blow to enterprises run by communes and production brigades, which relied on the domestic market for their existence.

Fifth, enterprises run by communes and production brigades were deemed a synonym for capitalism. For example, the plant run by the Xinqiao Commune in Danyang County, Jiangsu Province, was criticized in 1971 as "a capitalist seedling" and "a center of corrupt cadres," and was ordered to close down. Many of the backbone technicians in the industry run by communes and production brigades were considered problematic in the previous political movements or considered to have stains on their personal records, and were therefore resettled in the countryside from the cities. When a new political movement arose, those people were the first victims and the problem would often involve industry run by communes and brigades.

In 1975, Jiangsu Province organized a 100-person team to investigate bourgeois rights in Changzhou City. The team came to the conclusion that industry run by communes and production brigades had not only shaken the agricultural foundation and affected the implementation of the State plan for material supply and marketing, it had also corrupted the rural cadres and peasants by leading them to pursue self-interest. It was therefore capitalist in nature. Meanwhile, the team believed that industry run by communes and production brigades by working in coordination with the State-run factories stole profits from the State, thus undermining the cornerstone of socialism.

In the education drive in the Party's basic line with "class struggle as the key link" in 1975, the development of the private sector of the economy in Wenzhou, Zhejiang Province, was condemned as "virtually no different from Taiwan except that the Kuomintang flag was not hoisted." The authorities sent work teams to correct the situation.

A drive to criticize the "Gang of Four" and combat the sabotage of the class enemy and the onslaught of capitalism swept over China in 1977. In this movement, industry run by communes and production brigades in many places became targets of criticism for "taking money as the guiding principle," and being "the home of capitalism" and "the breeding ground of bourgeois rights." The critics believed that industry run by communes and brigades had squeezed State-owned industry, caused a loss to the State revenue and a waste of raw and other materials, and turning out many products that "had nothing to do with agriculture." The work teams in some places detained and interrogated leaders and marketing personnel of enterprises run by communes and production brigades.

It was against such a trend of thinking that enterprises run by communes and production brigades advanced. By the end of 1978, the total output value of enterprises run by communes and production brigades had already reached 30% of the total rural social output value of the country, and the peasants employed in industrial and commercial activities in such enterprises accounted for about one tenth of the total rural labor force.

Section 2 TVEs in the Early Stage of Reform and Opening-Up (1978-1983)

The Third Plenary Session of the CPC 11th Central Committee was convened in December 1978. That meeting was of monumental importance for it corrected and ended the catastrophe caused by the "cultural revolution," and ushered in a new stage of development, that is, carrying out economic reforms and opening up to the outside world. The session approved in principle the "Resolution (draft) of the Central Committee of the Communist Party of China on Some Issues Concerning the Development of Agriculture at an Accelerated Pace" and the "Working Regulations for Rural People's Communes (Draft for Trial Implementation)." The Resolution urges: "Enterprises run by communes and production brigades need a big development, so that by 1985 their combined output value should rise from the present 20% to more than half of the combined income of the economy at the three levels of the communes, production brigades and production teams."

In order to realize this goal, the Resolution stipulates: "All farm produce and sideline products fit for processing in the countryside should gradually be processed by enterprises run by communes and production brigades provided they conform to the principle of economic rationality. Factories in cities should place part of their products and machine parts fit for processing in the countryside with enterprises run by communes and production brigades to process, and the urban factories should support the latter with equipment and technical guidance. The State should adopt a policy of tax reduction or exemption for enterprises run by communes and production brigades in the light of the actual situation."

The Resolution points out that it is necessary to develop small towns in a planned way, which shall be "an inevitable approach to accelerating the country's modernization, narrowing the differences between cities and countryside, and between workers and peasants. We have 800 million people and 300 million able-bodied workers. With the advance of agricultural modernization, a large amount of agricultural labor power will be gradually saved. This surplus labor power should not all enter the existing large and medium-sized cities and industry, and other construction projects should not and need not all be in those cities. We must pay great attention to developing small towns and arming them gradually with modern industry and communications, modern commerce and service trades, and modern educational, cultural and health facilities as the advance bases for bringing about a new look to our countryside." [1]

The Resolution, while urging vigorous development of enterprises run by communes and production brigades, also urged the speeding up of the building of small towns. This approach to linking the two together shows that they are closely related, for enterprises run by communes and production brigades rest on the small towns as their bases, while the prosperity of small towns relies on the development of the enterprises of communes and production brigades. The revised "Working Regulations for Rural People's Communes" devoted its Chapter Seven to enterprises run by communes and production brigades. It stipulates: "Enterprises run by communes and production brigades should persist in the socialist orientation, primarily serve agricultural production and the people's livelihood, and serve large industrial enterprises and exports as well." The scope of development of enterprises run by communes and production brigades was defined as "running crop farming, animal raising and aquaculture, farm produce processing and sideline production, mining, construction, farm machinery, transportation and other industries in compliance with the local conditions by self-reliance and by making full use of local resources." The management of the enterprises "should enforce a system of responsibilities at each work post, quota control, business accounting and quality control." Distribution in the enterprises "should make the remuneration for labor equivalent to that for labor power employed in agricultural production, generally by the method of 'grade appraised by the factory, work points recorded in production teams, accounts settled between factories and production teams, and distribution done through production teams'." After that, enterprises run by communes and production brigades entered a new phase of development.

With approval from the State Council, the Ministry of Agriculture and Forestry back in April 1976 set up the Bureau for the Admini-

---

[1] Archive Research Center of the CPC Central Committee: *Major Archives since the Third Plenary Session of the 11th CPC Central Committee*, People's Publishing House, 1982, Vol. 1, p.191, p.198

stration of Enterprises Run by Communes and Production Brigades. The provinces, autonomous regions and municipalities directly under the State Council followed suit and set up their own administrative bureaus in this regard. The Ministry convened the first meeting on the work of enterprises run by communes and production brigades in April 1977, which was attended by leading members of the relevant departments from Hunan, Hubei, Guangdong, Guangxi, Jiangsu, Shandong, Anhui, Jiangxi, Hebei, Shanxi, Liaoning, Sichuan and Gansu provinces, and Beijing, Shanghai and Tianjin cities. A consensus was reached at the meeting to the effect that there was an urgent requirement for a document which should explicitly define the State guiding principle and policies and an administrative mechanism regarding the development of enterprises run by communes and production brigades.

Based on the views voiced at the meeting, the Ministry of Agriculture and Forestry submitted a report to the State Council. Before long, leaders of the State Council instructed the Ministry of Agriculture and Forestry to draft the "Provisions Concerning the Development of Enterprises Run by Communes and Production Brigades." After two years' painstaking discussion, coordination and drafting, the draft finally won the consent of the relevant departments, and was adopted by the State Council and promulgated as an interim draft on July 3, 1979.

The Provisions, for the first time in the form of a government decree, affirmed the political and economic status of enterprises run by communes and production brigades in China. It has explicit provisions for the development of the enterprises, their business scope, management and relations with relevant departments, their rights and obligations, State policy in support of the enterprises, and demand on the governments at all levels for setting up relevant institutions for the administration of the enterprises. In effect, it was China's first State decree on enterprises run by communes and production brigades.

The Provisions explicitly states: "Enterprises run by communes and brigades are economic institutions of socialist collective ownership, run and owned by the commune or by the production brigade. No institution or individual has the right to appropriate without compensation, products, equipment, raw or other materials from a commune or production brigade, or to borrow money from them, and their autonomy should be respected." On the question of business scope, the document added small articles of daily use, small chemical works, small blast furnaces and foundries, hotels, restaurants and export commodity centers.

The document also demanded that the prefectures, counties and communes and relevant departments of the central government should set up relevant administrative institutions for the administration of enterprises run by communes and production brigades. Guided by the spirit of the new resolution of the CPC Central Committee and the State Council, enterprises run by communes and production brigades displayed new zeal. Their 1978 output value rose 25.4% over that of the previous year, to reach 51.4 billion yuan, and their 1979 output value rose 10.9%, to reach 56 billion yuan.

In the course of developing the national economy in 1980, the targets set for industrial production were too high, and the number of capital construction projects launched was too large, thus affecting the people's daily consumption and causing a serious imbalance among the different economic sectors. In these circumstances, the planners failed to rectify the 'Left' tendency. Instead, they were too anxious for success, and announced impractical slogans and targets, and further increased the capital construction projects and imports of complete sets of equipment, thus straining the actual capacity of the country. The scale of capital construction remained too big after the Third Plenary Session of the 11th CPC Central Committee and the 22 large import projects which should have been suspended were not suspended. Meanwhile, many provinces and enterprises blindly started a large number of repetitive projects. That led to a serious imbalance in the national economy, and caused grave financial problems.

In face of this grave situation, the CPC Central Committee decided to make a major economic readjustment, and put forth three demands for 1981, namely, first, striving to strike a balance between revenue and expenditure; second, achieving a credit balance between payment and revenue; and third, basically stabilizing prices. To achieve this target, it was necessary first of all to curtail the investment in capital construction, and also to cut back defense allocation and administrative expenditure.[1] However, some departments, still fettered by old thinking, institution and concepts, harbored prejudice against industry, commerce and service trades run by peasants. Some critics asserted that enterprises run by communes and production brigades had grown by taking advantage of the chaos of the "cultural revolution" or through the patronage of certain high officials, and some even claimed that their growth was achieved to the detriment of the country as a whole, by distorting the arrangement of raw materials, energy, markets and funds.

Thereupon, the relevant department of the State Council drafted "Some Provisions on the Closing Down, Suspension, Merger or Shifting of Industrial Enterprises" at the end of 1980, demanding that the local governments report to the State Council on small enterprises in 26 categories that needed to be closed down, suspended, merged or have their lines of business changed. The 26 categories were: small iron and steel plants, small chemical fertilizer plants, small coal mines, small cement plants, small coke plants, small oil refineries, small cotton mills, small cotton textile mills, small knitwear mills, small silk factories, small chemical fiber plants, small dyeing and printing plants, small rubber product plants, small calcium carbide plants, small soap plants, small timber mills, small paper mills, small paint works, small plastics factories, small tanneries, small glass factories, small cigarette factories, small wineries, small machinery plants, small boiler plants and small home appliances plants.

The State Council called a routine meeting on January 20, 1981. Vice Premier Wan Li who was then in charge of the rural work pointed out: "Enterprises run by communes and production brigades should be exempt. We should work out another document especially pertaining to such enterprises. They should not be closed down or suspended rashly. So long as they can carry on production, and their

---

[1] Archive Research Center of the CPC Central Committee: *Major Archives since the Third Plenary Session of the 11th CPC Central Committee*, People's Publishing House, 1982, Vol. 1, p. 512

products have markets and they can supply themselves, we should allow them to continue. Don't close them down or suspend them. Let the market test them. If they have markets, they can survive. Those whose products have no market will naturally change their line of business or be merged with others. We should fix norms and those not up to the norm should be barred from the market. Why worry about the size of their batch production? Let them be tested by the market through competition. If their products are not needed by the market, they will automatically change their line of production. When designating certain products to factories, we tend to choose those enterprises under our administration, not always those with excellent quality. The localities rely on small plants to make profits. You cannot get rid of those small plants. If many small plants are shut down, a shortage of supply will appear in the market. We have just enlivened the market a little; why should we exert rigid control again?" Vice Premiers Yu Qiuli, Fang Yi, and Yang Jingren, and others also voiced their support for enterprises run by communes and production brigades.

It was also pointed out at the meeting that "the economic departments and administrative departments of our socialist country should support the peasants, help them, and give them guidance in enlivening the rural economy. We should not take measures to restrict them, block them or ban them from doing so, and especially we should not take dictatorial measures."

After the meeting, the State Agriculture Commission and the Ministry of Agriculture, Animal Husbandry and Fisheries drafted "Some Provisions by the State Council on Enterprises Run by Communes and Production Brigades in Implementing the Policy of Readjusting the National Economy." The State Council officially promulgated this document on May 4, 1981.

The new document clearly confirmed the positive role of enterprises run by communes and production brigades. It says, "Enterprises run by communes and production brigades have achieved obvious results in using and developing local resources, accommodating surplus rural labor power, consolidating and strengthening the collective economy, and helping increase the income of the commune members; have played a positive role in gradually changing the rural and agricultural economic structure, supporting agricultural development and enhancing the construction of small towns; and have made a contribution to the country in developing commodity production, enlivening the market, expanding exports and increasing State revenues. Enterprises run by communes and production brigades have become an important component of the rural economy, which is in compliance with the orientation of the all-round development of the rural economy." On the question of the readjustment of enterprises run by communes and production brigades, the document points out: "Enterprises run by communes and production brigades involve the economic interests of the peasants, the employment of nearly 30 million people and the market supply of some indispensable commodities. While it is necessary to make readjustments in the interests of the whole country, it is important to respect the autonomy of the communes and production brigades, necessary to take prudent steps and do a good job of making investigations and studies, understand the different States of affairs, let them play their positive role and restrict the negative elements, increase the production of commodities in short supply and curtail production of those in excessive supply, and help them develop in a healthy way."[1]

At the National Conference on Planning Work, held on November 14, 1981, a department under the State Council again put the document drafted at the end of 1980 which had already been refuted by the State Council, before the meeting for discussion. It met opposition from the representatives of all the provinces.

A representative from Anhui said that people should not mistake simply closing down small enterprises, suspending them, merging them or changing their line of operation for economic readjustment. The role of small enterprises should not be overlooked.

A representative from Shandong said, "Do not issue orders to cut back on small enterprises. The small enterprises will readjust themselves. They don't require you to readjust them. We think the prob-

[1] Archive Research Center of the CPC Central Committee: *Major Archives since the Third Plenary Session of the 11th CPC Central Committee*, People's Publishing House, 1982, Vol. 2, p. 1092

lem stems not from small enterprises but from larger ones. You and we think differently. We think the trouble lies with large enterprises. Small enterprises do not hamper large enterprises. Contrarily, they are a supplement to the large enterprises."

A representative from Sichuan said, "Your document gives one the impression that small enterprises are troublesome and larger ones are fine. The guiding thought of that document is questionable. Does our industry need small enterprises or not? It is impossible for our industry to do without small enterprises. Yet some departments prefer large ones to small ones."

A representative from Inner Mongolia said, "This document is incomplete. It is better not to issue it. First, it fails to understand the CPC Central Committee's principle of making all-round economic readjustment; second, it fails to reflect the spirit of Vice Premier Yao Yilin's proposal for the economic work in 1982, which put the focus on the readjustment and improvement of economic results; third, it reflects a poor attitude, as it passively stresses the measure of shutting down enterprises. The document gives people the impression that it tries to protect large enterprises and suppress the smaller ones, protect State-run enterprises and suppress collective-run enterprises, protect the more advanced areas and suppress the relatively backward areas. It runs counter to the spirit of the Party Central Committee."

A representative from Shaanxi said, "The problem we confront now lies not with small enterprises, but with larger ones. If small enterprises are to be shut down according to the standards laid down in this document, some 14,000 or more small enterprises in our province would be shut down. That would mean a loss of seven billion yuan of industrial output value, about half of the total. That would lead to serious consequences. The document gives the impression that it intends to suppress the small, local and non-government enterprises for the purpose of protecting the larger ones. The provinces are responsible for the collection of the State revenue, and the departments of the central government have no worries about that. At present, small enterprises are not burdens to us, but the large enterprises are. We hope that the central government will produce a plan for the readjustment of the large enterprises. Do not direct the spearhead of attack at small enterprises. Try to work out measures for the large enterprises."

The CPC Central Commission for Discipline Inspection, at its third meeting held in February 1981, pointed out: "There exists extensive malpractice in the economic field, such as irresponsibility toward work, departmental egoism, false reporting and cheating, hurting the public interest to boost private interests, bribery and corruption, and even extortion, which have put tremendous difficulties in the way of our modernization efforts." It urged "greater efforts to combat such malpractices." [1]

The CPC Central Committee published an urgent circular on January 11, 1982 which states that "those cadres who have committed crimes, primarily those cadres in leading positions who have committed crimes, must be arrested in accordance with the law, and severely punished by law, and the results of the trials of particular grave cases should be published in newspapers." [2] The document indicates that discipline inspection should focus on dishonest cadres who receive wages from government departments and State-run enterprises. It does not cover enterprises run by communes and production brigades, which are enterprises run by the common people. Furthermore, enterprises run by communes and production brigades are not included in the State plans and they rely on themselves, not on government allocations, for the purchase of raw materials and the marketing of their products. In many places, the rectification drive was aimed at those responsible for the purchase of materials and for the marketing of products by enterprises run by communes and production brigades, causing widespread uneasiness.

In view of this situation, Lu Dingyi, Chief of the Propaganda Department of the CPC Central Committee at the time, wrote a letter on November 14, 1981 to Hu Yaobang, then General Secretary of the Communist Party. He pointed out in his letter: "Enterprises run

---

[1] Jiang Huaxuan et al.: *Abstracts of Meetings of Communist Party of China*, Shenyang Publishing House, 1991, p. 654

[2] Archive Research Center of the CPC Central Committee: *Major Archives since the Third Plenary Session of the 11th CPC Central Committee*, People's Publishing House, 1982, Vol. 2, p. 1092

by communes and production brigades are many, and they have their role to play in industrial production, particularly in the countryside. (1) The surplus labor power cannot be absorbed without them. (2) In the better-off regions (particularly in areas that grow three crops a year), agricultural production needs subsidies from industry, and this state of affairs is bound to get more prominent. (3) In the better-off areas, the peasants rely rather on industry for their income than on farming. (4) This is important for the State revenue. Take Wuxi City for example. Local industry contributes half of the city's tax revenue. Attached to the letter was an internal publication of Xinhua News Agency carrying a report titled "Cadres of Communes and Production brigades in Suzhou Prefecture, Jiangsu Province, Speak on Corruption and Bribery in Enterprises Run by Communes and Production Brigades, and the solution."

Upon receiving the letter, Hu Yaobang wrote an instruction on it, reading: "Have this printed as a document for discussion at the Secretariat of the CPC Central Committee. Before discussion, let the Economic Commission and the Agricultural Commission make an investigation into the basic situation of enterprises run by communes and production brigades, and suggest how we should give guidance and control. Better produce a draft document in advance."

The CPC Central Commission for Discipline Inspection made investigations at the grassroots level. On the basis of their findings, the CPC Central Committee and the State Council adopted the "Resolution on Combating Grave Criminal Activities in the Economic Field." The document explicitly states: "We should never randomly extend the scope of this struggle to the broad masses of ordinary workers, peasants and other working people (excluding a few serious malefactors) in the cities and countryside. As for malpractice in the relations between rural enterprises run by communes and production brigades and industrial and commercial enterprises in the cities, except for a limited number of grave criminal cases, they should in general be resolved in the course of consolidating enterprises run by communes and production brigades, strengthening the administration for industry and commerce and the control of material supply. It is necessary to strictly delineate and correctly handle the two types contradictions which are different in nature. It is necessary to set apart errors in work from criminal activities, malpractice in economic activities from economic crimes, and smuggling, corruption and speculation from problems that arise from the imperfection of certain institutions or methods in the course of opening to the outside world in international economic activities and enlivening the economy at home."[1] The timely measures taken by the central government spared enterprises run by communes and production brigades grave losses.

Acting on the instructions of the CPC Central Committee and the State Council, enterprises run by communes and production brigades began readjustment and consolidation in 1980. The Ministry of Agriculture, Animal Husbandry and Fisheries called a meeting on the work of readjustment and consolidation in 1982. According to the analysis of enterprises run by communes and production brigades done by the local governments across the country before the work had started, the enterprises might fall into three categories: 35% of them were good, 50% were just the average, and 15% were not so good. The major problems with them were:

First, weak leadership; second, poor management; confused accounts; skewed picture of the actual state of operations; great waste resulting from handing out gifts and throwing banquets; third, faulty market targeting, smuggling, bribery, corruption, speculation and deception, and stealing State and collective property; fourth, overlooking economic accounting, high costs and low quality of products.

In view of the problems, the meeting proposed that consolidation should be combined with readjustment, with the technical transformation and reform of enterprises and with education in professional ethics. The meeting proposed that the enterprises be run as "civilian undertakings" rather than "government institutions." Meanwhile, it pointed out that it was necessary to delineate the policy of distinguishing proper business activities from speculation and profiteering,

---

[1] Archive Research Center of the CPC Central Committee: *Major Archives since the Third Plenary Session of the 11th CPC Central Committee*, People's Publishing House, 1982, Vol. 2, pp.1245, 1251

corruption and bribery from improper practice, errors in work from economic crimes, and confusion in policy from conscious criminality.

Through consolidation up to the end of 1983, according to statistics from 27 provinces, autonomous regions and municipalities, 560,000 or 42% of all enterprises run by communes and production brigades had been consolidated, and those with problems had been dealt with in the light of the actual cases. After the consolidation, the number of the enterprises was reduced by 178,000 from 1,524,000 in 1978 to 1,346,000 in 1983. But TVEs had survived and were making healthy progress. They had absorbed a greater amount of surplus rural labor and increased their output value. However, the pace of development was not as fast as it had been. Their annual increase of output value had been 24.8% before 1978, but the rate went down to 13.1% after that. (See Table 2-3)

Table 2-3 Development of Enterprises Run by Communes and Production Brigades 1978-1983

Year	Unit	1978	1979	1980	1981	1982	1983
Number of enterprises	10,000	152.4	148.0	142.4	133.7	136.2	134.6
Number of workers	10,000	2826	2909	2999	2969	3113	3234
Total output value	100 million yuan	514.4	560.7	678.3	767.2	892.3	1019.3
Industrial output	100 million yuan	388.7	424.9	519.1	585.2	649.4	754.2

Source: Statistics on TVEs, Ministry of Agriculture

Section 3 TVEs after the Disintegration of the People's Communes (1984-1988)

The economic restructuring began to deepen after 1984. The rural people's communes were disbanded, and local governments shed their function of managing enterprises. The original rural collective economy was replaced by a contracting system based on the individual peasant household. A large number of collective enterprises were disbanded, and a number of self-employed, private and cooperative enterprises mushroomed despite all sorts of obstacles.

In the new circumstances, the State Agricultural Commission and the State Economic Commission, acting on the instructions of Party General Secretary Hu Yaobang, organized a nationwide investigation of enterprises run by communes and production brigades. On the basis of the findings, the Ministry of Agriculture, Animal Husbandry and Fisheries drafted "A Report on the New Situation of enterprises run by Communes and Production Brigades," which was submitted to the CPC Central Committee. The Secretariat of the CPC Central Committee called a meeting on January 30, 1984 to discuss the report. At the meeting, Hu Yaobang said, "We must put an end to the State of affairs in which hundreds of millions of people are engaged in growing grain to feed the population. But the change should be gradual. Enterprises run by communes and production brigades, as a new phenomenon are promising, but we should support and guide them correctly so that they will grow in a healthy way. We should not weaken or restrict enterprises run by communes and production brigades, nor just let them drift regardless of whether they survive or die out. Enterprises run by communes and production brigades are not only a supplement to the State-run enterprises. They are important in three respects: First, they represent the road to wealth. The countryside cannot get rich without industry. Second, they constitute an important force in the national economy. Third, they serve as a supplement to State-run industry. They should be allowed to compete with State-run enterprises, and not be regarded as just a supplement. It is not bad for State-run enterprises to feel pressure." Hu proposed, "Enterprises run by communes and production brigades may undergo consolidation once every two years, but they should use methods different from those taken by the State-run enterprises, because they are collectives. For instance in consolidating the leading bodies, it will not do for us to impose cadres upon them. That would make things even worse, because that would deprive them of their independence. Shanghai does not agree to let enterprises run by communes and production brigades process farm produce and sideline products. But is it possible to gradually leave the processing of farm produce and sideline products to enterprises run by communes and production brigades along with the growth of the economy, while cities should stop expanding processing industry. We will not force the large processing enterprises to close down. But the cities should not expand such processing industry blindly. That is the prudent and safe way of development." After discussion, the Secretariat affirmed the value of the report: "Enterprises run by communes and production brigades serve as one of the roads for rural people to achieve common prosperity. They constitute an important force in the national economy, and serve as a major supplement to the State-run enterprises, for they can fill the gap left by State-run enterprises. Enterprises run by communes and production brigades and the State-run enterprises may spur each other forward. Our general principle for enterprises run by communes and production brigades is: Give them correct support, guidance and administration, and help them grow in a healthy way. We should use this general principle to unify the thinking of the whole Party. We should neither weaken them or block their development, nor treat them as a transitional measure, nor should we let them run their own course and grow aimlessly, not caring whether they survive or die out."

The Ministry of Agriculture, Animal Husbandry and Fisheries in its report says: "Considering the fact that communes and production brigades are gradually being transformed into township and village cooperative economic institutions and there have appear and a large number of cooperative enterprises run by several households or by people across different districts as well as associated enterprises and private enterprises run by individuals, and there is a tendency among them to gradually converge into small towns, their former name, enterprises run by communes and production brigades, can no longer reflect the latest development, so we propose that they be named 'township and village enterprises (TVEs) ."

On March 1, 1984, the CPC Central Committee and the State Council issued the "Circular on Distributing the 'Report by the

Ministry of Agriculture, Animal Husbandry and Fisheries on the New Situation of Enterprises Run by Communes and Production Brigades" (Document No. 4), which agrees to change the name of enterprises run by communes and production brigades to township enterprises (TVEs). [1] When the Circular reached the countryside, the broad masses of peasants and workers of TVEs hailed it as "having brought us a second spring, a timely rain which we have been awaiting for so long."

Before 1983, enterprises run by communes and production brigades had only two "wheels," namely, the commune-run enterprises and enterprises run by production brigades. Since 1984, TVEs have had four "wheels," namely, the township-run enterprises, the village-run enterprises, the cooperative enterprises and private enterprises. That has led to a vigorous growth in the number of enterprises, the number of workers, the total output value and the industrial output value.

However the distribution of Document No. 4 of the Party Central Committee and the State Council did not mean that the document immediately unified the people's thinking and removed all the obstacles to the development of TVEs. Some people were still prejudiced against TVEs.

An extraordinary letter signed by "Fan Zhuguan" On March 23, 1984, soon after the issue of Document No. 4, a letter signed with the pseudonym "Fan Zhuguan," which sounds in Chinese like the term "anti-subjectivism," wrote a letter to a leading comrade of the central government, criticizing the document for failing to give a proper appraisal to the roles of TVEs. It queried: "How can TVEs have such magic functions? Where does their vitality come from?" The letter said that "TVEs should not be made an independent force pitted against and developing in parallel with State-run enterprises." It demanded: "If commune-run industry could be relied on to achieve the task of eliminating the three major differences, why is there any need to build large- and medium-sized backbone industrial

---

[1] Archive Research Center of the CPC Central Committee: *Major Archives since the 12th CPC Congress*, People's Publishing House, 1986 Vol. 1, p. 439

projects? Such contentions as 'TVEs are of strategic importance in view of the reality of China' and 'It is a necessary historical step' are reminiscent of the slogans touted during the launching the drive to build industry in a big way during the Great Leap Forward in 1958." The letter believed Document No. 4 "did not draw upon historical lessons," asking, "Haven't we paid enough tuition fees? Can we rest assured that no more blind construction projects will spring up everywhere under such slogans again?"

The letter was from an individual, but it represented the mentality of some people who bore prejudice against peasants. That was an indication that the development of TVEs would not be plain sailing.

Criticism from an ecologist A Chinese ecologist, in an investigation report titled, "The Situation and Problems in the Development of TVEs in the Yangtze Delta in Jiangsu Province" and published in July 1985, sharply criticized TVEs. He said that he believed that the development of TVEs would "first of all cause an imbalance in the structure of agriculture. The townships and towns will overlook the importance of grain production because they believe that only industry can bring them wealth. Then they will pollute the environment, cause troubles with water resources and threaten people's health. Then, because of a shortage of raw and other materials, and energy, their competition with State-run enterprises and collective enterprises will intensify. TVEs obtain their raw and other materials through their own procurement personnel, who travel to all parts of the country and even engage in malpractice to obtain supplies. This practice can neither guarantee the supply nor help maintain good social conduct. TVEs mostly use only old equipment, some even produced in the 1920s and 1930s, and this will only result in high costs and low efficiency. That would mean a great waste of human, material and financial resources. In view of the 'super-high speed' growth of TVEs that has almost got out of control, it would be advisable to support those that merit support (those engaged in the processing of farm produce and sideline products) and close down those that should be closed down (such as those engaged in heavy industry and those causing serious environmental pollution)."

The view of an economic planner A specialist in economic planning published an article on July 12, 1985, titled, "Macro Control of TVEs Should Be Strengthened." The article pointed out that TVEs "have been growing so fast and so vigorously that they have brought about a series of problems. One is a serious shortage of funds. The fact that most of them rely on bank loans to tide over difficulties is more than the banks can bear. Second, TVEs have a serious shortage of material supply, which aggravates the strained situation in material supply, pushing up the prices and leading to a scramble for raw materials by TVEs and State-run enterprises within and outside the State plans. Third, TVEs vie with agriculture for land and labor power. Altogether, the current development of TVEs has gone far beyond the financial and material capacity of the country, and has begun to affect macroeconomic efficiency and social benefits in certain respects. Should this be allowed to go on without readjustment and proper control and guidance, it is bound to lead to an explosion in investment and credit that cannot be controlled."

A leading comrade said that loss of control in "four fields" had been caused by TVEs According to a leading comrade, control was being lost in four aspects of the country's national economy, namely, loss of control of bank loans, of the use of foreign exchange, of investment in capital construction and of consumption funds. In a speech at a national conference in 1985, he pointed out, "The loss of control in the four aspects has been caused by TVEs." He added that in 1984 "the over-rapid growth of TVEs and the excessive size of capital construction have gone beyond both objective and subjective capability. TVEs have grown too freely, and they have got too much loan support from the banks." He believed that owing to the excessive bank loans borrowed by TVEs, "there was a shortage of funds for the State purchase of agricultural products, and peasants got only unofficial IOUs." Under those circumstances, the banks believed "too much paper money was in circulation, and the first thing to be done was a tightening of control over bank loans to TVEs." He proposed stopping all loans to TVEs even if the formalities had already been completed or the loan was to be used on a project under construction.

All sorts of criticisms and attacks directed at TVEs from different quarters had one thing in common — exaggeration based on bias, although some of the problems they cited did exist to a certain extent. But was the loss of control in the four aspects caused by TVEs? The media published a series of articles that refuted this criticism with facts.

"The loss of control over foreign exchange" had nothing to do with TVEs, for they never used foreign exchange but only earned it.

"The loss of control over investment in capital construction" referred to the fact that government institutions at various levels increased investment in capital construction projects in disregard of the norms stipulated in State plans, thus giving the State budget a burden too heavy for the State coffers to bear. The total investment in fixed assets in the whole country reached 183.3 billion yuan, of which only 15.56 billion yuan, or 8.5% of the total, was spent by TVEs. The bulk of the funds used by TVEs were raised by peasants themselves. TVEs used 6.1 billion yuan from their profits to increase production, of which rural people raised three billion yuan from their own pockets. These two sources combined totaled 9.1 billion yuan, or 58.5% of the total investment in fixed assets by TVEs. The working capital of 500 million yuan granted by the State to the communes accounted for only 3.2% of the total investment. The Agricultural Bank of China lent TVEs 3.6 billion yuan, and the rural credit cooperatives gave them loans amounting to 2.36 billion yuan. The two put together totaled 5.96 billion yuan, or 38.3% of the total investment by TVEs, accounting for only 3.2% of the total State investment. So how could TVEs, which made up 8.5% of the total social investment in fixed assets, be held responsible for the problems that cropped up in the macro economy?

"The loss of control over consumption funds" was the result of government institutions freely raising wages and giving out bonuses beyond the State payroll plan. TVEs were peasants' enterprises, and their wages were not covered by State plans; therefore they had nothing to do with "the loss of control."

"The loss of control over bank loans"? The fact was that in 1984 it was decided that the loan targets for banks for the following year should be based on the credit balance of the current year in each bank. That broke up the division of labor among the four commercial banks — the Agricultural Bank of China, the Industrial and Commercial Bank of China, the China Construction Bank and the Bank of China — and led to competition in lending. The combined credit balance of the four banks at the end of that year amounted to 441.9 billion yuan. The Agricultural Bank lent TVEs a total of 18.9 billion yuan, accounting for only 4.3% of the total bank credit balance. So how could the 4.3% credit to TVEs be held responsible for the loss of control over bank loans? According to the Agricultural Bank, the bank credit balance to TVEs from the Agricultural Bank and the Rural Credit Cooperative came to 29.2 billion yuan at the end of 1984, while the deposits in the Agricultural Bank and the Rural Credit Cooperatives from TVEs came to 11.6 billion yuan, and deposits from individuals among the workers of TVEs came to 18 billion yuan. The two combined reached a total of 29.6 billion yuan, which was 101.4% of the bank credit to TVEs. That is to say, TVEs borrowed money from the Agricultural Bank and the Rural Credit Cooperatives through the deposits TVEs and their workers placed in the banks. They scarcely used State funds at all.

Vice Premier Wan Li, in a speech at a national conference attended by leaders of a number of provinces and municipalities in June 1985 said, "Last December we issued more currency than necessary, raised wages and bonus a little bit too fast, and issued more bank loans than we should have done. That primarily was a problem in policy. We have a habit of cutting back indiscriminately without taking into consideration the specific conditions. That practice benefits those with vested interests and incurs losses to the honest, with the result that it encourages people to inflate the basic figures. In some places, bonuses for bank clerks are based on the amount of loans issued. That will lead to the four banks vying with one another to issue loans."[1] Wan Li had laid bare the essence of the problem.

The Rural Policy Study Office of the Secretariat of the CPC Central Committee, the Rural Development Research Center of the State Council and the Ministry of Agriculture, Animal Husbandry

[1] *Selected Works of Wan Li*, People's Publishing House, 1995, 432

and Fisheries jointly organized investigation teams and sent them to 14 provinces. In July, August and September the teams investigated TVEs in more than 100 counties. Later, they received investigation reports from a dozen provinces.

The investigation teams reached the common conclusion that, following the promulgation of Document No. 4, TVEs in China entered a new phase of development, showing an excellent situation. By the end of 1985, the number of TVEs had reached 12.22 million, including 1.57 million run by townships or villages, accounting for 12.8% of the total; 280,000 cooperative enterprises in other forms, accounting for 2.3% of the total; 1.12 million associated enterprises run by peasants, accounting for 9.2% of the total; and 9.25 million private enterprises run by individuals, accounting for 75.7% of the total. Their combined output value in 1985 reached 272.8 billion yuan, up by 43.4% in terms of comparable prices and accounting for 44% of the total rural output value (the Third Plenary Session of the 11th CPC Central Committee put forth a demand for the output value of enterprises run by communes and production brigades to account for half of the total rural output value by 1985), including 182.7 billion yuan of industrial output value, accounting for 18.8% of the national total. The enterprises owned by townships and villagers had a combined asset worth 134 billion yuan, including 75 billion yuan of fixed assets and 59 billion yuan of circulating capital.

This fully proved that TVEs had become an important force in the country's national economy, especially in its rural economy. The history of TVE development is not a long one, but it has been displaying importance in both its position and functions in the country's rural economy and the national economy as a whole.

(1) The development of TVEs has caused the separation of industry, construction, transportation, commerce and the service trades from agriculture, thus diversifying the original mono-economy into a multiple economic structure in the countryside.

(2) After the household contract responsibility system was introduced in China's countryside, there appeared a big surplus of rural labor power. In a populous and relatively poor country like China, it would have been impossible to rely entirely on large-scale State

investment in building enterprises to absorb the surplus rural labor power. Nor is it possible to take the capitalist road of forcing a large number of peasants to swarm into the cities. TVEs have created a way of providing work for peasants "by leaving their farming work without leaving their native places." That helps resolve a major problem China has been confronted with in its national economic construction.

(3) TVEs have been built and grown with funds from agriculture when agriculture had developed to a certain stage, and with State support in policy and financing. And when TVEs have developed to a certain stage, they in turn give agriculture support to help it grow, through different forms of investment. Statistics show that the expenditure on agriculture from TVEs covers about 80% of the State agricultural support funds.

(4) TVEs have become an important source of State revenue. Between 1980 and 1985, TVEs paid a total of 37.9 billion yuan in taxes to the State, averaging 6.3 billion a year. In 1985 alone, they paid a total of 13.7 billion yuan in taxes, accounting for 7.5% of the State revenue. In addition, TVEs make indirect contributions to the State revenue, and share indirectly State expenditure.

First, TVEs pay a higher price than the State-run enterprises for the raw materials and fuel they buy. The market price they pay is bound to be higher than the State-fixed price which the State-run enterprises pay, and this price factor increases the income of the State-run enterprises. Investigations show that in 1985 TVEs bought 37 million tons of coal, eight million tons of rolled steel, 11.2 billion kwh of electricity, 3.66 million tons of diesel oil and 5.82 million tons of gasoline at market prices, which together meant an additional income of 10 billion yuan for State-run enterprises.

Second, TVEs assume the bulk of administrative expenditure and rural public welfare spending, thus saving the State expenditure and lightening the peasants' burden. TVEs handed to townships and villages 20 billion yuan, or 30% of their after-tax profits, during the Sixth Five-Year Plan period.

(5) The development of township industry, particularly the parallel economic association between urban and rural industries, has

broken through the mutual seclusion between town and country, and administrative divisions, thus enhancing the integration of town and country and peasants and workers into new relationships.

(6) The development of TVEs in connection with the traditional bazaar trade is giving rise to the formation of new towns as economic and cultural centers in the countryside. There were 2,600 administrative towns in rural China in 1980, but, thanks to the development of TVEs, the number increased to 6,600 in 1985.

(7) The development of the commodity economy in the countryside has abolished self-seclusion and complacency with the natural economy, accelerated the rhythm of the life of the Chinese peasants, spurred them to acquire more scientific knowledge, changed their thinking, and broadened their vision. This is particularly obvious among young people in the countryside, who display a hitherto-unknown thirst for knowledge. Marked changes have taken place in the mental outlook of China's peasants.

Investigation reports further point out that after a few years' economic development, there have appeared the following different types of regions in China:

First, the "Southern Jiangsu" type. Belonging to this type are the suburbs of large and medium-sized cities in the Yangtze Delta, the Pearl River Delta, the eastern Liaoning Peninsula and the eastern Shandong Peninsula, and Beijing, Tianjin and Shanghai. These have a combined population of more than 100 million, and township collective enterprises are in the absolute majority, while household-run and associated enterprises run by a number of peasant houses are in a small minority. TVEs are larger in scale, with a high level of management, advancing along the road of modernization, serial production and enterprise grouping.

Second, the "Wenzhou (Zhejiang)-Fuyang (Anhui)" type. This type represents regions where the local economy was relatively backward, and TVEs, which used to develop on a very limited scale, have grown rapidly in recent years. Here, TVEs are mainly run by individual peasant households and associated enterprises run by a number of households. The regions of this type are estimated to have a combined population of less than 300 million.

Third, the "Gengche (in Suqian, Anhui)-Langfang (Hebei) "type. This comes between the two types mentioned above. Enterprises here are of four different levels, run by townships, villages, associated peasant households and individual households, respectively. They are growing rapidly, almost doubling in number every two or three years. Generally, those run by townships and villagers are of the same number as those run by associated peasant households and individual households. These districts have a combined population of more than 300 million.

In an interview with some guests from Yugoslavia on June 12, 1987, Deng Xiaoping said: "The greatest, and most unexpected accomplishment in our rural reform has been the development of TVEs. They appeared all of a sudden, branching into multiple operations, running the commodity economy in all sorts of small enterprises, forming a shock force. This success should not be attributed to our Party's Central Committee. TVEs have achieved an annual growth of more than 20 percent for several years running. The development of TVEs has focused on industry, but they have also branched out into other trades. They present job openings for half of the rural surplus labor power. The peasants do not come to the cities, but have built a large number of new towns. If there is anything the Party Central Committee can take credit for, it should be the policy it has formulated to enliven the economy. This policy has yielded such good results that we know that we have done a very good thing. I personally had not anticipated it, nor had many comrades. It has been a pleasant surprise."[1]

On August 29 of the same year, Deng told some Italian guests: "How were we to dispose of the surplus labor power after the introduction of the responsibility contracting system in the countryside? Originally, we did not find any good way out. For centuries 70%-80% of the rural labor power had been tied to the land in this country. A person had only one or two fifteenths of a hectare of farmland to till on average. It was practically impossible to eke out a

[1] *Selected Works of Deng Xiaoping*, People's Publishing House, 1993, Vol. 3, p. 238

decent living by farming on such a tiny piece of land. What were we to do when surplus manpower appeared in the countryside? Our experience over the past decade shows that this problem could be solved only when the initiative of the grassroots organizations and the peasants themselves was mobilized to develop multiple economic undertakings and build new types of TVEs. TVEs are capable of absorbing about half of the rural surplus labor power. This good idea came not from us leaders, but was the creation of the agricultural institutions at the grassroots level and the peasants themselves. TVEs in turn have promoted agricultural development."[1] Deng's remarks may be considered a general summary of the debate over TVEs.

In order to give guidance to TVEs, and help them raise their operations to a new level, in 1988 the Ministry of Agriculture, the State Planning Commission, the State Scientific and Technological Commission and the State Education Commission jointly convened the National Conference on Technological Progress of TVEs, with the aim of helping speed up the technological transformation of TVEs. The meeting worked out the "Outline Program of Action for Accelerating the Technological Progress of TVEs." In 1987, the Ministry of Agriculture, the State Economic Commission and the Ministry of Foreign Economic Relations and Trade jointly convened the National Conference on the Export Business of TVEs. The meeting worked out a document titled, "Some Policy Provisions for Better Export Performance of TVEs" in an effort to help TVEs to develop as export-oriented enterprises. In order to commend those who had made outstanding contributions to the development of TVEs, the Ministry of Agriculture, via the Central Television Station, the Central People's Broadcasting Station and the *China Township Enterprises News*, sponsored a nationwide drive to select outstanding township enterprise activists. A citation meeting was held in the Great Hall of the People in Beijing in September 1987, at which State leaders personally congratulated such activists.

---

[1] *Selected Works of Deng Xiaoping*, People's Publishing House, 1993, Vol. 3, pp. 251-252

Encouraged by the excellent situation, the departments in charge of township industries and cadres at the grassroots level showed tremendous initiative in their work, and peasants showed great energy in running TVEs, which succeeded in boosting their output value by an average annual rate of 40% in the period. (See Table 2-4)

Table 2-4 Development of TVEs 1984-1988

Year	1984	1985	4986	4987	1988
Number of enterprises (unit: 10,000)	165	1,222	1,515	1,750	1,888
Number of workers (unit: 10,000)	3,848	6,979	7,937	8,805	9,545
Total output value (billion yuan)	142.1	272.8	371.7	505.5	750.2
Industrial output value (billion yuan)	102.1	182.7	244.3	341.2	499.3

Source: Statistics on TVEs, Ministry of Agriculture

Among the four "wheels" of the TVEs, there were rapid changes in the rate of increase of output and the ratio of each to the total. The ratio of collective enterprises run by townships dropped from 47.8% in1984 to 37.6% in 1988; that run by villages went down from 37.9% to 29.6%; that of cooperative enterprises rose from 7.4% to 8.6%; and that of enterprises run by individuals rose from 6.9% to 24.2%. Their annual growth rate of output value averaged 39.6%. The latter two "wheels" showed a faster increase in their ratio to the total.

Section 4 Readjustment and Consolidation of TVEs (1989-1991)

"The tree desires stillness, but the wind will not cease." In 1989, when the Chinese people were showing bubbling vigor in developing TVEs and boosting the rural economy in order to build a better-off life in response to the call of the CPC Central Committee, there broke out in China the "June 4" political incident. The incident was followed by the disintegration of the Soviet Union and upheavals in some East European socialist countries. For a time, some people came out into the open, capitalizing on the work of readjustment and consolidation, and hoisted the banners of "opposing peaceful evolution" "opposing liberalization" and "opposing capitalism." They demanded that it was imperative "to distinguish two different concepts of reform and opening to the outside world" and to "distinguish between capitalism and socialism in the reforms." They declared that to develop the private economy with the prerequisite of developing that of public ownership "is essentially advocating economic privatization." They criticized the theory that the fundamental task of socialism is to develop the productive forces, and condemned it as "a vulgar outlook on the productive forces." They clamored that to develop the market economy under socialism "is negating the dominant position of public ownership and the planned economy."[1]

For a time, TVEs came under fire. Some of the critics said that State-run industry continued to slide while rural industry soared, and they demanded "resolute measures to suppress the rural industry in defense of State-owned industry." In their view, "readjustment and consolidation means slashing back on TVEs." When TVEs were under attack from all sides and were facing many difficulties, the Agricultural Bank of China, on the pretext of "tightening circulation and checking inflation," announced that it would impose "zero growth" in loans to TVEs in 1990.

The broad masses of peasants and workers of TVEs were puzzled and worried in the face of such an abrupt turn in the situation. They said, "Yesterday we were praised for our contributions, but overnight we have become culprits." They saw a dark cloud looming over TVEs and the future of the Chinese countryside. During the three years of readjustment and consolidation (1989-1991), the "zero growth" of loans led to a "zero increase" in the transfer of labor power from agriculture to township industry and commerce, and the increase rate of the average income of the peasants plummeted to an all-time low of 0.7%.

---

[1] Ma Licheng and Ling Zhijun: *A Conflict*, China Today Press, 1998

In an interview with commanders of the PLA units carrying out martial law in Beijing, Deng Xiaoping said, on June 9, 1989: "Is the basic point of reform and opening policy wrong? No. The policy is correct. Without reform and opening up, we would not have what we have today. In the last decade, the living standards of the people have taken a big step upward. We should say that we have risen to a new height, despite inflation and other problems. The achievements in the reform and opening to the outside world in the last decade must be given full appraisal." [1]

In a conversation with some comrades from Shanghai, Jiang Zemin who had just been elected CPC General Secretary, said, "TVEs should continue, as they are the hope of the peasants for common prosperity. The role of TVEs lies not only in supporting agriculture and sideline production, but also in their close ties with large industries in the cities and the country's export business, and with agriculture and non-staple food production. Without TVEs, there will be no money. Not only will the 'vegetable basket' and 'rice bag' be empty, the State revenue and export earnings will also be affected. Our TVEs are a unique creation in the world. In a country with such a large rural population, the surplus laborers resulting from the development of agriculture have not converged on the cities, but found jobs locally. The principle of developing TVEs is correct. The CPC Central Committee always attaches great importance to them." [2]

On November 9, 1989, the 13th CPC Central Committee, in its 3rd plenary session, adopted the "Resolution on Furthering Readjustment and Consolidation, and Deepening the Reforms." The Resolution points out, "It is necessary to actively guide TVEs to develop in a health way, in accordance with the principle of readjustment, reform, consolidation and improvement. The development of TVEs in our country has made important contributions to agriculture, employment, national economic development, and the growth of State revenue and foreign exchange. They constitute a major pillar

---

[1] *Selected Works of Deng Xiaoping*, People's Publishing House, 1993, Vol. 3, p. 306

[2] *Shanghai Supply and Marketing News*, Nov. 22, 1989

in the rural economy and an important component of the national economy. All localities should make earnest efforts to consolidate TVEs, and make them develop energetically in compliance with the State's industrial policy. It is necessary to take resolute measures to shut down, merge or change the line of business of a number of TVEs that feature high consumption of raw and other materials, low quality of products, serious pollution and low efficiency, and compete with large enterprises for raw materials and energy. Through readjustment and consolidation, TVEs should undertake structural reform, improve their management and style of operation, and raise their technical level and efficiency."[1]

The CPC Central Committee in its documents, and the leaders in their speeches refuted all the erroneous views on TVEs, buttressed the confidence of the hundreds of millions of TVE workers, and helped TVEs avoid further losses.

When TVEs ran into difficulties, great efforts were made to have a correct understanding and ensure the healthy development of TVEs, such as in the following four aspects:

1. Launching a large-scaled publicity drive to provide guidance to public opinion The Rural Economy Team of the Research Office of the State Council and the Institute of Rural Development under the Chinese Academy of Social Sciences acting on the directives of the leaders of the State Council conducted a one-year long survey on "how to correctly understand and appraise the relations between TVEs and the national economy," with the aim of providing reference for adopting effective policies. A survey report was submitted to the leaders of the State Council, and excerpts of the report appeared in the *People's Daily.* The views of the report are:

(1) TVEs are not a major factor behind the overheated economy. TVEs are mostly labor-intensive, and their development relies heavily on absorbing a large number of rural laborers instead of on large-scale investment.

(2) Bank loans to TVEs are 8-9% of the national total, and that,

[1] Archive Research Center of the CPC Central Committee: *Important Archives since the 13th CPC Congress*, People's Publishing House, 1991, China, p. 675

too, constitute no principal cause of credit expansion.

(3) TVEs have a double-sided impact on inflation. On the one hand, their fast growth stimulates inflation and contribute to over-heated development, but on the other, they help increase effective supply, thus lessening the structural conflicts between supply and demand, and weakening inflation to a certain extent.

(4) In their relations with large urban industrial enterprises, TVEs are both rivals and assistants. As TVEs are market-oriented, they help ease shortages arising from the imperfect industrial structure and product mix of large industrial enterprises in cities, and enhance their capacity to satisfy market demand. Only TVEs whose combined output amounts to less than 15% of the total compete with large urban industries in some areas.

(5) TVEs had created a large number of jobs, and their employment index is much better than that of the State-owned enterprises. The growth of TVEs has facilitated the substitution of the country's rich labor force for the shortage of capital. Between 1980 and 1988, for every 10,000 yuan increase in output created by TVEs, 1.22 jobs and 2,300 yuan of fixed assets were added, whereas State-owned enterprises needed 10,800 yuan invested in fixed assets to increase output value by 10,000 yuan and create only 0.25 jobs.

(6) TVEs had contributed to the development of agricultural production and the progress of agricultural modernization. Between 1984 and 1988, China marked time in its grain production, with the per hectare yield going down from 3,615 kg in 1984 to 3,577 kg in 1988. The growth of TVEs should not be held responsible for this decrease. On the contrary, the development of TVEs had much to do with increases in grain yield. The per hectare grain yield increased 30 kg in this period in those areas where TVEs were more developed, and agriculture there had benefited from the subsidies provided by TVEs. On the other hand, the per hectare grain yield dropped by 65 kg in areas where TVEs were underdeveloped, and the yield dropped by 42 kg in areas where TVEs had developed moderately. [1]

---

[1] *TVEs: An Irreplaceable Engine to the Development of the National Economy*, *People's Daily*, Oct. 3, 1990

In March 1989, the *China Township Enterprises News* carried a series of eight signed commentaries on the erroneous views advanced by some departments, such as "resolute suppression of TVEs in defense of State-run industries." They were titled: "Can TVEs Hold Their Banners High for Long?" "Should Rural Industry Be Blamed for the Backsliding of Industry Owned by the Whole People?" "One of Our Fundamental Principles Is to Develop TVEs," "Township Industry Constitutes an Important Wing of China's Modernization," "Are Small Enterprises Pretty or Ugly?" "Resolute Suppression of TVEs Cannot Check the Backsliding of State-Owned Enterprises," "Any Slip of TVEs May Affect the Macroeconomy" and "TVEs Should Resolutely Implement the Policy of Readjustment and Consolidation." The commentaries explicitly pointed out that in face of those peddling erroneous fallacies, the broad masses of the peasants pleaded to society: "Help TVEs!" [1]

On June 6 of the same year, the *Economic Daily* published a signed commentary titled, "Some Understandings of TVEs in the New Circumstances." The writer refuted the fallacies that TVEs compete with State-owned enterprises for funds, raw materials and energy. The writer held that, first, when you look around the world, you find that a combination of large, medium-sized and small enterprises is a rational setup of enterprises in a country. Small and medium-sized enterprises are in the absolute majority in all countries, and their existence serves as a stimulus to large enterprises. They help solve unemployment problems, serve to supplement and fill out the national economy and are coordination partners for large enterprises. They play a role as equally important as that of large enterprises. All large enterprises developed from small and medium ones. Moreover, in China not all State-owned enterprises are large. The large ones account for only 0.6% of the total; the medium-sized ones account for 1.4%, and the small ones account for 98%. So the nature of ownership does not necessarily correspond to size. That way of thinking respects neither science nor facts.

Second, all the funds State-run enterprises used for development

[1] *China Township Enterprises News*, March 1989

and technological transformation came from State allocation. State-owned enterprises spent 229.8 billion yuan in 1987 on capital construction, renewal of equipment and other investment in fixed assets. The rural collective enterprises are part of the framework of socialist public ownership, but run by peasants and receiving few loans from the State. The bank loans to enterprises in 1988 totaled 1,055 billion yuan, but State-owned enterprises received 1,014.3 billion or 96.1%, and TVEs whose output value accounted for 23.5% of the social total, received only 40.7 billion yuan, a mere 3.9% of the total. How can we say they had competed against State-run enterprises for funds?

Third, TVEs were not just energy gobblers. They were energy producers. In 1988, they consumed 150 million tons of coal, but produced 320 million tons of coal. So they actually provided 170 million tons of coal to the State. In the same year, they produced 16 billion kwh of electricity and consumed 67.1 billion kwh. If the coal they provided to society were turned into thermal electricity, their energy consumption would equal their energy production. Furthermore, TVEs have financed the building of small power stations in their localities. China raised its coal output by 360 million tons between 1978 and 1988, and of the net increase 220 million tons or 69% of the total were attributable to TVEs, which used no State funds in the construction of new coal mines. State-run coal mines, however, spent more than 40 billion yuan granted by the State to increase coal output by 140 million tons. Besides, when there was a power shortage, the State-owned enterprises had priority for power supply, which was available to TVEs only where there was a surplus. And when there was a power cut, TVEs were the first to suffer. So it is groundless to say that TVEs competed with State-owned enterprises for energy.

Fourth, in the planned economy era, raw and other materials were controlled by the State. The State met the needs of State-owned enterprises in the supply of materials under the plans in the first place before selling materials to TVEs at the market prices. Because the Chinese producer goods market is a deficient, unstandardized and unfair market, TVEs could not get enough raw materials due to the short supply, and had to purchase them at negotiated price instead of buying them at par with the State-run enterprises, so some people with the power of material distribution sought personal gains by taking advantage of raw materials sales. All this caused an increase of the production costs for TVEs, which often suffered from shortages of materials, from higher prices and from extortion by corrupt officials. In fact, TVEs were not the trouble makers but the victims in the area of material supply.[1]

2. Resolutely implementing the plan of readjusting the national economy put forth by the Fifth Plenary Session of the 13th CPC Central Committee He Kang, Minister of Agriculture, who was in charge of TVEs at the time, made concrete arrangements for the work with regard to TVEs in view of the actual conditions, at the National Conference on TVEs on January 5, 1990. He pointed out that the structural readjustment of TVEs, which covered the industrial structure, trade structure and product mix, constituted the major content of the principle of "readjustment, consolidation, transformation and improvement." TVEs in China have the dual characteristics of rural and industrial economies and the dual functions of economic returns and social benefits. Therefore the readjustment of TVEs must comply with the State's industrial policies and at the same time proceed from the particular features of TVEs with a thorough understanding of the guiding thinking and principle of readjustment. Specifically, it is necessary to:

(1) Correctly handle the relationship between readjustment and development. It is necessary to actively push readjustment and through it to help TVEs grow in a healthy way. Readjustment is the means and healthy development is the purpose; the two must be well coordinated.

(2) Correctly handle the relationship between the planned economy and market regulation. It is necessary to support the production of items needed in the market and encouraged by the State's industrial policies.

(3) Correctly handle the relationship between preferential treat-

---

[1] *Economic Daily*, June 6, 1989

ment and restriction, and between ordinary and key enterprises. In dealing with different trades, enterprises and products, it is necessary to take into consideration the market demand, technological progress, their role in the earning of foreign exchange, economic returns, industrial connections, arrangement of labor power and other factors, to give different guidance, providing preferential treatment to those enterprises that produce energy and raw materials, process farm and sideline products, make parts and accessories for large industrial enterprises, export commodities, or turn out small commodities for people in urban and rural areas and products needed by agricultural production, supporting collectively-owned enterprises, and restricting in particular those enterprises characterized by high consumption of material, low quality, serious pollution of the environment and making very poor economic returns.

(4) Correctly handle the relationship between unified implementation of the State industrial policy and bringing regional advantages into full play. It is necessary for the eastern region mainly to develop the internal capacity of enterprises by developing technology-intensive and technology/labor-intensive enterprises with low consumption of materials and energy, and for the western region mainly to develop resources and resources processing, and to achieve a faster growth in the course of restructuring.

(5) Correctly handle the relationship between the technological composition of higher, middle and lower levels and the structural composition of large, medium and small enterprises. It is necessary to insist on the principle of constantly raising the level and at the same time adopt a pragmatic approach. That is to say, it is both necessary to develop advanced technology, intensified production and considerable scale of operation and at the same time to be aware of the rule of development by stages and the imbalance of regional development. It is necessary to develop different technologies of different levels to meet the diverse social needs, allow some traditional skills to continue to be practiced and refrain from randomly rejecting medium- and low-level technologies. It is necessary to decide the appropriate size of an enterprise in the light of the nature of the particular trade and the local social, economic and technical levels. The

appropriate size is the best size, not "the bigger the better." It is wrong to think that small enterprises must be backward, and it is even more mistaken to negate the role of small enterprises altogether.

(6) Correctly handle the relationship between a positive approach and a prudent attitude toward readjustment. The prerequisites for the work of readjustment is a stable development of the rural economy and social stability. The guideline is "fine-tuning of industry, steady readjustment of trades and fast readjustment of product mix." The key link to grasp at present is to readjust the problem of product mix. Unless it is absolutely necessary, enterprises are not to be closed down, and every effort should be made to transform, merge or change the lines of production of those enterprises it is deemed necessary to close down.

(7) Correctly handle the relationship between TVEs and agriculture. With the energetic development of agriculture as the prerequisite, it is necessary to actively develop TVEs, and make over-all arrangement concerning labor power for both agriculture and TVEs. It is necessary to give guidance to TVEs in constantly accumulating funds "to supplement and develop agriculture," and at the same time make great efforts to develop the processing of farm produce and sideline products. Enterprises which support agriculture should open new fields of such support, and gradually achieve the integrated development of agriculture and non-agricultural industries in the rural economy.

(8) Correctly handle the relationship between TVEs and urban industry. Township industry and urban industry should develop in a coordinated way, to achieve ultimate integrated growth. It is necessary to gradually achieve a rational industrial division of labor based on proper resource distribution and relevant guarantees.

3. Cultivation of the internal capability of TVEs in the course of readjustment and consolidation The Ministry of Agriculture in a circular in July 1989 demanded, "Implement in an all-round way the essentials of the resolution of the Fourth Plenary Session of the 13th Party Central Committee and Comrade Deng Xiaoping's important speeches, analyze the new circumstances confronting TVEs, sum up experience objectively, keep the future in mind, unify thinking, make active readjustments, deepen the reform, work hard, and make TVEs develop in a healthy, coordinated and sustained way."

In 1990, the Ministry of Agriculture further urged, "Focus on the readjustment of the industrial structure; cultivate the internal capability and improve management in an all-round way; optimize the composition of the factors of production and make great efforts to energize operations; strive to develop export-oriented enterprises; intensify the building of the service sector; make practical efforts to do political work well; and create a good environment for the consolidation of TVEs and the deepening of the reforms." On March 17, 1990, the ministry promulgated the "Resolution on Launching an 'Enterprise Management Year' among All TVEs across the Country." In the Resolution, the Ministry urged TVEs across the country to lay emphasis on the fundamental management of the enterprises in 1990, and on quality control in 1991. This "Year of Enterprise Management" campaign took the deepening of the reforms in enterprises as the driving force, made the improvement of economic efficiency the central link, and the improvement of product quality and the lowering of material consumption the focal points in work, and urged TVEs to achieve a shift from expansion of production by enlarging scale to expansion of production by internal improvement, a shift from speed efficiency to management efficiency, and a shift from management by experience to management by relying on science. The Ministry worked out the "Basic Working Methods of Management for TVEs." Thanks to all the measures taken, TVEs in China showed further improvement in quality, as follows:

(1) TVEs had laid an initial foundation for basic enterprise management and management in specific fields with fixed norms. Some of them introduced the 1,000-point inspection system for enterprise management. Certain enterprises were taken as pilot units for introducing modern enterprise management.

(2) On the basis of strengthening enterprise management, the work of raising enterprises to a higher level began. In addition to the State Grade I and Grade II enterprises and national advanced TVEs, the local governments selected some TVEs as provincial advanced enterprises, prefectural advanced enterprises and county advanced

enterprises. With the approval of the relevant authorities, 52 enterprises became State Grade II enterprises in 1990. This, plus the previous Grade I and Grade II enterprises, two TVEs became State Grade I enterprises, and 118 TVEs won the title of State Grade II Enterprise. In accordance with the "Trial Rules for Naming Advanced Enterprises among TVEs" formulated by the Ministry of Agriculture in 1990, the first batch of 32 TVEs became national advanced enterprises.

(3) TVE training centers were built at five levels across the country. By the end of 1990, there were 43 training centers for TVEs at and above the provincial level, and 395 training centers at the prefecture or county level. The number of TVE employees attending the training at different levels reached 930,000.

(4) The contract responsibility system of enterprises was further improved to cover at least 95% of TVEs.

(5) Eventually, 483 enterprises were cited by the Ministry of Agriculture as advanced enterprises in the "Year of Enterprise Management."

In the "Year of Enterprise Quality Control," the Ministry of Agriculture made work arrangements on March 9, 1991, as follows: Focusing on helping the township-run and village-run collective enterprises meet the norms for total quality control, disseminating the knowledge of quality control nationwide, popularizing advanced technologies, technological processes and management experience for the production of products that reach the national norms, and building a system of quality guarantee. TVEs across the country were to make the raising of product quality their central task, training in quality control the means and work measurement the link, to make a breakthrough, and raise awareness of the importance of quality in every department, so as to transform themselves from being quantity-oriented to being quality-oriented.

(1) The Ministry of Agriculture invested 15 million yuan and the provinces also made investment from 1986 to 1994 in building 50 quality inspection offices in 24 wholesale centers for products of TVEs nationwide;

(2) The provinces, municipalities directly under the Central Government and autonomous regions ran 200 training courses in quality

control, with 50,000 persons attending, in 1991;

(3) Quality control teams were set up extensively among TVEs, with 124 quality control teams cited by the Ministry of Agriculture for their good performance and eight teams cited by the State Council;

(4) With the deepening of the comprehensive quality control movement, 2,480 TVEs won certificates of comprehensive quality control worthiness issued by the Ministry of Agriculture;

(5) The products of TVEs began to show better quality, thanks to the quality control drive. Among them, 14 won national quality awards, and 689 won ministry-level awards. The Ministry of Agriculture and the Central Committee of the Chinese Communist Youth League jointly organized a national contest of production skills among young workers from TVEs.

4. Education in work ethics and moral integrity In order to strengthen confidence in overcoming difficulties, Vice Minister of Agriculture Chen Yaobang, on January 9, 1990, at a national conference on the work of TVEs, called on TVEs to launch an education drive among their workers in the Party's basic line, the basic government policies and the basic reality of China (the "Three Basics"), and in deepening love for the country, for socialism and for their own enterprises (the "Three Loves"), in the history of their enterprises, the family and themselves (the "Three Histories" for short) and in strengthening self respect, self protection and self improvement (the "Three Selfs" for short). He pointed out, "These are the essential part of the political and ideological work in TVEs, and constitute an important component of the socialist education movement throughout the country in the new era. The experience of some localities has proved that this education drive has not only helped enterprises persevere in socialist orientation in their development, but also mobilized the initiative of the workers, and strengthened their solidarity and the rallying power of the enterprises, which ensures their steady and healthy development amid difficulties."

On the basis of this drive, the Ministry of Agriculture and the Publicity Department of the CPC Central Committee, on January 5, 1991, jointly convened the "National Conference on Ideological and Political Work in TVEs." At the conference, Xu Weicheng, Deputy

Chief of the Publicity Department of the CPC Central Committee, said, "The basic task of the ideological and political work in TVEs is to educate their workers in patriotism, collectivism and socialism, constantly improve their moral quality, arouse their initiative, gradually bring up a contingent of a new type of workers characterized by high aspirations, moral integrity, good education and good discipline, who are united with one soul and one mind, and work hard to help their enterprises grow in a healthy way, and make continuous contributions to the task of building a socialism with unique Chinese features." At the conference, 102 enterprises were cited for their ideological and political work.

5. Boosting the morale of purchase and marketing personnel For their survival and development, TVEs rely on the market, not on the State plans. They expect the 10 million or so of their purchase and marketing personnel to bring back raw materials, energy and market information, and take their products to the market. To the purchase and marketing workers, the market is their battlefield, and their weapon is their tenacity of "traveling across the width and length of the country, of racking their brains to find good ideas, tiring out their tongues to convince their clients, and overcoming all sorts of hardships." When TVEs run into difficulties, it is the workers responsible for purchase and marketing who come to the rescue. The Ministry of Agriculture convened the National Conference on the Purchase and Marketing Work of TVEs on November 15, 1990, at which it cited the meritorious deeds of 148 supply and marketing departments in TVEs, as well as 680 outstanding purchase and marketing workers. Vice Minister Chen Yaobang said that the advanced purchase and marketing departments and outstanding purchase and marketing workers of TVEs had the following fine qualities in common:

(1) A tireless spirit of exploration;

(2) Tenacious credibility;

(3) Ability to overcome hardships and difficulties;

(4) The capacity to provide all-round services.

TVEs cultivated their internal capability through readjustment and consolidation under extremely subjective and objective difficulties in the period 1989-1991. The number of TVEs decreased by 190,000 in that period, and the number of their workers decreased by 2.8 million. The annual increase of total output value dropped from about 50% to 21.4% while their industrial output value rose at an average annual rate of 25.2%. (See table 2-5)

Table 2-5 Performance of TVEs 1988-1991

	1988	1989	1990	1991	Net increase in 1991 over 1988
Number of enterprises (1=10,000)	1,888	1,866	1,873	1,908	20
Number of workers (1=10,000)	9,545	9,367	9,265	9,613	68
Total output value (1=100 million yuan)	7,502	8,402	9,780	11,810	4,308
Of which, industrial output (1=100 million yuan)	4,993	6,100	7,097	8,699	3,696

Source: Statistics on TVEs, Ministry of Agriculture

Section 5 Period of High-Speed Economic Growth (1992-1997)

New problems cropped up in China's domestic economy in 1991. State-owned enterprises with independent accounting showed a drop of 15.3% in tax payments from 177.5 billion yuan in 1988 to 150.3 billion yuan in 1990, and a drop of 56.5% in profits from 89.2 billion yuan to 38.8 billion yuan. The percentage of loss-making State-owned enterprises rose from 10.9% to 27.6%, with the net losses rising from 8.19 billion yuan to 34.88 billion yuan — a 3.3-fold increase. The profits of State-run commerce and the supply and marketing cooperatives went down from 12.3 billion yuan to 670 million yuan — a 94.6% steep drop and the percentage of the loss-making enterprises grew from 9.9% to 26.7%, with the net losses shooting up from 4.8 billion yuan to 10 billion yuan — a 108% rise. That caused the country's GDP increase rate to slide from 11.3% to 3.8%, and its domestic industrial output increase rate to drop from 15.3% to 3.4%.

Deng Xiaoping, known as the "general architect of China's reform and opening-up drive," made an inspection tour of southern China in January 1992. The speeches he made on that trip of historic importance proved to be vital to the future of China.

On the basis of the essence of Deng Xiaoping's instructions made on his inspection tour to the South, the CPC Central Committee decided to adopt the general line of changing the socialist planned economy to a socialist market economy, and changing the socialist State-owned economy into a mixed economy, with socialist public ownership as the dominating form of ownership. That touched off the second round of reform across the country.

In the succeeding years between 1992 and 1996, China's GDP kept growing at an annual rate of at least 10%, rising from 2,161.8 billion yuan in 1991 to 6,788.5 billion yuan in 1996, for a 2.1-fold increase in five years. The added value of industry rose from 808.7 billion yuan to 2,908.3 billion yuan, a 2.6-fold increase in five years. For TVEs, the objective conditions improved tremendously, and among themselves enterprises of different types of ownerships competed for development, bringing the added value from 297.2 billion yuan in 1991 to 1,765.9 billion yuan in 1996, increasing 4.9 times, with the ratio to the GDP rising from 13.7% to 26%. Their added value of industry rose from 222.7 billion yuan to 1,262.8 billion yuan, increasing 4.7 times, with the ratio to the national total rising from 27.5% to 43.4%. The measures listed below were taken to help the development of TVEs:

1. Speeding up the development of TVEs in central and western China

The State Council convened the Conference for the Sharing of Experiences in Speeding Up the Development of TVEs in Central and Western China in Xi'an on November 18, 1992. That was the first national conference on the subject of TVEs convened by the State Council since their emergence. This fact was an indication of the importance the Chinese government gave to the work on TVEs.

Vice Premier of the State Council Tian Jiyun spoke at the conference on behalf of the State Council. He pointed out that TVEs "are a great creation by the Chinese peasants" and that "they have grown into a powerful economic pillar and made great contributions to the country within the short span of a little more than a decade. This is indeed a great miracle resulting from the policy of reform and opening to the outside world. The difficulty in realizing the target of reaching the level of a better-off life at the end of this century lies in the countryside. And the most important criterion for gauging the living standards of the rural population is the average per capita income. It will be very difficult to achieve an average annual increase of 5% in the per capita income of peasants. Our agricultural resources per person are rather poor and our agricultural productivity is low. For the country as a whole, it would be very difficult to rely solely on agriculture to reach the level of a better-off life in the countryside. We must make great efforts to develop the rural secondary and tertiary industries by relying on TVEs, if we wish to reach the target of a better-off life in the countryside, or even in the whole country at large." However, he said, "The development of the rural economy is starkly uneven between eastern China and the central and western regions, a major difference being among the TVEs. This disparity in economic development may affect not only the economic development of the central and western regions and their efforts to reach the better-off level, but also of the whole country. Now, in accordance with the spirit of the 14th Congress of our Party, while we continue to raise the development level of TVEs in the eastern region, we must speed up the development of TVEs in the central and western regions and areas where ethnic minorities live in compact communities, so that we may gradually close the gap between the two for the attainment of the goal of common prosperity for our 1.3 billion people. This is a historic mission we shoulder in building a socialist society with salient Chinese features, and an important strategic option in the course of accelerating the pace of development of the national economy and social progress."[1]

After the meeting, on February 14, 1993, the State Council promulgated the "Resolution of the State Council on Speeding Up the Development of TVEs in the Central and Western Regions." The document urged the provinces and autonomous regions to "persevere in the precondition of taking agriculture as the foundation, and pay equal attention to both large and medium-sized State-run enterprises and TVEs. The leadership of prefectures and counties should pay equal attention to both agriculture and TVEs. From now on, except for those projects under the unified State plan, the development of the secondary and tertiary industries at the county level in the central and western regions should gradually shift to the road of developing TVEs in those sectors. The comprehensive administrative departments in charge of industrial development and other relevant departments at all levels from the central government down to the grassroots should make active efforts to help the development of TVEs while at the same time serving the large and medium-sized State-run enterprises."

Between 1991 and 1996, the number of TVEs in the central and western regions grew from 12.42 million to 14.76 million — a net increase of 2.34 million. However, their ratio to the national total dropped from 65% to 63.2%, as the ratio of TVEs in the eastern region to the national total rose from 35% to 36.8%. The number of workers in TVEs in the central and western regions grew from 45.96 million to 68.53 million — a net increase of 22.57 million, and their ratio to the national total rose from 47.8% to 50.7%, while the number of the workers in TVEs in the eastern region in proportion to the national total dropped from 52.2% to 49.3%.

The total gross output (at current prices) of TVEs in the central and western regions grew from 393.1 billion yuan to 3,392.6 billion yuan — an average annual increase of 53.9%, and its ratio to the total output value of TVEs rose from 33.8% to 39.2%. The ratio of the eastern region to the national total output value of TVEs, how-

---

[1] State Council Research Project Team: *A Strategy for the Development of TVEs in the Central and Western Regions*, Xinhua Press, 1993, pp. 14, 16, 18

ever, dropped from 66.2% to 60.8% in the same period. And the industrial output value of TVEs in the central and western regions rose from 241.5 billion yuan to 2,030.4 billion yuan, at an average annual rate of 53.1%. And its ratio to the total national industrial output value grew from 27.7% to 31.8%, while that of the eastern region dropped from 72.3% to 68.2%. The figures indicate convincingly that TVEs in the central and western regions grew fairly rapidly, and the gap between the central and western regions on the one hand and the eastern regions on the other became narrower.

2. Formulating the "Township and Village Enterprise Law"

The Standing Committee of the Eighth National People's Congress, in its 22nd session on October 29, 1996, adopted the "Township Enterprise Law of the People's Republic of China," which was signed for promulgation by President Jiang Zemin on the same day. This was the first law for standardizing TVEs. The formulation of this law had undergone eight rounds of discussions and revisions after soliciting opinions from various ministries and commissions of the State Council, local governments and departments in charge of TVE work, economists and legal experts, township enterprises and peasants. Vice-Chairman of the NPC Standing Committee Tian Jiyun said: "The Party Central Committee and the State Council have formulated a series of policies, and promulgated more than 30 decrees and regulations, and the relevant departments have formulated 40 policy rules since 1978 with the aim of guiding, supporting and standardizing TVEs in the course of their development. These policies, regulations, provisions and rules form a basic legislative and policy system for the development of TVEs. But they are not laws. A law has the power of authority, stability, standardization and binding force; it is an expression of the people in a centralized form. The "Township and Village Enterprise Law" clearly defines the basic line, major principles and main tasks for the development of TVEs, clarifies the relationship of property rights, straightens out the management system of TVEs, defines their obligation to support agriculture and lays down the preferential measures for the development of TVEs as well as concrete requirements for the standardization of their conduct." The promulgation of this law is an important event in the history of TVE development. It allows TVEs to act in accordance with the law and prevents any department or individual from unlawfully interfering with TVEs, thereby protecting their legitimate rights and interests.

3. Deepening the reform of TVEs

Statistics from 1997 show that reforms were carried out in 520,000 rural collective enterprises, or 33.5% of the total number of rural collective enterprises. Among them, 4.07% were sold, 0.89% were merged with other entities, 0.22% were declared bankrupt, 0.39% were formed into enterprise groups, 21.23% were reorganized into joint stock cooperatives,[1] 1.53% were reorganized into limited liability companies, 0.53% into joint stock companies, and 4.66% into other forms of economic entities.

By 1998, the number of reorganized rural collective enterprises and joint stock enterprises newly set up by peasants reached 3.5 million, or 17.4% of the total number of TVEs. In Jiangsu Province, 74,002 rural industrial enterprises underwent one form or another of reform. They accounted for 79% of TVEs there. Among them, 55 were limited liability stock companies, 6,569 were other types of limited liability companies (8.87% of the total), 20,460 were joint-stock enterprises (27.65% of the total), 14,356 were leasing enterprises (19.4% of the total), 10,752 were contracted enterprises mortgaged against risks (14.53% of the total), 1,235 were reorganized enterprise groups (1.3% of the total), 14,150 were enterprises of public ownership turned into private ownership (19.12% of the total) and the rest, numbering 6,425 (9.13% of the total), were merged, went bankrupt, or were auctioned or sold.

---

[1] An enterprise form which combines fund and labor in cooperation, a creation by Chinese peasants.

4. Developing large and medium-sized enterprises

In order to keep in step with economic globalization and increase the competitiveness and efficiency of Chinese enterprises, in 1997 the Ministry of Agriculture in 1997 fixed the standards for large and medium-sized enterprises. On the basis of those reported by the relevant departments of local governments, the Ministry approved 6,376 TVEs to be up to the standards of large or medium-sized enterprises. Among them were the Shandong Wantongda Group, the Jilin Siping Hongzui Group, the Zhejiang Hengdian Group and two other enterprise groups cited as super-large TVEs, the Zhejiang Wanxiang Group and 273 others cited as Grade-A large TVEs, the Jiangsu Yilong Group and 1,265 others cited as Grade-B large TVEs, the Tianjin Longshen Industrial Company and 1,490 others cited as Grade-A medium-sized TVEs, and the Chenghai Hardware Tools General Factory and 3,343 others cited as Grade-B medium-sized TVEs.

Statistics concerning TVEs for 1995 show that at that time there were 736 State-class large TVE groups, 2,600 provincial-level large TVE groups and 4,531 large and medium-sized TVEs. They constituted only 0.036% of the total number of TVEs, but they possessed 10.8% of the total fixed assets, 6.5% of the turnover, 8.1% of the combined profits and taxes paid, and 13.2% of the total export deliveries of all TVEs. By1997, with the large TVEs as the nucleus, 1,039 national TVE groups had been formed through reorganization, and more provincial-level township enterprise groups had been formed.

5. Readjusting the industrial structure

A comparison between 1991 and 1996 shows that the number of township building enterprises grew at an annual rate of 46.8%, although their combined output value dropped from 9.6% to 7.8% of the total. The ratio of TVEs in tertiary industry to the total number of TVEs rose from 13.7% to 15.7%, at an annual rate of 46.7%. Among the rural industries, the number of those with farm produce as their raw material increased at an annual rate of 36%, although their ratio to the total dropped from 32.3% to 27.7%. The number of mining and raw materials enterprises based on local resources increased at an annual rate of 42.7%, and their ratio to the total rose from 15.3% to 16.6%. The products of TVEs delivered for export accounted for 10.3% of the total output of TVEs in 1991, and rose to 16.9% in 1996 — an average annual increase rate of 55.1%.

6. Improving the quality of the workforce

Measures were taken to improve the quality of the workforce through on-the-job training and recruiting new workers. Between 1991 and 1997, the number of township enterprise workers with a college education or higher rose from 0.4% to 1.6%; those with a senior secondary school or technical vocational school education of the same level rose from 18.3% to 27.2%; those with a junior secondary school or technical school education of the same level rose from 48.1% to 55.4%; and those with an education level lower than junior secondary school dropped from 33.2% to 15.6%. The number of technicians in the workforce rose from 2.76% to 5.4%. Among the technical workers, the number of technicians of the medium level or higher increased from 0.46% to1.6%, and that of the lower level from 2.3% to 3.9%. By introducing advanced technologies from outside, and through inventions and technological transformation to improve the technological level of the enterprises, the contribution from technology to the development of TVEs rose from 35% in 1991 to 45% in 1996.

To improve the management level, the relevant authorities in charge of TVEs encouraged them to strengthen their basic management, to modernize management, to organize public appraisal and to cite advanced enterprises, outstanding enterprise executives and enterprises of high efficiency. The annual per capita productivity of rural enterprises rose from 16,370 yuan in 1991 to 18,228 yuan in 1996. The output value of every 100-yuan-worth of fixed assets rose from 294 yuan to 498 yuan, and the taxable profits on the basis of every 100-yuan-worth of fixed assets rose from 25.3 yuan to 44.1 yuan. (See Table 2-6)

Table 2-6 Development of TVEs 1991-1996

Year	Number of Enterprises (1,000)	Number of workers (1,000)	Added value (billion yuan)	Industrial added value (billion yuan)
1991	19,090	96,140	297.2	222.7
1992	20,920	105,625	448.5	335.0
1993	24,530	123,450	800.7	593.6
1994	24,940	120,170	1,092.8	808.7
1995	22,030	128,620	1,459.5	1,080.4
1996	23,360	135,080	1,765.9	1,262.8
Average annual growth (%)	4.1	7.0	42.8	41.5

Source: Statistics on TVEs, Ministry of Agriculture

TVEs since 1997

In 1997 Asia was plunged into a financial turmoil. The currencies of some of China's neighboring countries depreciated drastically, and China's exports suffered heavily. Meanwhile, China's domestic market was dull, and most industrial departments reported a surplus of production capacity. The economic returns of State-run enterprises dropped, and many industrial sectors suffered losses. A large number of workers were laid off. In this situation, some people put the blame on TVEs. They said that since the State-run enterprises were in such difficulties, "it would be better to scrap the slogan of developing TVEs." Some said, "TVEs have fulfilled their historical mission. They should be called small and medium-sized enterprises."

In fact, small enterprises in 15 industrial sectors were ordered to close down or suspend production out of the need to deal with environmental pollution and enforce production safety measures. Most of these small enterprises were TVEs, for they were the worse hurt as they had inadequate environmental-protection norms and regulations, and received no government subsidies for environmental-protection facilities and measures. By 2001, most of the township-run small coal mines had been closed down, and the ratio of bank loans in the capital resources of TVEs dropped from 7.1% in 1996 to 5.4% in 1998. The number of TVEs dwindled from 23.36 million in 1996 to 20.85 million in 2002 — a net decrease of 2.51 million, and the number of their workers decreased from 135.08 million to 128.2 million, a net decrease of 6.88 million. TVEs once more found themselves in the doldrums.

In the course of overall economic restructuring, the State maintained a clear policy stand. President Jiang Zemin made several inspection tours of rural districts in Anhui, Jiangsu and Zhejiang provinces, and Shanghai, and in the speeches he made during the tours he held an affirmative attitude toward TVEs. He said: "Township enterprises are a great creation by the hundreds of millions of Chinese peasants, and also a great accomplishment our Party has made in implementing the policy of reform and opening up. Developing TVEs is an unavoidable way out for China's agricultural modernization, the only way for the countryside to become better off, and the only road to industrialization with Chinese characteristics. Developing TVEs is a major strategy and a fundamental, long-range principle. The development of TVEs has played an irreplaceably important role in enhancing the national economic growth and supporting the development of agriculture, helping the peasants increase their incomes and absorbing surplus rural laborers as well as in increasing the strength of the rural collective economy and supporting the rural public undertakings. Today, a significant portion of the new growth of our national economy is attributable to the role of TVEs. It is a task of great strategic importance, too, to actively build small towns."[1]

In April 2000, on the 3rd anniversary of the promulgation of the "Township and Village Enterprise Law," the NPC Standing Committee sent inspection teams to the countryside to examine the re-

[1] The Rural Work Team of the Policy Study Office of the CPC Central Committee: *General Secretary Jiang on Inspection Tours to Rural Areas*, China Agricultural Publishing House, 1998, pp. 244, 344, 345

sults of the implementation of the law. The inspectors found that the law still required complementary decrees and rules for its proper implementation, and that TVEs were still weighed down by heavy burdens and fell victim to frequent infringements upon their rights and interests. The inspection teams proposed to the State Council that it convene a national conference on the work in connection with TVEs as soon as possible so as to formulate some policy documents to protect and standardize the development of TVEs, and help them advance in a healthy way in the new century.

The authorities in charge of TVEs and TVE executives agreed that the way out for TVEs should be "a second wave of enterprise building." The TVE Bureau of the Ministry of Agriculture pointed out that in the second wave of enterprise building, it would be necessary to follow eight major strategies: 1. science and technology strategy; 2. market strategy; 3. brand name strategy; 4. enterprise group strategy; 5. specialty product strategy; 6. export-oriented strategy; 7. concentration strategy; and 8. strategy of the more advanced helping the less advanced. In addition, TVEs were required to achieve coordination in the following five fields, namely, coordination of the development of TVEs with the drive of industrializing the operations of agriculture, with the building of small towns, with the energetic development of the central and western regions, with the research work of scientific institutions and institutions of higher education, and with State-run enterprises.

In the period, the reforms deepened through reorganizing rural collective enterprises the ownership of which had been uncertain. By the end of 2000, this reorganization work had been completed in 80% of the rural collective enterprises across the country. Among them, 1% became joint stock companies; 5% became liability limited companies; 13% became joint stock enterprises; 8% became enterprise groups; 6% were contracted out; 8% were leased out; 15% were merged with others; 1% went bankrupt; 25% were sold, and 18% had mixed ownerships. Through the reorganization, the composition of the added value among the different types of ownership was: that contributed by collective enterprises dropped from 49.5% to 34.7% and that by private enterprises rose from 50.5% to 65.3%.

After three years of reorganization and consolidation, the number of TVE workers was reduced from 130.5 million in 1997 to 128.19 million in 2000 — a net decrease of 2.31 million. The number of enterprises rose from 20.15 million to 20.85 million — a net increase of 700,000. But as a whole, TVEs grew in strength and size, and made more profits and improvements in every way. There was a sharp drop in the number of enterprises that polluted the environment, wasted resources, made contraband or shoddy products, operated with hidden safety risks or were chronically in the red.

The added value of TVEs grew from 2,074 billion yuan in 1997 to 2,715.6 billion yuan in 2000, at an average annual rate of 9.4%. Their gross tax rose from 152.6 billion yuan to 199.6 billion yuan — a net increase of 47 billion yuan — at an average annual rate of 9.4%. Their after-tax profits rose from 435.5 billion yuan to 588.3 billion yuan, for a net increase of 152.8 billion yuan, averaging an annual growth of 10.5%. Their total wage payment rose from 582.7 billion yuan to 706 billion yuan, for a net increase of 123.3 billion yuan, averaging an annual growth of 6.6%. The original value of their fixed assets grew from 1,942.7 billion yuan to 2,622.4 billion yuan, for a net increase of 680.2 billion yuan, averaging a net annual increase in investment of 226.7 billion yuan which were raised mainly by TVEs themselves. It was a great feat for TVEs to achieve simultaneous growth in both size and profit. (See Table 2-7)

Table 2–7 Development of TVEs 1976-2000

Year	Enterprises (1,000)	Number of workers (1,000)	Added value (billion yuan)	Increased value of industry (billion yuan)
1996	23,360	135,080	1,765.9	1,262.8
1967	20,150	130,500	2,074.0	1,451.8
1998	20,040	125,370	2,218.6	1,553.0
1999	20,710	127,040	2,488.3	1,737.4
2000	20,850	128,200	2,715.6	1,881.2
Annual rate of increase (1996-2000) (%)	-3.6	-0.7	8.1	10.5

Source: Statistics on TVEs, Ministry of Agriculture

It should be pointed out that since 1997 China's agriculture has entered a new stage of development, marked by a transition from long-time shortages of agricultural products to a basic balance between supply and demand, with a surplus in years of good harvest, and from a seller's market to a buyer's market. This requires a strategic adjustment in agriculture and the rural economic structure. A prominent problem during this period is the falling prices of agricultural produce and the drop in the income growth of the peasants. This has not only affected the opening up of the rural market but also enlarged the income gap between urban and rural residents, which is unfavorable for social stability. Although, due to environmental control, some small coal mines and other polluting TVEs have been shut down, resulting in a drop of growth speed, TVEs have still maintained a development speed higher than the growth level of the national economy, playing a vital role in increasing the income of the peasants. In 1998-2000, the annual per capita net income of the peasants dropped by 3.4%, 2.2% and 1.9%. If labor service income from TVEs is deducted, the agricultural growth was negative, and such a negative growth increased year by year. The main source of net income growth of the peasants was labor service during that period.

Chapter III

The Position of TVEs in the National Economy

Section 1 Scale and Economic Efficiency of TVEs

TVEs have grown up in China out of the planned economy as an embryo of the market economy. Since China introduced its policies of reform and opening to the outside world, two decades ago, TVEs have emerged as a shock force in its march to a market economy, with a marvelous vigor that has attracted worldwide attention. They have become a leading force in China's rural economy and an important driver for social progress. They constitute an important component of the national economy.

1. Considerable scale and aggregate

There were 21.15 million TVEs in China at the end of 2001, employing a total of 130 million workers. Their added value of 2,935.6 billion yuan[1] accounted for 31.1% of the national total, and their industrial added value reached 2,031.4 billion yuan, almost half of the national total. They made 600 billion yuan in net profits and paid 230.8 billion yuan in taxes, accounting for 15.8% of the national total. Their deliveries for export reached 2,905.1 billion yuan-worth, or 42% of the national total. (See Table 3-1)

[1] Added value = the combined total output value of industry, agriculture, building, transportation and other industries minus the costs of raw and other materials, and the turnover of the commercial and service departments minus the value of the materials purchased from outside and the value of labor.

Table 3-1 Major Economic Indices of TVEs in 2001

Index	Unit	Total	Growth over 2000 (%)	Collective enterprises	Private enterprises	Individual enterprises
Number of enterprises	enterprise	21,155,389	1.48	668,786	2,007,103	18,479,500
Number of workers	person	130,855,754	2.07	33,721,812	36,938,473	60,195,469
Total output value	10,000 yuan	1,260,468,793	8.52	383,784,269	396,899,935	479,784,589
Industrial output value	10,000 yuan	898,454,409	8.96	313,050,335	320,076,251	265,327,823
Added value	10,000 yuan	293,563,886	8.10	91,177,562	89,473,475	112,912,849
Industrial added value	10,000 yuan	203,146,621	7.99	73,709,022	71,184,267	58,253,332
Operational income	10,000 yuan	1,165,854,685	8.12	351,683,184	347,649,343	466,522,158
Income tax	10,000 yuan	7,079,597	18.14	2,861,162	1,894,985	2,323,450
Net profit	10,000 yuan	60,015,002	2.02	16,642,839	16,704,854	26,667,309
Tax paid	10,000 yuan	23,080,856	15.61	9,731,765	7,228,661	6,120,430
Total payroll	10,000 yuan	77,320,632	9.51	22,456,521	22,467,189	32,396,922
Original value of fixed assets	10,000 yuan	290,515,945	10.78	135,144,950	85,987,116	69,383,879
Value of exported products	10,000 yuan	95,988,105	10.72			

Source: Bureau of Township Enterprises, Ministry of Agriculture

2. Sustained growth of economic aggregate of TVEs

TVEs have achieved continuous sharp increases in fixed assets, net profit, taxes paid and value of exported products and their economic returns are increasing.

(1) Total output value and added value

The total output value of TVEs in China reached 978 billion yuan in 1990, 6,956.9 billion yuan in 1995 and 11,615 billion yuan in 2000. The latter figure was 66.9% higher than that of 1995, or a 10.9-fold increase in a decade, and the total value rose to 12,604.7 billion yuan in 2001.

Their added value was 250.4 billion yuan in 1990, 1,459.5 billion yuan in 1995, and 2,715.6 billion yuan in 2000. The latter figure was 86.1% above that of 1995, or a 10.8-fold increase in a decade, and reaching 2,935.6 billion yuan in 2001.

Their average annual growth in added value was 37% in the 7th Five-Year Plan period (1986-1990); 42.3% in the 8th Five-Year Plan period (1991-1995); and of 13.2% in the 9th Five-Year Plan period (1996 - 2000). It rose only 9.14% in 2000 over the previous year.

Arranged in descending order, the added value of TVEs in different provinces, autonomous regions and municipalities in 2000 was: 283.9 billion yuan in Zhejiang; 265.9 billion yuan in Shandong; 244.1 billion yuan in Jiangsu; 218.8 billion yuan in Guangdong; 201 billion yuan in Hebei; and after those top five, Hunan, Liaoning, Henan, Fujian and Hubei each ranging between 100 billion and 190 billion yuan; Inner Mongolia and Sichuan each below 100 billion and over 85 billion yuan; Anhui and Shanghai each below 85 billion and over 60 billion yuan; Jilin and Shaanxi each below 60 billion and over 50 billion yuan; Shanxi and Jiangxi each below 50 billion and over 40 billion yuan; Guangxi and Tianjin each below 40 billion and over 35 billion yuan; Heilongjiang, Yunnan, Chongqing and Beijing each below 35 billion and over 20 billion yuan; Guizhou and Gansu each below 20 billion and over 16 billion yuan; Xinjiang 7.4 billion yuan; Hainan four billion yuan; Ningxia 3.8 billion yuan; and

Qinghai 1.7 billion yuan.

In 2000 the total added value of TVEs accounted for 64% of the total rural added value of the country and 30.4% of the added value of the national economy as a whole. TVEs in 2000 created 1,881.2 billion yuan of industrial added value, which was 47.3% of the total industrial added value in the national economy, which means that nearly half of the industrial added value in China was created by the TVEs.

(2) Fixed assets

The original value of the fixed assets of the TVEs was 285.7 billion yuan in 1990; 1,284.1 billion yuan in 1995; 2,622.4 billion yuan in 2000 which was twice the 1995 figure and 8.2-fold increase in 10 years, averaging an annual growth of 24.8%; and increased to 2,905.1 billion yuan in 2001. The leading provinces in terms of the original value of fixed assets in the descending order were Guangdong, Zhejiang, Jiangsu, Shandong and Hebei.

(3) Business turnover

The total business turnover of the TVEs in the country was 861.4 billion yuan in 1990, 5,729.9 billion yuan in 1995; and 10,783.4 billion yuan in 2000. The 2000 figure was 88.2% higher than in 1995 and the figure in 10 years grew 12.5 times, averaging an annual growth of 28.7%. And the 2001 business turnover reached 11,658.5 billion yuan. In 2000, the counties each having made at least one billion yuan by their TVEs numbered 1,614, the townships each having made at least 500 million yuan numbered 4,920, the villages each having made at least 100 million yuan numbered 9,101, and the enterprises each having made at least 100 million yuan numbered 4,121.

(4) Net profits

The net profits made by the TVEs reached 58.2 billion yuan in 1990, 325.1 billion yuan in 1995, and 588.3 billion yuan in 2000 which was 80.9% over that of 1995 and 10.1 times that of 1990. The five leading provinces in terms of net profits in the descending order in 2000 were Hebei, Zhejiang, Henan, Shandong and Liaoning.

The TVEs making a profit in 2000 numbered 20.12 million which accounted for 96.5% of the total. Only 3.5% of the TVEs were in the red. The percentage of loss-making enterprises has dropped markedly in recent years.

(5) Taxes paid

The TVEs paid taxes amounting to 31.3 billion yuan in 1990, 128 billion yuan in 1995, and 199.6 billion yuan in 2000 which accounted for 15.8% of the total State tax revenue, or 55.9% over 1995 and a 5.4-fold increase in 10 years, and 230.8 billion yuan in 2001. The five leading provinces in 2000 were Zhejiang, Jiangsu, Guangdong, Shandong and Hebei.

Tax contributions and profits per capita by TVEs in the country: 1,092 yuan in 1990; 4,128 yuan in 1995; 6,145 yuan in 2000, which was 5.6 times that of 1990 and an increase of 48.9% compared to 1995.

(6) Exports

A total of 139,500 TVEs produced 955.2 billion yuan-worth of products for export in 2000. Deliveries by TVEs for export reached 48.6 billion yuan-worth in 1990, 539.5 billion yuan in 1995 and 866.9 billion yuan in 2000, which was 60.7% higher than in 1995 and 17.8 times that of 1990, and reached 959.9 billion yuan-worth in 2001. The five leading provinces in 2000 were Guangdong, Zhejiang, Jiangsu, Fujian, and Shandong. The total exports of products made by TVEs accounted for 42% of the national total in 2000.

(7) Productivity

The labor productivity of the TVEs reached 21,183 yuan per person in 2000, or 94.5% higher than in 1990 and 86.7% higher than in 1995. The five leading provinces and municipalities in this field in 2000 were: Shanghai, with 42,700 yuan per person; Liaoning, with 37,600 yuan per person; Zhejiang, with 32,200 yuan per person; Tianjin with 29,200 yuan per person; and Jiangsu with 28,500 yuan per person.

(8) Rural surplus labor absorbed

The total employees of TVEs in the country reached 92.65 million persons in 1990, 128.62 million in 1995 and 135.08 million in 1996, but dropped to 128.2 million in 2000, which still exceeded the 1990 figure by 35.55 million. In seven of the past 10 years, the number of surplus rural laborers absorbed by TVEs was 3.44 million in 1991, 9.72 million in 1992, 17.64 million in 1993, 8.44 million in 1995, 6.46 million in 1996, 1.67 million in 1999 and 1.16 million in 2000. The number of employees of TVEs decreased in 1994, 1997 and 1998.

(9) Aid to agriculture

The TVEs supported agriculture with 16.7 billion yuan in 2000, which was 8.9 billion yuan more than in 1990 and 9.5 billion more than in 1995. The support-for-agriculture fund laid aside by TVEs in the past decade has more than doubled, averaging an annual increase of 7.9%. The five leading provinces in this respect, in descending order, were: Hunan, Zhejiang, Henan, Hebei and Shandong.

(10) Peasants' income

The average income of Chinese peasants from TVEs reached 760 yuan in 2000, which accounted for 33.7% of their net income.

Table 3-2 Major Economic Indices of TVEs 1990-2004

Year	Number of enterprises (million)	Number of workers (million)	Total output value (billion yuan)	Added value (billion yuan)	Original value of fixed assets (billion yuan)	Net profits (billion yuan)	Taxes paid (billion yuan)	Export delivery (billion yuan)
1990	18.73	92.65	978	250.4	285.7	58.2	31.3	48.6
1991	19.09	96.14	1,181	297.2	338.5	68.8	36.5	78.9
1992	20.92	106.25	1,788	448.5	454.0	104.8	49.4	119.3
1993	24.53	123.45	3,213.2	800.7	695.8	195.9	94.8	219.3

1994	24.94	120.17	4,612.4	1,092.8	886.8	228.6	103.5	339.8
1995	22.03	128.62	6,956.9	1,459.5	1,284.1	325.1	128.0	539.5
1996	23.36	135.08	7,677.8	1,765.9	1,492.4	388.6	130.7	600.8
1997	20.15	130.50	8,990.0	2,074.0	1,942.7	435.5	152.6	682.6
1998	20.04	125.37	9,669.4	2,218.6	2,156.6	463.5	158.3	685.4
1999	20.71	127.04	10,842.6	2,488.3	2,397.8	539.2	178.9	774.4
2000	20.85	128.20	11,615.0	2,715.6	2,622.4	588.3	199.6	886.9
2001	21.15	130.86	12,604.6	2,935.6	2,905.1	600.1	230.8	959.9
2002	21.32	132.88	14,043.5	3,238.6	3,569.8	696.2	269.3	1,156.3
2003	21.85	135.73	15,236.0	3,668.6	4,065.4	857.1	313.0	1,148.9
2004	22.13	138.66	17,251.6	4,181.5	4,787.2	993.2	365.8	1,693.2

Source: Bureau of Township Enterprises, Ministry of Agriculture

3. Trades and services operated by TVEs

The statistical data from 2000 categorized TVEs by trades in three ways:

(1) Grouping by trades according to the number of enterprises. The total number was 20.85 million: 151,000 in agriculture, 6.74 million in industry, 795,000 in construction, 4.125 million in transportation, 5.913 million in commerce, 2.492 million in tourism and services, and 630,000 in other trades.

(2) Grouping by trades according to added value. The total added value of TVEs was 2,715.6 billion yuan: 31.39 billion yuan in agriculture, 1,881.24 billion yuan in industry, 210.08 billion yuan in construction, 165.77 billion yuan in transportation, 262.56 billion yuan in commerce, 128.85 billion yuan in tourism and services, and 35.75 billion yuan in other trades.

(3) Grouping by added value according to three major departments, namely, primary, secondary and tertiary industries. The total added value of TVEs was 2,715.6 billion yuan: 31.39 billion yuan in primary industry, making up 1.2%; 2,091.3 billion yuan in secondary industry, 77%; and 592.93 billion yuan in tertiary industry, 21.8%.

4. Geographical distribution of TVEs (major economic indices)

(See Table 3-3)

Table 3-3 Major Economic Indices of TVEs in the Eastern, Central and Western Regions in 2001

Index name	Unit	Total	Eastern region		Central region		Western region	
			Total	%	Total	%	Total	%
Number of enterprises	enterprise	688,786	317,423	47.46	282,263	42.21	69,100	10.33
Number of workers	person	33,721,812	19,356,590	57.40	11,243,677	33.34	3,121,545	9.26
Total wages	billion yuan	224.6	150.2	66.87	60.7	27.03	13.7	6.10
Added value	billion yuan	911.8	657.2	72.08	209.8	23.01	44.8	4.91
Industrial added value	billion yuan	737.1	561.6	76.19	147.4	20.00	28.1	3.81
Business turnover	billion yuan	3,516.8	2,555.3	72.66	773.3	21.99	188.2	5.35
Total costs	billion yuan	3,285.2	2,396.0	72.93	712.6	21.69	176.5	5.37
Gross profits	billion yuan	195.0	141.2	72.41	45.2	23.18	8.7	4.41
Tax to be paid	billion yuan	142.8	103.2	72.27	31.9	22.34	7.8	5.45
Tax paid	billion yuan	97.3	74.8	76.88	16.8	17.27	5.7	5.86
Net Profit	billion yuan	166.4	119.4	71.75	39.5	23.74	7.6	4.56
Profit & tax	billion yuan	304.6	219.4	72.03	70.2	23.05	15.1	4.97

Source: Bureau of Township Enterprises, Ministry of Agriculture

Section 2 Forms of Ownership of TVEs

TVEs are non-State-owned enterprises set up mainly by peasants. In the days of the people's communes, the enterprises were owned by communes and production brigades. After China introduced the reform and opening-up policies, self-employed and other private enterprises developed rapidly. TVEs comprised four types of ownership. By 2001, of the 21.15 million TVEs, 660,000 were collectively owned, accounting for 3.1%; 18.47 million were self-employed individual enterprises, accounting for 87.3% and 2.02 million were private enterprises, accounting for 9.6% of the total.

Of the 128 million workers in the TVEs, 32.9 million or 25.7% belonged to collective enterprises; 59 million or 46.1% belonged to individual enterprises; and 36.1 million or 28.2% worked in privately owned enterprises.

TVEs registered 2,715.6 billion yuan in added value in 2000, of which 942.4 billion yuan or 34.7% was accredited to collective ownership, 1,028.6 billion yuan or 37.8% to individual enterprises, and 744.6 billion yuan or 27.5% to private ownership.

Of the 1,881.2 billion yuan industrial added value, 767.6 billion or 40.8% was created by enterprises of collective ownership, 536.3 billion or 28.5% came from individual enterprises, and 577.3 billion or 30.7% was generated by enterprises of private ownership.

The number of individual enterprises and private enterprises made up 96.9% of TVEs, employing 74.3% of the workers, generating 65.3% of total added value and 59.2% of the industrial added value, and 53.35% of taxes. This shows that TVEs were mainly individual and private enterprises, mostly small and medium-sized, at the end of 2001. Most of the medium-sized and small enterprises were joint stock cooperatives and most of the large ones were joint stock companies. The joint stock cooperative system was a creation by Chinese peasants, by which the peasants pool their labor and capital (in some places, the land contracted by individual peasants is used as their stock capital). Workers of a joint stock enterprise are both owners and workers. They elect shareholders' representatives to exercise the power of participation in policy decision-making, the power of disposing of their assets, distributing income and electing the managers.

Much progress has been made in recent years in converting TVEs into joint stock cooperatives, joint stock companies and enterprises of mixed ownership, in addition to enterprises of collective ownership, individual enterprises and private enterprises. By 2000, there were 162,600 joint stock cooperatives and 25,251 joint stock enterprises, totaling 187,851, of which 85,890 or 45.7% had been converted from collective enterprises and 48,542 or 25.8% had been converted from enterprises of individual and private ownership, and 28,168 or 14.9% were new ones. In addition, there were also enterprises of other ownerships (including joint ventures with foreign investors). Among the joint stock enterprises, some have been reorganized into enterprise groups and listed on the stock market, and some have set up branches overseas. Among them some have grown into giants with an annual turnover exceeding 100 million yuan. There were 6,956 such enterprises in 1998. Among these internationally known big companies are the Kelong Group of Guangdong, the Wanxiang Group of Zhejiang and the Yangguang Group of Jiangsu.

Available statistics show that self-employed and private enterprises are doing markedly better than collective ones. The self-employed and private enterprises among TVEs in 1998 achieved 1,221.5 billion yuan of added value, up 25.2% over the previous year, which was above the average for TVEs as a whole by 7.9 percentage points and above that of the collective enterprises by 16.4 percentage points. And they achieved 5,106.7 billion yuan of business turnover, up 11.6%, paid 71.7 billion yuan of taxes, up 7.5%, and made 293.8 billion yuan in net profits, up 12%, exceeding those of the collective-owned enterprises by 10.7, 6.7 and 14 percentage points, respectively — convincing proof of the tremendous vitality of individual and private enterprises.

In reorganizing TVEs, emphasis was laid on the ownership of the enterprises owned collectively by townships and villages and most of them were reorganized through contracting, leasing, merger or buy-up. However, this ownership reorganization was simplified into "buy-up" in some localities without an effective assets appraisal, open, fair and justified competition, or proper supervision. The buy-up was done under the table, and peasants' collective assets became the possessions of individuals, causing a loss of collective property, rise in the cost of the reforms, dissatisfaction among the peasants and social unrest. This phenomenon has aroused serious attention among governments at all levels.

Section 3 Contributions by TVEs to the National Economy

1. Boosting the rural economy and the national economic strength

TVEs in 1991 registered a total output value of 297.2 billion yuan, 36% of the added value of rural China. The added value registered by TVEs in 2000 rose to 2,715.6 billion yuan, 65.6% of the total rural added value of that year. Of the 3,240.7 billion yuan of net added value of rural China, that of the TVEs reached 2,418.4 billion yuan, 74.6% of the total. It is, therefore, safe to say that TVEs have played a vital role in bringing about robust growth in China's rural economy since Deng Xiaoping's 1992 South China inspection tour speeches were published. The development of TVEs is rapidly changing the poor and backward outlook of the countryside. In some localities, the peasants' living standard has reached the better-off line, and new socialist villages have emerged.

In 1991, the added value of TVEs accounted for 13.7% of the country's GDP of 2,161.8 billion yuan, and the 2000 figure accounted for 30.4% of the GDP of 8,940.4 billion yuan. Of the 6,778.6 billion yuan of the net added value in the country's GDP, TVEs contributed 2,418.6 billion yuan, 35.7% of the total.

2. Promoting rural industrialization and accelerating the pace of China's industrialization

China used to rely on just one leg — the cities — in its industrialization drive. The pace was slow, and it gave rise to a dual economic structure. But since China decided to "walk on two legs" by pushing industrialization in both the cities and the countryside, the pace has greatly quickened. The added value of township industry in 1991 reached 222.7 billion yuan, which was 27.5% of the national total industrial added value of 808.7 billion yuan. In 2000, the added value of township industry reached 1,881.2 billion yuan, accounting for 47.5% of the national total industrial added value of 3,957 billion yuan. Of the 3,148.3 billion yuan of net increase, township industry contributed 1,658.5 billion yuan, 52.7% of the national total industrial added value.

The proportion of township industry in the whole of industry was 83.6% in Zhejiang, 76.5% in Shaanxi, 73.4% in Hunan, 70.1% in Fujian, 69.8% in Shandong, 67.7% in Inner Mongolia, 67.2% in Guangxi, 66.8% in Hebei, 64.9% in Henan, 64% in Jiangsu, and below 60% in other provinces, regions and municipalities. Among them, Shanghai has virtually realized rural industrialization, and Tianjin, Beijing, Liaoning, Jiangsu, Zhejiang, Fujian and Guangdong have all initially realized rural industrialization.

3. Increasing State revenue

China's 1991 State revenue was 314.9 billion yuan, and the taxes paid by TVEs reached 36.5 billion yuan, 11.6% of the total. In 2000, the State revenue rose to 1,338 billion yuan, of which 199.6 billion or 15.9% came from TVEs.

Although State-owned enterprises constituted the main source of State revenue at that time, about 30% of the State budgetary expenditure, or about half of the taxes paid by State-owned enterprises, flowed back to them. On the other hand, TVEs paid taxes but received no returns from the State. Therefore theirs was pure contribution. In addition, TVEs made contributions of over 100 billion yuan a year to the State and the society through all sorts of channels, such as paying all types of fees and levies, sharing expenses for rural public amenities, cultural, educational and health undertakings, road and bridge construction, the building of new towns and villages, agricultural modernization projects and farm capital construction projects.

4. Bringing wealth to the peasants

The wages paid to peasant workers by TVEs in 2000 added 761 yuan to the purse of each peasant, on average, which was 33.8% of the average per capita income of the Chinese peasants that year. And this contribution to the income increase of the peasants has stood out all the more glaringly from the perspective that, owing to the ongoing restructuring of the country's agriculture, many places have not received increased incomes from bigger harvests, and in some localities peasants' income has even dropped. Take 1998 for example. The average net income of a Chinese peasant was 2,162 yuan in that year, 72 yuan more than in the previous year. Although the income from agriculture dropped by an average of 30.3 yuan per capita, the income from TVEs increased by an average of 81.4 yuan and the income from non-production undertakings increased by 19.6 yuan, thus ensuring a continued increase of the peasants' income.

The per capita net income of Chinese peasants in 1999 was 48 yuan more than in the previous year, despite a fall in the net income from crop farming of 45.2 yuan and 10.1 yuan in that of animal husbandry. The per capita net income from labor remuneration in the form of wages increased by 56.7 yuan, and that from family businesses in industry and services increased by 34 yuan. Again thanks to TVEs and family sideline production, the peasants managed to prevent their income from decreasing. Moreover, TVEs have become the main source of peasants' income in areas where TVEs are more developed. Taking rural China as a whole, since 1998, more than 50% of the newly increased income of Chinese peasants has come from TVEs — a proof of the fact that TVEs have become indispensable if the Chinese peasants are to achieve prosperity.

5. Reducing disparities between city and countryside

Developed industrial economies have succeeded in transferring part of the rural population to cities in the process of urbanization until the urban population accounts for more than 80% of the total. In China, the rural population is overwhelmingly large, and the development of industry in cities had helped reduce the rural population by only 16.1 percentage points by 2000 — from 89.4% of the total in 1952 to 73.3%.

When China ran into economic difficulties in the past, the cities had to send some of their residents to the countryside instead of continuing to absorb rural residents. To make things worse, China's rigid urban and rural permanent residence registration system made it extremely difficult for rural residents to flow into cities. So they built in their own local industrial, commercial, service, construction and transportation trades, which by the year 2000 had absorbed 128.2 million surplus rural laborers — 44% of the rural surplus labor power or 26.7% of the total rural labor power. That amounts to the equivalent of 60.3% of the total urban employment, which was 212.74 million at that time, and even exceeding the 50 million workers employed by State-owned enterprises.

Employment is of paramount importance in any economy, because it is vital to economic progress and social stability. TVEs in China have provided a solution to this important social issue by creating jobs for more than 100 million people. Chinese society is stable mainly because 100 million people have jobs and regular incomes. Together with their family members, the employed population totals about 400 million people, or half of the country's rural population. This is a major contribution of TVEs, which are also the driving force behind the elimination of the "three differences" — between the cities and the countryside, between workers and peasants and between mental and manual labor.

Where TVEs have developed faster than other places, small towns functioning as the local rural centers of politics, economy, culture, transportation, commerce, education and public health have taken shape. By 2000, there were 20,312 administrative towns, 12,356 more than in 1985. By 2000, a total of 9,397 small industrial districts and a large number of specialized wholesale marketplaces had been formed by TVEs, serving as the basis for urbanization. Meanwhile, new socialist villages have arisen where TVEs are more developed. The peasants there, while staying in the countryside, enjoy access to material and intellectual civilization. In some localities, the conditions are close to or even better than in many cities. Those localities may be considered to have realized urbanization. In some places, the dual economic structure has disappeared and the "three differences" are receding. Their number may not be very large in rural China yet, but they promise a bright future.

6. Increasing effective supply and ending the shortage economy

Under the planned economy, all supplies were subject to State plans, and people had to buy things against ration coupons due to shortage of supply. However, the domestic Chinese market began to change from a seller's market to a buyer's market in the mid-1990s, when supply and demand became virtually balanced, except for farm produce, which became surplus only after a good harvest. Manufactured products, in particular, were often over-supplied instead of being in short supply, and township industry played an important role in this respect.

Of the increase in the supply of industrial products between 1981 and 1997, township industry accounted for 71.5% of the increase of coal, 78.8% of that of machine-made paper and cardboard, and 47.4% of that of cement. Of the total industrial output value, township industry contributed 66.6% to food processing and manufacturing, 60.3% to the textile industry, 92.9% to the garment industry, 73.7% to the leather and tanning industry, 73.5% to the machine-made paper and cardboard industry, and more than 50% to the electrical appliances, handicrafts and arts, building materials, mechanical processing and manufacturing, and plastics industries. We may say that township industry has played a positive role in overcoming economic shortages, providing effective supply and meeting the daily growing social demand.

7. Emerging as a new force in exports

In 1980, the year after the Third Plenary Session of the 11th CPC Central Committee, China recorded only US$18.1 billion-worth of exports, way below the needs of the country's economic development. The CPC Central Committee proposed in 1985 that China should win international standing by allowing TVEs in its coastal regions to take the initiative. That year, China's exports reached US$27.3 billion-worth. Prior to that, TVEs in China only worked on orders for processing for foreign trade firms. In 1986, some TVEs began to set up factories on their own or in association with foreign trade firms and began to sell their products to foreign trade companies. Besides, some TVEs ran joint ventures with foreign investors or accepted orders for processing and assembly, with designs, materials or parts supplied by their foreign clients in the form of compensation trade. In recent years, some TVEs have been exporting by themselves or have set up subsidiaries overseas, greatly increasing their export earnings.

Export earnings by Chinese TVEs in 1986 reached US$2.8 billion, accounting for 9.1% of the US$30.9 billion of the total national export earnings. By 2000, their export earnings increased to US$104.8 billion, accounting for 42% of US$249.2 billion of China's total export earnings.

8. Introducing a fine operational mechanism

TVEs have been operating in the market economy outside State plans. The need to survive and develop has forced them to constantly improve their operational mechanism and product mix in compliance with the laws of market competition. Those capable of meeting market demands survive and grow, while those incapable of doing so are eliminated.

There is diversity among TVEs in terms of ownership. There are enterprises of collective ownership, individual ownership, joint ventures with State capital, joint ventures with foreign capital, joint ventures among collective enterprises, joint ventures between collective enterprises and private enterprises, joint ventures between private and State-owned enterprises, and joint ventures between private enterprises and foreign businesses.

TVEs are also diversified in their ways of operation. They include joint stock firms, joint stock cooperatives, contracted enterprises, leased enterprises, enterprises of mixed ownership and enterprises of sole ownership.

In terms of management, TVEs are entirely independent in accumulation, development, operation, and profit and loss.

In personnel policy, workers are free to come and go; executives are subject to promotion and demotion; wages are subject to raises and cuts; and operations may continue or stop.

A TVE makes decisions with its eyes wide open to market fluctuations and the changing needs of customers. It is quick in turning out new products, in responding to market changes and in taking decisions, and flexible in market strategy.

The experience of TVEs is useful for China's enterprise restructuring in the transition from a planned economy to a market economy.

9. Accelerating agricultural modernization

Agriculture is the foundation of the national economy. The State makes investment in agriculture out of macroeconomic consideration, focusing on capital construction projects vital to the whole country or a vast region. The State therefore cannot possibly pay attention to the needs of a specific village or rural household for capital construction, farming, or the purchase of modern farming implements.

One of the objectives of developing TVEs is to support agriculture, and help it make steady and continuous growth. TVEs earmark part of their profits every year as grants to agriculture. This fund between 1978 and 2000 exceeded 140 billion yuan. With 120 million rural able-bodied people transferred to TVEs, those still staying to engage in agricultural activities have found a much broader scope to display their abilities. They have found more land to contract or lease for farming on a larger scale and in a more intensive and modern way. Township industry depends on farm produce and sideline products for 28% of its raw materials. That provides an outlet for farm produce and at the same time lays a foundation for the industrialized operation of agriculture.

10. Accumulating experience for social transformation

A dual economic-social structure characterized by industrial cities and agricultural countryside has existed in China for a long time. In this society, peasants used to form a huge but disadvantaged community. This dual structure greatly retarded economic and social progress. The emergence and vigorous development of TVEs has directed a heavy blow at the dual structure, breaking through all restrictions that barred peasants from moving into cities to work and do business. They have played an extremely important role in correcting the traditionally unjust social policies, social structure and distribution of public resources, promoting population and labor force flow, accelerating the process of urbanization and enabling peasants to improve themselves and win an equal footing with their urban counterparts. Despite the immaturity of this process, it has yielded good results. This is a change of great social and historical significance, a valuable change the Chinese peasants have brought about by relying on their own unswerving efforts under the guidance and support of the Party's policy of reform and opening to the outside world.

While we fully recognize the success of TVEs, we should at the same time be fully aware of their weaknesses and shortcomings, and their defects of numerical multiplication at a low level. These weaknesses and defects are:

(1) Small scale and inadequate capital. On average, a TVE has only six workers, 126,000 yuan in fixed assets at the beginning, 557,000 yuan in output value, and 517,000 yuan in business turnover. An enterprise of such a scale can hardly cope with fierce market competition.

(2) Low economic returns. A township enterprise generates on average only 38,000 yuan in gross profits, or 28,000 yuan in net terms. With a low return on assets of 22.4%, a profitability of 5.5% or 4,588 yuan on a per capita basis, the enterprise would not have much left after paying the interest on loans. Such miserable economic returns handicap the enterprise's efforts to make technical innovations and expand production.

(3) Crude and outdated equipment. Some of the equipment used by TVEs, including some manufactured by the enterprises themselves, are products of the 1960s or 1970s. Production with such equipment can hardly guarantee product quality, low cost, safety and environmental protection.

(4) Product quality falling below State standards. Except for a limited number of products that have reached the State norms, many products made by TVEs are unable to meet State standards. A sample survey conducted by the State Bureau of Technological Supervision shows that only 60% of the products made by TVEs reach the State standards. Small batch production with low quality results in a high rate of unmarketable products, and even in shoddy ones or contraband.

(5) Government interference and unclear property rights. Especially in some collective enterprises, the governmental role is still significant. Township governments tend to treat the enterprises as their own property, and feel free to appoint executives, and use and keep their funds. On the other hand, factory directors or managers and other executives still look upon themselves as mere employees, lacking a sense of responsibility as masters of the enterprises.

(6) Inadequate investment, low technical level and duplicated products. TVEs mostly produce traditional products in traditional ways. Many TVEs are under great pressure from market competition, and do not hesitate to lower quality standards and economize on the use of raw materials at the expense of consumers.

(7) Inability to pay back loans. Some enterprises try to expand production by borrowing from rural credit cooperatives, which charge higher interest than State-owned banks do. But the enterprises find great difficulty in repaying their loans on time. As a result, the interest on bank loans often far exceeds the profits they can make. Thus, they are bogged down in a vicious circle: The more they produce, the more they lose.

(8) Low management level. Many TVEs are very wasteful and suffer from low efficiency. They lack a basic management system, and carry out production in disregard of the standards set by the State.

(9) Serious environmental pollution. Although TVEs do not constitute the major source of pollution in China, the pollution of the environment by TVEs has aroused serious attention because they are located all over the country. Unlike pollution caused by industry in cities at isolated points, pollution caused by TVEs is widespread, affecting the soil, river water, ground water, the air, farm crops, the human body and livestock.

(10) Lack of proper training and education on the part of executives. TVE executives generally have not received proper professional training or an appropriate education. Before assuming their present positions, they used to be rustic peasants with no skills or managerial experience and no training in marketing. In addition, they tend to be imbued with a strong patriarchal attitude, and to ignore laws and decrees.

(11) Lack of education, professional skills and discipline on the part of the workers.

These problems may become more outstanding, and may pose a still greater challenge to TVEs, following China's entry into the WTO, in the course of the on-going economic globalization and China's industrial modernization, and the development of the IT industry.

Chapter IV

Township Enterprises and Industrialization

Section 1 China's Unique Road of Industrialization

That an agricultural society develops into an industrial society is a general rule and tendency of the social development of all countries. However, the developed countries realized their industrialization under specific historical conditions, namely, through primitive accumulation at the expenses of the peasants and the plunder of colonies. Industrialization brings about urbanization — urbanization of industry and urbanization of population — resulting in a population composition characterized by the farmers accounting for only about 5% of the total population.

For a century and more since the Opium War in 1840, the Chinese people cherished the dream of industrializing their country. They hoped to pattern it after those of the Western countries, but suffered one setback after another. The great powers, which the Chinese took for their "teachers," turned out to be aggressors. Britain, France, Russia, Japan and other powers imposed a series of unequal treaties on China, forcing the Qing government to cede territory and pay indemnities. The 1905 War between China and Japan alone cost China an indemnity of 230 million taels (1 tael is about 37.8 grams) of silver to Japan, whereas China's national income that year was not much more than 70 million taels of silver. In 1901, the aggressor troops of eight Western powers invaded Beijing, and forced the

Qing court to sign an unequal treaty, including the payment of an indemnity of 450 million taels of silver, averaging more than one tael per person of the 400 million Chinese people. Such wars and plunder greatly retarded the pace of China's industrialization.

Industrialization has long been a cherished goal of the Chinese people and the Communist Party of China (CPC). In 1944, Mao Zedong, in a speech to the directors of factories and workers' representatives in Yan'an, said, "We must have industry if we wish to throw out the Japanese imperialists. We must achieve industrialization if we wish to have a powerful guarantee for our national independence. We Communists must do our best to realize China's industrialization. A main cause for our backwardness has been our lack of modern industry. Why did the Japanese imperialists dare to attack China? Because we have no powerful industry, and they take advantage of our backwardness. So it is the task of our entire nation to get rid of backwardness. People support the Communist Party, because we represent the demand of the nation and the people. But should we fail to solve our economic problem, build our new industry and develop our productive forces, we would lose the support of the people."[1]

On the eve of the founding of the People's Republic of China in 1949, the Chinese had already made the task of industrialization a state policy. The First Plenary Session of the National Committee of the Chinese People's Political Consultative Conference adopted the "Common Program of the Chinese People's Political Consultative Conference" on September 29, 1949. The Common Program lays it down that "we should rehabilitate and develop industry with emphasis on heavy industry in a methodical and planned way to lay a foundation for the industrialization of the country."[2]

The first "Constitution of the People's Republic of China," adopted on September 20, 1954, provides that "The People's Republic of

---

[1] *Mao Zedong's Works*, Vol. 3, People's Publishing House, pp. 146-147

[2] Archive Research Center of the CPC Central Committee: *Selected Important Archives since the Founding of the People's Republic of China*, Vol. 1, Central Archives Press, 1992, p. 9

China by relying on the State organs and social forces pledges to gradually eliminate exploitation and build a socialist society through socialist industrialization and socialist transformation."[1]

Old China left virtually no modern industry to New China. How to realize the country's industrialization became an issue of top priority confronting the Chinese leaders. Obviously it was impossible to rely on the Western countries and take the capitalist road of those countries. Moreover, the Chinese people badly lacked a proper economic foundation, technological conditions, management experience and the all-round quality of personnel. The only way out at that time was to learn from the Soviet Union. The Soviet Union was the first socialist country in the world, and had completed the task of industrialization in 1936. It had plenty of experience in this field, and was willing to help China.

So China adopted the Soviet road of industrialization, namely, the pursuit of a highly centralized planned economy with the emphasis on heavy industry and making agriculture help accumulate funds for industrialization by maintaining price disparity between industrial and agricultural products.

In the First Five-Year Plan (1953-1958) period, China faithfully followed the Soviet line and practice, and laid a foundation for industry. However, many problems cropped up. The Soviet Union at the time also exposed its own shortcomings and mistakes in the course of building socialism. In order to avoid a tortuous course of pushing industrialization in China, Mao Zedong made investigations and put forth his views on 10 major relationships in 1956.

Mao said: "We raised the issue of the 10 major relationships in 1956, and began to find a line in conformity with Chinese reality...and began to reflect the objective economic rules in China." [2] That line (concerning industrialization) was the same in principle as the Soviet one, but was different in methodology. It put greater stress

---

[1] Archive Research Center of the CPC Central Committee: *Selected Important Archives since the Founding of the People's Republic of China*, Vol. 5, Central Archives Press, 1993, p. 522

[2] *Mao Zedong's Scripts since the Founding of the People's Republic of China*, Vol. 9, Central Archives Press, 1996, p. 213

on flexibility in work and the dialectical relations between different economic departments. That is to say, while emphasizing the importance of heavy industry, it also paid attention to the development of light industry and agriculture; while developing industry in the coastal regions, it also paid attention to the development of industry in the inland regions; while emphasizing the importance of developing industry under the central government, it also paid attention to the development of local industry; and it advocated the need to pay simultaneous attention to both the national interest and the interest of the peasants in the course of accumulating funds for industrialization.

The CPC Central Committee called a meeting in Nanning, capital of the Guangxi Zhuang Autonomous Region, in 1958, at which delegates from various provinces and autonomous regions urged greater efforts to be made to develop local industry. After listening to their opinions, Mao pointed out that efforts should be made to make the output value of local industry (including the output of factories and mines which the central government had transferred to local governments and the output of handicraft and other industries originally owned by the local governments, but excluding factories and mines directly under the central government) exceed the output value of the local agricultural production within five years, or seven years, or 10 years.

Based on Mao's proposal, the State Economic Commission drafted "Some Ideas of the CPC Central Committee on the Issue of Developing Local Industry," which was adopted by the Party Central Committee at its Chengdu Meeting on March 23, 1958. The document for the first time put forth the idea of running industry "by the whole Party and at all levels," and stated that local industry should "include those run by counties, townships and agricultural cooperatives." [1] At a panel discussion at the Chengdu Meeting, Mao said that local industry should perform the four tasks of serving agriculture, serving large industrial enterprises, serving the daily life of urban residents and serving the country's export business. That was

[1] Archive Research Center of the CPC Central Committee: *Selected Important Archives since the Founding of the People's Republic of China*, Vol. 11, 1995, p. 223

how Mao put forth the policy of treating township and cooperative industry run by peasants as one of the tasks of running industry by the whole party and at all levels.

By the summer of 1958, Mao's concept of "ideal socialism" crystallized in the "Great Leap Forward," and through the form of the people's commune. The aim was to accomplish two transitions — the transition from collective ownership to ownership by the entire people, and the transition from socialism to communism. The organizational form of the people's commune was a five-in-one entity that incorporated industry, agriculture, commerce, education and military affairs into one and combined government administration with commune management.

When Mao visited Licheng County, Shandong Province, on August 9, 1958, on an inspection tour, he was briefed by Tan Qilong, the then Shandong Provincial Committee Secretary of the Communist Party, on the county's plan to set up a large number of big farms. Mao pointed out, "It would be better to set up people's communes to incorporate into one industry, agriculture, commerce, education and military affairs for the convenience of giving leadership.

The CPC Central Committee, at an enlarged meeting held in Beidaihe on August 29, 1958, passed the "Resolution on the Issue of Setting up People's Communes in the Countryside." As the Resolution says, "thousands upon thousands of small factories mushroomed in the country after the founding of the people's communes." Mao's thinking on the road for China to achieve industrialization also became mature at that time. That was to combine the industrialization drive with the commune drive, and take some "simultaneous actions," namely simultaneous development of industry and agriculture, simultaneous development of heavy and light industries, simultaneous development of central and local industries, simultaneous development of industry in the coastal and inland regions, simultaneous development of urban and rural industries, simultaneous development of large and medium-sized and small enterprises, and simultaneous development of industry by modern technology and indigenous skills.

In examining the first draft of the "40-Article General Program for Building Socialism in 15 Years (1958-1972)," Mao Zedong wrote in his comments and revisions in November 1958: "The task that confronts the Chinese people today is to develop social productivity at a high speed through the organizational form of the people's commune to enhance the industrialization of our country and the people's communes, and elevate agricultural production to the level of factory production."[1]

On November 10 of the same year, he wrote in his revisions of the "Proposal of the Zhengzhou Meeting on Some Issues Regarding the People's Communes": "In order to let the people's communes have powerful means of production, it is necessary to realize the industrialization of the communes, and make agricultural production like that in a factory (or mechanization and electrification)."[2] The Party Central Committee, in its "Resolution on Some Issues of the People's Communes," pointed out that "the people's communes indicate the road to the industrialization of the countryside of this country step by step."[3] Mao Zedong's thinking on the road to rural industrialization may be described in a more concrete way as follows:

(1) Achieving two transitions through rural industrialization. Mao, in his remarks on the 15-Year Program, said that the realization of commune industrialization "may step by step effect a transition from socialist collective ownership to socialist ownership by the whole people and a transition from incomplete socialist ownership by the whole people to complete socialist ownership by the whole people. Meanwhile, in the course of socialist construction, the elements of communism are bound to increase, thus laying a foundation in both material and mentality for the transition from socialism to communism."[4]

---

[1] *Mao Zedong's Scripts since the Founding of the People's Republic of China*, Central Archives Press, 1992, Vol. 7, p. 504

[2] *Mao Zedong's Scripts since the Founding of the People's Republic of China*, Central Archives Press, 1992, Vol. 7, p.515

[3] Archive Research Center of the CPC Central Committee: *Selected Important Archives since the Founding of the People's Republic of China*, Central Archives Press, 1995, Vol. 11, p. 599

[4] *Mao Zedong's Scripts since the Founding of the People's Republic of China*, Central Archives Press, 1992, Vol. 7, p 504

(2) Realization of rural industrialization will greatly enrich social commodity supplies. Mao, in his notes on *Economic Problems in Socialism in the Soviet Union*, wrote in November 1958 that without the realization of the industrialization of the communes and factory-like production in agriculture, it was impossible to have a very rich supply of commodities, or direct exchange and the abolition of commodity production. He added, "It is wrong to say that the economy of the people's communes is a self-sufficient natural economy. Communes should expand social exchanges and do their best to produce what they can to exchange for local products as well as products made in the same province, in the same country and even in other parts of the world. A people's commune should not be satisfied with 'small scope and small population,' but should embark upon diversified industrial crops, run industry and expand the production of things for exchange."[1]

(3) Industrialization of the countryside may turn peasants into workers without leaving their native place. Mao said that one of China's unique features is "the 600 million people and 166 million ha of farmland." The country would be in trouble, he said, if no special measures were taken. He went on, "More than 500 million rural residents are engaged in agricultural production, but they can not feed themselves. That is irrational. In the US, farmers account for only 13% of the total population, but they produce an average of 2,000 kg of grain per person. They produce more grain than we do. What should we do to reduce the rural population? They should not converge into the cities. Run factories in the countryside and turn local peasants into workers. In the future, half of our able-bodied people will be engaged in industrial production."

(4) Industrialization of the countryside will help eliminate the difference between the cities and the countryside. Mao said that workers were building the country in the cities and peasants were building the country in the countryside. The workers and peasants should cooperate and compete to bring the rural areas to the

[1] Tao Lujia: *Mao Zedong Teaches Us How to Be a Provincial Party Committee Secretary*, Central Archives Press, 1996, p. 180

level of the cities — that would be a worker-peasant alliance in the true sense. He said, "We should bring rural life to slightly below, or generally close to or even slightly higher than that in the cities, and each people's commune should have its own economic center." He added: "The collective farms in the Soviet Union do not run industry. That way it is impossible to eliminate the difference between the cities and the countryside."[1]

Under the guidance of Mao Zedong's "ideal socialism," people's communes and commune-run industry grew very rapidly. By the end of 1958, the output value of commune-run industry grew from zero to 6.25 billion yuan in the short span of just three months. But that was achieved through launching mass movements, adopting "human-wave" tactics and taking from the peasants without compensation. This malpractice, plus reckless guidance in production that ran counter to natural and economic rules, plus bad weather, caused crop failures for three consecutive years. The succeeding famine forced the leadership to correct errors in the work, call a halt to the practice of running everything "in a big way" and take measures to strengthen the agricultural frontline. In 1962, it was decided that the communes and their production brigades should stop running enterprises, and their industrial output value dropped to 420 million yuan in 1963. Commune-run industry came to a virtual standstill.

In the years from 1953, when China started its First Five-Year Plan to embark on the road of industrialization, to 1966, when Mao Zedong launched the "cultural revolution," the country's pace of urbanization was rather slow, although its industry made conspicuous progress. China's industrial output rose from 45 billion yuan to 162.4 billion yuan, with an annual increase of 10.4%, and accounting for 53% of the total social product and 64% of the combined industrial and agricultural product. Yet its urbanization rate was only 17.7%, with 83.5% of the country's population still working on farms. The peasants still mainly relied on manual labor and draft

---

[1] Tao Lujia: *Mao Zedong Teaches Us How to Be a Provincial Party Committee Secretary*, Central Archives Press, 1996, p. 108

animals to till an average of 0.17 ha of land per person, with very low productivity. The average able-bodied peasant made only 226 yuan a year. China remained a poor agricultural country. The production brigades of the communes were poor, with a gross annual income of 10,000 yuan, of which little was left after deducting the production costs. And the members of the communes could get only 52.4 yuan a year from distribution by the collective. In some places, after obtaining their ration of food grain, a peasant household not only could not get any money at all from the collective, they found themselves in debt to the collective. By the standards of the World Bank, that was "dire poverty."

After the "cultural revolution" began, the Chinese peasants found the cities were in chaos as the workers stopped production and students stopped studying to plunge into "revolutionary activities." Governments at all levels relaxed their administrative control, and domestic demand was plagued by painful shortages of commodities. The peasants saw their chance coming, and took advantage of this chaotic situation to find ways to increase their incomes. Production brigades and teams took the initiative in setting up industrial enterprises to turn out commodities to meet the market demand. By 1979, after the 11th CPC Central Committee convened its historic third plenary session, the output value of commune- and brigade-run industry had already reached 42.5 billion yuan, accounting for 9.5% of the country's total industrial output.

Barred by State policy from going to the cities to find jobs, Chinese peasants used to account for 84.2% of the country's total population and 72.5% of the total labor power. The surplus labor power in China's countryside — 140 million able-bodied persons — constituted one of the reasons for the low rural productivity. An able-bodied person on the agricultural front produced an average of 398 yuan of output a year, and the per capita annual income in the countryside from the collective distribution was only 86.7 yuan. Some 58.8% of Chinese peasants received less than 80 yuan a year each from the collective.

The Third Plenary Session of the 11th CPC Central Committee at the end of 1978 decided to initiate the policies of reform and opening to the outside world to enliven the economy. It urged "considerable development of the enterprises run by communes and production brigades." That further fired the enthusiasm of Chinese peasants for developing industry. Rural industry made headway by leaps and bounds in the midst of the tidal wave of reform. The combined output of township industry rose to 87.3 billion yuan-worth in 1986, accounting for 22.1% of the national total.

Commenting on the heartening vigorous development of industry in China's countryside, Deng Xiaoping told a state guest from Cameroon on March 27, 1987: "The fact that a large amount of the rural labor force is shifting to the newly emerging towns and small and medium-sized enterprises seems to be inevitable. It would not do to tie the peasants to tiny plots of land all the time. That would be hopeless."[1] Deng told a state guest from Yugoslavia on June 12, 1987: "The development of township enterprises, primarily industry, but also covering other trades, has created job openings for half of the surplus rural labor force. Peasants are no longer converging on the cities, but building a large number of small modern township enterprises."[2]

China's economy grew at a high speed in the 1990s. Spurred by this momentum, the country's township industry too developed rapidly, making increasingly important contributions to the countryside and society as a whole. Speaking on the issue of rural industrialization as one of the two wings of China's industrialization, Jiang Zemin made a very high appraisal of it. After he completed an inspection tour of the countryside in Jiangsu Province in 1998, he said, "The township enterprises, which have emerged like a shock force in the last 20 years of reform and opening to the outside world, have been developing rapidly and with great momentum. They have become a major force in our rural economy and an important component of our national economy. The development of township

---

[1] *Selected Works of Deng Xiaoping*, People's Publishing House, 1993, Vol. 3, pp. 213 - 214

[2] *Selected Works of Deng Xiaoping*, People's Publishing House, 1993, Vol. 3, p. 238

industry is the inevitable road to agricultural modernization, to a better-off standard of living in the countryside, and to rural industrialization with Chinese characteristics. It is a new path for the development of China's countryside and even the whole of society." He added, "The development of township enterprises is a major strategy and a basic principle of lasting significance, as is stepping up the building of small towns while developing township enterprises energetically. It is necessary to make serious efforts to sum up our experience in this respect, and further develop township enterprises and small towns. That should be the focus when promoting rural social progress." He pointed out that the emergence and development of township enterprises as a shock force in China had been "a great creation by the Chinese peasants. The township enterprise is a unique creative work in the world. It is our unique Chinese characteristic. The township enterprise is a great innovation by our millions upon millions of farmers, and a tremendous achievement made in the reform and opening to the outside world under the leadership of the Communist Party of China."[1]

Jiang, in his speech at the 1999 celebration marking the 50th anniversary of the founding of New China, said, "China, a country once very weak and poor, has undergone epoch-making changes through arduous struggles in the past 50 years, especially in the 20 years of reform and opening to the outside world. The industrious, brave and intelligent Chinese people, under the leadership of the CPC, have made world-shaking miracles in this old land of China." The dream which was cherished and fought for by many generations of the Chinese people has started to come true. The *Economic Daily*, declared, "China has grown from a traditionally agricultural country into a developing country which has succeeded initially in establishing fairly diversified industrialization." [2]

---

[1] Rural Work Team of the Policy Research Office of the CPC Central Committee: *General Secretary Jiang's Inspection Tours of the Countryside*, Agriculture Press, 1998, pp. 244, 342

[2] *Economic Daily*: National Day Focus page: "A Gradual Readjustment of the Industrial Structure" 2nd page of the paper on Sept. 22, 1999

Of the added value of industry and agriculture nationwide, that of industry grew from 63.2% in 1978 to 74.2% in 1999. The number of workers employed in secondary industry increased from 69.45 million in 1978 to 162.35 million in 1999 — from 17.3% to 23% of the entire workforce in employment. The urbanization rate of the country's population rose from 17.9% in 1978 to 30.9% in 1999. Township industry played an almost equal role to urban industry in the country's industrialization effort, as it accounted for 49.1% of the country's total added industrial value. Today, China's township industry is advancing toward modernization and informationization under overall strategic planning.

Section 2 Composition of Township Industry

Under the planned economy in the past, township industry in China was still handicapped by state industrial policy on issues like what products were allowed to be made, although the township enterprises basically operated by market economy rules. Meanwhile, they were forced by market forces to constantly readjust the mix of products, and even their industrial structure. More than 10% of the TVEs were closed down, merged with others, suspended or made to change their line of production every year.

The readjustment of the industrial structure was sometimes subject to objective conditions such as changes in market demand, new government policies forbidding the production of some seriously polluting products, state policies on regional industrial distribution, or the emergence of new technologies and new products that ousted old ones.

However, there exist many structural problems in TVEs. For example, those dependent on natural resources for raw materials usually make a single product without sufficient equipment for multiple uses of the resources, resulting in serious waste. Enterprises involving chemical processes usually lack sufficient funds and equipment to make their production environmentally friendly. Some township enterprises are incapable of making market investigations, and just follow others in making products in high demand, with the result of repetitive construction of the same type of plants in competition not only with State-run enterprises but also with other township enterprises. Still others have been built with old equipment discarded by large State-owned enterprises, and can produce only outdated and crude products.

TVEs have been growing in the course of constant readjustment from the first day of their inception. And such readjustment has been different in content under the influence of different State policies in different periods of time. During the time of the people's communes, for instance, the emphasis was on making commune- and brigade-run industry satisfy local needs in production and daily life by using local resources.

During the "cultural revolution," the CPC Central Committee and the State Council promoted the development of TVEs industry by focusing on the production of agricultural machinery, and the development of a three-level farm machinery manufacturing and repair network, small iron and steel plants, small machinery plants, small cement kilns, small chemical fertilizer plants and small coal mines under the guideline of accelerating agricultural mechanization.

In the 1980s, however, in face of a serious shortage of power supply nationwide, TVEs were largely engaged in developing small coal mines — generally small ones — wherever coal reserves were available. Township coal mines produced 107.11 million tons of coal in 1980, accounting for 17.3% of the national total, and the figure rose to 633.76 million tons in 1997, making up 46.8% of the national total coal output. These small collieries achieved a net increase of 527 million tons of coal in 17 years without using any state investment at all, whereas the total net increase of coal in those years nationwide was 736 million tons. The contribution made by the township collieries accounted for 71.6% of the national total.

In view of the international trend of economic globalization, which emerged in the late 1980s, the Party and State Council called on the country to develop the export-oriented economy, starting with making inroads into the international market with labor-intensive products. In 1986, TVES began their export-oriented operations by accepting orders for processing and assembly jobs with designs, materials or parts supplied by foreign clients in the form of compensation trade. In the same year, they achieved a total of 9.9 billion yuan-worth of export commodity deliveries, accounting for 9.1% of the national total exports. In 1998, the foreign trade deliveries by township enterprises reached 685.4 billion yuan-worth, accounting for 45% of the national total. The export commodities covered 13 industrial departments, with the focus on textiles, garments, light industry and handicrafts.

Toward the end of the 1990s, the domestic market was changing from a seller's market to a buyer's market. In order to maintain sustainable economic growth, those enterprises that wasted natural resources, polluted the environment, used outdated technology and equipment or had poor production safety records were forced to close down or suspend production. TVEs were the first to feel the blow, because many of them fell into the categories cited above. That wave of compulsory readjustment was the largest in scale in the history of China's industrialization, and involved the largest number of workers to be laid off and return to farming. In 1997 and 1998, the country's township industry not only absorbed no new surplus labor, but laid off more than 10 million peasant-workers.

Market demand is always a powerful driver for industrial readjustment in rural China. For example, there was an acute shortage of paper on the Chinese domestic market in 1980. That year, China produced only 5.35 million tons of paper, way below the market demand. For a time, printing houses even had difficulty in finding paper to print primary school textbooks and notebooks. The TVEs did not miss this opportunity. They used locally abundant supplies of wheat and rice straw as raw material, as well as ammonia, lime and sulfur to make cartons, glazed paper, packing paper and toilet paper. They turned out 13.65 million tons of paper and cartons in 1997, which was 63% of China's total output of 216.6 million tons. However, the small paper mills in the rural areas tended to pollute the ground water with their sewage, although the waste water was used to some extent for irrigation. In the interest of maintaining sustainable economic growth, the State was forced to order them to close down.

In the mid-1980s, small domestic appliances like electric fans, microwave ovens and water heaters were in vogue, and TVEs manufactured over 60% of such goods.

The readjustment of China's rural industry has stimulated the updating of products. The Guangdong Kelong Group, the Jiangsu Yangguang Group and the Zhejiang Wanxiang Group, for example, have sufficient funds for their own technological updating. They have the best equipment and produce the best products among all Chinese enterprises. Such TVEs, each with an annual turnover of at least 50 million yuan, now number 8,726, and among them more than 3,000 are enterprise groups.

All TVEs were collectively owned industrial enterprises before 1984. In the following year, 80% of the total TVE output value was produced by collectively owned ones. This ratio dropped to 51.5% in 1998, and to 45.5% in 1999 — for the first time lower than the production of privately owned TVEs. (See Table 4-1)

Table 4-1 Changes in China's Rural Industrial Structure

Content	Output value of township collective industry (in 100 million yuan)				Composition of township collective industry (%)			
Year	1980	1985	1991	1998	1980	1985	1991	1998
Township industry	516	1,846	8,709	69,127				
Collectively owned industry	516	1,478	6,518	35,569				
Proportion of collectively owned (%)	100	80.0	74.8	51.5				
Light industry	248	718	3,545	19,470	48.1	48.6	54.4	54.7
With farm produce as raw material	120	419	2,108	9,945	23.3	28.4	32.3	28.0

With non-industrial produce as raw material	128	299	1,437	9,525	24.8	20.2	22.1	26.7
Heavy industry	268	760	2,974	16,097	51.9	51.4	45.6	45.3
Mining	46	112	376	2,260	8.9	7.6	5.7	6.3
Raw materials	44	114	624	3,323	8.5	7.7	9.6	9.3
Processing	178	534	1,974	10,514	34.5	36.1	30.3	29.7

Source: *China Township Enterprises Yearbook*

The above table shows clearly that the proportion of heavy industry in the industrial composition was on the decrease — from 51.9% to 45.3% in 1999 — and that of light industry rose from 48.1% to 54.7%. TVEs reliant on local resources accounted for 53.6% of the total industrial output value, and those products meeting the popular demand on the local market accounted for 84.4% of the total industrial output value.

Readjustment of the industrial structure has been necessary for making the products of township industry constantly meet the demand on the domestic and international market, and indeed for them to survive. This is particularly true in the new century, which is expected to witness a transition from the epoch of the industrial economy to that of the information economy. China's township industry must seize this opportunity to make timely readjustments, and launch a second wave of development by consciously readjusting its industrial structure and product mix to meet the changing market demand.

Section 3 Distribution of Township Industry

Unlike agriculture, industrial production requires coordination on a social scale. Therefore, industrial production is relatively concentrated in the industrial districts of cities. Yet China's TVEs have tended to be scattered across the countryside from the very beginning. This phenomenon has a peculiar historical background.

Until the end of the 1960s, China had a socialist planned economy. The people's communes were a mixture of government and productive organization, and the rural population was tied to the countryside by a rigid household registration system. Peasants were not allowed to find jobs in the cities, and even demobilized soldiers had to return to their villages.

So when Chinese peasants began to run industry in their production brigades, they started with handicraft skills or semi-mechanized tools. They used abandoned warehouses, offices or even local temples as factory workshops. They did not have to invest in land, and found building materials locally. Those who were masons, carpenters and bricklayers acted as builders. They worked on their farm and in the workshops in their own villages, and slept at home. No dormitories or canteens were needed. When officials from higher up came on inspection tours, the workers simply closed the doors of the workshops and returned to the fields.

When the CPC Central Committee and the State Council, in government documents issued in 1978, officially sanctioned the running of industry by peasants, the peasants still had no way to set up industrial enterprises based on an association of several production brigades, or in the cities. This was because they could not buy, rent or borrow land. The production brigade had to find work for its surplus labor power, and therefore could not afford to set up enterprises far from the village. It was also impossible to solve the problem of the rigid household registration system. If peasants left their village to work elsewhere, they could not take care of the land they had contracted for farming from the collective. Finally, the production brigades simply could not win official approval to run enterprises in the cities. So they were forced to build and run enterprises locally. The result was that the vast Chinese countryside was dotted with a large number of small industrial enterprises in a highly scattered fashion.

The sparse distribution of TVEs was a matter of course. Yet

some rather serious problems surfaced. They were:

(1) They had to invest in infrastructure construction on their own, thus increasing the costs;

(2) The location of the factories in the villages and towns made it inconvenient to attract customers to conduct business negotiations;

(3) The transportation of raw materials and finished products over a long distance increased the costs, and often resulted in damage during shipment;

(4) For a small industrial enterprise in the countryside it was difficult to find production partners to make a complete product in coordination;

(5) The countryside with its relatively inconvenient living and working conditions was not attractive to engineers and managerial personnel; and

(6) Although the development of township industry is bringing modern culture to Chinese peasants and helps them overcome some backward or outdated ideas, the low level of pollution control that is common among township enterprises often damages the ecosystem.

In addressing these issues, the rural enterprises were gradually concentrated in small industrial zones of the townships and towns, where relatively workable infrastructure and pollution-prevention facilities were built. In order to receive business negotiators, the towns added service facilities. Gradually, there appeared marketplaces specializing in certain categories of industrial products, industrial raw materials and related materials. In the wake of this, commerce began to thrive. As time went by, new towns arose, and became rural political, economic, cultural, scientific, educational, public health and transportation centers. Chinese peasants, who were barred from working in the cities, built their own towns and small cities. So they not only created township enterprises to develop the rural economy but also built new rural towns and cities on their own.

Jiang Zemin spoke highly of the emergence of the large number of new towns in the Chinese countryside. During his inspection tour of Jiangsu and Zhejiang provinces, and Shanghai in October 1998, he said, "We have 1.3 billion people, and 900 million live in the countryside. With the rise of rural productivity and the development of TVEs, and the expansion of the scale farming in the more developed coastal regions, a large volume of rural surplus labor power needs to be transferred elsewhere. Transferring this surplus labor power to the newly emerging towns and TVEs in a planned and methodical way is the fundamental way out for the modernization of China's agriculture. Since we started the reform and opening-up, TVEs have developed rapidly, and spurred the development of towns and small cities. In this process, much surplus rural labor power and residents have moved to towns. Here we have found a way to achieve rural modernization in keeping with the reality of our country. Developing TVEs and promoting the building of small cities and towns are parts of a great strategy. We should sum up experiences carefully, and further develop TVEs and small cities and towns. That should be the focus of our work of promoting the social-economic progress of our countryside."[1]

In the late 1980s, the Ministry of Agriculture and Ministry of Construction joined hands in addressing the issue of building small cities and towns in the countryside, with emphasis on solving the problem of the over-scattered distribution of TVEs and the question of how to get TVEs to gather in small rural industrial districts as a way to speed up the building of small cities and towns. By the end of 2000, a total of 9,397 industrial districts consisting of TVEs had been built or were under construction. They included 200 pilot zones for demonstration, 287 industrial zones as good examples of cooperation between eastern and western China, and 8,910 other TVE industrial zones. The small industrial zones contributed an industrial output value of 621.6 billion yuan, accounting for 33% of the total made by China's township enterprises. The fact that the development of small industrial zones in rural towns has enhanced the construction of small cities and towns in the countryside is not an isolated example. It has formed a sweeping trend, constituting part of China's urbanization and rural modernization drive. It has become a major

[1] Rural Work Team of the Policy Research Office of the CPC Central Committee: *General Secretary Jiang's Inspection Tours of the Countryside,* China Agriculture Press, 1998

channel for diverting the surplus rural population, and a primary measure for overcoming the irrational and vastly scattered distribution of the rural industry. The peasants are taking the initial steps in building small cities and towns that may not be perfect at the start. But this is a new thing that will grow with amazing vigor and become mature. This is evident in the following passages quoted from news coverage by *Economic Daily* reporters on efforts made to change the scattered industrial distribution and the building of small cities and towns in the Chinese countryside:

According to the *Economic Daily* on September 23, 1999 and January 17, 2000, there were in all 19,216 administrative towns with a combined population of 170 million, accounting for 13.6% of the total population of the country. The towns had absorbed 30 million workers from agriculture, accounting for more than 30% of the surplus labor power in the countryside.

According to the *Economic Daily* on November 22, 1998, the leaders of Nanhai City in Guangdong Province said that they believed that the towns serve as powerful links between the city and the surrounding rural area, and are leading the city's rapid economic growth. The total income of the city's rural economy in 1997 reached 54.1 billion yuan, and of the 20 towns under the jurisdiction of the municipal government, 17 each had an annual income exceeding one billion yuan; three each had an annual income exceeding five billion yuan; one had an annual income exceeding four billion yuan; four each had an annual income exceeding three billion yuan; and five each had an annual income exceeding two billion yuan. The 20 towns were 20 pillars of Nanhai's economy. The city had more than 60,000 rural industrial and commercial enterprises in 1997, of which over 60 produced an output value of more than 100 million yuan each. The total output value of all Nanhai's rural industrial enterprises reached 43 billion yuan.

According to the *Economic Daily* on March 4, 1997, Longgang in Cangnan County, Zhejiang Province, used to be a typical economically backward village with practically no enterprises. But, spurred by the policy of reform and opening-up and the documents of the CPC Central Committee and the State Council encouraging the building of TVEs and the vigorous economic growth of the country as a whole, in 1985 the villagers of Cangnan and neighboring areas raised funds, and built roads, factory buildings, houses and a waterworks on a stretch of former marshland to set up enterprises. Now the place is a modern town of eight square km crisscrossed by 80-odd avenues lined with trees. It now has 140,000 residents and more than 10,000 industrial and commercial enterprises, which make a combined output value of three billion yuan a year, and provide 100 million yuan in revenue to the town government. Longgan has 38 secondary and primary schools, and other public amenities.

Longgang is known as "China's first town built by peasants." The State Commission for Economic Restructuring and 10 other departments under the State Council jointly made a resolution in August 1995 to designate Longgang as a pilot town in the overall reform of small cities and towns.

According to the *Economic Daily* on November 7, 1999 and April 11, 12, and 13, 2000, the State Council's "Systematic Plan for Towns in Zhejiang Province" set the targets for the development of Hengdian Town in the central hilly area of Zhejiang as follows: It should grow into a small city with at least 100,000 residents in the city proper by the year 2010.

The sponsor of Hengdian was a man by the name of Xu Wenrong, a peasant-turned-entrepreneur who founded the Hengdian Enterprise Group. From his personal experience, he believed that peasants would be happy to see industrial enterprises grow in their hometown, and to see their own town grow into a modern city. So he decided to invest in building his own native place, Hengdian, into a modern town.

Hengdian used to be a poor township in the depth of the mountains some 18 km from Dongyang City in Zhejiang Province. Xu set up a silk-reeling mill there in 1975. A large number of TVEs sprang up in Hengdian during the 1980s, and Hengdian became an administrative town with official approval from the local people's government. Xu Wenrong won approval from the authorities in the 1990s to organize an enterprise group by merging 200 small enterprises together, and established relationships with 800 more enterprises to form the Hengdian Enterprise Group, one of the five-largest township enterprise groups in China.

Hengdian encompasses three industrial zones: the general industrial zone, the electronics industry zone and the magnetic industry zone. Hengdian's 1998 output value amounted to more than five billion yuan. The development of local industry has absorbed a large amount of surplus labor power from agriculture. Now 65% of the able-bodied persons in Hengdian are working on the industrial front, and 25% in tertiary industry. Only 10% of Hengdian's workforce is engaged in farming.

The development of industry in Hengdian has brought about a fundamental change in the local economic structure. The composition of the primary, secondary and tertiary industries of the town was in a ratio of 1: 13.4: 2 in the year 1995, and became 1: 58.4: 11.4 in 1999. The group spent 10 million yuan on building 10 educational institutions, including kindergartens, and primary and secondary schools, and spent another 50 million yuan on building a technical school and a university. It plans to invest a total of one billion yuan on building a film shooting center and tourist center with settings of a Qin Dynasty Palace, a Hong Kong street and simulated scenes of the streets of the capital of the Song Dynasty. The cinematography center has provided settings for the shooting of the feature film *The Opium War* and more than 30 other films and TV plays. Hengdian's industrial development has also boosted its tertiary industry, which recorded an output value of 500 million yuan in 1999. The town received 800,000 tourists and made an income of 35 million yuan from tourism in the same year.

The group has allocated 1.98 billion yuan for the construction of the infrastructure of the town over the past 20 years. This includes public utilities, farm and water conservancy construction, education, social welfare, the film shooting center, exhibition halls and sports facilities. Since 1993, the group has spent 98.55 million yuan on reforestation of the surrounding hills; 100 million yuan on broadening the local waterways and building five dams, 14,000-m-long dykes, and a park along the Nanjiang River; and 165 million yuan on smoke emission and sewage treatment.

Thanks to the economic growth of the town, the annual income of Hengdian's residents has reached 5,780 yuan per person. The Dongyang municipal government has decided that Hengdian Town should reach out to include the neighboring 68 administrative villages of four townships to bring the number of its villages from 40 to 108 and the number of its residents from 24,000 in 1985 to 65,000. The town covers 18 sq km, and has 32,000 permanent residents and 20,000 temporary residents. The latter are mostly workers employed by the Hengdian Group. The town proper now has a population of more than 50,000.

On an inspection tour of Zhulin Town, Gongyi City, Henan Province, on July 9, 1996, President Jiang Zemin said that he was happy to see that the formerly poor township had become rich, with an annual output of 1.4 billion yuan, within 10 years.

The town used to be called Zhulin Village. It is situated in a valley deep in the Songshan Mountains. Owing to lack of water, the local bamboo groves died, and the hills became denuded. The villagers here could hardly grow enough grain to feed themselves. In 1983, Zhao Ming'en, the village leader, called a meeting of Communist Party members to discuss how to improve the local economy. They came to a consensus that the right way was to develop local industry.

First, the villagers built a refractory materials plant, and gradually added a number of factories and plants to produce magnesia bricks, chemical products, cardboard, furniture and pharmaceuticals, as well as a two-star tourist hotel. The local government agreed to change the administrative village into an administrative town in 1994. Zhao Ming'en said, "We just want to show people that socialism is a golden bridge to prosperity. We hope to attract people here to see for themselves that this road leads to paradise."

Although the work of readjusting the distribution of township industry has just begun, a feasible road seems to have been found. There are already a large number of successful examples and pilot projects, and people have come to a consensus on this matter. Jiang Zemin has pointed out the importance of concentrating a number of small TVEs to form industrial zones around rural towns. That has proved to be a feasible way to speed up rural industrialization, which in turn will accelerate the pace of constructing modern small towns in the vast Chinese countryside.

Section 4 TVEs and the Rural Economy

More than 40 years have passed since Mao Zedong first proposed the promotion of rural industrialization. But substantial progress in this respect began only after the Third Plenary Session of the 11th CPC Central Committee, held in 1978. That year, the output value of the country's township industry was only 5.8% of China's total industrial output value, whereas in 1996 township industry accounted for half of the country's total industrial output value. And this ratio has been kept up to this day. In terms of industrial added value, township industry accounted for 47.5% of the national total in 2000. Especially after Deng Xiaoping's remarks on his inspection tour of the South were published in 1992, all provinces, autonomous regions and municipalities directly under the State Council have speeded up the building of township industry. Since then, the overall output value of TVEs has been rising at an average annual rate of 30.3%, and their industrial output value has been rising at an average annual rate of 29.6%. The central and western regions have made even faster progress in this period. (See Table 4-2)

Table 4-2 Development of TVEs by Province, Autonomous Region and Municipality (Unit: 100 million yuan)

Area	Output value of TVEs			Output value of township industry		
Year	1991	1998	Annual increase (%)	1991	1998	Annual increase (%)
Beijing	280	690	11.9	216	394	7.8
Tianjin	265	1,337	22.4	253	1,099	20.2

Hebei	724	5,913	30.0	516	4,294	30.3
Shanxi	240	1,714	27.9	170	1,180	27.4
Inner Mongolia	70	2,835	36.3	34	769	47.7
Liaoning	550	5,762	34.1	416	3,773	31.7
Jilin	161	1,392	30.9	85	643	28.8
Heilongjiang	181	907	22.3	94	684	28.2
Shanghai	379	2,269	25.1	379	2,269	25.1
Anhui	376	3,018	29.7	225	1,879	30.4
Fujian	335	4,658	39.0	218	3,116	39.4
Jiangsu	1,664	9,510	24.3	1,527	8,449	23.8
Zhejiang	1,002	10,109	33.5	926	9,481	33.7
Jiangxi	200	1,292	26.3	132	852	26.3
Shandong	1,476	9,549	26.8	1,151	7,379	26.1
Henan	839	5,115	25.3	514	3,785	28.3
Hubei	393	5,653	39.6	249	3,596	39.6
Hunan	340	6,056	43.3	197	2,991	40.5
Guangdong	956	8,408	31.2	700	6,784	32.8
Guangxi	121	2,299	44.5	70	1,141	41.8
Hainan	17	117	27.3	6	63	34.2
Chongqing		669		406		
Sichuan	633	3,435	26.3	362	1,848	25.7
Guizhou	55	466	30.6	36	264	28.3
Yunnan	91	1,378	40.4	54	574	34.4
Shaanxi	184	1,671	31.8	108	991	31.9
Gansu	82	507	25.6	42	221	23.1
Qinghai	7	56	29.7	4	33	30.2
Ningxia	16	111	27.4	8	54	27.0
Xinjiang	30	246	30.1	16	111	27.4
Total	11,811	96,694	30.3	8,700	69,128	29.6

Note: (1) Chongqing was still under the jurisdiction of Sichuan Province in 1991, and therefore not separated from Sichuan in calculation in 1991. (2) Tibet is not listed for lack of data. (3) Source: *China Township Enterprises Yearbook* (1999)

The uneven development of TVEs is obvious in the proportions of each of the provinces, autonomous regions and municipalities. (See Table 4-3)

Table 4-3 Proportion of Township Industry in China's Rural Economy

Area	Proportion of township industry in total rural industrial and agricultural output value (%)	Township industry workers in total rural labor power (%)
Beijing	79.6	57.0
Tianjin	89.5	66.5
Hebei	79.7	25.6
Shanxi	82.7	32.8
Inner Mongolia	81.7	9.2
Liaoning	85.6	45.5
Jilin	67.6	39.0
Heilongjiang	55.2	16.0
Shanghai	91.6	65.0
Jiangsu	83.7	30.6
Zhejiang	91.0	37.6
Anhui	71.5	20.9
Fujian	82.7	42.5
Jiangxi	63.7	19.7
Shandong	81.4	33.8
Henan	73.7	18.9
Hubei	83.1	35.6
Hunan	83.1	31.5
Guangdong	83.9	44.5
Guangxi	72.6	17.8
Hainan	32.5	11.9
Chongqing	60.6	10.3
Sichuan	71.1	14.9
Yunnan	69.2	20.7
Guizhou	53.7	7.2
Shaanxi	77.7	28.1
Gansu	60.1	15.8
Qinghai	47.9	13.6
Ningxia	58.4	26.5
Xinjiang	33.1	20.6
Total	80.7	27.0

Sources: *China Statistical Yearbook* and *China TVE Yearbook*

Rural industry in China is still in the initial, and in some parts of the country in the foundation-laying, stage. But in the more developed provinces and regions, township industry has set an example of rural industrialization for the whole country. It has shown the Chinese peasants the bright future of a new socialist countryside, and shown the world the vitality of township industry. The development of township industry has helped accelerate China's industrialization, and helped increase the national strength. It has increased peasants' income and absorbed surplus rural labor power. Moreover, it serves as a stabilizer of rural social order, and is creating conditions for rural modernization, contributing to the country's foreign exchange earnings and the state coffers. It helps accelerate the process of urbanization of China's countryside and helps change the traditional conservative mindset of the Chinese peasants by introducing them to modern cultural concepts, thus helping to transform China's countryside into industrial society.

Chapter V

TVEs and Urbanization

Section 1 Process of Urbanization

The rapid development of TVEs has also been a course of rural industrialization and urbanization. The emergence and growth of TVEs have accelerated the urbanization of the rural areas, which has in turn enhanced the entire process of urbanization. The process of urbanization has brought about social progress, helped to absorb a large amount of surplus rural labor and to increase the peasants' income, raised living standards in the countryside, and narrowed the gap between town and country.

In contrast to the countryside, a city is a concentration of population, industry and commerce, serving as the political, economic and cultural center for its surrounding area.

Urbanization is a process of the movement of rural population into cities, and a process in which the number of cities increases. Urbanization is an inevitable process of modernization and industrialization. Urbanization stimulates economic growth. The developed countries have virtually all become urbanized, and so will the developing countries in the future. The world today is deeply concerned about environmental pollution caused by urbanization, the treatment of "urban illnesses" and how to make development sustainable.

Urbanization is a major manifestation of industrialization. In China, however, the course of urbanization has not gone side by side with industrialization, as urbanization has lagged behind industrialization, and small and medium-sized cities have lagged behind large ones. Consequently, urbanization remains at a low level, and is concentrated mainly in the large and medium-sized cities. The level of urbanization is particularly low in central and western China. This is an important indication of the country's economic backwardness as well as a marked feature of the dual character of its economic structure. Thanks to the rise of TVEs since China began to implement its reform and opening-up policies, the country's urbanization process has gathered momentum. (See Table 5-1)

Table 5-1 China's Urban and Rural Populations 1990-2000

(Unit: 10,000 persons)

Year	Total population	Urban population	Rural population	% in total	
				Urban	Rural
1990	114,333	30,191	84,142	26.41	73.59
1991	115,823	30,543	85,280	26.37	73.63
1992	117,171	32,372	84,799	27.63	72.37
1993	118,517	33,351	85,166	28.14	71.86
1994	119,850	34,301	85,549	28.62	71.38
1995	121,121	35,174	85,947	29.04	70.96
1996	122,389	35,950	86,439	29.37	70.63
1997	123,626	36,989	86,637	29.92	70.08
1998	124,810	37,942	86,868	30.40	69.60
1999	125,909	38,892	87,017	30.89	69.11
2000	126,583	45,844	80,739	36.22	63.78

Source: *China Statistical Yearbook 2001*

There were 40,370 administrative towns and townships in China in 2001 (the decrease resulting from mergers), including 20,012 townships and 20,358 towns.[1] The number of towns exceeded that of townships. But with the development of TVEs, towns are bound to increase in number and size.

[1] Administrative townships and towns are both the grassroots level administrations, each covering a number of villages in a neighborhood. The difference between a township and a town lies in that a town is a small city with a concentrated population and relatively developed industry and commerce while a township has no obvious concentration of population in one locality and the township government is a purely rural administration.

The rapid development of industry has brought about tremendous changes in the distribution of cities. In the last decade of the 20th century, the number of cities in China increased from 467 to 663. Among them, the number of cities each with a population of at least two million rose from nine to 13, those with a population ranging from one million to two million rose from 22 to 27, those with a population ranging from 500,000 to one million rose from 28 to 53, those with a population ranging from 200,000 to 500,000 rose from 117 to 218, and those with a population of less than 200,000 rose from 291 to 352.

One of the salient features of China's urbanization is the relatively rapid increase in the number of small and medium-sized cities. The cities with a population of less than 500,000 each account for 85.9% of the total number of cities in the country. Among them, those with a population of less than 200,000 each account for 53.1% of the total and those with a population between 200,000 and 500,000 each account for 32.9% of the total. The number of small cities with a population of less than 200,000 increased by 21% and that of cities with a population between 200,000 and 500,000 increased by 86.3% in the 1990s.

Table 5-2 Number of Cities in China 1990-2000

Year	Number of cities	Population 2 million +	Population 1-2 million	Population 500,000–1 million	Population 200,000-500,000	Population less than 200,000
1990	476	9	22	28	117	291
1991	479	9	22	30	127	297
1992	517					
1993	570	10	22	36	160	342
1994	622	10	22	42	173	375
1995	640	10	22	43	192	373
1996	666	11	23	44	195	393
1997	668	12	22	47	205	383
1998	668	13	24	48	205	378
1999	667	13	24	49	216	365
2000	663	13	27	53	218	352

Source: *China Statistical Yearbook*

China's urbanization in the 1990s was a gradual process. The urban population has been growing, while the rural population has been on the decrease. Of the total population, the urban population made up 19.4% in 1980, 26.4% in 1990, 29.0% in 1995 and 36.2% in 2000 (The 2000 census showed a total population of 1.265 billion, with 458 million urban residents and 807 million rural residents).

The development of urbanization is uneven among the provinces, autonomous regions and municipalities directly under the State Council. Leading the way are Shanghai (88.31%), Beijing (77.54%) and Tianjin (77.99%). Regions with an urban population exceeding 50% of the total are Guangdong (55%), Liaoning (54.24%) and Heilongjiang (51.54%). Next come Jilin (49.68%), Zhejiang (48.67%), Fujian (41.57%), Jiangsu (41.49%), Hubei (40.22%), Hainan (40.11%) and the rest (below 40%). (See Table 5-3)

Table 5-3 Distribution of Urban and Rural Population in China in 2000

Area	Total population (million)	Urban population (million)	Rural population (million)	% in total	
				Urban	Rural
National	1265.83	458.44	807.39	36.22	63.78
Beijing	13.82	10.72	3.10	77.54	22.46
Tianjin	10.01	7.21	2.80	71.99	28.01
Hebei	67.44	17.59	49.85	26.08	73.92
Shanxi	32.97	11.51	21.46	34.91	65.09
Inner Mongolia	23.76	10.14	13.62	42.68	57.32
Liaoning	42.38	22.99	19.39	54.24	45.76
Jilin	27.28	13.55	13.73	49.68	50.32
Heilongjiang	36.89	19.01	17.88	51.54	48.46
Shanghai	16.74	14.78	1.96	88.31	11.69
Jiangsu	74.38	30.86	43.52	41.49	58.51
Zhejiang	46.77	22.77	24.00	48.67	51.33
Anhui	59.86	16.65	43.21	27.81	72.19
Fujian	34.71	14.43	20.28	41.57	58.43
Jiangxi	41.40	11.46	29.94	27.67	72.33
Shandong	90.79	34.50	56.29	38.00	62.00
Henan	92.56	21.47	71.09	23.20	76.80
Hubei	60.28	24.24	36.04	40.22	59.78

Hunan	64.40	19.16	45.24	29.75	70.25
Guangdong	86.40	47.53	38.89	55.00	45.00
Guangxi	44.89	12.64	32.25	28.15	71.85
Hainan	7.87	3.16	4.71	40.11	59.89
Chongqing	30.90	10.23	20.67	33.09	66.91
Sichuan	83.29	22.23	61.06	26.69	73.31
Guizhou	35.25	8.41	26.84	23.87	76.13
Yunnan	42.88	10.02	32.86	23.36	76.64
Tibet	2.62	0.50	2.12	18.93	81.07
Shaanxi	36.05	11.63	24.42	32.26	67.74
Gansu	25.62	6.15	19.47	24.01	75.99
Qinghai	5.18	1.80	3.38	34.76	65.24
Ningxia	5.62	1.82	3.80	32.43	67.57
Xinjiang	19.25	6.51	12.74	33.82	66.18

Note: This table is based on the results of the census collected at 00:00 hours, Nov. 1, 2000. The national total includes members of the PLA as well as urban and rural residents, but the populations of the provinces do not include PLA members.

Source: *China Statistical Yearbook, 2001*

The calculation of the non-agricultural population of the provinces, autonomous regions and municipalities shows some differences. (See Table 5-4)

Table 5-4 Non-Agricultural Population of Cities in the Provinces, Autonomous Regions and Municipalities in 2000

Area	Number of cities	Size of non-agricultural population of cities				
		above 2 million	1 million-2 million	500,000-1 million	200,000-500,000	below 200,000
National	663	13	27	53	218	352
Beijing	1	1				
Tianjin	1	1				
Hebei	34		3	3	5	23
Shanxi	22		1	1	4	16
Inner Mongolia	20		1	1	7	11
Liaoning	31	2	2	6	7	14
Jilin	28	1	1		11	15

Heilongjiang	31	1	1	6	10	13
Shanghai	1	1				
Jiangsu	41	1	3	3	23	11
Zhejiang	35		1	2	7	25
Anhui	22		1	4	10	7
Fujian	23		1	1	4	17
Jiangxi	21		1		8	12
Shandong	48		3	6	23	16
Henan	38		2	7	8	21
Hubei	36	1		4	12	19
Hunan	29		1	3	8	17
Guangdong	52	1	1	2	29	19
Guangxi	19			2	4	13
Hainan	9				2	7
Chongqing	5	1			3	1
Sichuan	32	1		1	12	18
Guizhou	13		1		3	9
Yunnan	15		1		2	12
Tibet	2					2
Shaanxi	13	1			5	7
Gansu	14		1		2	11
Qinghai	3			1		2
Ningxia	5				2	3
Xinjiang	19		1		7	11

Source: *China Statistical Yearbook, 2001*

Section 2 Reform of the Household Registration System

The existing household registration system in China is a major obstacle to urbanization. China is one of the very few countries that carry out a household registration system barring peasants from moving into cities. This system makes a rigid delineation between the urban household register for urban residents and the rural household register for rural residents. The system was enforced in the period of the planned economy, when the purchase and marketing of food grains was strictly controlled by the State, and the system has been implemented for decades. Since China started its reform and opening to the outside world, peasants have been moving into cities to work in increasing numbers. A system that hampers the movement of people is obviously a handicap to any country's economic development. Some localities began to adapt to the changing situation by allowing peasants to move into small cities and towns, and issued special passes to differentiate them from permanent urban residents.

China has reformed its household registration system four times since the mid-1980s, as follows:

(1) In 1984, the State Council approved the Ministry of Public Security's "Circular on the Issue of Peasants Settling in Rural Towns," which allowed peasants to be registered in towns provided they took care of their own supply of food. In accordance with this document, the public security departments provided permanent residence registration as non-agricultural households for peasants and their families who applied for permission to work, do business or provide services in rural towns. The newcomers still had to take care of their own food supply. Nevertheless, this was an important breakthrough in reform of the rigid household registration system.

(2) In June 1997, the State Council approved the Ministry of Public Security's "Tentative Plan for Pilot Projects for Reform of the Household Registration System in Small Cities and Towns." The document stipulated that permanent residence could be granted to those who went to small towns to work or to run businesses in secondary or tertiary industry, to be employed as functionaries, managerial personnel or technicians, or who had legitimately bought or owned permanent houses in towns, had lawful and steady incomes from non-agricultural or other sources and had been residing in a permanent residence in a town for at least two consecutive years. The same applied to their family members. The towns mentioned in this document were no longer just rural towns, but urban areas too.

(3) In March 2001, the State Council approved the "Circular on Promoting the Reform of the Household Registration System in

Small Cities and Towns" of the Ministry of Public Security, which pointed out that permanent urban residence permits could be granted on a voluntary basis to those who had permanent residence, a stable job or stable source of income, together with their direct family members in towns and cities up to the county-seat level. There were no quotas for such permits. By mid-December 2001, a total of 1,386,000 people had received permits for permanent residence in small cities and towns in Tianjin and Chongqing cities, and Liaoning, Jiangsu and Henan provinces, and the Xinjiang Uygur Autonomous Region.

(4) In 2002, the State Council approved the "Circular on Resolving Some Outstanding Issues Regarding Household Registration Control" of the Ministry of Public Security, which pointed out that permits for permanent residence in cities could be granted to rural people, together with their direct family members, who invested, set up enterprises or bought commodity houses, had legitimate and permanent houses, and legitimate and stable jobs and income in an urban area, had lived there for a certain period of time and met other relevant regulations promulgated by the local governments. The cities mentioned here included large and medium-sized ones. The new document abolished the traditional distinction between "agricultural" and "non-agricultural" households in the household registration system, and introduced a unified household registration system.

In accordance with the new rules, Guangdong, Fujian, Ningxia, Jilin and Hunan provinces began to implement a unified household registration system for both urban and rural households. That was a major step forward in accelerating the process of urbanization in China. It is understandable, however, that it may take some time for the new settlers in the cities to gain access to all the rights to social security their urban counterparts enjoy.

The process of urbanization is gathering speed across the world, as an increasing number of rural people in developing countries are pouring into cities. According to data from the UN International Bureau of Economic and Social Affairs, 38% of the world's population lived in cities in 1975, and the percentage rose to 47% in 2000. It predicted that about 60% of the world's population will live in cities by the year 2025. Half a century ago, i.e., in 1950, however, only 41% of urban residents lived in developing countries, but this percentage rose to 64% in 1995. Some 80% of the world's urban population is expected to live in developing countries by 2015.

However, in some countries and regions, urbanization brings about unemployment, poverty, hunger, disease, traffic jams, housing shortages, environmental pollution and many other problems. There has even appeared a reverse trend of moving from cities to the countryside in some countries and regions. Urbanization requires greater efforts in infrastructure construction such as housing, water source protection, sewage disposal, transportation and communications, public health, culture and education. Governments need to draw up scientific and rational plans for and give positive guidance and support to urbanization.

China, a developing country, has an extremely large rural population, and the increase in population in the near future will occur mostly in the countryside. Consequently, it remains a pressing task for China to accelerate the process of urbanization. For this, the government should pay great attention to improving the functions of large cities and the development of the surrounding satellite towns and small cities. China should develop large cities in an appropriate proportion, and make vigorous efforts to develop small and medium-sized cities, with particular attention given to the development of small cities and towns. The development of the small cities and towns is expected to stimulate the economic and social progress of the countryside. But the task has to be performed in a progressive way, instead of in a rush.

The central government should formulate effective policies to guide the work of urbanization so that it will proceed in a healthy way. It is important to protect the ecosystem and use land economically. It is also important to follow the path of economic, social and cultural development in harmony with the ecosystem by paying attention to quality and efficiency.

Chapter VI

TVEs and the Disintegration of Rural Labor

Section 1 Dual Structure and "Hereditary Peasants"

China is a big agricultural country, with a time-honored history of farm production. Having passed the stages of collecting, hunting, and crop and animal farming, it ultimately became a cradle of a brilliant agricultural civilization in the Orient. Geological findings of grains and traces of domestic animals at Neolithic sites indicate that agricultural development dates back to some 8,000 years in China, starting primarily in the Yellow River basin in the north and the Pearl River basin in the south. [1] Excavations at the Hemudu Ruins in Yuyao, Zhejiang Province, found evidence that rice cultivation dates back some 7,000 years ago there. Siliceous rice seeds 10,000 years old discovered in the Niulan Cave at Yunling, Yingde City, Guangdong Province, pushes the history of rice cultivation 3,000 years further back.[2]

Since ancient times, the laborers tilling the land have been called tillers, farmers or peasants. The *Shuo Wen Jie Zi* (*Origin of Chinese Chracters*) says: "a farmer is one who cultivates crops on the land."

---

[1] Sun Daren: *On the Changes of China*, Central Compilation & Translation Press, 1996

[2] Guo Shutian: "China's Ecological Agriculture in the 21st Century," *Chinese and International Scientific and Technological Information*, Issue No. 10, 2001

The Book of Han: Chapter on Food says: "One who tills the land to grow grain is a farmer." The *Book of Guliang: First Year of the Duke of Cheng* has this to say: "There were four types of citizens in ancient times: the scholar, the merchant, the farmer and the worker." Emperor Yan taught his people the skill of farming and was known as "Shennong" ("the divine farmer"). The "people" here refers to peasants tilling the land. Peasants have long been the driving force behind agricultural production and rural social progress in China.

The agricultural civilization of China has traversed the four stages of primitive agriculture, ancient agriculture, modern agriculture and contemporary agriculture. So far, the greater part of China remains at the stage of traditional agriculture. The 2001 census showed that there are 1,276,270,000 people in China, of which 480,640,000 were urbanites, accounting for 37.6% of the total, and 795,630,000 were rural residents, accounting for 62.4% of the population. So, more than half of the population were engaged in agricultural activities. In 2001, the proportion of agriculture dropped to 15% in the GDP, which might serve as an indication that China had reached the middle stage of industrialization. But the rural population and labor employed in agriculture still made up a considerable proportion of the total population, which however constitutes a basic feature of an agricultural society. That is both a feature of the Chinese economic-social structure and an outstanding weakness of that structure. It is a major cause of the numerous contradictions that keep cropping up in the course of China's economic-social development. In other words, the dual nature of the economic-social structure of China is yet to undergo fundamental changes. This should be the most basic appraisal of the reality of China.

Agriculture is the foundation of the national economy, and the issue of the peasants has been a basic on throughout the country's revolution and construction. By relying on the Chinese peasants, the Communist Party of China (CPC) built revolutionary base areas in the countryside, adopted a strategy of encircling the cities from the rural areas and after 28 years of arduous struggle ultimately overthrew the rule of imperialism, feudalism and bureaucrat capitalism, and founded the People's Republic of China in 1949. Following the founding of New China, the CPC launched the land reform, in which the dream of "land to the tiller" came true. It took only three years for the Chinese people to heal the wounds of war, and bring agricultural production to the pre-war peak of 1936.

Beginning in 1953, China set out on a large-scale industrialization drive. The drive was launched under a highly centralized planned economy, patterned in the main after the Soviet model and based on 156 major projects with direct aid from the Soviet Union. That wave of industrialization was characterized mainly by the following five aspects:

— State-owned enterprises dominating enterprises;
— Heavy industry dominating industry;
— Mainly State investment;
— Large projects dominating projects;
— Mainly carried out in large cities.

That drive gained a tremendous achievement by building an independent and complete industrial system, and greatly strengthened the country's comprehensive strength and national defense. And it was on this industrial basis that China successfully made its nuclear and hydrogen bombs and space satellites. Nevertheless, that industrialization drive had its obvious problems and drawbacks. In addition to the structural and institutional problems and drawbacks which have been or are being overcome with the deepening of the reform and opening-up policies, the most glaring problem and drawback was the neglect and exclusion of the countryside and the peasants.

The peasants were forced to contribute to the primitive accumulation (amounting to 600 billion yuan between 1952 and 1978) for the country's industrialization through the scissors difference in the prices of farm products and manufactured goods (which Stalin called "ultra tax"). The enforcement of a household registration system that rigidly separated the rural from the urban areas contained the huge rural labor force in the countryside, making the rural residents in effect "hereditary peasants," thus further ossifying the duality of the country's economic-social structure. That has been a major cause for the economic backwardness of China.

The 11th CPC Central Committee convened its Third Plenary

Session toward the end of 1978, at which it was decided to carry out reform and opening to the outside world. The prelude to this began in the Chinese countryside. While a responsibility system of land contracting by individual households was being introduced in the rural areas, TVEs mushroomed, blazing a trail of industrialization with unique Chinese features — the path of rural industrialization. This was the start of industrialization of the countryside with TVEs as the mainstay. Compared with the industrialization in cities, rural industrialization has these five distinct features:

— With the non-State-owned enterprises dominating;

— With light industry dominating;

— With small and medium-sized enterprises dominating;

— With investment by peasants dominating; and

— With the countryside as the dominant area.

The industrialization of the countryside can also be considered as one with peasants as the mainstay. Based on agriculture, it was born out of agriculture, and is inalienable from peasants' interests. It manifests itself in the following ways:

(1) Directly absorbing and transferring labor power from agriculture;

(2) Helping increase the income of peasant households;

(3) Serving agriculture by providing subsidies, promoting agricultural development through strengthening farmland capital construction and farm mechanization, increasing socialized services, promoting agricultural modernization and socialization, and helping raise agricultural productivity;

(4) Developing public amenities in rural communities and strengthening social stability, and helping narrow the difference between the cities and the countryside; and

(5) Contributing greatly to the State revenue.

The first four items have not been accomplished by urban industrialization. The transfer of labor power from agriculture to non-agricultural activities is costly. In the cities, the State has to pay at least 20,000 yuan as the cost of the employment of one worker by a State-run enterprise. In the countryside, however, peasants themselves pay the costs involved in their employment by TVEs. This is another difference in the forms of industrialization in the cities and the countryside.

Section 2 The Process of the Disintegration of Labor

Rural industrialization provides a vast scope for the splitting up and transfer of labor in the countryside. At the time of the people's communes, before the reform and opening-up era, communes and their production brigades set up industrial enterprises under the guideline of integrating industry, agriculture, commerce, education and military affairs into one. Rural labor began to be split up and transferred within the communes. Mao Zedong called for industry to be run by communes and production brigades, and spoke highly of the significance of commune-run industry. He pointed out that the industry run by communes and production brigades "promises a bright future." The guideline at the time was "to run industry centering round agriculture and run industry well to promote agriculture." In response to his call, industry run by communes and brigades developed rapidly, and absorbed 17,344,000 able-bodied persons, accounting for 7% of the total rural labor force. Industry run by communes and brigades was the predecessor of TVEs, a sector of the market economy or a budding market economy in itself under the highly centralized planned economy and the highly centralized commune system. This was because industry run by communes and brigades had no share of the production, supply and marketing covered by the national economic plan, and had to survive at the mercy of market forces.

The vigorous growth of TVEs in the general setting of the reforms and opening to the outside world since 1979 has brought the country's rural industrialization to a new phase. It has been serving as the leading force in the Chinese market economy, touching off a large-scale disintegration and transfer of rural labor.

As many as 135 million rural workers had been transferred from agricultural to non-agricultural activities by the end of 1996. That amounted to 27.5% of the total rural labor force, an all-time high.[1] In addition, there were 60 million-70 million rural seasonal or permanent workers working away from their native places. This was a situation without parallel in Chinese history, and probably a rarity in the world. One may say it was a mammoth-scale emancipation of the productive forces, a remarkable example of social progress in China, a major breakthrough in the dual economic-social structure, a major turning point and big stride forward in the transition from traditional to modern civilization.

The split-up and transfer of rural labor, under the impact of the State macro economic policy, has been proceeding by stages.

The first stage covered 1979-1983. In this period, collective land was contracted to individual households for tilling. Peasants thus won autonomy in their farm production. This, plus a generous raise of the purchasing prices of farm produce by the State, boosted peasants' income and fired their enthusiasm. The result was big increases in the yield and output of all farm products. Meanwhile, the enterprises run by communes and production brigades also developed, and the labor force they employed grew from 29.09 million in 1979 to 32.35 million in 1983, increasing by 3.26 million and accounting for 9.3% of the total rural labor force.

The second stage cover 1984-1988. In this period, the people's communes were disintegrated, and township governments were instituted. Beginning in 1984, the enterprises originally run by communes and production brigades were renamed TVEs, which began to grow with new vigor, as did the transfer of rural labor. In 1984, TVEs employed a total of 38.48 million persons — 6.13 million more than in the previous year. They accounted for a record 10.9% of the total rural labor power. By 1988, TVEs employed a total of 95.45 million people — 63.1 million more than in 1983 and accounting for 23.8% of the total rural labor force. In five years, an

[1] TVE Bureau of the Ministry of Agriculture: *The Basic Situation of TVEs in the Country and an Analysis of Their Economic Operation*, 1996

annual average of 12.62 million peasants moved to non-agricultural activities, equal to the entire population of Zhejiang Province or of France. This period was the "golden time" for the development of TVEs and the movement of rural labor.

The third stage covered 1989-1991. This period witnessed drastic drops and fluctuations in the output of grain, cotton and other major farm produce, inflation, imbalance in the relationship between industry and agriculture in the national economy and the implementation of the policy of "readjustment and consolidation." The bank credit interest rates were raised, and currency circulation tightened. Agricultural production recovered, and output began to increase again. But TVEs bore the brunt of the blow. Banks stopped extending loans to TVEs, and the movement of rural labor came to a standstill. The labor force of TVEs of a little over 96.14 million people in 1991 was almost the same as in 1988. In the three years, peasants' income dropped, averaging an annual increase of merely 0.7%, and even -1.7% in 1990, the lowest point since the initiation of the policy of reform and opening up.

The fourth stage covered 1992-1996. In this period, inspired by Deng Xiaoping's remarks made during his South China inspection tour, TVEs developed at a high speed, and the movement of rural labor to other industries accelerated. TVEs employed a total of 135 million workers in 1996 — 38.94 million more than in 1991 and averaging 6.49 million a year. The total figure for these six years was equal to the entire population of Canada. Thanks to a good harvest and increased income from wages paid by TVEs, peasants' income rose 9% in 1996, an all-time high for the 1990s.

The fifth stage covered 1997-2000. Due to the impact of the East Asian financial crisis and the Chinese government's economic readjustment policy, a large number of TVEs were closed down, merged or switched to other lines of production, and once more the movement of rural labor slowed down. The number of TVE workers dropped to 125.37 million in 1998, nearly 10 million less than in 1996. The number rose to 128.2 million in 2000, but was still below the 1996 level. Meanwhile, the prices of farm produce dropped due to excessive supply, and peasants' income nosedived.

The farmers' net income averaged 2,253 yuan in 2000, up by only 2.1% as compared with the previous year. The income derived from farming actually decreased, buoyed by wages paid by TVEs. (See Table 6-1)

Table 6-1 Changes in TVE Labor Force

Year	Total rural labor (10,000)	TVE labor (10,000)	Percentage of TVE labor in total rural labor (%)
1978	30,638	2,827	9.2
1979	31,025	2,909	9.3
1980	31,836	3,000	9.4
1981	32,672	2,970	9.1
1982	33,867	3,113	9.2
1983	34,690	3,235	9.3
1984	35,968	3,848	10.7
1985	37,065	6,979	18.8
1986	37,990	7,937	20.9
1987	39,000	8,805	22.6
1988	40,063	9,545	23.8
1989	40,939	9,367	22.9
1990	42,010	9,265	22.1
1991	42,093	9,614	22.3
1992	43,802	10,625	24.8
1993	48,784	12,345	25.3
1994	48,786	12,017	24.6
1995	48,854	12,862	26.3
1996	49,035	13,508	27.5
1997	49,393	13,050	26.6
1998	49,279	12,537	25.4
1999	49,572	12,704	25.6
2000	49,876	12,820	25.7

Source: *China Statistical Yearbook*

The changes in the movement of rural labor to TVEs may lead to these conclusions:

First, TVEs constitute the main absorber of surplus rural labor. The proportion of rural labor taken in by TVEs rose from one tenth of the total rural labor in the 1980s to more than a quarter in the 1990s. That may be deemed the most important contribution made by TVEs in changing the duality of China's economic-social structure.

Second, the transfer of rural labor proceeded at a more rapid rate than the increase of rural labor. Between 1978 and 1990 the country's rural labor force increased by 37.1%, whereas the number of rural people absorbed by TVEs grew 127.6%. Between 1991 and 2000, the rural labor force grew by 18.5%, and the number of TVE workers rose by 33.3%.

Third, TVEs have a tremendous potential for absorbing labor from agriculture. They took more than 10 million workers from agriculture in each of the years 1985, 1992 and 1993, with the figure in 1985 hitting a record 30.71 million. It is to be noted that the speed of the movement of rural labor to non-agricultural activities depends on the macro economic policies of the State.

Fourth, since 1992, more than 100 million people have taken jobs in industries and services run by TVEs, more than the number of those who have taken jobs in industries and services run by the State in cities. In 2000, State-owned enterprises had 81.02 million workers, while TVEs had 128.2 million, 58.2% more.

Section 3 Forms of the Split-Up of Rural Labor

The large-scale split-up and transfer of rural labor since the introduction of the policy of reform and opening up have taken place on a voluntary basis, with the exception of people moving into education, joining the armed forces or becoming non-rural residents after the farmland they tilled was requisitioned by the State for capital construction projects. The movement of rural labor has taken on a variety of forms. They include:

1. Leaving farmland but not home

This is the most common form of the split-up of rural labor. Employed by TVEs in the same communities, rural labor is transferred locally, resulting in a breakthrough in the industrial structure and in the structure of ownership.

First of all, it represents a break with the original principle that communes and their production brigades must "run industry centered on agriculture and run industry to promote agricultural production," and the principle that commune industry must rely on locally available raw materials in their production and market their products by themselves. While agriculture aims to develop simultaneously farming, forestry, animal husbandry, sideline production and fisheries, TVEs seek to engage in industry, commerce, construction, transportation, and service trade.

Second, it represents a break with the original single ownership — collective ownership. TVEs may be owned collectively, individually or privately. There have appeared peasant households engaging in both agriculture and industry. Among the 240 million peasant households in 2000, the number of pure farmers accounted for 59.3% of the total; those engaged in other trades as well as farming accounted for 18.2%; and those engaged in occupations having nothing to do with agriculture accounted for 22.5%. The proportion of households engaged in both agricultural and non-agricultural activities was bigger in the eastern part of the country than in the central and western parts. This has led to a marked change in the industrial and labor structures.

2. Leaving both farmland and home

With TVEs growing rapidly, some peasants have left their villages and entered county seats or cities to start up industrial and service enterprises. The local governments of some cities and counties have offered them preferential policies with the aim of boosting the local economy. The common practice is to help the peasants solve the problem of obtaining permanent residence permits in cities and enjoy equal treatment as their urban counterparts after paying some "fees for urban construction."

The flexibility of the local policies has played a positive role in promoting the split-up and movement of rural labor and the economic development of cities. However, the lack of a unified national policy led to such malpractices as "selling household registration" in some places in the mid-1980s, and this policy was banned later. The authorities of some big cities granted "blue-sealed household registration booklets" to peasants who came to cities to start up industrial or service enterprises. The Beijing Municipal Government, for example, issues three different types of household registration certificates for temporary residence. In 2001, Guangdong, Fujian and some other provinces lifted restrictions on household registration in their provincial capitals to provide convenience for peasants to move into cites. They allowed peasants to obtain legitimate urban household status with slightly different treatment from that meted out to the original urban residents.

3. Leaving home but not farmland

Most of the peasants who have moved into cities engage in industrial and service activities, with only a minority of them still engaged in agriculture. This is because the overwhelming majority of the peasants on the outskirts of big cities have abandoned farming and moved to non-agricultural activities, and the farmland there has been subleased to peasants coming to settle from other rural areas. Such leasing may be seasonal or annual. This is the case of leaving home without leaving farmland.

4. Farmers' towns

Some new towns have grown in the seats of township governments, with the investment in the infrastructure coming from peasant entrepreneurs. A typical example is Longgang Town in Cangnan County, Wenzhou City, Zhejiang Province. This modern town, with a population 130,000, sprang up on a stretch of coast with money raised from levying municipal construction fees and selling land-use rights (42 sq m per household) in the mid-1980s. This practice has spared peasants the need to lease land for farming, and facilitated the management of large tracts of land on a large scale. There are now 138 such new towns that have sprung up in the Wenzhou area, with the peasants' total investment amounting to 10 billion yuan. The birth of Longgang Town has furnished valuable experience for the country to accelerate the pace of urbanization.

Farmers' towns like Longgang are mushrooming across China. Thanks to the development of TVEs, many towns and central administrative villages have not only absorbed all of the local surplus rural labor but also large numbers of peasants from other areas. In some places, peasants from other parts of the country outnumber the original local population.

Chang'an Town in Dongguan City, Guangdong Province, originally had 30,000 residents and 1,330 ha of farmland. Following the vigorous development of TVEs, the proportion of agricultural output value was only 0.2% of the total, while that of secondary and tertiary industries rose to 99.8% in 1998. Some 300,000 peasants from other parts of the country have settled in the town, outnumbering the original population by 10 times.

5. Flocking to cities to seek jobs

Despite some initial hostility to job-seeking peasants, the growing need of urban construction for labor, especially in areas where workers are hard to find locally, has become a natural "pull." Such a "pull," interacting with the "push" of rural surplus labor, has resulted in a continuous growth of the waves of peasants flocking to cities to seek jobs.

A survey made by the Ministry of Agriculture in 1993 showed that as many as 64.5 million peasants were involved in this large-scale movement across regional, provincial and county borders, a figure very much close to the figure of 70 million estimated by the Ministry of Labor. This amounted to 15% of the total rural labor force and 7% of the total rural population. In recent years, this movement of surplus rural labor has remained at levels ranging from 70 million to 80 million (with the increase of layoffs from State-run enterprises in cities). This is of great significance in Chinese history. Of the peasants on the move, 20% move within their own county, 30% within their own province, and 50% across provincial borders. Of them, 51.9% are men and 48.1% are women.[1]

This mammoth movement of rural labor serves as a big school for Chinese peasants to learn the operation of a market economy and at the same time it yields a huge amount of funds for the development of agriculture in China. Some 10 million peasant-workers from Sichuan Province and Chongqing, or about 10% of the local populations of those places, work away from their native towns. The money that Sichuan or Anhui migrant workers remits back home exceeds the revenue of each of those provinces. The total remittances from Sichuan peasant-workers reached 20.2 billion yuan in 1996, and this increased to 40 billion in 2000. Of the 3.5 million able-bodied workers in Nanchong City, Sichuan Province, 1.8 million work in other provinces. They remit back home a total of 5.4 billion yuan every year, averaging 3,000 yuan per person and six times the revenue of the municipal government.

Naturally the mobile peasant-workers have fallen victim to censures from all quarters. They have been blamed for disruption of social order and for putting pressure on transportation. But what they are criticized for most is excessive reproduction, making it difficult to implement the family planning program. However, a survey shows that those who have stayed relatively longer in cities and accepted the urban way of life have become more conscientious about birth control. At any rate, the huge army of mobile peasant-workers

[1] Guo Shutian: "An Analysis of Tidal Waves of Peasant-Workers — Cross-Border Movement of Rural Labor," in *The Movement of Population and Control of the Trend in China*, China Population Press, 1995, p. 196

has proved to be indispensable for the cities. They have made great contributions to the construction of cities and to changing the dual character of the economic structure. Some have melted into city communities to become part of the urban population.

6. Villages in cities

Some mobile peasant-workers have settled down on the outskirts of big cities, forming their own communities, such as "Zhejiang Village," "Henan Village" and "Xinjiang Village" in suburban Beijing. These people rent houses from local peasants, and produce whatever they can to sell locally or to other parts of the country (including even export items). In some villages, the new settlers outnumber the local people. The local governments have given them certificates of temporary residence and business licenses. But they have to rely on themselves in such matters as children's education, medical care and even security. Some of the new settlers are members of the Chinese Communist Party or the Communist Youth League, but they are still affiliated to the organizations in their home villages and organize themselves into temporary Party or League cells at the places of their residence. These "villages" are actually on the move, as the residents are.

7. New Chinatowns abroad

Among the Chinese peasants who have gone abroad, some have become wealthy entrepreneurs. These people usually chose to settle in Chinese communities, which either expanded the existing Chinatowns or added new ones in foreign cities. "Wenzhou Street" in Paris is a typical one. This quarter comprises six adjacent streets in the Third District of downtown Paris. The Chinese settlers there mainly deal in quality fashionable leather goods. These people from Wenzhou, Zhejiang Province, have made their success by relying on their diligence, skills, business acumen and competitive prices, despite the exotic language, culture, and customs and habits of Paris. There are some 300,000 people from Wenzhou doing business in more than 60 foreign countries. The experience of the Wenzhou people shows that China, with its rich human resources, has much to offer the vast global labor service market.

8. Restarting enterprises back home

Restarting enterprises to a reverse movement of rural labor from cities back to their native places. After the peasant-workers have mastered the knowledge and skills of modern enterprise management in the course of running industries and services in cities, many have become entrepreneurs of considerable financial strength. Some of them have returned to their native places with the funds and skills to start new enterprises. The peasants who returned home to restart enterprises in Sichuan Province in 1996 alone numbered 340,000. Each of them took back an average of 100,000 yuan in capital, and their total investment in their own areas reached 34 billion yuan. The Sichuan Provincial Government set up a special committee in January 1997 to provide services for those returned entrepreneurs.

The split-up of the rural labor force in China bears the features of the transition from a planned economy to a socialist market economy, from a closed, semi-natural economy to a commodity economy, and from traditional agriculture to modern agriculture. The split-up of the rural labor force is in keeping with the general trend of the development of world economic and social progress. It helps make up for the losses brought by the former closed-door policy and narrows the gap between China and the advanced world economic levels.

Section 4 Rural Labor Fragmentation and the Economic Structure

The split-up and movement of rural labor has caused a change in agriculture and the overall rural economic structure, which, in turn, has created the conditions for further fragmentation and movement of labor.

1. The internal structure of agriculture

The internal structure of agriculture is on two levels.

One is the internal structure of crop farming. In the 1978-1995 period, the percentage of the sown areas of cereal crops in the total sowing area dropped from 80.34% to 73.43%, while the percentage of the areas sown to such cash crops as cotton, oil- and sugar-bearing crops, vegetables and fruits rose from 11.3% to 26.1%. The areas sown to grain crops dropped to 69.39% in 2000, whereas the areas sown to cash crops rose to 28.9%. (See Table 6-2)

Table 6-2 Crop-Sown Areas

(Unit: 1,000 ha)

Year	Total crop sown area	Grain crops		Cash crops						
		Area	%	Cotton	Oil-bearing crops	Sugar-bearing crops	Vege-tables	Fruits	Total	%
1978	150,104	120,587	80.34	4,867	6,222	879	3,331	1,657	16,965	11.3
1995	149,879	110,060	73.43	5,422	13,101	1,820	10,616	8,098	39,057	26.1
2000	156,300	108,463	69.39	4,041	15,400	1,514	15,237	8,932	45,124	28.9

Source: Ministry of Agriculture, *China's Agricultural Development*, 1995, 1996 and 2001

The other level is the internal structure of agriculture as a whole. In the 1979-1995 period, the proportion of the output value of crop farming in the total output value of farming, forestry, animal husbandry and fisheries dropped from 78.07% to 58.43%, while that of forestry dropped from 3.58% to 3.49%, that of animal husbandry rose from 16.82% to 29.72% and that of fisheries rose from 1.53% to 8.36%. If calculated by new indicators following the adjustment in 2000, the percentage of crop farming was 59.4%, forestry 4.5%, animal husbandry 24.9% and aquatic products 11.1%. Meanwhile, the proportion of labor in agricultural activities rose from 284.556 million to 323.34 million, but the percentage of the total rural labor dropped from 92.9% to 71.8%. (See Table 6-3)

Table 6-3 Changes in the Agricultural Industry and Labor Structure 1979 c.f. 1995

	1979	1995
Crop farming	78.07	58.43
Forestry	3.58	3.49
Animal husbandry	16.82	29.72
Fisheries	1.53	8.36
Agricultural labor force	92.9	71.8

Source: Ministry of Agriculture, *Report on China's Agricultural Development*, 1995, 1996 and 2001

This shows that the decrease in the proportion of agricultural labor is in keeping with the decrease in the proportion of agricultural output value in the total social output value. Within agriculture, the percentage of crop farming went down, while that of diversified operations went up. Within crop farming, the proportion of grain-sown areas dropped, while that of cash crop-sown areas rose. Such changes have not only played an important role in improving the market supply of agricultural produce to satisfy the national demand, but also exhibited significant results in tapping the potential of rural labor and increasing the income of rural families.

2. Internal economic structure of the rural areas

From 1979 to 1994, the proportion of agricultural output value in the total rural social output value dropped from 68.6% to 25.7%, and the output value of non-agricultural activities rose from 31.4% to 74.3%, or roughly three-quarters of the total social output value, with the proportion of industry rising from 19.5% to 58.4%, of construction dropping from 6.6% to 6.4%, of transportation rising from 1.7% to 4.1%, and of commerce and the service trades rising from 3.7% to 5.4%. This shows that rural industry has grown rapidly, giving rise to a pattern of integrated operation of industry, commerce, construction, transportation and services. (See Table 6-4)

Table 6-4 Changes in the Rural Economic Structure 1978-1994 (%)

Year	1978	1994
Agricultural output value	68.6	25.7
Non-agricultural output value	31.4	74.3
Of which, output value of industry	19.5	58.4
Output value of construction	6.6	6.4
Output value of transportation	1.7	4.1
Output value of commerce and the service trades	3.7	5.4

Source: Ministry of Agriculture: *Agricultural Development in China*, 1995, 1996, 2001

Meanwhile, great changes have also taken place in the labor structure. Compared with 1978, the percentage of non-agricultural labor in 1994 rose from 7.1% to 26.8%, and that of agricultural labor dropped from 92.9% to 73.2%. In 2000, the percentage of agricultural labor dropped further to 68.4%, and that of non-agricultural labor rose to 31.6%. Of the non-agricultural labor force, the part in industry numbered 74.67 million persons, accounting for 58.2% of the total employed by TVEs; that in construction numbered 15.81 million, making up 13.2%; that in transportation numbered 8.98 million, making up 7%; that in commerce reached 15.57 million, making up 12.1%; and that in catering and tourism reached 8.64 million, accounting for 6.7%.[1]

During this period, the ownership structure of the non-agricultural sectors also underwent significant changes. By 1996, the operational

[1] TVE Bureau of the Ministry of Agriculture, *China TVEs Yearbook*, 2001, China Agriculture Press, 2000

income of TVEs had reached a total of 6,834.3 billion yuan, with 3,661.7 billion accredited to rural collective enterprises, accounting for 53.58% of the total, and 3,172.6 billion to non-collective enterprises, such as individual, associated partnerships and private enterprises, accounting for 46.42% of the total. The original value of fixed assets of TVEs was 1,605 billion yuan, with 1,114.9 billion accredited to collective enterprises, accounting for 69.46% of the total, and 490.1 billion to non-collective enterprises, accounting for 30.54%. This shows that the non-collective sectors were no longer mere "useful and necessary supplements," but "important components" of the socialist rural economy, which has developed in parallel with the rural public sector.

Private enterprises have grown by leaps and bounds, with the total number reaching 20.04 million in 2000, accounting for 96.2% of the total number of TVEs. They employed 89.87 million workers, accounting for 70% of the total rural labor force. Their total output value reached 7,587.2 billion yuan, 65.3% of the overall total. Their operational income reached 7,095.1 billion yuan, 65.8% of the total. In addition, they paid 106.5 billion yuan in taxes, 53.4% of the total tax payments made by TVEs. Their net profit reached 414.9 billion yuan, 70.5% of the total made by all TVEs. All their economic indicators are higher than the average for TVEs. Individual and private enterprises have become the mainstay of TVEs, an important force and a new engine of growth in the country's rural economy. (See Table 6-5)

Table 6-5 Ownership Structure of TVEs in 2000

	Collective (%)	Non-collective (%)
Number of enterprises	3.8	96.2
Employment	30.0	70.0
Turnover	34.2	65.8
Net profit	29.5	70.5
Tax payment	46.6	53.4

Source: TVE Bureau of the Ministry of Agriculture, *China TVEs Yearbook*, 2001

The changes in the industrial and labor structures are bound to be reflected in the changes in the income structure of peasants, which feature rises in cash income and drops in income in kind. The average income of the Chinese peasants was 134 yuan in 1978. It rose to 1,926 yuan in 1996, with the percentage of cash income rising from 41.92% to 68.66%, and that of income in kind dropping from 58.08% to 31.34%. Meanwhile, the percentage of income derived from agricultural activities dropped from 92.08% to 69.39%, and that of income from non-agricultural activities rose from 7.92% to 30.61%. The peasants' per capita net income hit 2,253 yuan in 2000, 43 yuan more than in 1999, up by 2.1%. The income from labor service increased by 90 yuan. If this income is deducted, the income derived from agriculture dropped by 47 yuan or 2.1 percent. This shows that income from labor service has played a decisive role in the changes from a growth of -2.1% to a growth of 2.1%. (See Table 6-6)

Table 6-6 Structure of Peasants' Income 1978 c.f. 1996

	1978 (%)	1996 (%)
Cash income	41.92	68.66
Income in kind	58.08	31.34
Income from agriculture	90.08	69.39
Income from non-agriculture	7.92	30.61

Source: Ministry of Agriculture: *Agricultural Development in China*, 1995, 1996

3. The urban and rural economic structures

The split-up and movement of rural labor have brought about great changes to the rural industrial structure, thus creating a new situation featuring the common development of the primary, secondary and tertiary industries, with agriculture as the foundation. This has contributed greatly to the total and incremental volume of the national economy. The rural GDP (including the primary, secondary and tertiary industries) in 1993 accounted for 53.2% of the national total, for the first time surpassing that of the urban GDP, which was 46.8% of the total. That was an amazing change. The country's rural GDP in 1995 accounted for 57.1% of the national total, while that of cities was 42.9%. What merits particular attention is the GDP of secondary industry, which was 24.7% in rural areas and 24.1% in urban areas. Only the GDP of tertiary industry was lower in the rural areas (12.5%) than in the cities (18.8%). As for primary industry, it was 20.6% in the rural areas but zero in the cities.

The situation developed even further in 1996, when the rural GDP hit 58.3% of the national total, with 20% in primary industry and 26.9% in secondary industry and 11.4% in tertiary industry, whereas the urban GDP was zero in primary industry, 22% in secondary industry and 19.7% in tertiary industry. The lower percentage of rural tertiary industry is expected to grow with the development of small towns until it is on a par with or even higher than that of the cities. In terms of incremental value, the national GDP in 1996 grew 9.7% from the previous year, with the rural areas contributing 8.33% and the cities contributing 1.37%. This shows that high-speed growth was sustained by the rural GDP. (See Table 6-7)

Table 6-7 GDP Growth 1992-1996 (%)

	1992	1995	1996
GDP growth	14.2	10.5	9.7
Urban	5.09	1.21	1.37
Secondary	3.11	0.14	0.20
Tertiary	1.98	1.07	1.17
Rural	9.11	9.29	8.33
Primary	1.15	1.03	1.04
Secondary	5.80	6.74	5.69
Tertiary	2.16	1.52	1.60

Source: Rural Development Institute of the Chinese Academy of Social Sciences, *Economic Green Book, 1995, 1996*

The added value of GDP in 1992 was 14.2% nationally, with the rural areas contributing 64.16% and cities, 35.84%. It was 10.5%

nationally in 1995, with the rural areas contributing 88.5% and the urban areas 11.5%. It was 9.7% nationally in 1996, with the rural areas contributing 85.88% and the cities 14.12%. This shows that the rural areas have been the main contributors to the double-digit growth of the national economy since 1992. Although this contribution dropped to a certain extent after 1997, it was still over 50% in the period 1997-1998, and close to 50% in the period 1999-2000. (See Table 6-8)

Table 6-8 Contributions by the Rural and Urban Areas to National GDP Growth 1997-2000 (%)

	1997	1998	1999	2000
National GDP	8.8	7.8	7.1	8.0
Primary	7.2	7.7	6.5	4.7
Secondary	66.0	64.6	63.3	67.2
Urban	30.8	27.0	31.8	37.8
Rural	35.2	37.6	31.5	29.4
Tertiary	26.8	27.7	30.2	28.0
Urban	11.9	15.8	19.5	20.5
Rural	14.9	11.9	10.7	7.5
Urban total	42.7	42.8	51.2	58.3
Rural total	57.3	57.2	48.8	41.7

Source: Rural Development Institute of the Chinese Academy of Social Sciences, *Economic Green Book,* 2000

Section 5 Rural Labor Split-Up and the Social Structure

1. Population structure

As the history of China's agricultural society is long, and industry is underdeveloped, the rural population has traditionally been a large proportion of the total — above 80%. Although China began to introduce industrialization after the founding of New China in 1949, the pace of urbanization seriously lagged due to the policy of mainly developing heavy industry, and the proportion of the rural population remained virtually unchanged, resulting in a very low level of urbanization. During the nearly 30 years from 1949 to 1978, the proportion of the rural population dropped from 89.4% to 83.6%.[1] The rural population did not begin to move to non-agricultural activities until after the country introduced the reform and opening-up policies, thus reducing the proportion of the rural population. In 1995, the national population reached 1211.21 million, of which the rural population amounted to 859.47 million, accounting for 70.96%, and the level of urbanization reached 29.04%. The rural population dropped to 61% or 782,410,000 in the national population of 1,284,530,000 in 2002, elevating the level of urbanization to 39%.[2]

2. Rural occupational structure

The disintegration of the rural labor force is mostly reflected in the split-up of occupations. According to a study by Lu Xueyi, director of the Institute of Sociology of the China Academy of Social Sciences, the rural population has, to a large extent, become a concept of a household registration or area of residence. In reality, they have split into agricultural laborers, village workers (including township enterprise workers and peasant workers), village hired hands, peasant intellectuals, self-employed villagers engaged in industry and business, village private business owners, TVE managers and rural managers. And they all have different interest demands. Agricultural laborers make up about 55-57% of the total rural population; village workers make up about 24%; village hired hands make up about 4%;

---

[1] Policy and Law Department of the Ministry of Agriculture, *40 Years of China's Rural Economy*, Zhongyuan Peasant Publishing House, 1989, P. 409

[2] State Statistical Bureau, *China Statistical Yearbook* 1996, China Statistics Press, 1996, P. 20

peasant intellectuals make up about 1.5-2%; self-employed villagers engaged in industry and business make up about 5%; rural private businesses owners make up about 0.1%-0.2%; TVE managers make up about 3%; and rural managers make up about 6%.[1]

This data reflects the realities of the rural occupational structure in 1998 and shows that the concept of "peasant" is quite different in meaning from in the past. Among this group of people, the "pure peasants," who engage in crop and animal farming make up about 55-57% while those who are engaged in non-agricultural activities make up about 43-45%. In other words, nearly half of the peasants have become non-agricultural.

As TVEs mainly engage in industry, which has a diversity of sectors, the labor force in township industries is scattered in almost all industrial sectors, including metallurgy, machine-building, electronics, chemicals, light industry and textiles, garments, construction and energy. The composition of TVE workers in 1996 was as follows: agriculture, 2.48%; industry, 58.19%; construction, 14.42%; commerce, 10.25%; services, 6.76%; and communications and transportation, 7.9%. Primary industry (agriculture) accounts for 2.48%; secondary industry for 72.61%; and tertiary industry for 24.91%.[2]

3. Rural family structure

(1) Property structure. After the people's communes disintegrated, rural households became independent production units and, with the labor split-up and changes in the job pattern, rural families have acquired sizable means of production, thus turning from "people without property" into "people with property."

In 1978, the fixed assets of the people's communes totaled 84.9

---

[1] Lu Xueyi, *The Chinese Society in Transition*, Heilongjiang People's Publishing House, 1994, P. 41

[2] Policy and Law Department of the Ministry of Agriculture, *40 Years of China's Rural Economy,* Zhongyuan Nongmin Publishing House, 1989, p. 409

billion yuan, and by 1986 the productive fixed assets in the rural areas had reached 239.3 billion yuan, with collectives and rural households sharing 50-50.[1] By 1995, the original value of fixed assets of TVEs was 1284.1 billion yuan, with private enterprises possessing 371.8 billion yuan, accounting for 28.95%. Up to 2000, the original value of fixed assets of TVEs reached 2,622.3 billion yuan, with private and self-employed ones jointly possessing 1,253.8 billion yuan, accounting for 47.8%.[2]

Rural households have made most of the rural fixed assets investment. In 1981, the fixed assets investment by collectives was 8.371 billion yuan, while that made by rural households was 16.63 billion yuan. By 1995, the investment made by collectives had reached 241.26 billion yuan, and that made by rural households had reached 191.99 billion yuan.[3] All these show that rural families have become production and operational units with a considerable amount of assets. This is a major achievement of the rural reform.

(2) Family operation patterns. The patterns of family operations have been transformed from single agricultural operations to diversified operations, and from only engaging in agriculture to extending their operations to both industry and services. In some areas, especially the economically developed eastern areas and suburbs of large cities, family operations have been transformed from agriculture to going in for industry and commerce. A similar trend can be seen in the central and western parts of the country. This is an inevitable evolution due to economic development and changes in the occupational patterns in the rural areas.

(3) Family population structure. Rural families are becoming smaller and smaller. In the past, three generations or even four generations lived in one family. Now, such families are few and far be-

---

[1] Policy and Law Department of the Ministry of Agriculture, *40 Years of China's Rural Economy*, Zhongyuan Peasant Publishing House, 1989, P. 409

[2] TVE Bureau of the Ministry of Agriculture, *The General Picture of TVEs in the Country and the Analysis of Their Operations*, 1996

[3] State Statistical Bureau, *China Statistical Yearbook 1996*, China Statistics Press, 1996, P. 20

tween. Families of three to four members make up over 70% of the total. The economic base of the family, formed in the prolonged period of feudal society is disintegrating. This is social progress for the rural areas. But the family networks formed of relatives still play a powerful role in rural social activities and the rural economy.

4. Rural marriage structure

The opening up of the rural areas, especially the movement of labor, has brought about major changes in marriage.

(1) The scope of intermarriage has been expanded. In the past, due to autarchy, the scope was limited, and there were many instances of marriage of near relatives, resulting in a lot of mentally retarded children. Following the movement of labor, the scope of marriage partners has increased. This has not only contributed to the improvement of the population quality but also to exchanges among different regions in economy and culture.

(2) The number of late marriages and planned births has increased following the increased mobility of labor.

(3) Voluntary marriage has increased. According to a sample survey, voluntary marriages in the rural areas make up 53.2%, while those arranged by parents make up 46.8%.[1] The proportion is even higher in areas where more rural laborers have moved into non-agricultural activities. This represents a revolutionary change in China's rural areas.

(4) The social status of women has risen. In the past, men used to dominate rural families. In recent years, however, more and more women have begun to take to industry and commerce in their native place or elsewhere. Some have even become business managers or heads of households. This has helped change the status of women in their families. This is an important hallmark of women's liberation. Although these changes are local, they are of great social significance nationwide.

---

[1] *China Sociology Yearbook* 1989-1993, p. 342

5. Rural cultural structure

The people in the rural areas, whether they work in local TVEs or do hired labor elsewhere, have a higher education level. A 1993 survey shows that 10.3% of the rural laborers who had worked in areas other than their native places had a senior secondary education and 45.5% had a junior secondary education. The number of laborers with a secondary or higher education who had worked away from home made up 20.3% of the total number of laborers with a similar education in the rural areas. Among laborers working elsewhere, 33.7% have some kind of skill, accounting for 29.9% of the total of such laborers in the rural areas. People working elsewhere were mostly young and middle-aged, with those below 35 accounting for 71.8%, or 21.2% of the total number of labors of similar age.[1]

According to statistics released by the TVE Bureau of the Ministry of Agriculture, in 1996 the rural collective enterprises employed 59.53 million workers, of whom those with a college education accounted for 1.3%, those with a secondary vocational education accounted for 2.9% and those with a technical school education, senior secondary school education or lower accounting for 95.8%. In rural collective enterprises, those holding senior technical titles made up 0.3%, those with intermediary technical titles accounted for 1.4% and those with primary technical title accounted for 4%. Workers below 35 years old made up 64.9%, those in the 36-50 age group made up 29.7%, and those above 50 made up 5.4%.[2]

By 2000, in rural collective enterprises 2.7% of the workers had at least college education, 5.5% who had secondary vocational school education, and those with senior secondary school education made up 31.7% — higher than at the end of the "Eighth Five-Year-Plan" period.[3] In addition, with the changes in the employment pattern,

---

[1] Guo Shutian, *Peasant Worker Tide — Analysis of the Trans-regional Movement of Rural Labor*, People's Population Publishing House House, 1995

[2] *China TVE Yearbook* 2001

[3] *China TVE Yearbook* 2001

family income has increased. There are fewer children dropping out of compulsory education. The family spending on education has also increased. All these are favorable for the improvement in the educational levels of the rural people as a whole.

In recent years, a large number of university graduates, including postgraduates, have taken jobs in the rural areas, principally in TVEs, and have brought about fresh changes in the educational quality of the rural population.

TVEs have strengthened technical education. More and more enterprises are following the practice of providing pre-job training. In 1996 alone, 7.19 million people received such training in rural collective enterprises, accounting for 12% of the total workers. In areas where a large number of rural laborers moves out to work, labor service departments cooperate with units that absorb such workers in providing pre-job training, thus creating better conditions for the employment of rural people.

The split-up of rural labor, the movement from agricultural to non-agricultural activities and movement from rural areas to cities and towns, represent a great revolution, both economically and socially. Millions of peasants are rapidly changing the rural outlook and themselves in the spirit of perseverance in the drive for developing the market economy. The rural areas are marching from traditional civilization to modern civilization. This is a major turning point, representing a glorious page in the annals of the progress and development of the Chinese peasants.

Of course, it will take a long time to complete the reorganization of labor, and it is also an arduous task in terms of both the existing large numbers of laborers and in terms of the increase in the laborers moving to non-agricultural activities. Demographers predict that by 2030, when China's population peaks at 1.6 billion, the increased population will mainly be in the rural areas, posing a huge employment problem. Due to great disparities in economic and cultural development among different regions, the changes and the speed in the changes of the employment pattern vary greatly.

But agricultural modernization and the rise in agricultural productivity, and the income growth of farmers are, in the final analysis, preconditioned by the movement of surplus rural labor into the non-agricultural activities. In the economically developed coastal areas, the population density is high, and the per capita cultivated land area is far below the national average. But, owing to the high levels of industrialization and urbanization there, there is a serious shortage of labor and, therefore, a lot of labor has to be taken from elsewhere. In many townships and towns, the amount of migrant labor has exceeded that of local labor. However, as noted, some people working in other areas return to their native places, and create businesses with the skills and management experience they have learned, thus giving a big impetus to the development of the local rural economy.

These facts give us food for thought. In China, where the population is large and the cultivated land is limited, agricultural modernization can be realized at an accelerated rate by way of promoting industrialization, urbanization and cooperation between the eastern and western parts of the country. We should adopt positive and effective policy measures to create the conditions for the movement of agricultural laborers and other people to non-agricultural sectors. Experience over the years has shown us that it is groundless to worry that the split-up and movement of rural laborers would affect agricultural development and social stability.

But the negative effects, such as the scattering of industrial distribution, occupation of cultivated land, serious environmental pollution and dropping of the educational qualities of agricultural laborers, also merit attention. These problems have to be resolved while implementing the sustainable development strategy and the strategy of invigorating the country by relying on science and education as well as in the course of realizing the transition of the economic system and growth pattern, and by providing policy guidance and macroeconomic control. It is infeasible to weaken the position of agriculture as the foundation of the economy due to the drop in its proportion in the national economy. On the contrary, it is imperative to increase the input into agriculture, strengthen the agricultural infrastructure, develop rural culture, education, health, and science and technology, improve the ecological environment, improve the quality of life, and enhance the capabilities of the rural people to resist natural adversities and market risks. Following China's accession to the WTO, we should make better use of the WTO's "green box" policy to give more powerful support to agricultural and rural development, so as to make real efforts to change the dualistic economic and social structure.

Chapter VII

TVE Management Systems

Section 1 Diversified Forms of Operation

In 1958, when the people's communes had just started to run enterprises, TVEs were single collective economic entities owned by communes, with the management, and the arrangements for employment, income and spending all subject to the unified control of the people's communes. The peasant workers enjoyed free meals and other essential supplies. After the country corrected the egalitarian practice of "sharing all things in common" and established the "system with ownership at three levels, with the production teams as the base," some of the commune-run industrial enterprises were returned to production brigades, and the rest were left under direct management by the communes. In 1962, the Central Committee of the CPC and the State Council deemed it improper for communes and production brigades to run industry, and therefore ordered the closing down of all rural industries.

When the "cultural revolution" started, virtually all State-owned enterprises stopped production, and the market was badly in need of means of industrial production and consumer goods. The communes and production brigades revived their industrial production spontaneously in accordance with market demand. At that time, enterprises were owned by those who ran them, with laborers assigned by production teams, and the workers got their pay from where they came from and according to the work points they earned. The enterprises had neither accounting systems nor had they formed independent economic entities. Common sense dictates that enterprises run by a commune or production brigade should be owned by the whole commune or the whole production brigade. But at that time, it was what leaders of communes or production brigades said that counted. In reality, they were "official enterprises" that had no clear definition of either property rights or powers and responsibilities.

In 1978, the 11th CPC Central Committee held its third plenary session, from which issued the policies of rural reforms and opening up. This kindled the spirit of reform among the peasants and grassroots cadres. TVEs also began to reform their ownership systems and forms of management.

1. The contract responsibility system

(1) The economic responsibility system. At the beginning of the 1980s, there was a kind of household-based responsibility system for contracting the tilling of land, with remuneration tied to output. TVEs in some areas followed suit. They introduced the economic responsibility system that fixed employment size, output value, capital, profit and loss, and awards and penalties for those who produced in excess of the fixed quotas and those who failed to fulfill the fixed quotas, respectively. Most places introduced the management system in their TVEs. TVEs also introduced a similar system among their workers who were required to do the fixed amount of work according to a fixed quality standard. Some enterprises also introduced the responsibility system to their management personnel, supply and marketing personnel, and technicians.

The essence of such a responsibility system was to replace direct intervention by communes and production brigades in enterprises with economic assessment, so that enterprises acquired a certain degree of autonomy. This was of great significance in displaying the initiatives of enterprises in carrying out their production and operational activities, and in seeking economic accounting. But, as the management system, which integrated government with enterprises in the rural areas, did not change, the enterprises found it hard to exert autonomy in economic policy decisions, appointment of personnel and use of profits. They were still bogged down in the egalitarian practice of "everybody eating from the same big pot," as there was no separation of government from enterprises.

(2) Contract responsibility system. In the mid-1980s, TVEs tried the system of "contracting for fixed quotas of profits," which, in essence, linked the operations of enterprises with the interests of contractors. The Commune and Production Brigade-run Enterprise Bureau of the Ministry of Agriculture (predecessor of the TVE Bureau of the Ministry of Agriculture) called a meeting in Beijing to urge all commune and production brigade-run enterprises to adopt the contract responsibility system by drawing on the household-based contract responsibility system that ties family income to output. The main forms of contracting are as follows:

1) Collective contracting, mostly for fixed quotas of profits. Some contracted for the amount of profits to be delivered while retaining the surplus for use in expanded production, welfare and bonuses of workers; some adopted the profit-sharing system in the ratio of 3:7, 4:6 or 50-50; some introduced the system of sharing profits after profit delivery. Inside an enterprise, every level of operation sub-contracted for fixed quotas of profits, delegating the targets down to the shop floor and even to shifts or individuals. Workers got basic wages plus bonuses or received piecework rates plus bonuses.

2) Contracting by factory directors, managers, partnerships or individuals. This was similar to collective contracting. Larger or more profitable enterprises adopted collective contracting, while smaller ones or loss-making enterprises or enterprises not producing marketable products were mostly contracted out to factory directors or managers, partnerships or individuals.

With the spread of the contract responsibility system, some places introduced the "objective management system during the tenure of factory directors," which was designed to correct the short-term behavior of stressing consumption to the neglect of accumulation and overworking the equipment. Some places introduced the practice of contracting for the rolling increment in the value of assets by measuring the base figures for contracting and value increment co-efficient so as to enable enterprises to increase the value of assets in a rolling fashion. Some places introduced the contracting system by risk mortgage, to enable contractors to bear risks and ensure that assets would not be drained.

Contracting by marketing personnel is a system widely adopted in enterprises. The main forms are as the follows: (a) Contracting for the basic fulfillment of the tasks of purchase, marketing and overhead expenses. When the tasks were fulfilled, the contractors would get their basic wages, plus bonuses, while those who failed to fulfill the tasks would have their basic wages reduced and overhead expenses withheld. (b) Contracting for all marketing operations; (c) Contracting for expenses, with remuneration floating; (d) Income sharing from what was gained from marketing, according to a fixed proportion; (e) Contracting for the tasks of marketing, purchase and sales and recovery of payments, with basic wages and bonuses linked to actual performance. All these forms of contracting played an important role in production and operations.

(3) "One contracting and three reforms," that is, contracting for operations and reforms in the cadre appointment system, the worker's employment system and the wage system. The idea was to enable cadres to adapt to the situation of both promotion and demotion, workers to adapt to the practice of both employment and unemployment and both high and low wages.

This form of contracting was created by Yanqiao Township in Wuxi County, Jiangsu Province, and it had a big impact on the TVEs throughout the country. It was actually a development of the contract responsibility system. Jiangsu was then noted for the progress made by its TVEs, and Yanqiao was one of the best in this regard. They borrowed the idea of linking payment to production as in agricultural activities, and applied it in the operation of TVEs. This practice injected renewed vigor into enterprises, encouraged industrious people and made it tough for lazy ones.

The practice soon spread in the whole of Jiangsu Province, and the TVE Bureau of the Ministry of Agriculture recommended it to other places in the country. It was then developed and enriched. By

1987, most of the collective TVEs had adopted the practice.

(4) Leasing. Some service enterprises which were small in scale or operating with thin profits or losses were leased out to individuals. Relatively speaking, as the interests of the leased enterprises were closely linked with those of the lessees, the latter exerted themselves and ran the enterprises better.

In order to provide guidance for the spread of the contract responsibility system, the Ministry of Agriculture, Animal Husbandry and Fisheries issued a document titled, "Minutes of the Forum on the Rectification of Commune and Brigade-run Enterprises" in November 1982, urging all places to adopt the contract system, sum up experience and make improvements. In May 1983, the ministry circulated the "Investigation Report on the Contract Responsibility System in Commune- and Brigade-run Enterprises," which presented several forms of contract responsibility system for reference. In July 1987, the Ministry of Agriculture issued the "Proposals for Improving the Contract Responsibility System of Village Collective Enterprises." In April 1990, it issued the "Regulations on the Contract Responsibility System of TVEs."

The contract responsibility system played the following roles:

1) Breaking the pattern featuring one-level ownership, one-level accounting, putting everything under the monopoly of communes, and unclear definition of responsibilities and main players.

2) Introducing the competition mechanism into enterprises, helping them improve the practice of selecting leading bodies by township and village leaders and providing the opportunities for a large number of competent personnel in the rural areas to compete for the position of enterprise leader.

3) Implementing the principle of income distribution of "to each according to his work" and other ways of distribution. Some introduced the system of two-level accounting, three-level management and progressive piecework wages; some introduced the practice of making workshops branches to which power was delegated and remuneration made according to contract provisions. Some enterprises tied remuneration to output for workers, to efficiency for technical personnel, and to performance for marketing and management per-

sonnel. Some even introduced the system of calculating wages according to work results.

4) Elevating the level of management. All enterprises paid much more attention to financial management, quality control, basic management and specialized management, and improvement of the responsibility system.

5) Reducing unnecessary interference by township and village leaders, as the autonomy of enterprises was expanded and competitiveness improved.

2. Joint stock cooperatives

In the early 1980s, following the spread of the household-based contract responsibility system in the rural areas, the amount of surplus labor increased, and it was impossible for TVEs to absorb all of it. Some surplus workers took the initiative to pool funds to run joint stock enterprises. This method spread not only among farm households but also between farm households and village collectives, among collectives and between urban and rural enterprises. Such an innovation bore both the features of a joint stock economy and of a cooperative economy. They were therefore called joint stock cooperatives, which was then a form of collective enterprise, favorable for displaying the advantages of the joint stock system and cooperation.

In order to promote this new form of collective enterprise, in 1990 the Ministry of Agriculture issued the "Provisional Rules for the Governance of Joint Stock Cooperatives in the Rural Areas." There were mainly the following forms of joint stock cooperatives:

(1) New joint stock cooperative enterprises formed by peasants. These were set up by individual peasants pooling their funds or by several big households taking the lead and encouraging the pooling of funds by others.

(2) Joint stock cooperative enterprises established jointly by collective enterprises and individual peasants pooling their funds. These joint stock enterprises covered a wide range of participants and some were trans-regional, trans-industrial and trans-ownership associations. Some people offered money and labor as their shares; some offered factory premises or equipment, some offered research achievements, and some offered raw materials. Township collective enterprises, State-owned firms, and research institutions, universities and colleges all displayed their respective advantages. The ownership structure of such enterprises belonged to the mixed economy, with one enterprise having two or three types of ownership. The principle was equality and mutual benefit and voluntariness. Profits were divided according to the size of the individual shares and all participants shared risks and interests on an equal footing.

(3) Old enterprises converted into joint stock enterprises by breaking the assets up into shares on the basis of liquidation according to their different sources. As for investment by rural collectives, the assets originally belonging to those acquired through accumulation or with bank loans were taken as collective shares, and the assets originally acquired through acquisition were distributed to individuals with certificates for dividends, which, however, could not be withdrawn, transferred or inherited. Some enterprises expanded the amount of their shares according to funds needed for subscription by workers and peasants. Such shares could be inherited, transferred or withdrawn. Some enterprises absorbed workers who contributed a certain amount of money as shares.

In profit distribution, people who held controlling shares could get dividends but not interest, with risks shared among them. Some were paid interest but not dividends. Some enterprises distributed profits in proportion to the contribution by labor and by investment. Some divided up profits while retaining interest. The form of distribution depended on decisions taken by shareholders. Enterprises that became joint stock cooperatives underwent the following changes:

(a) Management personnel were appointed or dismissed at shareholders' meetings rather than by the town government or village committee.

(b) The operations were contracted out by the board of directors elected at the shareholders' meeting instead of by the township or village government.

(c) Profits were distributed according to the size of shares, and the township and village governments also got their due dividends according to the size of the shares they held. Enterprises no longer delivered profits to the township and village authorities.

(d) The enterprises were owned by the shareholders, with the manager appointed or dismissed by the board of directors.

(e) Workers were both shareholders and ordinary operatives, with their immediate interests closely tied to the efficiency of the enterprises.

(f) The enterprises became producers with independent accounting and management, entirely responsible for their operations, profits or losses, and exercising self-regulation, thus ending the egalitarian practice of "everybody eating from the same big pot."

By the end of 2000, there were 162,600 joint stock cooperatives, making up 20.3% of the total number of collective enterprises. Their combined added value reached 177.7 billion yuan, accounting for 18.9% of the total added value of collective enterprises.

3. Enterprise groups and companies

The State promulgated a number of laws and regulations, including the "Company Law," concerning the conversion of enterprises into modern models, namely, into modern companies. Large TVEs also went along with the tide, and formed themselves into companies or enterprise groups.

(1) TVE groups. In the face of fierce competition, some places came to realize the necessity of combining with others to achieve scale advantages. In Jiangsu, Shandong, Guangdong and other provinces, some large enterprises began to form enterprise groups. In January 1992, the Ministry of Agriculture issued the "Provisional Rules on the Formation and Development of TVE Groups." The provisional rules made it clear that the purpose of the formation of enterprise groups was to further deepen enterprise reform, adjust the organizational structures, optimize the allocation of the factors of production, display group advantages and raise competitive power and scale efficiency.

Strong TVEs acted as the core of the groups, and other enterprises and institutions were free to join on the basis of voluntariness, equality and free consultation. The groups were united joint stock economic entities organized by enterprises of different levels.

The groups, according to the objective demand of social production, adopted their methods of production according to division of labor and cooperation, acquiring such functions as production, foreign trade, technology development, financing, information service and business management. The qualifications for a national TVE group were:

(a) The core enterprise of an enterprise group must be one that was the strongest in financial strength and technology development with a high level of management in the locality or among similar enterprises;

(b) Leading products were the most market competitive or with export potential.

(c) Apart from the core enterprise, there must be a number of closely-knit enterprises, a number of less closely-knit enterprises and some scattered enterprises. They were required to form an integral whole bonded by assets, production and operations. They had to have articles of association that all members had to abide by, with each knowing its interests and responsibilities, and a sound management system and accounting system.

At the same time, the Ministry of Agriculture formulated the "Model Articles of Association for TVE Groups," clearly defining the scale, mode of management, organizational setup, rights and interests of members, and the functions and responsibilities of the board of directors, chairman of the board and general managers, as well as requirements for accounting and profit distribution of the core enterprises and closely-knit enterprises.

The Ministry of Agriculture drew up some rigid rules for applicants in terms of scale of operation, efficiency, and quality. They included:

(a) A core enterprise had to have total assets of more than 100 million yuan, the annual turnover had to be at least 200 million yuan (in the case of export earnings, they had to be more than 10 million

US dollars annually) and the gross profits before tax had to be more than 20 million yuan.

(b) A core enterprise had to be a holding company, and members had to include trans-regional, trans-sectoral and trans-ownership enterprises.

(c) Leading products had to have high popularity, and the technology development capability and management level of the enterprise had to be in the lead nationally.

Only enterprises that met all these requirements were allowed to file applications with provincial TVE bureaus, and the Ministry of Agriculture undertook to verify and approve the applications and make them public. By the end of 1998, there were 1,235 enterprises meeting the prescribed requirements. They were at the core of the TVEs, and became well known enterprises nationwide. Many of them gained a foothold in the international market.

(2) Companies. According to the requirements of the "Company Law" and related rules and regulations, the Ministry of Agriculture formulated rules on the establishment of a modern enterprise system among TVEs, which provided guidelines on how to convert TVE enterprises into limited liability companies and joint stock companies according to the requirements of the "Company Law."

The document pointed out: In the new situation, TVEs should maintain high efficiency, and sustainable, rapid and healthy development. They must deepen their reform, improve their general quality and enhance their market competitiveness. The central point is still how to improve and innovate the operational mechanism and build modern enterprises with a clear definition of property rights, powers and responsibilities, clear independence from government interference and scientific management.

It also says that a modern enterprise requires first a clear definition of property rights, improves the corporate system and ends the situation in which there is no distinction between property rights and between enterprises and government, so as to make enterprises genuinely independent corporate persons with property rights, capable of exercising civil rights and undertaking civil responsibilities.

Second, TVEs must have an organizational setup in line with

modern enterprises, and transform and standardize their operations according to the requirements for joint stock companies, so as to seize the time to convert themselves into companies when the conditions are ripe.

Third, it is necessary to set up modern employment, wage, accounting and auditing and other internal management systems. By 2000, the number of joint stock enterprises had reached 25,000 among TVEs, accounting for 3.1% of the total of the collective enterprises. Their added value totaled 81.7 billion yuan, making up 8.7% of the total added value of the collective enterprises.

The development of TVEs has gone through a transition from collective ownership to common ownership, from an appendage to township and village authorities to corporate persons, from the workers being employees to being the masters of their enterprises, and from the egalitarian practice of "everybody eating from the same big pot" to the practice of holding shares and getting payment according to the size of their shares and labor. Such big changes are the result of innovations by TVEs in the context of general reform throughout the country.

Section 2 Innovation of Operational Mechanism

TVEs were born in the days of the planned economy, when everything operated according to plans. TVEs were neither owned by the State nor by urban collectives. They were not covered by State or local plans. Some people compared TVEs to wild birds, which had to seek their own food, winter or summer, rain or shine; otherwise, they would starve to death. It is exactly in such an environment that TVEs seek survival, hence the mechanism dependent on the market. This mechanism developed, grew and improved with the development of enterprises. The development may be divided into three stages:

1. "Seeking food for survival" stage

At the beginning, TVEs operated under the highly planned economy and the market was not open. The State monopolized the supply of materials. There was no way for TVEs to get raw materials, fuel and other materials from channels of planned supply. They had to seek them from the market. At that time, they followed the "marketing — supply — production" pattern. As they were short of funds, they had to seek orders first, and got the money for buying materials and fuel before starting production. They had to rack their brains to get raw materials and fuel.

Often, they used locally produced rice, wheat flour, vegetable oil and animal by-products or native produce as gifts for knocking open the doors of officials in power. With the gradual reform of the material control system, the channels for the purchase of materials were expanded, too. TVEs began to get some materials by way of forming associations and processing supplied materials. Some places had township supply and marketing companies to purchase and organize material exchange. By means of parallel cooperation, they gradually established their own stable bases of raw materials and energy. Some local surveys indicated that TVEs got 85% of their raw materials and fuel by the ways mentioned above up to 1986. What was allocated, directly or indirectly, by State and local plans made up only 15%.

They could not get the funds from the planned channels either, and so they had to raise or accumulate the funds by themselves. At the beginning, there were instances of commune members taking their sewing machines to a workshop and setting up a garment factory; blacksmiths pooled their funds to run a farm tool repair shop, using equipment rejected by urban State-owned enterprises and bought cheaply. With the expansion of production, their efficiency rose, their capital grew, and new equipment was added.

In 1986, the State Economic Commission and the Ministry of Agriculture issued a document titled, "Proposals on the Distribution of Profits in TVEs," requiring that enterprises retain no less than 60% of the after-tax net profits, most of which was to be used to expand production. In the same year, the Ministry of Finance and the Ministry of Agriculture issued a document on the "Financial System of TVEs." The document required commune-run enterprises to pay income tax from the profits realized. About 45% of the amount after tax (including profits delivered to communes and retained by enterprises) was to be used for expanded production and the setting up of new enterprises, about 40% should be used to support agriculture, and the other 15% should be used as bonuses and for collective welfare. The funds needed for the development of TVEs were mainly accumulated by the peasants and collectives, and only a very small part came from bank loans and the State.

2. Reliance on the market

TVEs evolved their unique operational methods, persisting in planning production according to market demand and orders, and developing production by market promotion.

(1) Taking prompt decisions in response to market changes. Competition was fierce in the changing market. Before the market was opened, competition first came from State-owned enterprises under the protection of administrative departments at all levels, then from urban light industrial enterprises operating under local government protectionism, and finally from other TVEs. As TVEs were excluded from the State plans, they had no need to ask for permission concerning production nor ask for approval. They started production whenever they saw fit and seized the time to put their products on the market first. Once they discovered that the products were no longer needed on the market, they lost no time turning out new products or new varieties.

They arranged their production and operations according to the cyclical changes in the development of commodities. Usually, as soon as a new product was put into production, they started developing another or new products, so that when the product in production was put on the market, they began to arrange the production of new ones, and when the product was at the sales peak, they started producing new ones. When the old product showed signs of sluggish sales, they put new ones on the market. The process was often described as like a boy eating sweets: "One in the mouth, one in the hand, eye another one and think of one more." To adapt to the capricious market, some enterprises set up R&D institutions to devote all their energy to the development of new products and new models to keep the market well supplied with new products in time. Their production process was described as "producing a prototype in three days, putting it in batch production in five, and putting the products on the market in seven."

(2) Winning out with variety and superior quality. TVEs planted their feet firmly in the market by paying full attention to quality. Some enterprises succeeded in reducing material consumption and non-production costs by improving quality and strengthening quota management. Even when they paid higher prices for raw materials than State-owned enterprises did, their selling prices were lower than those of the State-owned enterprises, thus achieving the results of good quality products at low prices and selling more at low profits.

Some enterprises adopted the strategy of "producing what others do not have, producing something newer than others, having superior products when others have new ones, having cheaper superior products when others offer superior ones, and transferring to other products when others also have cheap superior products," to win out with something new and superior.

Some enterprises produced only what was lacking or what was previously non-existent in the market, and arranged production to cater to different seasonal demands and consumers of different age groups.

Some enterprises accepted orders the large industries rejected, and filled in the gaps in city industries. They were ready to produce all the products that city enterprises refused or were unwilling to produce, such as products in small batches, products with particular specifications and special processes, products in multifarious types, products that were costly in labor, time and energy, products that needed urgent delivery, products requiring consummate skill, and products with low output value and low profits.

They thus satisfied the market demand and displayed their advantages in flexibility. Some people described the practice of TVEs as "all-penetrating, omnipotent and full of surprises."

(3) Keeping themselves well informed to open up the market. TVEs set great store by information about the market, economic development and progress in science and technology. They collected information through multiple channels, including their supply and marketing agents, so that they became very adept at applying the information, in launching projects when information indicated that it was timely to do so, in responding to the market and in putting new products on the market.

Being well informed, they were able to produce many good items and seize the market. In order to expand the market, they upheld creditworthiness, honored their commitments and offered good after-sales services. They set up service points wherever products were sold, committed themselves to having products returned, repaired or replaced if flaws were found, and offered warranty for quality, timely delivery and the teaching of the use of products. They offered warm and sincere services irrespective of sales amount, the whereabouts of customers or the cost of transportation, thus winning good reputations.

(4) Devoted to the development of variety. With the development of production and increase in products, China began to make the transition from a "shortage economy" to a "surplus economy." At this juncture, TVEs began to shift their production and operation model from "supply — production — marketing" to "marketing — supply — production." Many enterprises updated their ideas to "production according to sales" and "using sales to promote production," by and by putting product marketing in the lead of all production and marketing activities. They adopted the methods of door-to-door sales promotion, associated marketing, setting up sales points, appointing sales agents and attending all kinds of fairs and sales promotion exhibitions. Some places opened "specialized markets" for selling products made by TVEs, thus forming a unique rural commodity flow network.

(5) Expanding supply and marketing contingent throughout the country. Gradually, TVEs formed a supply and marketing contingent of more than 10 million operatives, who were responsible for collecting information, procuring raw materials and promoting sales. They established connections with all cities, universities and colleges, research institutions and administrative departments. They were able to grasp and transmit information, deliver tens of thousands of products to customers and bring back feedback from them. They acted as advisors to policy decision makers and got involved in economic accounting, careful calculation and strict budgeting, seeking reasonable prices while maintaining good quality and pursuing profits by selling more, thus achieving good economic results. Thanks to their hard work, TVEs secured adequate supplies of materials, sold their products briskly and developed smoothly

3. Improving quality and upgrading products

Entering the 1990s, TVEs faced fiercer competition and challenges from both State-owned and foreign enterprises. They became aware of the fact that only by improving quality and upgrading production scale, efficiency and level of technology and management would it be possible to withstand the market competition. At the same time, they knew that it was necessary to handle the relationship among development, management and reform, and to seize the fleeting opportunity to make innovations, as follows:

(1) To improve the operational and management mechanism and closely link the immediate interests of every worker to the development of the enterprise;

(2) To concentrate efforts on the development of famous, superior, specific and famous brands, to win out with quality;

(3) To promote association among strong enterprises, to form so-called "aircraft carriers" or "joint fleets," to make the enterprises bigger and stronger in competition.

(4) To deepen reform by recapitalization through leasing, auc-

tioning, acquisition and bankruptcy, and optimizing the internal operational mechanism.

TVEs created in practice and exploration a full set of unique operational mechanisms, which can be summarized as: development mechanism by self-accumulation and independent development, independent and rapid mechanism of policy decision-making, distribution mechanism by tying remuneration to economic efficiency, reward and punishment mechanism, the mechanism of self responsibility for losses, the mechanism of making officials adaptable to both promotion and demotion; and the mechanism of employment featuring flexible entry and exit.

Section 3 Innovation in the Management System

TVEs were subject to administration by government departments at many levels. At the national level, it was the TVE Bureau of the Ministry of Agriculture that took charge of them; at the provincial (city and autonomous region), city (autonomous prefecture) and county (county-level city and autonomous county) levels, there were TVE offices. Although these administrative departments were responsible for TVEs, they were different from other administrative organizations in that they did not administer enterprises directly. They had no money, materials or power. They only mapped out long-term indicative development plans instead of mandatory plans.

Their main functions were: Charting the course of development for TVEs, coordinating their relations, improving the business environment and standardizing operational behavior. Their responsibilities were: formulating development plans, providing information, strictly enforcing administrative rules and regulations, giving guidance to enterprises with restructuring, supervising their management and promoting technical progress. This showed that the tasks of the government administrative departments for TVEs at all levels were not to administer enterprises but to serve them. These departments, therefore, gave priority in their work to conducting investigations and studying and spreading the experience of advanced enterprises.

The rules and regulations were worked out first by TVEs using lessons learned from their practice, and were later upgraded to regional rules and regulations, which were summed up by the State to become relevant State industrial policies or national rules and regulations after trial implementation and soliciting comments from TVEs throughout the country.

When issued to the grassroots, these rules and regulations may be further made more concrete and more comprehensive by enterprises, according to their actual circumstances. The development of TVEs, therefore, has followed a unique management model.

TVEs paid attention not only to static management, i.e., basic and specialized management, but also to the dynamic management of personnel in their production and operational activities. The production and operational activities have fostered a large contingent of managers who know how enterprises should be managed and operated, and a host of skilled workers, who helped raise the production level and general quality. The ranks of managers and workers have grown in strength with the development of enterprises, while enterprises have grown in strength with the growth of the ranks of managers and workers. The management system of TVEs has evolved by and large in three stages:

(1) "From have-not to have," featuring traditional family management.

At the initial period, all workers of TVEs were peasants who had just put down their hoes, and most of the management personnel were village cadres. On the one hand, the latter had the experience of developing production and had a strong craving for knowledge, while on the other hand they had a low level of education and no experience of industrial management. They had to learn from practice based on their experience in farm production. Such family management played a useful role at the primary stage, when industrial production was small and simple, often in the form of handicraft workshops.

(2) "From few to many," featuring "rule-of-the-thumb" management.

During this stage, the original handicraft workshops were gradually replaced by machines and technologies rejected by urban industries, and the technical forces were stiffened by retired technical workers from cities. This brought about corresponding changes in management. In addition, new enterprises cropped up, covering all sectors of the economy and with diversified management methods. At the same time, there emerged a large number of accountants, managers, technical workers, and marketing and supply personnel. Some of them became factory directors or managers, or department managers. They studied hard to learn from others' experiences, adopting the method of what they called "take-and-use," that is, take whatever is useful to serve the purpose of the development of TVEs.

(3) "From small to big," featuring institutional management. With the deepening of reform and opening up, TVEs greatly improved their production conditions, and there appeared many backbone enterprises. By absorbing the management methods of urban industries and applying them to practice, they have formed a whole set of management systems best suited to the conditions of these enterprises.

1. Basic management

(1) Carrying out upgrading activities. In order to strengthen the management of State-owned enterprises, the State Council issued the "Decisions Concerning Management Problems of Industrial Enterprises." TVEs studied the document, and followed the major principles therein, in a bid to raise their management levels. As TVEs were excluded from State plans, the Decisions did not mention TVEs. But thanks to efforts made by the Ministry of Agriculture, the State Council Enterprise Upgrading Office agreed to list TVEs in the ranks for upgrading. Through strict examination, the Hangzhou Universal Joint Manufactory passed assessment to become a State Second-Class Enterprise in 1987. This was the first TVE to win such an honor.

In order to provide guidance for the upgrading activities, in 1988 the Ministry of Agriculture issued a circular on upgrading and the "Detailed Rules for the Implementation of Upgrading TVEs to State-level Enterprises," demanding that the upgrading of enterprises follow the three standards prescribed in the decisions of the State Council. The three standards were:

(a) Upgrading the indices to the advanced provincial, domestic and international levels in terms of quality, materials consumption and efficiency;

(b) Upgrading the basic and specialized management levels by gradually introducing modern management methods;

(c) Upgrading the qualities of personnel politically, culturally and technically to enhance enterprises' technological level and contribution to society.

The circular stressed that indices upgrading was the main content, management upgrading was the means, and personnel quality upgrading was the guarantee. Following the issuing of the document, the work of enterprise upgrading spread throughout the country. By the end of 1996, two enterprises had been approved as first-class enterprises in the country, and 118 others approved as second-class enterprises.

The Ministry of Agriculture decided to confer the honorary title of "Advanced Township Enterprise" according to the standards of State-class enterprises. By the end of 1994, a total of 357 enterprises had been given that title.

At the same time, the Ministry of Agriculture formulated the "Rules for Reviewing State Class TVEs." Enterprises which failed to keep up the standards would be ordered to correct the situation within a prescribed time limit; if they failed to do so, their titles would be revoked. The enterprise upgrading activities enabled the relevant government departments to have a deeper understanding of TVEs. They admired the hardworking spirit and aggressiveness of these enterprises. They confirmed that there were indeed many good TVEs, and regretted that many of them could not be listed as State-class ones because of the limited quota.

(2) "Year of Enterprise Management" activities. The Ministry of Agriculture designated 1990 the "Year of Enterprise Management," and issued a circular, urging all TVEs to concentrate their efforts on making their management systematic, scientific and standard as soon as possible. The activities centered on deepening reform, raising economic efficiency, improving product quality and lowering material consumption, so as to realize intensive expanded production instead of extensive expanded production, seek efficiency by improving management instead of speed and realize scientific management instead of "rule of thumb." The priorities were:

(a) To improve basic management, including standardization, measurement, quotas, information, rules and regulations, basic education and the building of shifts and work teams;

(b) To strengthen specialized management in quality, accounting, equipment, materials and production safety;

(c) To introduce modern management methods and facilities;

(d) To do a good job of enterprise upgrading; and

(e) To improve the responsibility contract system.

Besides, the Ministry also urged the strengthening of leadership and personnel training, especially the training of management personnel, improving the style of work and work methods, summing up experience properly, and publicizing exemplary enterprises. At the same time, the Ministry of Agriculture issued the "Rules for the Basic Management of TVEs." After some years of solid work, TVEs became better aware of the importance of management. Their management levels improved, as did the general quality of enterprises, laying a foundation for strengthening the overall management of enterprises.

(3) Strengthening supervision and the management of production and operations. TVEs are widely scattered, their development levels are spotty, and the quality of their products varies. In the late 1980s, TVEs in some places resorted to the production of counterfeit and shoddy goods. These goods appeared not only on the home markets but also entered the markets of neighboring countries through border trade, seriously damaging the image and reputation of TVEs. Governments at all levels paid full attention to this, and began to crack down on such activities in accordance with the law. At the same time, they strengthened supervision and management in the spirit of "protecting the flowers while killing the pests." As a result, this unhealthy phenomenon gradually faded, and some enterprises succeeded in turning out products with prestigious brand names.

2. Specialized management

At first, TVEs adopted the cash receipt and payment accounting method, or accounting in money and in kind, and single-entry and double-entry book-keeping used by rural production brigades. Some adopted the accounting system used by supply and market cooperatives, the commercial accounting system or the industrial accounting system.

At the end of the 1970s, the Ministry of Agriculture and the Ministry of Finance jointly issued documents providing trial rules for the principles and methods of financial management and accounting for commune- and brigade-run enterprises. These later became a nationally unified accounting system, and a contingent of professional accountants began to emerge.

Later, the Ministry of Agriculture checked the accounting statements of commune- and brigade-run enterprises. In 1985, these enterprises were renamed TVEs, and in September 1986 the Ministry of Finance and the Ministry of Agriculture issued the "Financial Systems for TVEs," the "Accounting Systems for TVEs" and the "Regulations on the Coverage of Cost Spending of TVEs." The new system was then applied to all enterprises engaged in agriculture, industry, commerce, construction, transportation and communications, catering and other types of enterprises in the rural areas.

In 1992, with the approval of the State Council, the Ministry of Finance issued the "General Rules for the Financial Affairs of Enterprises" and the "Accounting Norms for Enterprises," as well as guidelines for financial systems and accounting systems for specific industries and trades. Now, TVEs follow the "Methods for Implementing the Financial and Accounting Systems for TVEs" issued by the Ministry of Agriculture in April 1993.

Apart from financial management, there were also management rules for quality, materials, equipment and production safety.

3. Modern enterprise system

Entering the 1990s, the State decided to establish the modern enterprise system, in order to internationalize the operations of enterprises. In 1994, the Ministry of Agriculture issued the "Proposals for the Establishment of a Modern Enterprise System by TVEs," and in 1995 issued a circular on carrying out experiments for establishing the modern enterprise system.

The proposals urged TVEs to straighten out the property right relationship, improve the corporate person system, and establish a modern enterprise organizational system and modern enterprise management system. The establishment of a modern enterprise system was thus conducted in the light of different levels of development and different types of enterprises.

The work started with experiments in different types of enterprises on the basis of voluntariness. The contents of the experiments included the property right system, organizational setup and management system. An enterprise may carry out experiments for a single item or for several items combined, which must reflect the realities of the enterprises concerned. The experiments laid a good foundation for converting TVEs into modern enterprises.

4. Fostering a contingent of entrepreneurs

Factory directors and managers come mainly from two sources. One is the rural cadres and the other is skilled workers. They have certain traits in common — fearing neither hardship nor fatigue and having a strong pioneering spirit, and, especially the latter, a strong sense of the market.

But their common weakness is low educational level and inadequate professional knowledge. Directors often work in their factories by day and study modern management at home in the evening. They also take time out to go to universities or colleges to learn management and gain specialized knowledge. They master enterprise management the hard way. Each step forward and each achievement by TVEs is tinged with their sweat and wisdom.

The Ministry of Agriculture cited 100 peasant-turned entrepreneurs in 1987, 500 in 1991 and 1,000 in 1994 with honorary titles for their contributions to the State and society.

In 1995, the Ministry of Agriculture went on to issue rules on the management of executives of TVEs, clearly defining the qualifications for assessing rural entrepreneurs and made the election of excellent factory directors and managers a regular affair. The entrepreneurs elected are entitled to corresponding benefits. Their names are then archived, and they are subject to dynamic management and regular review. Those who make outstanding contributions will be upgraded, and those who are found to be no longer up to standard will have their honorary titles rescinded. The document of the Ministry also called for the training of more entrepreneurs.

After the issuing of the document, the Ministry gave training to 1,000 entrepreneurs between 1995 and 1997.

TVEs have accumulated a wealth of experience in innovations in ownership, business models, operational mechanism and management system, which has proved to be useful for the reform of Chinese enterprises, and has therefore received close attention and high praise from the general public.

Chapter VIII

Technical Progress of TVEs

Section I Course and Achievements of Technical Progress

1. Stages of technical progress of TVEs

The history of the development of TVEs is, to a certain extent, the history of technical progress. Technical progress of TVEs has undergone four major stages over the past four decades:

The first stage, covering the period from the late 1950s to the late 1970s, was a state of accumulation and preparation for starting up new enterprises. During the late 1950s, the equipment level of Chinese industry as a whole was very low, being mostly hand-operated. Electricity was available only to the few places where there were pumping stations. Most of the production equipment was self-made or self-repaired. Most of the employees were from rural backgrounds. Up to the late 1960s, farm machinery manufacturing and repair shops appeared in the eastern coastal areas, with the workforce reinforced by a large number of laid-off technical personnel and educated youth from cities.

The formation of industrial enterprises independent of farm production, the emergence of farm machinery manufacturing workshops and reinforcement by technical equipment from urban industries, especially a large number of machine tools, boosted the level of equipment in TVEs. By 1978, hand operations had been replaced by semi-mechanized operations, and coal-fired power stations had become the main source of motive power.

The second stage, covering the period of the early 1980s, featured the introduction of urban technologies. Professional people from the cities, especially retired technical personnel, plus "Sunday engineers," gave a great boost to TVEs. Production was no longer confined to traditional products, but was extended to cover metallurgy, power, coal, chemicals, machine building, building materials, textiles, garments, food processing, paper making and stationery, which assumed some of the features of modern industry. During this period, TVEs mainly copied technologies passed from enterprise to enterprise. Some enterprises made efforts to tap their potential, and made some technical improvements.

The third stage, covering the period from the mid-1980s to the early 1990s, featured the importation of advanced applicable technologies and equipment. With the development of export-oriented operations of TVEs and the upgrading of domestic consumption structure, TVEs began to spread to the interior from the coastal areas, resulting in a technology-import "fever." The overall personnel quality improved after due attention was given to recruiting and training technical personnel. The number of technical personnel in TVEs by that time had reached 1.87 million, 4% of the total employment. Technical progress contributed to an estimated 30% of the total added value of TVEs.

The fourth stage, covering the mid-1990s to the early years of the 21st century, marked the beginning of technology development and innovation. During this period, instead of importation, TVEs began to develop technologies independently or jointly. During the Ninth Five-Year Plan period (1996-2000), technology-development enterprises made up 20% of the 5,286 TVEs whose annual business returns were above 10 million yuan each. More than 50,000 enterprises set up R&D organizations. 1,127 research achievements made by TVEs won Scientific and Technical Progress and TVE Science and Technology awards from the Ministry of Agriculture. Nearly 50,000 technical achievements won provincial awards, almost half of which were made by enterprises that had cooperative relations with research institutions and universities. During this stage, more than 50,000 research institutes were set up either by enterprises on their own or in cooperation with research units and universities. The number of professional technical personnel in TVEs reached three million, or 6% of the total employment in rural collective enterprises. It is estimated that technical progress accounted for 45% of the output growth of TVEs.

2. Main achievements in technical progress

(1) Technical innovation capabilities enhanced. This mainly manifested itself in the following:

(a) The general qualities of entrepreneurs improved. The drive for technical progress brought forth a third-generation contingent of entrepreneurs imbued with ideals, moral integrity, education and discipline. The 1,000 entrepreneurs cited by the Ministry of Agriculture in 1994 were their representatives. Fundamental changes also took place in the composition of personnel at the policy decision-making level. The enterprises recruited and trained a large number of innovative management personnel with rich experience and professional knowledge of technology, economics and management. During the Ninth Five-Year Plan period, 85% of the research achievements nationwide that won technical progress awards were made by TVE workers, and 90% of the leading personnel in accomplishing the achievements were leaders in technical innovation.

(b) Forming stable R&D institutions with stable technology development forces working in close cooperation with research institutes and universities. Independent and joint R&D boosted the capacity of TVEs to absorb and digest new technologies. Some enterprises set up R&D organizations abroad. The Guangdong Kelong Group, for instance, moved its R&D center to Japan and Jiangsu Senda Group Corporation set up its design department in Italy.

(c) The technical level improved markedly and technical innovation capacity was enhanced. From the beginning of the 1990s, TVEs actively adopted advanced applicable foreign technology and equipment to transform their traditional technology and products, and built computer information systems to promote technical upgrading and management modernization. Twenty provinces (autonomous regions and municipalities directly under the State Council) rewarded research achievements made by TVEs. The 401 enterprises which won the Scientific and Technical Progress Award granted by the Ministry of Agriculture during the Eighth Five-Year Plan period (1991-1995) developed 105 state-level and 258 province-level new products, and completed 124 state-level and 256 province-level projects contained in the State "Spark Program" and other programs for making breakthroughs in science and technology.

(d) Investment in science and technology kept increasing. The ratio of R&D investment to turnover among TVEs rose from 0.3% at the end of the 1991-1995 period to 0.5% at the end of the 1996-2000 period, with that in some large and medium-sized enterprises reaching over 3%. A large proportion of investment in technology went to technical transformation and the development of new products, and importation of advanced technology and equipment. Of the total fixed assets investment in 1995, 135.9 billion yuan was used to purchase equipment, accounting for 46% of the total.

In Jiangsu Province, more than half of the fixed assets investment by TVEs went into advanced technology and equipment. Textile enterprises have all rejected the traditional iron and wooden frames, and installed shuttleless frames imported from abroad. Machine-building enterprises have added a large number of digitally programmed machine tools and flexible processing centers imported from abroad. In some TVEs, the investment in technical transformation makes up 70% of the total investment, 70% of the investment for equipment renewal and 70% of the investment for advanced equipment in the total of newly added equipment.

(e) The technical equipment levels of many enterprises have reached advanced levels both internationally and domestically. TVEs in Zhejiang Province completed nearly 30,000 technical transformation projects during the Eighth Five-Year Plan period, with a total investment of 41 billion yuan and yielding an additional output value of 150 billion yuan. The reason is that they have imported a large number of advanced technologies and equipment, and there have emerged a large number of technology-intensive backbone enterprises of considerable size.

In Shaoxing County, Zhejiang Province, home of light and textile goods, TVEs imported more than 4,000 shuttleless frames and a number of items of advanced textile and dyeing equipment, and more than 100 leading enterprises have installed automatic textile-dyeing production lines that use advanced modern technologies.

The Xi'an Wancheng Magnetic-Electric Co. Ltd invested 4.3 million yuan to import a whole set of automatic production and testing equipment from Japan and the United States to produce floppy disks for computers. Testing by the State quality testing center shows that most indices of the company's products have reached the standards of internationally famous brands.

(f) Establishing science and technology parks. By the end of 2001, there were 150 TVE science and technology parks across the country. Technical innovation has become an engine of economic growth. In 1998, some 57 TVE science and technology parks realized a total sales revenue of 82.8 billion yuan, with 28.8 billion yuan coming from the sales of new- and high-tech products, accounting for 34.8% of the total sales, following the investment of 2.63 billion yuan in technical innovation. The number of technical and engineering personnel holding intermediate professional titles and above in TVEs makes up 15.5%. Moreover, 94 national model TVEs realized a combined turnover of 42.3 billion yuan, and recorded profits and taxes of 5.2 billion yuan.

(2) System to ensure scientific and technological progress being perfected. In addition to the "Township and Village Enterprise Law," "Law on the Progress of Science and Technology" and "Law on the Application of Research Achievements," TVEs have benefited from cooperation between the Ministry of Agriculture and a number of state departments, including the State Planning Commission, the State Economic and Trade Commission, the Ministry of Science and Technology, the Ministry of Education and the Ministry of Personnel, in mapping out the "Proposals for Accelerating the

Technical Progress of TVEs," "Outline Program for Scientific and Technical Progress in TVEs," "Circular on Improving Assessment of Professional Technical Titles in TVEs" and the "Regulations on TVE Workers' Education." These laws, rules and regulations have greatly helped to promote the technical progress of TVEs.

Besides, technical, information, quality control and training and other TVE service organizations have formed networks which are playing an important role. In the mid-1990s, there were more than 60,000 bases run by TVEs, higher educational institutions and social organizations for training TVE workers, and there were nearly 200,000 management personnel working in this area. The Ministry of Agriculture set up the TVE Management College to train management personnel for TVEs. Zhangjiagang, in Jiangsu Province, launched the first university for training technical and management personnel for TVEs. Some institutions of higher learning have since set up similar colleges.

(3) Market-oriented technical innovation mechanism taking shape. A large number of research institutions, universities and technical personnel have cooperated with TVEs in R&D. A large number of backbone TVEs have invested heavily in recruiting technical personnel and buying technologies and patents, or directly absorbing technical shares. Some universities provide higher education courses in cooperation with TVEs to better integrate education and research with production.

3. Experience in technical progress

(1) Adhering to market-oriented technical innovation. Since the Eighth Five-Year Plan period, more than 70% of TVEs have carried out technical innovations, and the number of innovative products and processes average six per enterprise, with the main purpose of opening up new markets. Jiangsu Shuangliang Group and Wanxiang Group in Zhejiang have set up state-level technology centers. TVEs in Wujin City, Jiangsu Province, have established more than 60 joint institutions with research units, and 236 R&D

centers on their own. These organizations have become the main force in technical innovation, and help enterprises absorb, digest and make research achievements. Technical progress has contributed to about 70% of the production and profit growth of TVEs so far.

(2) Paying particular attention to human resources development. TVEs undertake to train whatever personnel they need, and run all kinds of schools best suited to their needs. In selecting personnel, they stick to the principle of stressing actual performance and the correct handling of the relationship between competence and educational level. In the use of personnel, they carry out both training and assessment, and have established a personnel incentive mechanism. In personnel management, they strictly observe policies and ensure due benefits to personnel, thus absorbing and stabilizing a large number of technical and management personnel. They now follow the principle of bringing up their own human resources pool instead of borrowing from elsewhere, as they used to do, thus ensuring a stable workforce and a contingent of entrepreneurs well versed in science and technology and management.

(3) Persisting in the interest-oriented principle and stressing exemplary demonstration. Following the setting up of its awards for technical achievement in 1987, the Ministry of Agriculture set up an award for adult education in 1993, and cited 50 advanced units and 100 individuals excelling in adult education. At the end of 1995, the Ministry commended 500 advanced units for excelling in technical progress and 1,000 individuals who had made outstanding progress in technology. Many places carried out projects for creating science and technology-oriented enterprises and high-tech enterprises.

(4) Persisting in technical transformation and stressing application of research achievements. More than 50% of the patents applied for in China have come from TVEs. In 1993, Shandong Province introduced the policy of "carrying out more technical transformation and building fewer new projects" and "giving priority to technical transformation." The province has incorporated technical transformation of TVEs into the provincial development program, earmarking 40 million yuan for this every year.

(5) Persisting in development in the light of local conditions, stressing classified guidance. Economically developed areas stress scale, technical level, upgrading of products and improvement, while the less-developed areas stress both development and improvement. In underdeveloped areas, work started with poverty relief and the use of adaptable technology to transform the traditional technology and the development of locally available resources. All areas give equal stress to capital-, technology- and knowledge-intensive enterprises as well as labor-intensive ones, traditional industries and resource-processing industries, and introduce advanced adaptable technology to carry out technical transformation. For large and medium-sized enterprises, emphasis is placed on upgrading technical equipment to the levels of the most advanced at home and abroad. Medium- and small-sized enterprises are encouraged to import adaptable technology according to the principle of small but specialized production of exquisite and unique products.

(6) Persisting in policy support and stressing investment in science and technology. Policy support includes encouragement measures for technical transformation, tax reimbursement for expenses incurred in the development of new technology and new products, tax exemption or reduction for new products, tax reduction or exemption for the import of advanced technology and the encouragement of personnel to move to TVEs. In 1996, the Ministry of Agriculture and the Ministry of Personnel issued a joint document on the granting of professional technical titles in TVEs to pave the way for the assessment and management of TVE personnel. Many local governments have adopted positive measures and formulated their own detailed rules for the implementation of the document. TVEs have increased investment in science and technology by raising funds on their own, borrowing from banks, winning financial support from the Central Government or overseas investment. Many enterprises devote 50% of their new investment to technology development.

At present, the general technological level of TVEs is low. The proportion of professional technical personnel is only about 2%, far lower than the national average. Most of the TVEs are short of technical personnel and have not established R&D centers. Their technical innovation capabilities are weak and an independent innovation mechanism has not taken shape within them. The level of technical equipment is also low, and so is the technical content of their products. Overall production is still at a low level. Great efforts are needed for improvement.

Section 2 Strengthening Quality Control

1. Quality control of TVEs in the 1980s

There are two stages by which TVEs may comprehensively upgrade their quality control by relying on science and technology:

(1) The first stage involves the formulation of documents for improving TVEs' product quality. In order to strengthen quality control, the State Economic Commission, the Ministry of Agriculture, Animal Husbandry and Fisheries and the State Administration for Industry and Commerce issued a joint statement in 1996 on quality control of industrial products produced by TVEs. In May 1987, the State Economic Commission issued a supplementary document on banning the production and sales of products without certificates and formulated detailed rules on overall quality control of TVE products. In June 1987, the three government departments jointly issued the "Regulations on Quality Control of Industrial Products of TVEs." In the same year, the State Standards Bureau and the Ministry of Agriculture, Animal Husbandry and Fisheries issued the "Regulations on Strengthening Standardization of TVEs."

In September 1987, the State Measurements Bureau and the TVE Bureau of the Ministry of Agriculture, Animal Husbandry and Fisheries formulated rules for the management of measurements in TVEs. In order to strengthen the management of quality products, the TVE Bureau of the Ministry of Agriculture formulated the "Detailed Rules for the Selection of Quality Products made by TVEs." All these documents, rules and regulations are aimed at raising the efficiency of quality control.

(2) The second stage features standardization, measurement control and selection of quality products.

(a) Strengthening standardization. After 1984, some provincial level administrative and standardization departments organized training of TVEs in standardization. By the end of 1989, more than 85% of the TVE products had reached the standard level, and some of the better-established TVEs began to adopt international standards. According to statistics from 14 provinces in 1987, 149 enterprises' products were accepted after inspection as standardized, and obtained international standard certificates.

(b) Improving management of measurements. By the end of 1989, 14,000 enterprises had obtained certificates of standard measurement or for single item acceptance after inspection, including 330 with second-class measurement qualification certificates. The testing instruments and devices of many enterprises have reached the domestic advanced level.

(c) Product quality contests. Since the Ministry of Agriculture, Animal Husbandry and Fisheries initiated selection of quality products in 1982, the level of quality products has been rising continuously, especially in 1986 and 1987. The number of products that won ministerial awards increased from only 32 in 1982 to 444 in 1989, including six national quality products. In 1986, quality products at the ministerial level were subject to review. The results were: All the 294 products that won the ministerial awards from 1982 to 1984 maintained a very good level; only one enterprise was found to have lower quality.

(d) Introducing total quality control. Since TVEs began to introduce overall quality control in 1982, the number of enterprises practicing such control rose from 384 in 1985 to 30,000 in 1989. Starting in 1985, the Ministry of Agriculture set up a ministerial quality control award to promote overall quality control in all TVEs. By 1989, 294 TVEs had won province-level quality control awards, and 30 had won ministerial-level quality control awards.

2. Quality control of TVEs in the 1990s

(1) Aiming at overall quality control standards. From 1991 to the end of 2000, a total of 24,000 enterprises had met the standards for overall quality control at the ministerial level.

(2) Name brand strategy. Since the early 1990s, the Ministry of Agriculture has recommended 216 name brand products made by TVEs, and a large number of other products have been recognized as name brands in their own provinces. There are also a number of state-class and even world-class name brands made by TVEs. By the end of 2000, there were 40 trademarks recognized as nationally known trademarks, such as Youngor, Kelong, Senda, Red Bean, Yefeng, Wanxiang, Midea, Galanz, Robust, Chuangshi, D'sily, Wensli, Hengli and Anerle. In addition, 350 TVEs have won titles recognizing them as "major enterprises which have created famous brands."

(3) Improving quality. In order to implement the "Program of Action for Improving Quality" and the "Law of the People's Republic of China on Product Quality," the Ministry of Agriculture decided to launch activities to improve the quality of TVE products in 1997. In 1999, the Ministry of Agriculture issued a circular on selecting major enterprises which had created famous brands, and commended 192 enterprises, including the Beijing Xingguang Film and Video Equipment Group.

(4) Quality control group activities with mass participation. The formation of QC groups provides incentives for workers, and fires their zeal for innovation and creation. At the same time, such activities encourage workers to participate in enterprise management, and enhance their awareness of being the masters of their enterprises. According to incomplete statistics, there were 902 QC groups in 1985, and the number had soared to 11,457 by 1987. By 1989, the number of registered QC groups had reached 60,000. Fifty QC groups from TVEs were honored as province-level outstanding QC groups, 18 as ministerial-level outstanding QC groups, and four as State-level QC groups. In addition, 160 achievements recommended by QC groups were selected and submitted by provincial TVE bureaus to the Ministry of Agriculture.

(5) GB/T19000-ISO9000 standards and certification. The ISO9000 is the standard document for a total quality control system. In April 1998, the TVE Bureau of the Ministry of Agriculture called a national conference on quality, at which the GB/T19000-ISO9000 quality management and quality control standards were highly stressed, demanding that all TVEs management departments and enterprises pay great attention to them.

Administrative departments in charge of TVEs in all places have made specific arrangements, provided guidance and actively coordinated certification organizations and consulting units to provide certification consulting services to TVEs. By the end of 2000, more than 5,000 TVEs had obtained quality management and quality guarantee system certification. A sample survey showed that about 95% of the large and medium-sized TVEs met the prescribed standards.

(6) Licensing. In July 1987, the TVE Bureau of the Ministry of Agriculture drafted the "Regulations on Problems Concerning Production Licenses of TVEs." By the end of 1989, some 6,000 TVEs had obtained production licenses, accounting for one third of the TVEs in the entire country. More than half of China's provinces have set up TVE production license offices.

(7) Monitoring and testing. Starting in 1987, the Ministry of Agriculture invested a considerable amount of money in building a number of product testing stations for TVEs. By the end of 1998, the number of such testing stations set up jointly by the Ministry of Agriculture and local governments had reached 73. By the end of 2000, more than 80 monitoring and testing stations had been set up in cooperation with localities, and 100 more were built by provincial, prefectural and county governments. Among them, there were 18 designed for testing building materials, 11 for testing foodstuffs and beverages, eight for testing metal products and six for testing fireworks. By the end of 2000, qualification rate of items tested by the building materials testing stations rose from 50% to more than 80%.

Section 3 Improving and Protecting the Environment

TVEs rely on science and technology to improve and protect the environment. The work has so far been carried out in three major stages:

1. In the 1980s

(1) Management of environmental protection by TVEs. In the 1980s, pollution caused by TVEs aroused extensive concern. In 1983, the Ministry for the Protection and Construction of the Urban and Rural Environment called a national work conference on environmental protection, which put forward suggestions concerning environmental pollution caused by TVEs.

In September 1984, the State Council issued the "Regulations on Strengthening the Management of Environments of Township and Neighborhood Enterprises." The document pointed out that the main reason for the environmental pollution caused by TVEs was improper selection and irrational distribution of products, and backward technical equipment. It called for strengthening leadership over environmental management and adopted strict measures to control new pollution sources and resolutely check the transfer of pollution from cities to the countryside.

Toward the end of 1984, the TVE Bureau of the Ministry of Agriculture, Animal Husbandry and Fisheries set up an Environmental Protection and Safety Management Division, and decided to carry out a general survey of environmental pollution caused by TVEs from April 1985 to April 1986. For this purpose, a survey training class was organized by the Ministry's Environmental Protection Scientific Research and Monitoring Institute of the Ministry of Agriculture, Animal Husbandry and Fisheries.

The result of the survey showed that in 1984, the total industrial output value of TVEs made up 14.7% of the national total; waste water discharge made up 10.69% of the national total; waste gas discharge made up 9.34%; and the discharge of solid waste made up 11.1%. In terms of the three types of waste generated per 100 million yuan of output value, TVEs generated 259.4 tons of waste water, 64,000 standard cu m of waste gas and 4.8 tons of solid waste, while the figures for the country as a whole were 357.6 tons, 97,000 standard cu m and 6.4 tons, respectively.

In October 1986, the Ministry of Agriculture, Animal Husbandry and Fisheries, the Ministry of Public Health and the State Administration for Environmental Protection called the National Conference on Labor Hygiene and Environmental Protection in TVEs. The conference drew attention to environmental pollution, which concerns the public health, and urged all enterprises to pay full attention to environmental protection. The conference played a stimulating role in strengthening environmental protection among TVEs.

In its 1991 Report on China's Environment Strategy, the World Bank said that TVEs were growing at an alarming rate; the industrial output value of TVEs accounted for 25% of the total industrial output value. "Many people blamed TVEs for China's environmental pollution." "Although there are many problems with industrial TVEs, their pollution discharge is still lower than that of State-owned enterprises in terms of the national average and according to the proportion in industry. Waste water discharged by TVEs makes up only 10.7% of the national total, the discharge of pollutants into the air makes up 9.4%, and the discharge of solid wastes makes up 11%."

(2) Pollution control. TVEs began to control pollution as soon as the appropriate technologies were available.

(a) Renovating indigenous methods for making coke and sulfur, in order to eliminate pollution. In Jiexiu County, Shanxi Province, where the coking industry is the most developed, technical transformation was carried out to replace former indigenous coking oven with a new improved one, which reduced coal consumption by 20%, raised tar recovery by 20 kg and recovered part of the coal gas for utilization. Pollution was basically brought under control, and economic efficiency was raised from 1-4.5 yuan per ton of coal to 12-20 yuan. Jiaokou

County adopted a new process for refining sulfur, which raised the sulfur recovery rate from 40% to 80%, and the waste gas discharge met the State set standards. In October 1987, the Ministry of Agriculture, Animal Husbandry and Fisheries held a national meeting in Xiexiu County and recommended this experience to all TVEs.

(b) Eliminating pollution caused by small paper mills. At the beginning of 1987, the Dongfeng Paper Mill in Dazhu County, Sichuan Province, bid for the development of technology for controlling pollution caused by small paper mills offering soda recovery technology for the heat insulation-reflection furnace. This was one of the scientific research projects organized by the State Science and Technology Commission for the Seventh Five-Year Plan period (1986-1990). After winning the bid, the paper mill rapidly achieved success, and the technology was spread to other parts of the country. Up to 20% of the black liquid discharged by township and village paper mills was brought under control.

(c) Pollution caused by electroplating plants brought under control. In 1985, Guangzhou City cut the number of its electroplating plants by half, and strengthened the control of chromium-containing waste water. This experience was also spread to other parts of the country.

(d) Cement dust control. There were 3,817 cement plants in the country at the end of 1986, producing 7.69 million tons of cement a year. But dust and soot from them caused serious pollution. In 1987, the Zhuyou Cement Plant of Longkou City, Shandong Province, and the Shijing Cement Plant of Guangzhou City developed technologies to control dust and soot. In September of the same year, an on-the-spot national meeting was called at the plant in Shandong Province to recommend their experience.

2. Environmental protection in the "Eighth Five-Year Plan" period (1991-1995)

(1) During the Eighth Five-Year Plan period, TVEs continued to implement the "Environmental Protection Law of the People's Republic of China." The Ministry of Agriculture produced the "Program of Action for Environmental Protection by Township and Village Enterprises." By 1995, the waste water discharge per 10,000 yuan of added value of TVEs was 56.9 tons, and the waste gas discharge was 31,500 standard cu m and solid waste discharge was 1.57 tons, deceases of 52.3%, 49.9% and 50.6%, respectively, from 1990.

(2) Major achievements by TVEs in environmental protection in the Eighth Five-Year Plan period

(a) Environmental protection management network took shape;

(b) The legal system of TVEs concerning environmental protection improved, and local TVE management departments formulated local regulations on environmental protection.

(c) Investigation and studies of environmental protection carried out in major industries. During the Eighth Five-Year Plan period, investigation and studies were completed in 10 industries and small industrial zones, covering the industries of brick making, coking, casting, cement, pottery and porcelain, lime, beer, starch, ferro-alloys and iron.

(d) Pollution control demonstration projects. TVEs have constructed 16 environmental protection and energy conservation demonstrative projects, involving nine industries, including chemicals, energy, building materials and metallurgy.

(e) Environmental protection service systems improved. The Ministry of Agriculture, together with TVE bureaus in Shanghai, Tianjin, Shanxi and Dalian, invested about 14 million yuan in building regional energy-efficient product testing and environment monitoring centers.

(f) Practical results achieved in environmental protection in seriously polluted areas. In close cooperation with the TVE bureaus of related provinces, the Ministry of Agriculture has adopted such measures as shutdown, stoppage of production, technical transformation and shifting to other products, with regard to seriously polluting enterprises and indigenous coking and sulfur-making enterprises in the Shanxi-Shaanxi and Inner Mongolia area, the Henan, Anhui, Shandong, Huaihe River basin, and the Yunnan, Guizhou and Sichuan area.

(g) Progress made in winning international technical and economic cooperation. In 1992, the World Bank provided technical aid for carrying out studies of energy conservation and pollution control by TVEs in the brick making, coking and casting industries in Sichuan and Shanxi provinces, and Tianjin City. By the end of 1993, technical training had been carried out and demonstration projects and environmental protection service systems had been built in the cement, brick making, coking and casting industries.

3. Environmental protection during the Ninth Five-Year Plan period (1996-2000)

During the Ninth Five-Year Plan period, the main task was to consolidate the protection of resources, the environment and arable land, and implement the "Regulations on Strengthening Environmental Protection Among TVEs," which was part of the sustainable development strategy, and aimed to:

— Halt the building of new polluting enterprises;

— Resolutely implement the environmental effect assessment, pollution control and elimination systems;

— Develop a number of exemplary environmental protection zones in townships and villages in conjunction with the building of TVEs and small towns.

Section 4 Improving the Quality of Enterprises and Employees

1. Improving the quality of TVEs and employees by relying on scientific and technological progress

(1) The number of enterprises of a considerable scale increased. By the end of 2000, the number of TVEs with an annual business income of more than 10 million yuan each had reached

53,178, some 815 more than in the previous year, with a combined operational income of 2,556 billion yuan, accounting for 23.7% of the total generated by TVEs. Among these enterprises, those with an annual operational income of more than 50 million yuan each had reached 10,760, or 1,606 more than in the previous year, and their combined operational income had reached 1519.1 billion yuan, accounting for 14.1%; the number of enterprises with an annual operational income of more than 100 million yuan each had increased by 720, and their combined operational income had reached 1020.6 billion yuan, accounting for 9.5%. The total value of assets had increased from 4,511.5 billion yuan in the previous year to 4,871.1 billion yuan at present, a net increase of 359.6 billion yuan. All TVEs are moving steadily toward intensified and scale operation.

(2) Management level raised. About 80% of the TVEs completed their tasks for the improvement of seven kinds of basic and five kinds of specialized management. Their internal rules and regulations and supervisory and disciplinary mechanisms have been made more scientific, regular and properly planned. A number of backbone enterprises have actively introduced modern management. In 1998, there were 6,956 TVE groups, 549 more than in the previous year, and the number of national TVE groups confirmed by the Ministry of Agriculture came to 1,039.

(3) Technical progress accelerated. More than 50% of the increased investment by TVEs has gone into R&D. A survey of 4,523 TVEs showed that the R&D funds of 1,000 enterprises accounted for over 4% of the total sales revenue.

(4) Product quality improved. The variety of name brands, excellent, new and specialty products has increased steadily. Among the 60 national famous brands, 20 belong to TVEs.

2. Improving the quality of employees by relying on technical progress

(1) The total number of personnel and the quality of ordinary employees have markedly improved. A contingent of senior professional personnel who have mastered modern science and technology has taken shape. The ranks of modern entrepreneurs with innovative operational ideas have been expanded. The proportion of professional personnel holding intermediate professional titles and employees with college and secondary specialized school education has been rising.

(a) In terms of workteam structure. In 2000, there were 38.33 million employees in collective enterprises. They included 2.77 million engineers and technicians, accounting for 7.2%; 29.33 million workers and apprentices, 76.5%; the number of management personnel came to 3.19 million, making up 8.3%; and the number of service and other personnel reached 3.04 million, accounting for 7.9%.

(b) In terms of age, there were 24.91 million employees under the age of 35, accounting for 65%; people in the 36-50 age group numbered 11.36 million, accounting for 29.6%; and the number of people above the age of 51 was 2.06 million, accounting for 5.4%, in 2000.

(c) In terms of education in the same year, the number of people with a university or college education was 1.03 million, accounting for 2.7%; the number of people with a secondary vocational school education was 4.38 million, accounting for 11.4%; and the number of employees with a senior secondary education or below was 32.92 million, accounting for 85.9%.

(d) And in terms of technical titles, the number of people holding intermediate level technical titles was 1.05 million, accounting for 2.7%; and the number of people holding primary technical titles was 2.33 million, accounting for 6.0%.

(2) The ranks of specialized personnel grew. In 1996, the Ministry of Agriculture and the Ministry of Personnel jointly issued the "Circular on Improving the Assessment of Professional Technical Titles in TVEs." The following year, the Ministry of Agriculture and the former Ministry of Labor issued another joint circular on the skill training and assessment of employees and people with technical titles in TVEs. A number of provinces and cities performed well in implementing the spirit of these circulars. They included Hebei,

Zhejiang and Shaanxi provinces, and Chongqing, Tianjin cities. They all formulated a series of awards and built housing for experts and outstanding personnel, and set up post-doctoral stations to attract talented personnel. By the end of 1999, the number of professional and technical personnel in all specialties had reached 3.12 million, accounting for 7.1% of the total number of employees in rural collective enterprises.

3. Training system of TVEs

(1) General plans for education and training. In order to implement the spirit of the document issued by the CPC Central Committee on the training of a large number of TVE managers who are sound politically, have a pioneering spirit, and know how to operate and manage enterprises, the Ministry of Agriculture issued a circular in July 1997 on the improvement of the qualifications of TVE executives. Administrative departments in charge of TVEs in all places organized post credential training classes for directors, managers and senior management staff members, including engineers, economists, accountants and reserve personnel, at the level of the training carried out by the State in business management, and they must have training certificates for their jobs. The first round of training of all directors, engineers, economists and accountants of backbone TVEs was completed in four years.

(2) Running schools. One method of carrying out such training is to run schools with the backing of universities and colleges; another is for TVEs to run their own junior colleges, and secondary vocational schools; and a third is to set up training centers at the provincial, prefectural, county and township levels. By the end of 2000, there were 150 TVE training centers in the country, including 11 key training centers.

(3) Personnel growth incentive mechanism. This means setting up an environment and mechanism favorable for attracting, utilizing and fostering new personnel. The Ministry of Agriculture and the Ministry of Personnel issued a document on how to encourage skilled people to move to TVEs in an attempt to solve the latter's personnel shortage problem.

(4) Continuing education of technical personnel and employees strengthened. According to proposals advanced by the Ministry of Agriculture and the Ministry of Personnel, TVEs carry out training with special purposes in mind. Career and skill training helps raise the quality of employees. The enterprises also strengthened the skill development and performance assessment of their employees. Now some departments employ only workers holding training certificates.

(5) Education and training in TVEs in the western part of the country spurred. The TVE Bureau of the Ministry of Agriculture has directed the national TVE training centers to help enterprises in the western part of the country train management personnel. In November 1995, the first training course started to train personnel for a demonstration zone for cooperation between the eastern and western parts of the country. The trainees came from 32 demonstration zones in 12 provinces, and they got the certificates for their jobs issued by the Ministry of Agriculture. The Bureau also arranged for management and technical personnel from TVEs in the western part of the country to make study tours of the southeastern coastal and other economically developed areas.

In July 1995, the Ministry of Agriculture cited Huaxi Group Corporation in Jiangsu Province for its achievements in training management personnel for TVEs in the central and western parts of the country. The group was the first to start projects in this less-developed region. In 1994 and 1995, the group invested more than one million yuan in providing free training to technical and grass-roots management personnel for TVEs in the central and western parts of the country.

Chapter IX

Financing and Liabilities of TVEs

Section 1 Methods and Features of Financing of TVEs

Funding is the lifeblood for the development of an enterprise, indispensable for its production and operation. The sources of funds or channels from which enterprises get funds are of paramount importance for the development of enterprises.

1. Limitation of agricultural accumulation for development

Before 1976, TVEs mainly relied on internal accumulation from agricultural production for financing. That is why TVEs were obliged to support agriculture. Before and in the first few years after the founding of the People's Republic of China, carpenters, bricklayers, blacksmiths, bamboo chip makers and tailors were active in the vast countryside. They did farming during the busy seasons and pursued their own professions during the slack seasons, playing an important role in the rural areas. But in 1956, during the socialist transformation period, rural handicrafts industry joined rural production cooperatives and later people's communes. During the Great Leap Forward period, starting in 1958, a big campaign was waged to boost industry, and enterprises belonging to communes and production brigades gained much ground as the result of requisition.[1] But due to excessive speed of development and poor management, the assets accumulated by hard labor were virtually all wasted in the short span of two years.

With the development of TVEs, the internal financing channels were expanded. On the one hand, they reinvested their profits, and on the other, after the introduction of the land contract system, they used some of the accumulation from agriculture, mainly from individuals instead of collectives as in the past. In 1998, TVEs invested a total of 251.7 billion yuan in projects absorbing more than 50,000 yuan each. Part of the money — about 47.18 billion yuan — came from bank loans, 25.16% less than in the previous year. The proportion of total investment from bank loans dropped 3.01 percentage points from 21.36% in the previous year to 18.35%. Their own funds were 113.75 billion yuan, accounting for 45.2%. Plus funds coming from other sources, the funds raised through internal channels made up 81.65%.

As the realization of the importance of raising funds through internal accumulation for development was enhanced, the proportion of investment of their own funds by TVEs increased. The capital public accumulation and surplus public accumulation both increased to reach 120.9 billion and 119.2 billion yuan, respectively, by the end of the year, increases of 11.39% and 3.37% over the amounts in the previous year. More individual rural dwellers also increased their investment.

In 1998, the capital invested by individuals in TVEs reached 127.119 billion yuan, accounting for 15.39%, or 22.28% more than in the previous year. But in terms of total capital, the proportion of the capital contributed by individuals would have been much bigger. By the end of 1998, the proportion of the original value of fixed assets of private and individual enterprises was 37.67%.[2]

---

[1] The egalitarian practice to transfer and use the means of production or capital of subordinate agricultural production unit without compensation.

[2] See the TVE Bureau of the Ministry of Agriculture: *Analysis of the Basic Conditions and Economic Operation of TVEs in China*, Vol. 1999, pp. 22, 23 and 72. The proportion was calculated on that basis.

2. Outside financing began with associated enterprises

Associated enterprises refer to joint operations by township, State-owned and urban collective enterprises. Such association became an outside source of financing, marking the first step out of agricultural accumulation. As early as 1975, Deng Xiaoping said, "It is a major task for industry to support agriculture and stimulate agricultural modernization. Industrial areas and cities must bring along their neighboring rural areas, helping them develop small industries and do farm production well, and incorporating this into their own plans."[1]

The practice of cities supporting rural areas, industry supporting agriculture, and association of enterprises among State-owned or urban collective enterprises and TVEs did not develop until the beginning of the 1980s. Urban enterprises in the eastern coastal areas began to outsource their parts and accessories to the rural areas, and some moved the production of heavily polluting items to the rural areas. Others began to build factories in the rural areas for the purpose of expanding production or for the purpose of utilizing agricultural and sideline produce and cheap rural labor. Modes of investment included direct investment and investment in equipment and technology. The celebrated Bailan Washing Machine Plant in Yingkou, Liaoning Province, cooperated with rural enterprises in the production of parts and accessories by providing equipment and technology. Similar instances can be found in Shanghai and Jiangsu Province.

The attempt to use outside investment enabled TVEs to raise their operational levels. First of all, the total output and size were expanded. In 1983, rural enterprises run by communes and production brigade had a total employment of 32.35 million, with the total output value breaking the 100-billion-yuan mark to reach 100.8 billion, 80.52% and 232.67%, respectively, more than in 1976.

---

[1] *Selected Works of Deng Xiaoping*, July 1983, first edition, p. 28

Secondly, technical levels rose, with production equipment and technological processes transformed and manual labor reduced. Thirdly, the market was expanded, with products serving big industries and urban residents. Fourthly, great changes took place in the organizational forms of production, with a number of small but proficient enterprises specializing in the production of parts for large industries in the cities.

With the deepening of reform and the intensification of market regulation, rural-urban associated enterprises have been consolidated and developed. By the end of 1998, there were 7,692 rural-urban associated enterprises, with 3,925 in cooperation with State-owned ones and 3,767 in cooperation with urban collective enterprises, with a total employment of 710,000, added value of 20.2 billion yuan, business revenue of 83.5 billion yuan, profit of 4.25 billion yuan, and the original value of fixed assets standing at 37.872 billion yuan.

3. Bank loans boost increment of rural enterprises' capital volume

The limited use of bank loans began in the early period of commune- and production brigade-run enterprises. But the use of large amounts of bank loans gave a further stimulus to the development of outside sources of financing for TVEs. The total amount of bank loans outstanding at the end of 1978 was 2.2 billion yuan, equivalent to 6.77% of the original value of the fixed assets and circulating assets combined of the commune- and production brigade-run enterprises. In July 1979, the State Council issued the "Regulations on the Development of Commune- and Production Brigade-Run Enterprises (Draft)," deciding that no less than half of the investment by the State in people's communes should be used to support poor production brigade-run enterprises and that the Agricultural Bank of China should provide a certain amount of low-interest loans to rural enterprises to expand their sources of financing. But the use of bank loans by TVEs did not begin in earnest until 1984.

In 1984, the former enterprises of communes and production brigades were renamed township and village enterprises (TVEs) after the people's communes were dissolved. Then, the central authorities formulated a series of new policies for the development of rural industry. That year, the amount of bank loans broke the 10-billion-yuan mark to reach 19.8 billion yuan, 102.04% more than in 1983 or nine times the figure for 1978. The growth of bank loans brought about rapid development for TVEs. By the end of 1984, the amount of the original value of fixed assets and circulating assets of TVEs had reached 57.5 billion yuan and 39.9 billion yuan, respectively, 20.80% and 51.71% more than in the previous year or 1.5 and 3.2 times more than that of 1978.

In the years that followed, the indices of TVEs almost grew synchronously with the growth of bank loans. The amount of bank loans used by TVEs broke the 100-billion-yuan mark to reach 112.8 billion yuan by 1990, and reached 207.1 billion yuan by the end of 1992, when the number of TVEs reached 20.92 million, with a total employment of 106.25 million. The bank loans used in 1993 reached 310.7 billion yuan, and the proportion of added value of TVEs reached 53.8% of the total rural added value, and the TVE industrial added value made up 41.9% of the total industrial added value in the whole country.

The balance of bank loans used by TVEs at the end of 1998 reached a historical high of 579.6 billion yuan. Correspondingly, the original value of fixed assets and circulating assets also reached historical highs of 2,156.7 billion yuan and 2,070.6 billion yuan.

4. Use of foreign capital accelerated the pace of internationalization of TVE operations

TVEs then extended their sources of financing from domestic sources to overseas sources. The utilization of foreign capital has not only increased the amount of capital funds, it has also expanded production scale and introduced advanced management and technology, enriched the experience of TVEs in dealing with foreign investors and enhanced their international competitiveness. Enterprises that used foreign capital made fast progress in production technology, and realized mechanization and semi-automation. They have implemented the human-based management ideas, strengthened cost accounting, improved labor organization and raised labor productivity. TVEs began to use foreign capital at the beginning of the 1980s, but the utilization capital did not reach a meaningful scale until the beginning of the 1990s.

In October 1988, the central authorities decided to carry out consolidation of the national economy, and tightened the policies toward TVEs. As a result, the latter's domestic market shares dropped. TVEs had no choice but to turn to foreign markets. On the one hand, they increased exports and built enterprises abroad, and on the other, they used foreign capital on a larger scale. By the end of 1992, the value of goods delivered for export by TVEs topped 100 billion yuan, and TVEs had launched more than 10,000 joint ventures with foreign or Hong Kong, Macao, or Taiwan enterprises. From then on, they continued to expand the utilization of both the internal and external markets.

In 1998, the value of goods delivered for export by TVEs hit a historical high of 685.4 billion yuan, accounting for 40% of the national total, including 530 billion yuan in direct exports. The year 1997 saw the biggest number of joint- or cooperative-venture TVEs, which was 29,779. Due to the impact of the 1998 Asian financial crisis, the amount of foreign capital used in the year dropped. During the year, only 20,937 cooperation agreements were signed, and US$4.56 billion of foreign capital was used, US$950 million or 17.24% less than in the previous year. The amount of foreign capital actually used reached US$3.55 billion, some US$540 million or 13.20% less than in the previous year. The number of joint-venture or cooperative enterprises launched in the year shrank by 2,121 or 7.12%, as compared with the previous year. But the scale of operation of joint ventures or cooperative enterprises continued to expand, and economic efficiency continued to rise. (See Table 9-1)

Table 9-1 Operations of Joint-Venture TVEs in 1997 and 1998

	Added value		Business revenue			Profit	
	Total (billion yuan)	Per capita average (yuan)	Total (billion yuan)	Growth (%)	Profitability (%)	Total (billion yuan)	Per capita average (yuan)
1997	100.9	29,000	436.2	23.1	4.8	21.1	6,070
1998	110.1	30,200	467.2	23.6	4.9	22.8	6,263

Source: Based on the TVE Bureau of the Ministry of Agriculture: *Analysis of the Basic Conditions and Economic Operation of TVEs in China*, 1999

5. Modernization of capital structure and financing methods gave rise to a number of large TVEs

With the establishment of the modern enterprise system, the capital structure and financing methods of TVEs also began to develop toward modernization. First, more and more enterprises introduced the joint stock system; second, a number of large enterprises had their stocks listed on the stock market, realizing the modernization of financing means. The number of TVEs hit a historical high in 1994, reaching 24.95 million. But it fell in the following few years, to 20.04 million by 1998, some 19.68% less than in 1994. The figure rose to 21.32 million in 2002, still 14.5% less than in 1994.

The number of enterprises was reduced because: (1) heavily polluting enterprises were shut down; (2) small enterprises, enterprises with thin profits and enterprises running in the red were merged or acquired by larger ones to form joint stock enterprises or enterprise groups. However, the average size of enterprises increased, and the total output rose. More than 40 TVEs had their stocks listed on the stock market. Although small in number and proportion, these enterprises were super-large ones and export-oriented, with good economic returns. Statistics show that the number of TVEs with an annual business revenue ranging from 50 million yuan to 100 million yuan reached 8,788 in 2002; the number of enterprises with an annual business revenue topping at least 100 million yuan came to 6,091.[1]

Section 2 Financing Structure of TVEs

1. 20 years of financing scale expansion

The scale of funding of TVEs is the value expression of the scales of production, operation and resources. These can be divided into tangible resources value and intangible resources value. Within the tangible resources value, there are values of fixed assets and circulating assets.

Table 9-2 Fixed, Current and Intangible Assets of TVEs in Major Years

Item	1978	1980	1985	1990	1995	1998
1. Fixed assets						
Absolute amount (billion yuan)	23	32.6	82.3	285.7	1284.1	2156.7
Growth (times*)		0.4	1.5	2.5	3.5	0.7
Average annual growth(%)**		18.3	20.1	28.5	35.1	18.9
2. Current assets						
Absolute amount (billion yuan)	9.5	17.7	64.7	263.2	1449.3	2070.6
Growth (times)		0.86	2.66	3.07	4.51	0.43
Average annual growth (%)		37.8	27.0	30.6	37.4	23.6
3. Intangible assets						
Absolute amount (billion yuan)					12.7	38.4
Growth (times)						2.0
Average annual growth						44.6

*Growth as compared with the previous year. The same below.

** Average growth as compared with the previous year. The same below.

Sources: TVE Bureau of the Ministry of Agriculture: *Glorious TVEs in China*, New Star Publishers, 1999. *Analysis of the Basic Conditions and Economic Operation of TVEs in China*, 1996, 1998. Growth times and average annual growth are calculated on the data given in the above books.

[1] TVE Bureau of the Ministry of Agriculture, *Analysis of the Basic Conditions and Economic Operation of TVEs in China*, Vol. 1999, p. 30

Funds are the material basis on which TVEs grow. Without sound financial resources, it would have been impossible to have large-scale output. Since the reform and opening up policies were introduced over two decades ago, as the most active component of the Chinese economy TVEs have made indelible contributions to the rapid development of the Chinese economy, and this is inseparable from the rapid expansion of financial resources.

Features of the growth of funds:

First, rapid growth in fixed assets. In the period 1978-1998, the original value of fixed assets grew by 92.9 times, from 23 billion yuan to 2156.6 billion yuan, averaging an annual growth of 25.5%. During the 20 years, it took five years to double the original figure, and then the figure doubled every three years. By 2002, the original value of the fixed assets of TVEs reached 3,569.8 billion yuan, or 65.5% higher than the 2,156.6 billion yuan of 1998.

Second, the floating assets grew in a similar fashion. They rose from 9.5 billion yuan in 1978, to 2,070.6 billion yuan in 1998, and to 2,964.5 billion yuan in 2002, an increase of 43.2% in mere four years.

Third, brand names and other intangible assets that represent the fame and credibility of the producer grew from nil, and growth has been accelerated in recent years. In 1995, the intangible assets of TVEs were worth a total of 12.7 billion yuan. This figure had grown to 38.3 billion yuan by 1998, averaging an annual growth of 44.8%.

The rapid expansion of the aggregate assets of TVEs laid the foundation for the growth of output. In the period 1978-1998, the output growth of TVEs was kept in step with the expansion of total assets. In 1978, the added value of TVEs was 20.8 billion yuan, and it rose to 2,218.6 billion by 1998, growing by 106 times and averaging an annual growth rate of 26.3%; business revenue rose from 43.1 billion yuan to 8,935.1 billion, growing by 206 times and averaging an annual growth rate of 30.6%. The added value reached 3,238.6 billion yuan, and business revenue reached 12,976 billion yuan in 2002, up 46.0% and 45.2% as compared with 1998. (For details of major economic indices, see Table 9-3)

Table 9-3 Growth of Major Economic Indices of TVEs in 1978-1998

Item	1978	1980	1985	1990	1995	1998
1. Number of enterprises (million)	1.52	1.42	12.23	18.73	22.03	20.04
Growth (times*)		-0.7	7.6	0.5	0.2	-0.9
Average annual growth (%)**		-3.3	53.8	8.9	3.3	-2.0
2. Employees (million)	28.27	30	69.79	92.65	128.62	125.37
Growth (times)		0.6	1.3	0.3	0.4	-0.3
Average annual growth (%)		3.0	18.4	5.8	6.8	-0.5
3. Added value (billion yuan)	20.8	28.5	77.2	250.4	1459.5	2218.6
Growth (times)		0.4	1.7	2.2	4.8	0.5
Average annual growth (%)		16.8	22.1	26.5	42.3	8.7
4. Business revenue (billion yuan)	43.1	59.6	256.6	866.4	5729.9	8935.1
Growth (times)		0.4	3.3	2.4	5.6	0.6
Average annual growth		17.6	33.9	23.2	51.1	9.3

Source: TVE Bureau of the Ministry of Agriculture: *Glorious TVEs in China*, New Star Publishers, 1999. Growth times and growth percentage are calculated based on the data given in the book.

The dynamic changes in the assets and output of TVEs reveal the following points:

(1) The expansion in number in the mid- and late 1990s was not as fast as in the previous 10 years. In the three years from 1995 to 1998, the original value of fixed assets grew only 0.7 times, averaging an annual growth of 18.9%, 6.6 percentage points lower than the average growth in the period 1978-1998.

(2) Due to limitations in capital expansion, the number of enterprises and employees dropped from historic highs, but the added value and business revenue increased. This shows that enterprises had become larger, and their equipment and capital composition had been improved. In 1978, the added value realized per TVE was less than 14,000 yuan, and the fixed assets (original value) per employee was only 810 yuan. These figures rose to 111,000 yuan and 17,000 yuan, respectively, in 1998, close to the national average.

(3) Both the tangible and intangible assets of TVEs grew year by year. This shows from one angle that the quality and market competitiveness of TVEs had improved.

With the rapid expansion of TVEs, the major economic indices began to take an increasingly larger proportion in the national economy, and their positions have become increasingly important. In 1998, the added value of TVEs occupied 27.9% of the GDP and 60.8% of the total added value in the rural areas. The added value of township industries occupied almost half of the national industrial added value, reaching 46.3%. The proportion of employees in TVEs was 27% of the total labor force in the rural areas. The per capita wage of rural people derived from TVEs was 31.8% of the net income (for details, see Table 9-4). Now every three percentage points of growth of TVEs contribute to one percentage point of GDP.

Table 9-4 Major Economic Indices of TVEs

Item	1978	1980	1985	1990	1995	1998
% of added value in GDP	5.8	6.3	8.6	13.5	25.0	27.9
% of added value in rural total	17.0	17.3	23.3	33.3	54.9	60.8
% of industrial added value in national total	9.9	10.9	15.0	27.0	43.7	46.3
% of employees in total rural labor force	9.2	9.4	18.8	22.1	28.6	27.0
% of per peasant's TVE wage in total net income	8.0	7.6	14.1	16.6	30.0	31.8

Source: *Glorious TVEs in China*, p. 57

2. Changes in financing structure

After 20 years of development and reform, internal financing remains the main source of financing, and in the external financing, indirect financing remains the dominant form. Private and self-employed businesses in the rural areas mainly rely on internal financing, bank loans making up only a very small part.[1] There are virtually no other

[1] Bank loans borrowed by private and self-employed TVEs were only about 9.4% of the year-end balance of the original value of fixed assets and current assets combined, which is calculated based on data available in p. 223 and 224 of the *Analysis of the Basic Conditions and Economic Operation of TVEs in China*, 1999

forms of financing.

Collective enterprises also rely on their own accumulation for financing, followed by bank loans, corporate financing, individual financing and the use of foreign capital, State funding and appropriations by superior organs and stocks. Funds coming from the State made up less than 1% at the turn of the century. Funds appropriated by superior organizations are also small, less than 2%. Loans provided by banks and credit cooperatives make up 20-25%; imported capital make up over 20%, with foreign capital accounting for over 10%. Self-owned funds make up the biggest proportion, over 40%, with funds raised by individuals accounting for about 6%. Funds from other sources make up 8-10%.

So, the major sources of financing in the order of importance are: self-owned funds, bank and credit cooperative loans, imported funds, other funds, funds appropriated by superior organs and funds from the State.

Such direct financing as stocks and bonds is limited. As China's capital market is underdeveloped and non-standard, and subject to credit line management, State-owned enterprises are given priority, and only a tiny number of TVEs have entered the stock market. TVEs are effectively barred from bond financing.

For details about sources of funds in TVE fixed assets investment, see Table 9-5:

Table 9-5 Sources of Fixed Assets Investment of TVEs

(Unit: 100 million yuan)

	1987	1990	1992	1994	1997
Actual amount of investment in the year	243.2	206.3	1,046.8	2,542.8	2,952
Supporting funds from the State	8.7	7.2	19.2	22.0	19.5
Funds appropriated by superior organs	17.2	15.3	45.8	73.5	41.7
Loans provided by banks and credit cooperatives	117.7	420.3	420.3	717.6	630.4
Imported funds	16.5	149.3	149.3	442.1	653.6
Of which foreign capital	3.0	64.0	64.0	229.6	318.2,

Own funds	64.4	357.8	357.8	1,042.9	1,188.1
Of which funds raised by employees	11.5	59.1	59.1	240.4	167.6
Other sources	18.8	89.3	89.3	244.8	251.0

Source: *China TVE Yearbook*, 1988, 1991, 1993, 1995, 1998

The changes in the financing of fixed assets show that the sources of financing have become narrower instead of broader. Although such changes are of positive significance in a certain sense, as financing by administrative means has become less and market restriction has become stronger, broad sources of financing have remained the necessary conditions for a fast and healthy development of TVEs. This is determined by both the changes in the external ideas and relaxed policies, and on the improvement of TVEs' qualities and their competitiveness in the market to absorb more investment.

Section 3 Liabilities of TVEs

1. Liability level

The total liabilities of township collective enterprises came to 1,550.1 billion yuan in 1997, some 7.2% more than in the previous year, with the asset/liability ratio being 61.2%. (See Table 9-6)

Table 9-6 Liabilities and Losses of Township Collective Enterprises 1996-1997

	1996	1997
Total liabilities	1446.2 billion yuan	1550.1 billion yuan
Total asset	2333.7 billion yuan	2533.5 billion yuan
Asset/liability ratio	62.0%	61.2%
Growth of liabilities over previous year	15.7%	7.2%

Source: *China TVE Yearbook*, 1997 and 1998

Although the liability growth and asset/liability ratio dropped from the previous year, liabilities of TVEs were still at a fairly high level. Concomitant with the high liabilities was the high level of losses. The loss-making enterprises in 1997 accounted for 6.84%, and the loss rate was 10.57% (see Table 9-7). The high levels of both liabilities and losses indicated that the operational conditions were deteriorating.

Table 9-7 Losses Sustained by Township Collective Enterprises 1996-1997

	1996	1997
Total number of enterprises	1,548,932	1,291,912
Number of loss-making enterprises	88,436	88,393
% of loss making enterprises	5.81	6.84
Losses sustained	21.2 billion yuan	21.5 billion yuan
Profits of profit-making enterprises	203.6 billion yuan	203.4 billion yuan
Rate of loss (%)	10.41	10.57

Source: *China TVE Yearbook*, 1997 and 1998

2. Liability structure

Firstly, the total current liabilities of township collective enterprises were 1,306.4 billion yuan in 1997, 84.4% of the total liabilities; while the long-term liabilities were 242.1 billion yuan, 15.6% of the total. (For details, see Table 9-8)

Table 9-8 Liability Structure of Township Collective Enterprises in 1996-1997

	1996		1997	
	Absolute figure (billion yuan)	%	Absolute figure (billion yuan)	%
Total liabilities	1446.2	100	1550.1	100
Current liabilities	1202.7	83.3	1306.4	84.4
Long-term liabilities	243.1	16.7	242.1	15.6
Bank loans	432.6	29.9	457.2	29.5
Accounts payable	531.7	44.2	588.7	45.1

Source: Calculated based on data in *China TVE Yearbook*, 1997 and 1998

The above table shows that floating liabilities are the main form, as short-term credit is an important factor sustaining the development of TVEs. Floating liabilities include short-term loans, bills payable, accounts payable, wages payable and welfare funds payable. They reflect the short-term credit relationship between enterprises and banks, among enterprises, and between enterprises and employees. Although it does not require enterprises to pay high interest, enterprises have to commit to speedy realization. Once any part of the credit relationship is out of joint, it poses a direct threat to the whole course of trading, especially with the floating liabilities among enterprises. So, a high proportion of floating liabilities may bring about the risk of a debt crisis.

Secondly, the bank loans borrowed by township collective enterprises totaled 457.2 billion yuan in 1997, and 29.5% of the total liabilities; accounts payable came to 588.7 billion yuan, 38% of the total liabilities, and 45.1% of the current liabilities. (See Table 9-9)

Table 9-9 Liabilities of Township Collective Enterprises 1988 c.f. 1997

	1988		1997	
	Absolute figure (billion yuan)	%	Absolute figure (billion yuan)	%
Total liabilities	183.0	100	1550.1	100
Total asset	318.5	--	2533.5	--
Asset/liability ratio	--	57.4	--	61.2
Bank loans	76.2	41.6	457.2	29.5
Accounts payable	63.0	34.4	588.7	38.0

Source: *China TVE Yearbook*, 1989 and 1998

The amount of accounts payable was much bigger than the amount of bank loans, indicating that TVEs mainly owed money to other enterprises, and not to banks. It also means that bank support was inadequate, and TVEs had to rely on other enterprises for money, thus resulting in debt chains. In 1997, the accounts payable in TVEs were as high as 588.7 billion yuan, while accounts receivable reached 620.3 billion yuan, 46% of the floating assets. This shows that the debt chains of IOU or UOM were serious. The large amount of uncollected receivable accounts was the major adverse factor in the normal operations of TVEs.

3. Historical comparison of TVE liabilities

The liabilities of TVEs in 1997 underwent great changes as compared with those in 1988. During the period 1988-1997, total assets increased 7 times, and total liabilities increased 7.5 times, with the asset/liability ratio rising by 3.8 percentage points from 57.4% to 61.2%. The liability structure showed that bank loans were reduced and accounts payable rose. In the period 1988-1997, bank loans dropped by 12.1 percentage points in total liabilities, from 41.6% to 29.5%, although the amount of bank loans increased five times. Accounts payable in total liabilities rose by 3.6 percentage points, from 34.4% to 38%, and the total accounts payable increased 8.3 times.

Liabilities were maintained at a very high level in that there was no capital market that offered free choice of financing, and TVEs could not get financial support from the government as the planned economic system gave priority to State-owned enterprises with regard to financial support. Liabilities thus became the main means for TVEs to operate and develop.

4. Assessment of liabilities of TVEs

To judge the liabilities conditions, it is necessary to view the liability ratio and the debt repaying abilities and profitability combined, instead of by the absolute amount or the level of liability ratio. In 1997, the asset/liability ratio (61.2%) and percentage of indebted enterprises (24.6%), which reflect the long-term debt paying abilities of TVEs, both dropped as compared with 1996. (See Table 9-10)

Table 9-10 Debt Paying Ability and Profitability of TVEs 1996 c.f. 1997

	1996	1997
Liquidity ratio	104.9%	103.27%
Quick ratio	62.8%	62.89%
Turnover days of accounts receivable	31.1	32.8
Turnover of inventories	7.79	7.64
Total profit/current liabilities	16.9%	15.6%
Asset/liability ratio	62%	61.18%
Long-term liability/proprietor's rights	27.4%	24.6%
Return on total assets	12.8%	11.65%
Capital gain	25.1%	22.37%

Source: Calculated on the basis of data given in the *China TVE Yearbook*, 1997 and 1998

As shown in the table, it seems that the abilities of TVEs to pay long-term debt increased. But the current ratio and quick ratio that reflect the abilities of TVEs to pay off short-term debts were 103.27% and 62.89% in 1997. Furthermore, the turnover speed of floating assets of enterprises also slowed, the turnover days of accounts receivable increased, and the number of turnovers of inventories was reduced gradually. The profit indices (total profit/floating liabilities) that could be used to directly pay off floating liabilities also dropped. All these facts indicate that the ability of TVEs to pay off short-term debts deteriorated.

The liability structure was irrational, in that the proportion of floating liabilities was too big (84.4%), the proportion of long-term liabilities too low (15.6%), the proportion of debts among enterprises too high (45.1%), and that of bank loans too small (29.5%).

As regards the profitability of TVEs, in 1997, the capital gains of TVEs reached 22.37%. Although the performance was not bad, the gains dropped by a large margin as compared with the previous few years. In 1997, the returns on total assets were 11.65% (see Table 9-10), far lower than in the previous few years and only slightly higher than the interest rates on bank loans during the same period

(The interest rates on one-year working capital and capital construction loans on May 1, 1996 were 10.98% and 11.52%, respectively; the same interest rates on August 23, 1996 and on October 23, 1997 were 10.08% and 8.64%, respectively). This shows that the current profitability level sounded the warning: Be cautious about increasing liabilities, otherwise, the increase in debt will lead to greater risks and rise in costs instead of gains.

Section 4 Orientation of TVE Investment

Financing and investment are interrelated concepts. Financing refers to the sources of funds, while investment refers to the use of funds.

1. Industry as the main focus of investment, supplemented by diversified operations

The main orientation of investment by TVEs should be diversified operations, with industry as the main operation. The overwhelming majority of investment should go to industry, while the rest should go to such areas as agricultural projects run by enterprises, construction, transportation, commerce, tourism, catering and other services. Investment by TVEs has assumed the following features over the past few years:

(1) Investment mainly went to industry, but the proportion dropped. At the end of the 1970s and the beginning of the 1980s, investment of collective township enterprises in industries reached more than 90%, but it began to drop after that, until it reached about 70% in some years, before it rose again to 84.9% by 1996. But it dropped again in 1997 and 1998, to reach 79.47%.

(2) Investment in agriculture also dropped. In 1998, it accounted for only 4% of the total.

(3) Investment in construction and transportation rose, but faster investment was recorded in wholesale and retail sales, tourism and catering. As is shown in the following table, from 1996 to 1998 the investment in wholesale and retail sales rose from 3.4% to 4.1% and then to 5.2%, and investment in tourism and catering trade rose from 2.6% to 3.0% and 3.5% (for investment orientation of TVEs in the period, see Table 9-11).

Table 9-11 Orientation of Investment in Fixed Assets by Township Collective Enterprises 1996-1998

Year	Absolute amount (AB)(billion yuan) & %	Total invest-ment	Agri-cul-ture	Indus-try	Constru-ction	Transport-ation	Whole & retail sales	Tourism & catering	Oth-ers
1996	AB	312.69	9.74	265.59	8.99	3.09	10.53	8.06	6.69
	%	100	3.1	84.9	2.9	1.0	3.4	2.6	2.1
1997	AB	295.2	12.03	244.84	7.98	3.02	12.35	9.05	5.93
	%	100	4.1	82.9	2.7	1.0	4.1	3.0	2.0
1998	AB	257.13	10.16	204.35	8.56	2.66	13.35	9.03	9.03
	%	100	4.0	79.5	3.3	1.0	5.2	3.5	3.5

Source: Calculated on the basis of data provided by the TVE Bureau of the Ministry of Agriculture: *Analysis of the Basic Conditions and Economic Operation of TVEs in China*, 1996, 1998

The output structure of the three types of industry also underwent corresponding changes.

Table 9-12 Added Value of TVEs in the Three Types of Industry in Years with Major Changes

(Unit: %)

Industry	1978	1985	1990	1995	1997	1998
Primary	8.4	2.2	1.6	1.9	2.1	1.6
Secondary	81.6	86.4	84.2	82.8	83.6	78.0
Tertiary	10.0	11.4	14.2	15.3	14.3	20.4

Source: *Glorious TVEs in China*, 1999, p. 67

Take added value for example. The added value of primary industry in the total added value of all trades and services was 8.4% in 1978, which was the highest. In the following 20 years, it dropped year by year, until it fell to the lowest point of 1.6% in 1998. The proportion of added value of secondary industry was 81.6% in 1978, and reached the peak of 86.4% in 1985. It was spotty in the ensuing 15 years, never reaching the level of 1985 again, and even dropping to 78% in 1998. The proportion of the added value of tertiary industry was 10% in 1978, which was the lowest, and it assumed an upward trend in the ensuing 20 years, although with some small fluctuations until it reached a record 20.4% in 1998.

2. Main body of TVEs

At the beginning, there were only collective enterprises. With the deepening of the policies of reform and opening up, private and self-employed businesses began to develop. In 1996, the total assets of private and self-employed businesses were 824.8 billion yuan, and they had risen by 33.7% to 1,102.7 billion yuan by 1998, 20.9 percentage points higher than the growth rate of 12.8% for collective enterprises.

After 20 years of development, private and self-employed businesses have become an important component part of TVEs, with stock assets making up one third of the total. Specifically, the total assets of private and self-employed businesses account for 29% of TVEs' total; floating assets, 33.1%; original value of fixed assets, 37.7% (for stock assets of major types of TVEs in 1996 and 1998, see Table 9-13) .

Table 9-13 Stock Assets of Major Types of TVEs 1996 c.f. 1998

		1996			1998		
		Total	Collective	Private	Total	Collective	Private
Absolute figure	Total assets	3158.5	2333.7	824.8	3734.3	2631.6	1102.7
	Current assets	1698.9	1261	437.9	2070.7	1385.9	684.8

(billion yuan)	Original value of fixed assets	1605	1114.9	490.1	2156.7	1344.3	812.4
Per-centage	Total assets	100	73.9	26.1	100	70. 5	29.5
	Current assets	100	74.2	25.8	100	66.9	31.1
	Original value of fixed assets	100	69.5	30.5	100	62.3	37.7

Source: Calculated on the basis of the data in *Analysis of the Basic Conditions and Economic Operation of TVEs in China*, 1996, 1998

Table 9-14 Proportion of Main Indices of Private and Self-Employed Businesses in TVEs (1998)

	Number of enterprises (million)	Employment (million)	Total output value (current price) (billion yuan)	Added value (billion yuan)	Business revenue (billion yuan)	Net profit (billion yuan)	Tax paid (billion yuan)
Amount	18.974	77.079	5339.59	1221.51	5106.7	293.75	71.68
%	94.7	61.5	55.2	55.1	57.2	63.4	45.3

Source: Calculated on the basis of data in *Analysis of the Basic Conditions and Economic Operation of TVEs in China*, 1998, p. 72

The number of private and self-employed enterprises, their employment, added value, business income, profits and tax payments rose with the steady increase of their stock assets among TVEs' total assets. Now they occupy an important position in TVEs, and are an important force behind the development of the rural areas and even the whole national economy.

Section 5 Comparison of TVEs and State-Owned Enterprises

In China, TVEs and State-owned enterprises are two different kinds of enterprises, with different ownerships. The comparison between the two kinds of enterprises in financing, liabilities and fund efficiency may reveal from one angle the allocation of funds and the results of their use. The comparison is confined to industrial enterprises. TVEs include the collective industrial ones at the township and village levels, and State enterprises include industrial enterprises with independent accounting. Both include their holding companies.

1. Sources of funds and structure

First, the two categories of enterprises vary in both sources of funds and structure. For TVEs, the main source of funds is still internal financing, with external financing — principally indirect financing — as a supplement, with only a small amount of direct financing from the stock market and by means of bonds. This shows that TVEs are far from the market in terms of financing. This presents a sharp contrast to their market-oriented production.

But for State-owned enterprises, external financing is the principal source of funds, and direct financing from the stock market has developed rapidly. There are also ways of direct financing, such as by issuing bonds. With regard to financing, State-owned enterprises are much closer to the market than TVEs. Yet, the products of State-owned enterprises are less market-oriented. This is another sharp contrast which shows how China's economic system has been distorted.

Second, not only the size of investment and financing of TVEs is much smaller than that of State-owned enterprises, the composition of indirect financing between them also varies greatly.

(1) The funds covered by the State budget are much smaller for TVEs than for State-owned ones. Although the funds of State-owned enterprises covered by the State budget have been dropping since 1984, they are still maintained at about 5% (see Table 9-15). But the funds for TVEs coming from the State are less than 1%.

Table 9-15 Sources of Investment in Fixed Assets in the State Sector of the Economy 1994-1997

	1994		1995		1996		1997	
	absolute figure (billion yuan)	%	absolute figure (billion yuan)	%	absolute figure (billion yuan)	%	absolute figure (billion yuan)	%
Total sources of funds	961.6	100	1089.8	100	1205.6	100	1309.2	100
Funds covered by State budget	47.8	4.97	54.5	5.00	55.7	4.62	61.3	4.68
Domestic loans	247.1	25.70	257.8	23.66	285.1	23.65	300.8	23.00
Foreign capital	69.0	7.18	85.9	7.88	81.1	6.73	66.3	5.06
Self raised	490.5	51.01	530.7	48.70	614.2	50.95	690.3	52.73
Others	111.8	11.63	173.2	15.9	173.1	14.36	186.6	14.25

Source: National Bureau of Statistics of China: *China Statistical Yearbook*, 1995, 1996, 1997 and 1998

(2) TVEs get fewer bank loans than State-owned enterprises. Although the domestic loans for State-owned enterprises are not big in name (23% in 1997) and they are assuming a downward trend, the proportion of their self-raised funds and other sources of funds is big (the two items combined is close to 67%), and it is assuming an upward trend. As self-raised funds and other sources of funds are also loans, the changes in essence reflect the rise of loans by banks or other financial institutions. Suppose 50% of the self-raised funds and other sources of funds are loans, plus domestic loans, the proportion of this part of funds accounts for over 55%, far above the level of 20-30% borrowed by TVEs from rural credit cooperatives.

(3) The total amount of foreign capital used by collective industrial TVEs is no less than that used by State-owned enterprises, and it is assuming an upward trend in contrast with the downward trend for State-owned enterprises.

Third, the big difference in financing and investment between

TVEs and State owned enterprises is being narrowed. With the deepening of reform of the economic system, enterprises have to rely more and more on the market for financing, no matter what kinds of enterprises they are. This is an inevitable result of the Chinese economy deepening its market orientation.

2. Stock assets

TVEs have much fewer stock assets than State-owned enterprises. In 1998, the assets of industrial enterprises owned by the State totaled 7,491.6 billion yuan, 3.4 times the total of 2,172.2 billion yuan owned by TVEs.

In the period 1987-1998, the fixed assets (original value) of township collective industrial enterprises grew 6.6 times, from 122.67 billion yuan to 938.03 billion yuan; those of State-owned enterprises grew about 5.2 times, from 767.79 billion yuan to 4791.33 billion yuan.

In the same period, the floating assets of industrial TVEs grew 8.9 times — from 113.46 billion yuan to 1125.5 billion yuan — while those of State-owned enterprises grew 15.3 times, from 221.5 billion yuan to 3612.27 billion yuan.

TVEs and State-owned enterprises record the same speed of the expansion of fixed assets, but State-owned enterprises are much faster than TVEs in expanding their floating assets. That is why the proportion of floating assets among the total assets of TVEs dropped by two percentage points from 54.2% in 1987 to 52.2% in 1998, and that of State-owned enterprises rose by 19.6 percentage points from 28.6% to 48.2% in the same period.

The movement of floating assets of the two kinds of enterprises in opposite directions shows that the composition of assets of State-owned enterprise is becoming more and more rational, while that of collective industrial TVEs is becoming more and more irrational. Although the proportion of floating assets of TVEs in the total assets was four percentage points higher than that of State-owned enterprises in 1998, the debt chains among TVEs were more serious.

The accounts receivable in TVEs' floating assets in 1998 totaled 319.1 billion yuan, 38.4% of the total floating assets.[1]

3. Liability structure

In 1997, the asset/liability ratio of State industrial enterprises practicing independent accounting was 64.8%, 3.6 percentage points higher than that of township and village collective enterprises. But the liability structure of TVEs was not as good as that of State-owned enterprises, because State-owned enterprises had a higher proportion of long-term debts — about 35.6%, 20 percentages points higher than that of TVEs. (See Table 9-16)

Table 9-16 Liabilities of Collective TVEs and State-Owned Industrial Enterprises with Independent Accounting in 1997

	State-owned enterprises		TVEs	
	Absolute figure (billion yuan)	%	Absolute figure (billion yuan)	%
Total assets	5910.8	--	2533.5	--
Total liabilities	3831.5	100	1550.1	100
Current liabilities	2467.5	64.4	1306.4	84.4
Long-term liabilities	1363.9	35.6	242.1	15.6
Asset/liability ratio	--	64.8	--	61.2

Source: *China Statistical Yearbook*, 1998 and *China TVE Yearbook*, 1998

As the current liability rate is high, TVEs have bigger pressures than State-owned ones in the course of debt payment.

4. Fund efficiency

(1) State-owned enterprises are better off than TVEs in

[1] Figures calculated on the basis of the data available in *China Statistical Yearbook* of the corresponding years and the article *Analysis of the Basic Conditions and Economic Operation of TVEs in China*. The same below.

terms of equipment availability, but the two are similar in labor productivity, if calculated by added value. In 1997, the original value of fixed assets per employee in State-owned enterprises was about 100,000 yuan, three times that of TVEs, which was only 32,000 yuan. This shows that the level of production technology and equipment of State-owned enterprises is much higher than that of TVEs, but there is little difference in labor productivity if calculated in terms of added value. Labor productivity was 23,000 yuan/person/year in State-owned enterprises in 1997, 11.4% higher than the 20,000 yuan/person/year in TVEs. The main cause of lower labor productivity in State-owned enterprises is the bloated workforce.

(2) The average amount of funds varies greatly, and so do fund efficiency. State-owned enterprises have far more funds than TVEs. But in terms of fund efficiency, those of TVEs are far higher than those of State-owned ones. In 1997, there were 74,388 industrial enterprises practicing independent accounting owned by the State, with total assets of 5,910.8 billion yuan, averaging 79.46 million yuan per enterprise. In the same year, the number of collective industrial TVEs was 844,050, with total assets of 2,106.1 billion yuan, averaging 2.5 million per enterprise, only a little over 1/32 that of State-owned ones. Yet, the net profit realized in the year by collective industrial TVEs was 134.5 billion yuan, while the net profit realized by State-owned enterprises was only 42.8 billion yuan, 1/3 that of TVEs.

The difference in profitability on assets is even bigger. In 1997, the average profitability on assets in TVEs was 6.4%, while that of State-owned enterprises was only 0.7%, less than 1/9 that of TVEs. Even large State-owned enterprises with good economic efficiency realized only 1.6% in profitability on assets, a quarter of that of TVEs.

It should be pointed out that the economic efficiency of TVEs has also assumed a downward trend, with more and more enterprises running in the red and the amount of losses growing. In 1997, there were 90,000 collective TVEs running in the red, accounting for 6.9% of the total, 1.1 percentage points higher than in the previous year, and the total losses amounted to 21.5 billion yuan, 300 million more than in the previous year, averaging 239,000 yuan per enterprise. This may be attributable to the law of average profitability dropping with the increase in market competition. But blind investment, backward technology and extensive management are also contributing factors.

Chapter X

Striving for an International Standing

Section 1 Course of Development and Major Achievements

Since 1979, when China introduced its reform and opening-up policies, the country has been following a path to industrialization which is different from either the traditional one or the one of export-led burgeoning industrial countries which are overly dependent on the industrially developed countries. It is a path with Chinese characteristics, and this industrialization is taking place in both urban and rural areas. The rise of TVEs is part of rural industrialization. Such enterprises not only serve the home market, they are also striving for a niche in other parts of the world. The export trade and international economic and technological cooperation carried out by TVEs have experienced a gradual development process, showing the great vitality of TVEs. This course of development may be divided into three stages:

1. The initial stage (before 1985)

As early as in the 1960s, some rural enterprises began to export arts and crafts, native produce, fireworks, carvings, drawn works, straw-, bamboo- and willow-plaited works, overalls, sealing rings, small farm implements, hardware and tools, cotton yarn, gray cloth, silk, mineral ores and other products under the arrangement of foreign trade department or factories turning out products for export. In 1965, commune- and brigade-run enterprises in Pingxiang, Jiangxi Province, exported 15,000 boxes of fireworks. Before 1980, the number of export production enterprises in China was less than 1,500. After 1980, some qualified enterprises began to export canned food, wine, soy sauce and gourmet powder, in addition to the traditional export products.

Some also began to batch-produce textiles, knitwear, middle-grade garments, refined carpets and toys. Some machinery with high added value began to find its way into the world market. It included electric fans produced in Guangdong, hoes produced by the rolling casting process made in Tianjin, microwave acupuncture devices developed by the Jiangdu Radio Factory of Jiangsu Province in cooperation with the No. 11 Electronics Institute of the Ministry of Electronics Industry. This device, which combines microwave technology with traditional acupuncture skills, can treat more than 20 kinds of chronic diseases, including heart trouble. Markets for it were found in Europe, the United States, Japan, Hong Kong and Macao.

The characteristics of exports during this period were:

(1) Export enterprises were few in number and situated mostly in coastal areas, such as the Zhujiang River Delta, Shanghai and southern Jiangsu, as well as the suburbs of Qingdao, Yantai, Tianjin, Beijing and Dalian. By the end of 1985, the number of export production enterprises had reached more than 2,400. In addition, there were more than 5,900 enterprises which exported more than 50% of their products.

(2) More than 90% of the export products were traditional ones, primarily processed farm products and resources of the labor-intensive type. Exports of machinery and electronic products that had a high added value were insignificant. Before 1980, fewer than 500 kinds of such products were exported. But by the end of 1985, the variety had reached 3,500.

(3) Export enterprises in general were small in scale, with outdated equipment. More than 80% of the enterprises each had fewer than 100 workers. Apart from a few enterprises in Guangdong Province

that used advanced equipment to do processing by using supplied materials or samples, or assembly by using supplied parts, or compensation trade, most of the enterprises used traditional processing tools, and even hand tools.

(4) After 1980, enterprises doing processing trade grew rapidly in number in Guangdong. The number of such enterprises in Shunde, Dongguan, Zhongshan and Nanhai counties, neighboring Hong Kong and Macao, had reached 3,500 in 1984, with an annual earning of about US$120 million. By 1985, the number had reached 5,300, with annual total earnings shooting up to US$180 million.

(5) Some enterprises in the coastal areas, which had good conditions, began to launch joint ventures and cooperative enterprises, the number of which had topped 110 by 1983, and had reached 235 by 1984. They were mostly concentrated in coastal Guangdong and Fujian provinces. All these enterprises had to keep their own balance of payments in foreign currency, and exported more than 50% of their products.

(6) TVEs began to launch joint operations with State-owned foreign trade companies. This form of association was most welcome to TVEs. By 1985, the number of such joint companies had reached 2,400, and they were the backbone export exchange earners at the time.

2. High-speed development stage (1986-1993)

In order to stimulate TVEs to better develop exports and international economic and technical cooperation, the State foreign trade departments concerned raised the slogan of giving full scope to TVEs in their roles as a new emerging force in export, and adopted a series of incentive measures. From August 27, 1986 to September 5 of the same year, the Ministry of Agriculture and other ministries held the First TVE Export Commodities Exhibition in Beijing. During the 10-day run, diplomatic missions of 54 countries and representatives of foreign firms, totaling more than 620 people, visited the exhibition, in addition to more than 120,000 local people.

In December 1987, the Ministry of Agriculture and the former Ministry of Foreign Trade and Economic Cooperation held the Work Conference on TVE Exports in Beijing. The conference summed up the experience of the export performance of TVEs since the introduction of reform and opening up, and put forward the policies and measures for building trade-industry-agriculture export production bases approved by the State Council.

Starting in 1988, the production base program officially started. All export production TVEs meeting the following requirements were eligible for membership of production bases: enterprises that had launched joint enterprises with State foreign trade companies; enterprises that mainly produced export products and exports made up 60% of their annual sales volume; enterprises with an annual export volume of more than US$1 million or having annual export earnings of more than US$5,000 per capita; enterprises that had raw materials and energy sources as well as advanced production technology and processes, capable of producing famous, quality, unique or new products that were in demand on the international market; and enterprises that were good at carrying out export contracts.

In July 1988, the Ministry of Agriculture and the Ministry of Foreign Trade and Economic Cooperation jointly issued "Regulations on Implementing the Policies to promote exports by TVEs." They urged all government departments to treat TVEs the same as they did State-owned enterprises, and make support for TVEs a long-term policy.

In September 1989, the Second TVE Export Commodities Exhibition was held in Beijing, which demonstrated the tremendous potential of TVEs for earning foreign exchange.

In December 1989, the UN Asian and Pacific Economic and Social Committee held the International Forum on TVEs in Wuxi, Jiangsu Province. Representatives from eight countries in the Asian and Pacific region and six international organizations, and observers from a number of other countries attended the forum, discussing the issues of international economic cooperation and trade of TVEs with Chinese representatives from some TVEs and government departments concerned.

In May 14-18, 1992, the Second Work Conference on TVE Exports was held in Beijing. The conference summed up the experience of export business of TVEs from 1986 to 1990, and discussed the related plans for 2000. The conference cited 649 export-oriented TVEs and 25 townships, towns, counties and cities, and sanctioned 193 trade-industry-agriculture export production bases.

The development of exports by TVEs in this stage assumed the following characteristics:

(1) Export earnings increased greatly, and development was rapid. The value of export goods made by TVEs accounted for only 4.3% of all the goods purchased for export in the country in 1984. But the proportion rose to 9.3% in 1986, 19.1% in 1988, 23.7% in 1990 and 32.4% in 1992, averaging an annual growth rate of over 32%. The earnings from processing and compensation trade rose from 1.06 billion yuan in 1986 to 2.94 billion yuan in 1988, to 8.03 billion yuan by 1990 and to 19.73 billion yuan by 1992, averaging an annual growth rate of about 35%. TVEs played a vital role in the batch production of some industrial products: 89.7% of garments, 63.7% of arts and crafts, 54% of silks, 53.2% of chemical products, 38.7% of textiles and 36.2% of foodstuffs. Great development was also recorded in the export of medium-sized and small machinery, home electrical appliances, electrical engineering supplies, medical apparatus, medium- and high-grade textiles and garments.

Table 10-1 Volume of Goods Offered for Export by TVEs

Year	Annual volume of goods supplied (billion yuan)	Annual growth (%)	% in total goods purchased for export in the country
1986	9.9		
1987	16.1	62.6	14.9
1988	26.8	66.4	19.1
1989	37.1	38.4	21.9
1990	48.5	30.7	23.7
1991	88.3	82.1	29.7
1993	219.3	74.2	35.8

(2) The number of export enterprises swelled, and their average size increased. By the end of 1992, the number of export-oriented TVEs had reached 84,750, including 48,500 specializing in export production or exporting most of their products. Their total employment reached 7.5 million. There also emerged a number of townships and towns whose value of goods delivered for export exceeded 100 million yuan each, and counties and cities whose export value exceeded 500 million yuan each. A number of export processing industrial clusters appeared in Guangdong, Jiangsu and Fujian provinces, and Shanghai and Dalian cities.

Table 10-2 Development of Export-Oriented TVEs

Year	Number of export-oriented TVEs	Number of TVEs exporting over 50% of their products	Total
1985	2,400	5,900	8,300
1986	4,100	6,000	10,100
1987	7,800	9,700	17,500
1988	14,300	10,700	25,000
1989	20,800	24,200	45,000
1990	22,000	35,800	57,800
1991	28,700	45,900	74,600
1993	39,400	45,105	84,505

(3) Export enterprises improved quality, and became larger, creating a number of prestigious brands.

(a) A large number of highly competitive large enterprises with advanced equipment, good management and superior products appeared. The Ministry of Agriculture and the Ministry of Foreign Trade and Economic Cooperation approved 193 trade-industry-agriculture export production bases. In 1987, each of these enterprises had export earnings of US$3.166 million to their credit, with an average export earning cost of 3.64 yuan, averaging US$3,630 per person, and the export earnings per 10,000 yuan in fixed assets was US$5,480. Among them, three enterprises had export earnings exceeding US$10 million each, and 23 others had earnings of more than US$5 million each. In 1988, the export earnings per enterprise were US$4.05 million, averaging US$4,700 per person, US$7,000 per 10,000 yuan in fixed assets. Among them, six enterprises had export earnings exceeding US$10 million each and 56 had export earnings of more than US$500 million each.

In 1989, the number of enterprises whose export earnings exceeded US$1 million each had reached 2,800, and the number of enterprises whose export earnings exceeded US$3 million each had reached 750; the number of enterprises whose export earnings exceeded US$5 million each had reached 150; and the number of enterprises whose export earnings topped US$10 million each had reached 22. By the end of 1992, 4,200 enterprises had attained annual export earnings of US$1 million each; 820 each earned more than US$5 million and 70 earned more than US$10 million each. By the end of 1993, nearly 500 each delivered goods with an export value of US$6 million, and 98 each delivered goods, of more than US$100 million. More than 3,000 enterprises each earned more than US$3 million annually, and 103 enterprises each earned more than US$10 million annually. The export products improved in quality, grade and packaging to adapt to the international market, and the goods of more than 80% of enterprises specializing in export production reached international standards or standards provided by customers. All of them introduced total quality control.

(b) Technical transformation accelerated. From 1985 to 1992, TVEs imported more than 190 items of equipment and production lines, of which 60% reached the world level of the 1970s and 1980s.

(c) Inviting professional technicians, experts and professors. More than 60% of patented technologies were adopted by TVEs and hundreds of thousands of experts, professors and experienced technicians served TVEs directly or indirectly. During the Seventh Five-Year Plan period (1986-1990), 35 products made by TVEs won international gold or silver medals. Enjoying a high reputation were such products as those of the Beicai Embroidered Clothes Factory of Shanghai, the Silk Fashion Knitwear Factory of Zhenjiang, the Baihe Garment Factory, and the Midea and Yuhua brands electric fans, and

TMT and SMC ceiling fans made in Shunde, Guangdong Province.

(d) A number of export processing zones and export enterprise clusters with international prestige appeared in the coastal areas and some big cities. They included a base for the manufacture of home electrical appliances in Shunde, toys in Dongguan and Zhongshan, silk garments in Chuansha, Shanghai, Wujiang in Suzhou and Nantong in Jiangsu, sports shoes in Putian, Fujian, garments in Shunyi near Beijing and Yangshufang in Dalian, and cashmere sweaters in Beijing's Pinggu District.

(e) Exports of machinery and electronic products grew at an annual rate of 50%. Home electrical appliances, hand tools, auto parts, storage batteries, standard parts, fasteners and foundry equipment all became bulk export goods. By the end of 1987, 1,053 TVEs were exporting machinery and electronic products.

(4) Foreign-funded enterprises (Chinese-foreign joint ventures, co-operative enterprises and exclusively foreign-owned enterprises) developed rapidly. By the end of 1992, there were 16,400 such enterprises, including more than 5,000 funded by Taiwan business people. The foreign-funded enterprises, plus loans provided by international financial institutions and foreign governments, witnessed a capital inflow of US$8.85 billion. In 1993, China approved 15,000 joint ventures and cooperative enterprises launched by TVEs, 87.5% more than in 1992. Their total contractual foreign capital reached more than US$15 billion, and US$4.958 billion was put in place.

Table 10-3 Growth of Fees Collected by TVEs from Processing Business and Compensation Trade

Year	Processing fees (billion yuan)	Growth (%)
1986	1.06	
1987	2.43	129.2
1988	2.94	20.9
1989	5.12	74.1
1990	8.03	56.8
1991	14.07	75.2

Table 10-4 Joint Ventures and Cooperative Ventures Launched by TVEs

Year	Number
1986	2,405
1987	2,996
1988	4,762
1989	5,915
1990	6,987
1991	8,456

(5) Exports took up an increasingly large proportion of TVE products, and many items occupied important positions. Starting in 1991, the State scrapped subsidies for State-owned foreign trade companies, and the prices of goods purchased by these companies for export were reduced. According to data from 11 provinces and cities, TVEs found their income dropping by three billion yuan. The following table shows the significance of TVEs in the export activities of various provinces, municipalities and autonomous regions:

Table 10-5 Proportion of Goods Delivered by TVEs for Export in the Total Goods Purchased for Export in China

(Unit: 100 million)

Category	Volume delivered in 1998	% in national total	Volume delivered in 1990	% in national total
Clothes	30.2	49.6	63.8	72
Arts and crafts	37.9	39.04	61.3	45
Chemicals	15	23.6	24.7	27.3
Silk	13	21.4	29.01	24.3
Light industrial goods	28.7	19.3	63.5	28.5
Textiles	42.9	16.4	80.9	21.88
Machinery	11.2	16.2	26.39	21.8
Foodstuffs	27.1	12.9	41.86	15.5
Minerals	13.6	12.5	24.5	15.8
Others	32.7	25.2	44.7	24.5

Note: The amount of goods for export supplied by TVEs does not include those for indirect export. For export products of many State-owned enterprises processed by TVEs, only processing fees were computed.

Table 10-6 Proportion of Goods Delivered for Export by TVEs in the Localities

Area	1990 (%)	1991 (%)
Beijing	24.52	34.43
Tianjin	35.95	44.68
Hebei	27.26	30.43
Liaoning	17.19	21.51
Shanghai	21.24	26.92
Jiangsu	41.57	53.11
Zhejiang	47.11	56.97
Fujian	41.05	52.52
Shandong	28.2	35.31
Guangdong	21.41	23.3
Dalian	9.81	59.49
Qingdao	60.36	70.33

What merits attention is that export goods made by TVEs in those two years occupied more than half of the total exports from Jiangsu, Zhejiang, Fujian, Dalian and Qingdao, and more than a quarter of Shanghai's exports. From 1991 to 1993, the value of goods delivered for export by TVEs increased at an average annual rate of 57.5 billion yuan, 2/3 of the net increase in the annual national export earnings.

(6) Export enterprises spread from south to north and from coastal areas to the hinterland. After 1985, export-oriented TVEs began to grow at a rapid rate in the central and western parts of China.

During this period, border trade also began. Although small in amount, it played an important role in promoting the economy of the border regions. Border trade mainly takes place on the borders of Heilongjiang, Jilin, Liaoning, Yunnan, Guangxi, Xinjiang and Tibet, and with such countries as the Commonwealth of Independent States, Vietnam, Myanmar, Laos, the Democratic People's Republic of Korea, and Nepal. The border trade volume in 1993 increased by 66% from the previous year. Non-coastal provinces and cities also increased their exports to neighboring countries.

TVEs started late in setting up factories abroad. By the end of 1991, there were only 19 TVEs investing abroad — to the tune of US$15.4 million. By the end of 1993, the number of enterprises that launched enterprises abroad reached 450, with a total investment of 400 million yuan.

Table 10-7 Volume of Goods for Export by TVEs in Central and Western China

(Unit: million yuan)

Region	1987	1991	1993
Shanxi	120	380	1060
Inner Mongolia	24	100	159
Jilin	46	240	650
Heilongjiang	74	200	375
Henan	250	1347	3340
Hubei	278	900	2450
Hunan	371	980	2140
Sichuan	410	1120	1690
Guizhou	47	106	148
Yunnan	60	119	220
Shaanxi	36	150	418
Gansu	30	79	160
Qinghai	9	89	138
Ningxia	15	51	96
Xinjiang	8	43	69

3. Upgrading stage (after 1994)

In July 1997, the Third Work Conference on TVE Exports and the Third TVE Export Commodities Fair were held.

Among the 1,000 TVEs cited in 1995, 913 were located in the eastern part of the country, including nearly 200 that had close business relations with the central and western parts of China; 83 were in the central area and four were in the western area. In terms of trade, 214 were in the machinery and electronics industry; 186 were in the garment trade; 182 in textiles, 80 in arts and crafts, 79 in chemicals; and 259 in other sectors.

The development of TVEs during this stage assumed the following characteristics:

(1) Continued high-speed development. In 1996-2000, TVE exports grew at an annual rate of 10%. The total export of textiles and garments by TVEs accounted for 70% of the national total, 15% of the world's total and 35% of the total in Asia.

The value of goods delivered for export by TVEs in 1999 was 774.4 billion yuan, 12.99% more than in 1998, with the proportion of national exports rising from 34.8% in 1998 to 37.8% in 1999.

Table 10-8 Exports by TVEs

	1994	1995	1998	2000
Number of export TVEs	110,913	118,151	123,663	139,549
Number of employees (million)	8.022	10.262	9.535	11.275
Total output value of export goods (billion yuan)	403.21	623.52	773.62	955.26
Value of goods delivered for export (billion yuan)	339.83	539.45	600.79	886.94

(2) Joint ventures and cooperative ventures developed rapidly. The size and volume of investment of wholly foreign-owned, joint-venture and cooperative enterprises used to be very small, with foreign investment ranging from US$100,000-300,000. Now, these enterprises have become much bigger. In Jiangsu Province, the number of foreign-funded enterprises engaging in export production increased by 1,365 in 1995, with foreign investment averaging US$2.01 million per enterprise. In Dalian, the total number of foreign-funded enterprises launched between 1996 and 2000 was 1,364, with total contractual foreign capital reaching US$3.62 billion and the amount actually used reaching US$1.46 billion, averaging US$2.66 million per project. In 1998, the national exports experienced zero growth, but TVEs realized a growth of 2.5%, making their contribution to resisting the Asian financial turmoil.

Table 10-9 Joint Ventures and Cooperative Ventures Funded by Foreign Businesses

	1994	1995	1998	2000
Number of joint ventures and cooperative enterprises added in the year	17,000	16,016	20,937	12,427
Cumulative number of joint ventures and cooperative enterprises put into operation	19,453	28,023	27,658	25,566
Cumulative total of foreign capital used (US$ billion)	15.68	31.8	45.35	50.7
Total export by joint ventures and cooperative enterprises (billion yuan)	67.9	128.5		
% of the total exports contributed by TVEs	20	23.8		
Total profits of joint ventures and cooperative enterprises (billion yuan)			22.81	28.98
Income from processing fees (billion yuan)	34.87	74.64	54.35	39.72

(3) Export scale expanded and export enterprise groups appeared. By 1999, there were 48,000 TVEs whose value of goods delivered for export exceeded one million yuan each and the total value realized reached 650.6 billion yuan, 84% of the total value of TVEs' export volume. In 2000, the average value of goods delivered for export per enterprise reached 6.21 million yuan and 614 TVEs each exported over 10 million US dollars-worth of goods in that year.

Of the 1,000 TVEs whose business revenue exceeded 220 million yuan in 2000, some 780 made export products, and the total business revenue of the first 20 topped 2.5 billion yuan. The Mozhihua Group of Zhejiang earned US$150 million from exports in 2000. There were also more than 100 enterprise groups whose annual export earnings topped US$10 million each, making up over 40% of the total export value produced by TVEs in the province. They included the Hengdian Group, Wanxiang Group, Feiyue Group, Yefeng Group and Shengda Packaging Group.

In terms of gross profit (net profit plus tax payment), an indicator of the performances of enterprises, there were 14 TVEs whose annual gross profits topped 300 million yuan. They included Midea of Guangdong (970 million yuan), Hengdian Group of Zhejiang (679 million yuan), Wanxiang Group of Zhejiang (616 million yuan), Guoping Iron and Steel Company of Hebei (510 million yuan),

Youngor Group Corporation Ltd of Zhejiang (448 million yuan), Longcan Group of Chongqing (328 million yuan) and Yangguang Group of Jiangsu (317 million yuan).

(4) General qualities of TVEs have risen and a number of strong ones have begun to implement the strategy of creating famous brands.

(a) According to data from 10 provinces and cities, including Jiangsu, Beijing, Dalian and Zhejiang, TVEs have recruited 1,135,000 technical personnel, including 748,000 with junior college education and intermediate-level technical personnel.

(b) By virtue of their price advantage, TVEs have shifted to competition in non-price advantage areas, such as brands, product quality, performance, style, packaging, advertising, sales channels, after-sales service, and corporate culture and image.

In the 1990s, TVEs created quite a number of famous brands, such as Rongsheng refrigerators, Kelon air-conditioners, Midea air-conditioners, Galanz microwave ovens, Shinko hi-fi systems, Haitian plastics injectors, Feiyue sewing machines, Longxin motorcycles, Bird mobile phones, Yangguang woolen fabrics, Youngor garments, Trend Western-style clothes, Senda leather shoes and Hongdou shirts. By 2000, the Linghua Group of Shandong Province had acquired 16 State-owned enterprises which were on the verge of bankruptcy, to become the world's No. 4 gourmet powder producer, with an annual output of 120,000 tons. The Yangguang Group of Jiangsu Province devoted 5% of its business revenue to technology development, and imported advanced equipment from Germany and France to produce high-grade woolen fabrics.

(c) Introducing total quality control and building ISO9002 quality certification system. The Changchun Haoyue Halal Meat Company of Jilin Province implemented the health standards of the European Community, and a quality guarantee system that meets the ISO9002/1994 standards. It acquired the British QM certification in December 2000. The company produced 56 kinds of quality beef products in four major series, and exported them to 17 countries in the Middle East, North Africa, Southeast Asia and Europe, realizing a sales revenue of 350 million yuan and earning US$15 million from exports.

(d) First TVE listed on the stock exchange. In 1993, the Midea

Group Company floated its "MD A" stock on the market. This was the first TVE listed on the stock market. From 1998 on, the relevant government departments have urged equal treatment for TVEs and lifted the control over ownership of B shares. Ten TVEs were listed on the stock exchange from May 13 to September 13 1999. They included Shandong Jiangquan Industry Stock Co. Ltd, Zijiang Enterprise Group Co. Ltd, Jiangsu Yangguang Group, Nanshan Industrial Co. Ltd, Shandong Zibo Wanjie Industrial Co. Ltd, Lanzhou Huanghe Enterprise Co. Ltd, Fuxing Science and Technology Co. Ltd, Zhongsheng Pharmaceutical Co. Ltd, Guangdong Kelong Electrical Holding Co. Ltd and Jiangsu Huaxi Group Corporation. By the end of 1999, the number of listed TVEs had reached 40. In July 1996, Guangdong Kelong Electrical Holding Co. Ltd was listed on the Hong Kong stock exchange, and in July 1997 it introduced ration shares, raising HK$1.6 billion.

(e) Export product mix further optimized. In 2000, TVEs exported 12 major categories of goods, and all showed sharp increases, with the export of machinery and electronics products increasing the fastest to reach 17.17%.

Table 10-10 Export Mix of TVEs

Category of products	1994		2000	
	Value of goods delivered (billion yuan)	%	Value of goods delivered (billion yuan)	%
National total	339.8	100	886.94	100
Chemicals	18.65	5.5	44.0	5
Machinery	24.2	7.1	74.36	8.4
Minerals	14.87	4.4	33.2	3.7
Light industrial goods	60.7	17.9	204.35	23.0
Foodstuffs	22.28	6.6	52.85	6
Native produce	5.74	1.7	13.24	1.5
Animal by-products	10.35	3.0	18.9	2.1
Textiles	50.4	14.8	78.79	8.9
Silk fabrics	11.05	3.3	8.55	1.0
Garments	54.9	16.2	130.3	14.7
Arts and crafts	34.8	10.2	73.2	8.3
Others	31.84	9.4	154.80	17.4

The above table shows that exports of deep-processed and high-added-value products such as machine-processed items and light and textile industrial goods increased sharply.

(5) Export channels and ways became diversified. The Asian financial turmoil served as a grave lesson to all economies. After 1995, TVEs began to diversify their export destinations, increasing exports to markets other than in Asia. The proportion of exports from Beijing, Shandong and Guangdong to Japan and Hong Kong dropped from 50% in 1995 to 40% in 2000, while the proportion of exports to Europe rose from 8.5% to 19%. Before the Asian financial crisis, TVEs in Shandong exported only 25% of their products to markets other than in Asia. But the percentage rose to 45% in 2000. The proportion of exports from Zhejiang's TVEs to Southeast Asia dropped from 70% to 37%. The proportion of exports by TVEs in Ningbo to Asia dropped from 70% to 53%, and the proportion of their exports to Europe and the United States rose to 47%. At the same time, Jilin, Heilongjiang, Guangxi and Yunnan provinces expanded border trade, and Zhejiang Province began to implement its "outward-going" strategy. In 2000, some one million people from the province went to border regions and foreign countries to run factories or provide labor services.

Table 10-11 Diversified Exports by TVEs

Item	1994	1995	1999	2000
Direct export volume (billion yuan)	228.39	347.18	612.2	694.9
Export handled by TVEs themselves (billion yuan)	67.9	105.1	274.2	334.4
Number of enterprises empowered to export	250	396	2,500	9,457
Number of enterprises launched abroad	586	673	1,631	1,886
Total volume of investment abroad (US$ billion)	2.564	4.4	8.8	16.5

Section 2 Advantages and Features of the Export-Oriented Economy

The main advantages and features of TVEs in developing foreign economic and technical cooperation and foreign trade are:

1. TVEs have the backing of the abundant cheap labor and bountiful agricultural produce and natural resources of the rural areas. They can build export production and processing bases to ensure a ceaseless supply of export goods.

TVEs export all kinds of products, except those for military use and large complete sets of equipment. The products are available in all grades, including traditional ones and modern manufactured ones. Statistics show that there are more than 1.2 million kinds of commodities worldwide, and Chinese TVEs produce 550,000 kinds.

By the end of 2000, there were 139,549 export production TVEs, with a total employment of 11,275,000. The number of foreign-funded TVEs was 25,566, with a total employment of 3,703,000. The number of enterprises launched by TVEs abroad had reached 1,886, with a total investment of US$16.5 billion.

2. In 1987 the Chinese government approved the establishment of trade-industry-agriculture export production bases, which exhibit the following advantages:

(a) Trade-industry-agriculture export production bases are closely associated with foreign trade companies. As TVEs are not as well informed as foreign trade companies, their association is very favorable for production and trade, and thus is beneficial to both sides.

(b) Trade-industry-agriculture export production bases (trade-industry-stockbreeding, and trade-industry-fisheries) are three-in-one arrangements, with producers, processors and marketers operating in concert to respond to market changes, adjust product mix, improve quality, increase varieties and lower costs.

(c) The general qualities of export TVEs have improved. Cooperation with foreign businesses and foreign trade companies has helped TVEs improve their quality certification system, acquire advanced technical equipment and introduce a high level of management, thus making them quite competitive on the international market and developing toward large export groups.

(d) The production bases have demonstrative and diffusion effects. Many TVEs in the production bases play a flagship role in promoting exports.

(e) The production bases have made it possible to build export enterprises in accordance with the requirements of the market, and motivate localities to develop export-oriented undertakings by making full use of locally available resources.

In a word, the construction of export commodity production bases that combine trade, industry and agriculture has given rise to a number of large and better-performing export-oriented enterprise groups and foreign trade industrial zones.

Table 10-12 Trade-Industry-Agricultural Export Production Bases

Year	Number of enterprises	Total investment (million yuan)	Additional export (US$ million)
1988	213	512.99	551.57
1989	72	96.99	118.71
1990	154	230.20	234.43
1991	122	251.64	225.09
1992	110	234.27	179.17
1993	78	319.85	299.83
1994	82	337.74	220.29
1995	84	542.99	279.92
1996	105	790.83	371.28
1997	115	996.65	437.18
1998	85		
1999	118		
Total	1337	4314.15	2916.77

In the period 1988-1996, there were 1,019 export commodities production bases in the country, with the value of goods delivered for export reaching a total of 80 billion yuan, averaging 78,508,000 yuan per enterprise or 12% of the total export by TVEs. Every 1.5 yuan of input yields one US dollar in earnings.

By the end of 1997, there were five cities whose annual export volume exceeded 13 billion yuan each. They were Panyu in Guangdong Province (13.4 billion yuan), and Wujin (13 billion yuan), Wujiang (13.5 billion yuan), Wuxi (18.1 billion yuan) and Jiangyin (20.7 billion yuan), all in Jiangsu Province. There were also five towns whose annual export volume topped 2 billion yuan each. They were Beijiao in Shunde (2.1 billion yuan), Xiaolan in Zhongshan (2.3 billion yuan) and Chang'an in Dongguan (2.9 billion yuan), all in Guangdong Province, and Shengze in Wujiang (2.1 billion yuan) and Yangshe in Zhangjiagang (4.2 billion yuan), both in Jiangsu Province.

3. TVEs export their products in accordance with market demand and international standards. The operational mechanism of TVEs can well meet the demand of the international market. As they are independent in their operations and have fewer levels of management, TVEs can take quick and flexible decisions in response to the market, and their abundant cheap labor and low production costs make their products highly competitive. Their multifarious products can meet all kinds of demands of different economies. In order to secure a niche in the world market, they uphold the principle of "quality first, reputation first and timely delivery first." A German customer placed an order with a TVE in Shanghai for some blue jeans. He ordered two styles and three specifications for each, but only four to six dozen for each specification, all for delivery within a month. The enterprise accepted the order without a hitch. But the customer demanded modifications to 132 pairs of jeans of two specifications only two days in advance of the delivery time. The factory director immediately put on a night shift to make the modifications. The customer came to accept the goods the following morning, and was amazed to find that everything was ready. He immediately placed another order, worth US$1.03 million.

4. All the workers in TVEs come from the countryside, and 95% of overseas Chinese have their roots in Chinese countryside. This furnishes opportunities for TVEs to forge close relations with overseas Chinese or foreign nationals of Chinese origin. This has made it favorable for TVEs to update their information about the international market — one reason why the TVEs in the coastal areas of Guangdong, Fujian, Zhejiang, Shandong and Dalian have developed so fast.

The processing and compensation trade was started and developed mainly by overseas Chinese or foreign nationals of Chinese origin who came to visit their homeland after China started its reform and opening up policy, some two decades ago.

In 1979, the total fees from processing and compensation trade in the country came to only US$27 million. It rose to US$340 million by 1986, with 82.8% attributable to TVEs. By the end of 1987, the number of TVEs doing processing and compensation trade had reached 13,800. The processing fees earned in the period 1984 to 1987 totaled US$1.03 billion.

Table 10-13 Development of Processing and Compensation Trade

Year	Number of enterprises engaged in processing and compensation trade	Earnings
1984	3,500	US$ 120 million
1987	13,800	US$ 450 million
1990	24,500	8.03 billion yuan
1995	31,800	52.31 billion yuan
2000		39.7 billion yuan

The table shows that processing and compensation trade developed rapidly before 1995. After that, many such enterprises became joint ventures or cooperative enterprises, and some began to export their own products. But the processing and compensation trade made indelible contributions to promoting the development of the export-oriented TVEs.

Table 10-14 Exports by TVEs in 2001

Region	Number of enterprises	Number of people at year-end	Export output value (million yuan, current price)	Value of exported goods (million yuan)	
				Total	Direct export
National total	153,886	12,376,845	1,064,859.12	959,881.05	785,472.11
Beijing	644	112,158	7,375.39	6,309.27	4,433.51
Tianjin	1,331	216,496	16,842.11	17,152.90	11,238.05
Hebei	15,694	488,044	33,055.56	26,429.27	14,865.50
Shanxi	389	77,004	6,356.87	5,625.75	3,816.87

Inner Mongolia	284	33,585	3,453.49	1,631.07	1,010.01
Liaoning	8,642	370,857	46,227.75	36,186.32	26,099.78
Jilin	1,516	33,544	2,020.84	1820.20	900.50
Heilongjiang	161	17,555	1,639.42	942.23	611.61
Shanghai	2,496	363,209	34,395.58	63,261.51	51,757.18
Jiangsu	10,602	1,391,166	149,543.10	145,375.59	115,849.36
Zhejiang	36,428	2,060,895	220,903.68	203,092.89	169,051.10
Anhui	3,804	201,760	9,815.93	8,926.66	4,148.92
Fujian	10,487	1,154,779	106,401.82	97,499.76	97,499.76
Jiangxi	1,965	87,312	4,279.08	3,686.65	1,685.44
Shandong	10,892	1,130,010	106,818.97	8,261.11	58,643.44
Henan	5,646	246,516	14,715.49	10,203.14	4,848.69
Hubei	609	116,926	9,369.25	9,391.08	4,678.04
Hunan	5,733	279,470	17,670.78	16,141.34	6,814.04
Guangdong	30,775	3,615,846	251,653.06	243,018.70	225445.49
Guangxi	3,662	148,648	5,708.07	4,985.07	2,729.05
Hainan	15	825	116.90	78.13	77.13
Chongqing	289	57,829	4,406.19	3,070.13	2,025.34
Sichuan	720	68,176	4,731.94	3,576.03	2,250.62
Guizhou	114	18,122	1,696.94	1,011.95	526.15
Yunnan	93	21,066	1,963.45	1,685.19	1,182.25
Tibet					
Shaanxi	286	29,864	1,445.78	1,191.74	579.66
Gansu	514	18,827	952.53	655.08	311.19
Qinghai	9	3,205	310.09	129.72	125.72
Ningxia	80	8,694	808.89	707.60	604.37
Xinjiang	6	4,457	180.17	180.17	62.66
Separately-listed cities in State plan	14,656	1,887,921	130,801.06	121,817.72	105,202.88
Dalian	1,208	155,594	22,514.31	21,510.51	16,606.03
Qingdao	4,421	175,650	21,712.91	19,600.69	14,701.74
Ningbo	4,412	428,319	52,089.53	48,669.39	43,745.36
Xiamen	449	75,360	7,951.55	7,054.50	7,054.50
Shenzhen	7,161	1,052,514	26,441.46	24,919.52	23,046.04
Xinjiang Construction Corps	5	484	91.30	63.11	49.21
Eastern region	127,991	10,903,460	973,217.02	888,849.85	747,847.99
Central region	20,832	1,186,092	75,005.79	59,224.66	30,633.41
Western region	5,063	287,293	16,636.31	11,806.54	6,990.71

But the foreign trade development of TVEs is uneven among the eastern, central and western regions of the country. In 2001, the value of goods delivered for export by TVEs in the eastern region accounted for 92.6%, while that of the central region accounted for only 6.2%, and that of western region accounted for a mere 1.2%.

Table 10-15 Joint Ventures and Cooperative Enterprises Launched by TVEs

Region	Number of enterprises	Average number of people per year	Added value (million yuan)	Business income (million yuan)	Total profit (million yuan)	Tax payable (million yuan)
National total	26,147	3,936,471	147,075.58	608,350.42	33,709.33	20,312.20
Beijing	569	57,963	1,569.79	7,597.48	336.96	303.68
Tianjin	372	69,992	3,621.13	10,003.06	1,305.72	952.03
Hebei	719	120,220	4,359.49	15,768.61	1,436.69	522.86
Shanxi	62	18,074	639.67	2,474.32	138.23	161.53
Inner Mongolia	24	4,812	190.59	604.59	52.78	26.88
Liaoning	1,504	106,704	3,789.96	17,350.47	1,027.05	553.94
Jilin	48	3,657	161.90	566.64	79.60	51.40
Heilongjiang	44	6,158	278.65	917.21	49.78	28.11
Shanghai	2,629	337,469	18,971.84	85,183.26	4,700.68	2,254.91
Jiangsu	4,194	556,706	24,752.66	101,932.48	4,790.13	3,921.42
Zhejiang	4,003	576,505	22,637.89	103,379.67	6,831.10	4,345.49
Anhui	136	27,454	623.49	2,195.03	115.34	114.45
Fujian	1,893	270,516	8,369.97	32,129.86	1,725.37	874.19
Jiangxi	112	11,803	436.11	1,670.82	119.25	40.20
Shandong	2,822	452,053	16,891.87	59,089.59	4,670.53	2,175.41
Henan	179	31,421	1,671.53	8,784.52	336.16	132.59
Hubei	155	41,532	1,783.32	8,805.13	280.83	245.86
Hunan	192	16,818	459.71	1,611.80	120.17	61.89
Guangdong	6,195	1,180,151	33,700.64	136,140.14	5,108.67	3,073.13
Guangxi	49	11,193	234.64	976.21	81.31	57.55
Hainan	5	79	0.75	2.85	0.34	0.08
Chongqing	29	5,704	402.15	1,852.20	92.35	82.47
Sichuan	118	17,527	1,087.59	3,973.39	193.39	237.86

Guizhou	16	1,868	58.62	173.02	12.17	5.41
Yunnan	23	2,444	123.24	759.39	42.02	29.23
Tibet						
Shaanxi	26	2,464	105.21	440.44	12.47	25.13
Gansu	12	3,656	84.49	335.15	21.81	20.24
Qinghai	2	207	0.80	4.00	0.03	0.24
Ningxia	10	581	43.94	173.91	9.14	11.43
Xinjiang	5	740	23.94	155.18	19.26	2.59
Separately-listed cities in State plan	4,370	530,040	15,073.63	63,499.02	4,597.35	2,598.67
Dalian	1,068	58,482	2,251.06	9,699.72	586.08	295.66
Qingdao	946	115,660	2,757.95	10,920.34	563.37	450.21
Ningbo	1,483	175,191	6,714.60	32,216.71	2,675.35	1,487.65
Xiamen	4	573	20.38	322.74	3.71	10.38
Shenzhen	869	180,134	3,329.64	10,339.51	768.84	354.77
Xinjiang Construction Corps						
Eastern region	24,900	3,728,279	138,665.24	575,874.62	31,932.90	18,977.06
Central region	1,075	180,148	7,544.12	28,851.06	1,525.10	1,156.36
Western region	172	28,044	866.22	3,624.74	251.33	178.78

In terms of added value created by joint ventures and cooperative enterprises set up between TVEs and foreign enterprises in 2001, Guangdong ranked first with 33.7 billion yuan, Jiangsu, second, with 24.7 billion yuan, Zhejiang, third, with 22.6 billion yuan, Shanghai, fourth, with 18.9 billion yuan, and Shandong, fifth, with 16.8 billion yuan.

Great changes have taken place in recent years in the export product mix of TVEs. The proportion of garments, textiles and foodstuffs has dropped, and that of light industrial goods and chemicals and machinery has risen. The leading export products of TVEs are light industrial goods. In 2001, the value of light industrial goods delivered for export was 241.5 billion yuan. This was followed by garments (141.9 billion yuan), chemicals and machinery (126.4 billion yuan), textiles (83.6 billion yuan), arts and crafts (72.8

billion yuan), foodstuffs (54.5 billion yuan), mineral products (38.1 billion yuan) and others (201.1 billion yuan).

Table 10-16 TVE Export Product Mix and Delivery Values in 1997-2001

	1997 (%)	2001 (%)
Light industrial goods	21.1	25.1
Garments	16.3	14.8
Textiles	12.5	8.7
Chemicals and machinery	12.6	13.2
Foodstuffs	8.8	5.7
Arts and crafts	8.7	7.6
Minerals	3.9	3.9
Others	16.1	21.0

References

The sources of the data in the charts and tables are:

1. *China Yearbook of Foreign Economic Relations and Trade*, 1991, p.644

2. China Foreign Economic Relations and Trade Press: *TVEs Go International*, 1991

3. International Business Department, Agricultural Bank of China: Information provided for 1992 training class (Haikou) of the Asian Development Bank

(1) International Economic Situation and China's Exports in 1990s

(2) TVEs in China today, problems and prospects

4. *A Strategy for Checking Rural Poverty*, UN Asian-Pacific Economic-Social Conference 1990, Bangkok (English edition)

5. The China-Japan Friendship Association: *TVEs Constitute a Primary Force for the Reinvigoration of China's Rural Economy,* Documents of the 1993 Forum on Comparisons between the Chinese and Japanese Local Economies

6. China Society of Industrial Economy (1991): *The Idea of Increasing the International Competitive Power of Large Enterprises, in View of the Development of Export-Oriented TVEs,* a document of the 1991 Forum on the International Competitive Power of Large Enterprises

7. The foreign trade section in *China TVE Yearbook* 1988, 1989, 1990, 1991, 1992, 1993, 1994, 1995, 1996, 1997, 1998, 1999

Chapter XI

TVEs: Historical Mission and Prospects

Innovation is the soul of a nation. The rise and development of TVEs is a great creation by the people of China's rural areas under the guidance of the policy of reform and opening up and a great event toward the end of the 20th century that has had a huge impact on the economic and social development of China as a whole. The Chinese central authorities make this judgment on TVEs: "A leading force that has propelled China's market economy forward, a vital pillar of the rural economy and an important component of the national economy." As early as in the 1960s, Mao Zedong regarded the enterprises run by communes and production brigades, the forerunners of TVEs, as "where the bright and splendid hopes lie." In the 1980s, Deng Xiaoping described the rise of TVEs as "a new force suddenly coming to the fore." In the 1990s, Jiang Zemin said that "development of TVEs is a major strategy, a fundamental principle of long-term importance and a road to industrialization with Chinese characteristics." This is the latest appraisal and summation of TVEs.[1]

Section 1 Historical Role of TVEs

The course of development of TVEs shows that they have had a tremendous impact on the rural areas and on the whole national economic and social development.

---

[1] Guo Shutian, "WTO and TVEs," *TVEs News*, Issue No. 7, 2001

First, they have played a major role in the high-speed growth of the national economy.

Figure 11-1 Added Value of TVEs and National GDP Growth

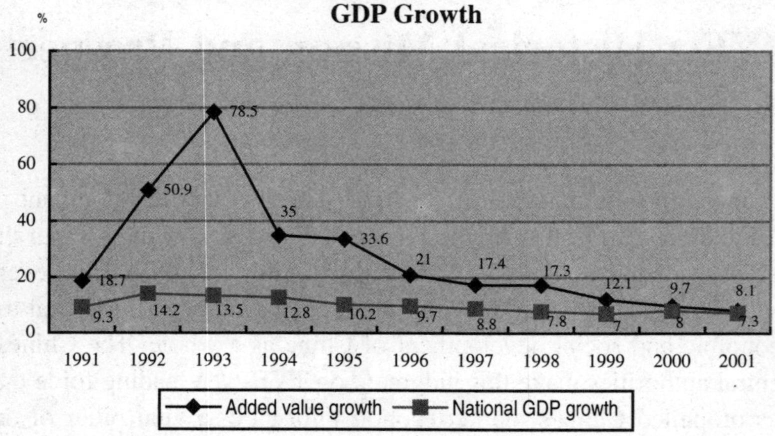

Sources: *China TVE Yearbook,* 2001 and *China Statistical Yearbook,* 2001

The graph shows that figures for all the years, except those for 1992 and 1993 which were unable to be verified and corrected due to some abnormal factors, reflect the correlation between the growth speed of added value of TVEs and China's GDP growth. Despite the fact that the growth since 1994 has dropped year by year, the added value of TVEs in 2001 was still 2,935.6 billion yuan, 8.1% more than in the previous year.[1] And it was still higher than the 7.3% growth of the national economy. So it is safe to say that China's high rate of economic growth would have been impossible without high TVE growth.

Second, after 1994, the growth of added value of TVEs dropped year by year, but the absolute value rose year by year, still occupying a big proportion of the GDP.

---

[1] Qi Jingfa, "Processing of Agricultural Produce Will Be the Main Thrust of Efforts by TVEs," *Peasants' Daily*, April 14, 2002, P.1

The added value of TVEs in 2000 reached 2,715.6 billion yuan, 10.8 times more than in 1990 or 64% of the total rural added value created, or 30.4% of the national GDP. This indicates the significant position of TVEs in the rural areas and in the nation as a whole.

Figure 11-2 Added Value of TVEs

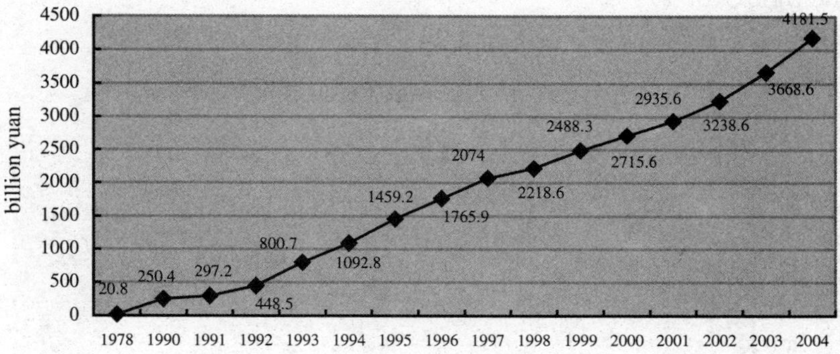

Sources: *China TVE Yearbook,* 2004 and *China Statistical Yearbook,* 2004

Third, the fixed assets of TVEs have risen year by year, indicating the scale and strength of the non-agricultural sector of the rural economy.

Figure 11-3 Fixed Assets of TVEs

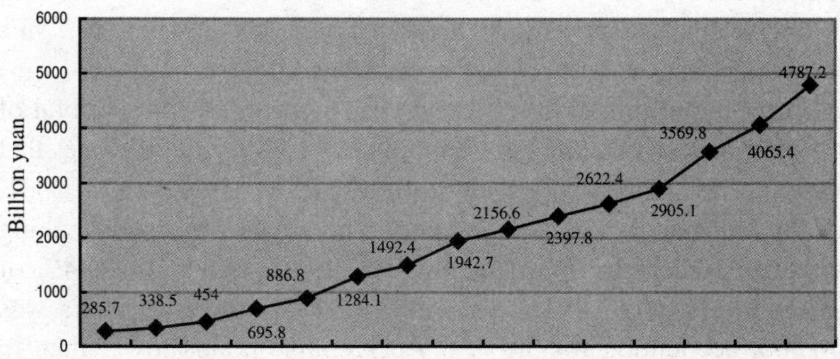

Sources: *China TVE Yearbook,* 2004 and *China Statistical Yearbook,* 2004

The total fixed assets of TVEs in 2000 reached 2,622.4 billion yuan, 9.2 times that of 1990 or 9.37% more than in 1999, quite in step with the growth of added value.

Fourth, TVEs mainly relied on their own accumulation for development, and their floating assets rose year by year to reach 2,395.3 billion yuan by 2000, 6.5% more than in 1999 or 9.1 times the figure for 1990.

Figure 11-4 Current Assets of TVEs

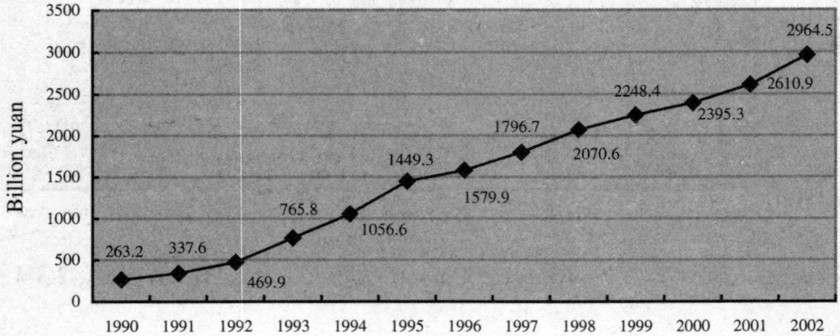

Sources: *China TVE Yearbook,* 2002 and *China Statistical Yearbook,* 2002

The balance of bank loans granted to TVEs in 2000 was 628.2 billion yuan, 600 million less than in 1999. But the added value of TVEs accounted for 30% of the GDP, while their loans accounted for only 6%. This shows that the high-speed development of TVEs was realized on the basis of self-accumulated funds.

Fifth, the profits of TVEs grew year by year, reaching a total of 648.2 billion yuan in 2000, 8.3% more than in 1999 and 9.5 times that in 1990. They generated a total profit of 670.9 billion yuan in 2001, 3.5% more than in the previous year. The number of profit-making enterprises reached 20.1 million in 2000, accounting for 96.4% of the total number of TVEs. The number of loss-making TVEs was 750,000, accounting for 3.6%, 6.5 percentage points lower than in 1999, and the total losses came to 84.1 billion yuan, 26% less than in 1999.

Figure 11-5 Profits of TVEs

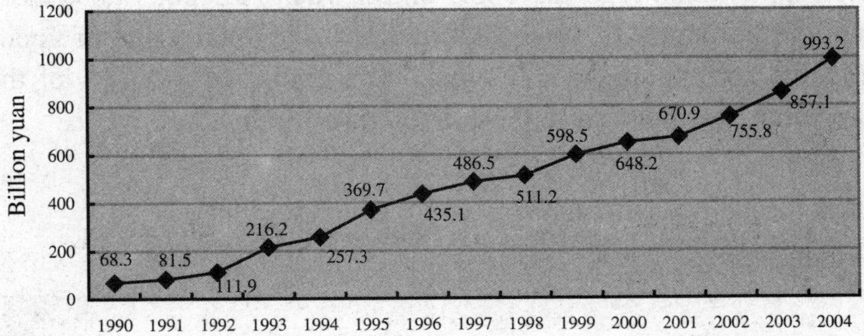

Sources: *China TVE Yearbook,* 2004 and *China Statistical Yearbook,* 2004

The total payroll of TVEs in 2000 was 706 billion yuan, 7% more than in 1999 and averaging 5,508 yuan per worker. This is fairly low compared with that of State-owned enterprises. That is why the cost of TVEs is low. The per capita wage in State-owned enterprises was 9,552 yuan in 2000, 35.3% more than in TVEs. The income derived by rural workers from TVEs in 2000 was 760 yuan per capita, 33.7% of the per capita net income of rural people as a whole.

Sixth, the total tax payment by TVEs also rose year by year, reaching 199.6 billion yuan in 2000, 11.57% more than in 1999 and accounting for 15.8% of the national total.

Figure 11-6 Total Tax Paid by TVEs

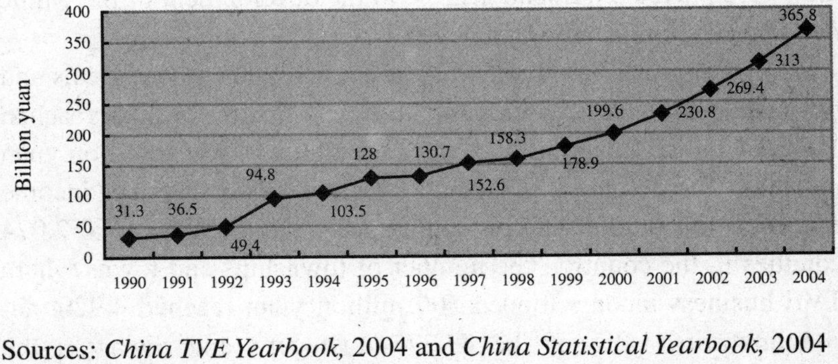

Sources: *China TVE Yearbook,* 2004 and *China Statistical Yearbook,* 2004

Seventh, the total value of goods delivered for export by TVEs rose year by year, reaching 886.9 billion yuan in 2000, 14.5% more than in 1999 and 18.2 times that of 1990. The total value of goods delivered for export by TVEs in 2000 accounted for 33.7% of the total value of exports from the country as a whole.

Figure 11-7 Value of Goods Delivered for Export by TVEs

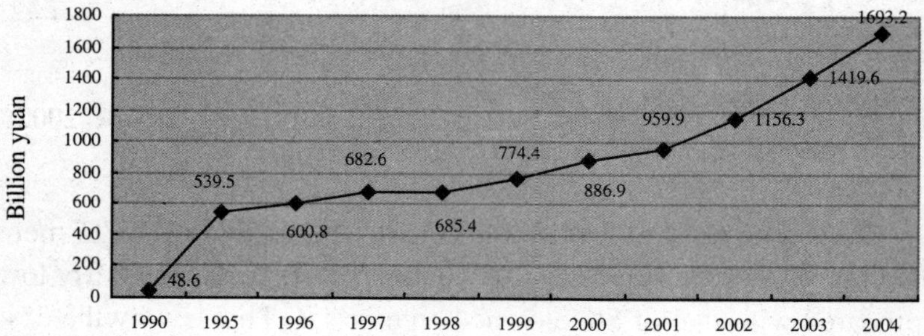

Sources: *China TVE Yearbook,* 2004 and *China Statistical Yearbook,* 2004

All the above show that TVEs developed from small to big, from grassroots enterprises to modern undertakings, exhibiting strong vitality. They have not only absorbed a large amount of surplus rural labor and increased the incomes of rural families, they have also made great contributions to promoting the modernization of agriculture and the development of welfare undertakings in the rural areas. In short, they have played a tremendous role in the development of the whole national economic and social development.

TVEs are distributed at two levels in the countryside: towns and townships, and villages. Their total business income in 2000 reached 10,783.4 billion yuan, or 12.5 times the figure of 861.4 billion yuan in 1990. There were 1,614 counties whose TVE business income exceeded one billion yuan, accounting for 77.8% of the total 2,074 counties in the country. The number of townships and towns where TVE business income topped 500 million yuan reached 4,920, accounting for 11.2% of the 43,275 townships and towns in the country. The number of villages where TVE business income topped 100 million yuan reached 9,101, accounting for 1.2% of the 740,000 administrative villages in the country. The number of enterprises whose business income exceeded one million yuan was 53,178, accounting for 0.26% of the total number of 20.847 million TVEs, but their combined business income reached 2,556 billion yuan, accounting for 23.7% of the total business income of 10,783.4 billion yuan of the TVEs. The number of enterprises whose business income topped 100 million yuan reached 4,121 and their business income topped 1,020.6 billion yuan, accounting for 9.5% of the total business income of TVEs. The 100-million-yuan villages and 100-million-yuan TVEs are the backbone force of the rural areas. Many of them have been listed on the stock exchange and have attained an international standing. It is incorrect to say that all TVEs are small and medium-sized enterprises. The Wanxiang Group, headed by peasant entrepreneur Lu Guanqiu, boasts total assets of six billion yuan, and it has acquired part of the equities of the US Ford and GM automobile companies. This is a new bright spot in the rural economy, and also the hope for the future of the Chinese rural economy. These 100-million-yuan villages and enterprises assume the following 10 features:

(1) The proportion of the output value of agriculture and agricultural labor in the whole of the rural economy has dropped to less than 10%, and labor in non-agricultural activities (including workers leaving the land but not their native place and those leaving both the land and their native place) rose to over 90%, basically the same as in developed countries. Even in places where land is scanty on a per capita basis and population density is high, they have realized full employment of local agricultural labor, and in addition absorbed a large amount of agricultural labor from elsewhere. In some villages, labor from elsewhere outnumbers local labor by seven or even a dozen times.

(2) With the drop in the proportion of agriculture (to less than 2%), TVEs spend more money on building high-standard irrigation and other water projects, buying modern farm equipment and strengthening social services to agriculture, thus giving a big boost

to the modernization of agriculture in their localities. The technical level of agriculture in the localities, the technical content of agricultural products and labor productivity of agriculture are all very high. Their products are very competitive on the world market. The income of people engaged in agriculture is higher than those engaged in business. This shows that the status of agriculture as the foundation of the economy can be realized only by developing TVEs.

(3) TVEs invest or import outside capital in building enterprises to process farm, animal and aquatic products and streamline production, processing and marketing. They have formed specialized cooperative organizations (associations or cooperatives), such as company + cooperatives + farming households to provide services in the entire process of production and in the process of converting primary products to end-products and, through the secondary distribution, return part of the profits to agriculture so as to increase income of farmers and help them resist natural adversities and market risks. The flagship enterprises have become bridges between petty farming and large markets.

(4) With the support and assistance of TVEs, rural communities have realized all-round social development in culture, education, medical and health services, and other welfare undertakings. Children in these places receive free education from kindergarten to senior high school, and those who are admitted to universities can get local scholarships. Medical services are partly or entirely free. All these communities have set up public funds to cover major medical expenses. Old people get pensions or live in homes (apartments) for the aged. There are also village TV stations and village newspapers, and entertainment and sports centers. In such respects, there is virtually no difference between these communities and the cities.

(5) The level of material and cultural consumption of the people in the areas where TVEs have been set up is high. The per capita living area is larger than in the cities, and the housing quality is not inferior either. Average incomes are higher than those for city dwellers, and the Engel coefficient is close to or even lower than that in the cities. Illiteracy has been eliminated basically and people's awareness of the importance of law and science has been enhanced. The

development of eco-agriculture and eco-homes has made great improvements to the village environment.

(6) These villages enjoy improved social security. Criminal cases are few and far between. Family planning has become the conscious action of villagers. All the families live in harmony. Disputes are settled by people's organizations. All the contradictions in the communities are nipped in the bud. The whole atmosphere gives the impression of a "peaceful world."

(7) All the villages have introduced villagers' autonomy and grassroots democracy. The roles of villagers' self-government organizations have been given full scope to ensure democratic election, democratic policy decision making, democratic supervision and democratic management, so as to make the villagers feel that they are the true masters of the country. The autonomous organizations handle village affairs in an open fashion, especially administrative and accounting affairs. The peasants have changed their status from one of being governed to one of "self-government." Village party branches, villagers' committees and economic organizations have fewer but better staff members, and their work efficiency is high.

(8) The development of village economies has not only provided superior farm produce for the market, but also more deposits in banks and more taxes for the State.

(9) Local peasants are free from all social burdens, as such burdens are all taken care of by the village administrations. The grassroots cadres wholeheartedly serve the local people, thus resulting in a good relationship between the local people and the former.

(10) The villages with TVEs have brought forth a large number of grassroots cadres and a contingent of entrepreneurs. They come from among the peasants and thus cherish profound feelings for them. They implement the State policies and principles in the light of local conditions, and serve the people heart and soul. These villages and their enterprises boast a large number of well-educated technical personnel and managers, as well as peasants-turned entrepreneurs. The workers and staff members of TVEs are young, with those below 35 accounting for 65%, eight percentage points higher than in State-owned enterprises, those in the 36-50 age bracket ac-

counting for 29.6%, and those above 51 accounting for 5.4%.

Longshan Village in Dantu County, near Zhenjiang City in Jiangsu Province has a population of 1,000. It used to be a poor village. Its per capita annual income in 1986 was only 260 yuan. Later, the village began to breed eels, and exported them to Japan. In the 10 years up to 1996, the village earned 4.5 billion yuan and US$450 million in foreign exchange, averaging 5,000 yuan per person a year. But the market has not been good in recent years, and their business income has dropped to a certain extent. The village has opened up new avenues of income. Its 2001 business income still reached 1.2 billion yuan, averaging 7,000 yuan per person. The village has a golf course and an international conference center, and has become a tourist attraction.

Qizhong Village on the outskirts of Shanghai has more than 1,000 people. By developing sideline production and industry, the village raked in 1.3 billion yuan in business income in 2001. It has become a retreat for Shanghai residents.

Other villages that have become nationally known for their wealth include Wanfeng in Shenzhen, Guangdong; Huaxi in Jiangyin, Jiangsu; Nanjie in Linpin, Henan; Hancunhe in Beijing; Jianchangying in Chifeng, Inner Mongolia; and Hongzuizi in Siping, Jilin Province.

In 2001, there were nearly 10,000 villages with an annual income of more than 100 million yuan each. All these villages have realized rural industrialization, urbanization and modernization by developing TVEs. This is the fundamental way for peasants to get wealthy and the hope for the future of Chinese rural areas.

Here, it may be interesting to present a case study concerning Zhejiang. It is known to all that Zhejiang is small in land area but large in population. Before the introduction of the reform and opening-up policies under the policy of taking the food grain as the key link, Zhejiang, with the least land per capita, had the highest multi-crop index of 300% (three crops a year, with two rice crops and one wheat crop) and the highest unit grain output of 6,000 kg per hectare (the first to attain the target set in the "Agricultural Development Program"). Yet the farmers were still poor.

But in the course of the reform and opening-up, TVEs developed very rapidly, bringing about a fundamental change in the outlook of agriculture and the rural areas.

(1) The total added value of Zhejiang's TVEs reached 69.5 billion yuan in 1995, placing the province behind only Guangdong, Shandong and Jiangsu. This figure reached 160.6 billion yuan to outstrip Guangdong in 1996. The following year, it reached 191.6 billion yuan, overtaking Shandong; and it reached 211.8 billion yuan in 1998, throwing Jiangsu behind, to rank first in the country. Zhejiang maintained its lead in 1999, with 244.2 billion yuan, and in 2000, with 283.9 billion yuan, up 15.2% and 16.2% than the previous year, and higher than the national average by 3.1 and 6.5 percentage points, respectively.

(2) The per capita net income of Zhejiang's peasants in 2000 was 4,254 yuan, 7.8% more than in the preceding year and 5.7 percentage points higher than the national average increase of 2.1%. The income of TVEs accounted for 50% of the per capita net income of rural dwellers, 17 percentage points higher than the national average.

(3) TVE industries made up 4/5 of the industries in the whole province and contributed 2/3 of the local revenue, all far higher than the national average.

(4) The labor force of TVEs made up over 40% of the total rural labor, 13 percentage points higher than the national figure. Some 17% of the total arable land in the province was tilled by specialized households. There were more than 300 specialized industrial belts each covering at least 667 hectares. Specialized grain-growing households fulfilled 80% of the grain purchasing tasks of the province. In 2000, the province exported US$2.4 billion-worth of agricultural products, 42.6% more than in the previous year.

(5) Some 98% of collective TVEs completed the conversion into joint stock companies, succeeded in separating government administration from enterprise management, and solved the problems of unclear delineation of property rights and inflexibility of operational mechanisms. They have become truly independent market players, developing toward large grouping, high technology and export-oriented operations. The added value created by private

businesses in 2000 made up over 80% of total TVE added value.

(6) The province has experienced a big migration of rural labor. More than three million rural laborers are active in other places, including some one million participating in the development of the western part of the country. About one million are working abroad. The urbanization rate reached 48.7% in 2000, 12.7 percentage points higher than in the country as a whole.

(7) There were 4,400 specialized markets, with a transaction volume reaching nearly 400 billion yuan in 2000. They include three whose annual transactions have reached 10 billion yuan-worth and more than 70 whose annual transactions have reached one billion yuan-worth.

(8) While maintaining the collective ownership of land and the land contracts by peasants remaining unchanged, the province has set up a land-use turnover mechanism. It has set up more than 5,000 specialized cooperatives to serve as a bridge between flagship enterprises and rural households. Some new cooperative financial organizations have appeared. The local governments have made great progress in shifting their functions to meet the requirements of market development.[1]

Section 2 Stern Situation Confronted by TVEs

Over the past 20 years, TVEs have made achievements that have attracted worldwide attention. But there are also many practical difficulties and problems. They are facing a stern situation since China became a WTO member.

[1] Gu Yikang: "An Analysis of the Peasants' Income Growth Features and Mechanism in Zhejiang Province;" *An Analysis and Forecast of the Rural Economic Situation in China*, 2000-2001. "How Does Zhejiang Develop County Town Economy," *Economic Daily*, January 4, 2002, P. 7

1. Development speed drops after 1994. The development speed of TVEs dropped to 12.1% in 1999, down to 9.7% in 2000, and further to 8% in 2001. Although still higher than country's overall GDP growth, the speed dropped below 10% for the first time since the inception of TVEs. This slowdown has a direct bearing on the transfer of surplus rural labor. In 1996, the total employment by TVEs was 135 million. But it had dropped to 125 million by 1998. This has brought about a new backflow of rural labor in recent years, and that has directly affected the income of peasants. In 1999, it rose to 127 million, and to 129 million by 2000. But still it did not reach the historical high. That has affected not only the income of peasants but also the relations between town and country. The income gap between urban and rural residents in 2000 was 2.68:1, outstripping the level before 1978, when reform and opening-up began, with the Gini coefficient being as high as 0.42, thus threatening social stability.

2. Unfavorable external environment slows TVE development. In addition to the elimination of heavily polluting enterprises, some of taxation and credit policies in favor of TVEs have been scrapped; the burdens on TVEs have increased and their economic performances have therefore dropped. Since 1995, decreases have been recorded in all the economic indices, such as profitability on business income, profitability on investment, turnover of working capital, capital gains and gains on total assets. In 1992-1997, the funds raised by TVEs rose from 33.1% to 42.7%. In 2000, capital flow was clogged, with finished products occupying 210.3 billion yuan of funds, accounting for 15.4% of the floating assets. Accounts receivable came to 585.1 billion yuan, accounting for 42.6%. The total of the above two items added up to 795.4 billion yuan, accounting for 58% of the floating assets. This shows that stockpiling of products and inability to recover loans have become bottlenecks in TVE development.

3. Government departments at five levels collect more than 1,000 kinds of fees from TVEs, with 100 collected nationwide. The total fees to be paid by TVEs account for 20% of their profits or 3-5% of their sales revenue. That is too much to bear. It is necessary to go through more than a dozen departments and more than 20 procedures and at least three months to get a new TVE started. These heavy burdens hamper the normal development of TVEs, and so it is urgent for the government to push ahead with reform of the political structure. The superstructure formed under the planned economy has in many ways been unable to promote, or even hinders, the normal operation of the market economy.

4. The inherent drawbacks of TVEs are also quite outstanding. TVEs are small in scale and widely scattered. There were 20.04 million TVEs in the country in 1998, averaging 141 per township. They included 1.065 million collective enterprises, accounting for 5.3%, and 18.975 million private businesses, accounting for 94.7%. The added value of collective enterprises made up 44.9% while private businesses, 55.1%. The value created by the non-public sectors is more than that created by the public sector. This is a major change. Collective enterprises are larger, with each one possessing fixed assets worth 1.261 million yuan on average. They each created 935,000 yuan of added value in 1998, and employed an average of 42.3 people. In the same year, each private business had fixed assets worth 44,000 yuan, created 65,000 yuan of added value and employed an average of 4.1 people. They are mostly family businesses, but their economic performances are better than those of the collective ones. In 2000, the original value of fixed assets of each TVE was 120,000 yuan, while that of private enterprises was only 35,000 yuan. Due to their small size, they can not withstand market risks, and lack the ability to embrace technical innovation and competitiveness. Since the early 1990s, private businesses began to develop in the direction of joint stock cooperatives, while collective ones began to sell small enterprises operating at thin profits or in the red, and move to a joint stock system, so as to enable managers to have greater autonomy. By 2000, more than 90% of collective TVEs had been converted into joint stock companies. But due to imperfect internal governance structure, some new problems cropped up, and the problem of non-separation of administration from enterprise management was left unresolved.

5. The difference between TVEs in the eastern region and the central and western parts of the country grew. In 2000, the business income of TVEs in the eastern region grew 12.08% while that in the central and western regions dropped by 0.52%. The added value of TVEs in the eastern area grew by 11.45%, but that in the central and western regions increased by only 5.76%. The proportion of business income of TVEs in the eastern region in the national total rose from 58% in 1999 to 70.5% in 2000, while that in the central and western regions dropped from 42% to 29.5%. In 2000, the total investment in fixed assets in the eastern area was 1.3 times that in the central and western areas, and the total export deliveries by the eastern TVEs were 11.3 times that of the other two areas.

6. Irrational industrial structure of TVEs. In 2000, the proportion of primary industry among TVEs was 1.16%, that of the secondary industry, 77.01%, and that of tertiary industry, 21.83%. This is virtually an economic structure with industry as the mainstay and underdeveloped tertiary industry. The industrial added value of TVEs in the same year was 1881.2 billion yuan, accounting for 47.3% of the national total. The added value of the construction trade was 210.1 billion yuan, accounting for 35.3% of the national total. The added value of communications and transportation was 165.8 billion yuan, accounting for 33.7% of the national total. That of commerce and catering came to 391.5 billion yuan, 53.6% of the national total. In terms of investment structure, the proportion of secondary industry was 84.05%, and that of the tertiary industry was only 12.6%. In terms of sources of investment, bank loans made up 16.3%; funds raised by TVEs accounted for 52.6%; and State grants formed only 1.34%.

7. General quality of TVEs low. Among TVE workers in 2000, those with university and junior college degrees made up 2.7% of the total; those with a secondary vocational education made up 11.4%; and those with a senior secondary general education and below made up 85.9%. Technicians with professional technical titles of middle rank and above made up 2.7% and those with elementary professional technical titles made up 6%. A considerable part of small TVEs have a low management level, backward technical equipment, low product quality, and accidents are frequent. All these factors damage their competitiveness.

Section 3 Starting Anew

China is now a WTO member, and that has made it inevitable for the Chinese economy to become part of the world economy. This represents China's most extensive and most comprehensive opening-up in history. TVEs are sure to appear on the world arena with a renewed image and renew their former glory. In 2000, TVEs delivered 320.8 billion yuan-worth of goods for export to foreign trade companies, and handled 334.4 billion yuan-worth of exports by themselves. Labor-intensive export products, such as light industrial goods, garments and textiles, made up 48.7% of the total exports by TVEs. A total of 9,457 TVEs had been empowered to handle their own exports, realizing 225.1 billion yuan of export earnings in 2000. TVEs had launched 1,886 enterprises abroad, with a total investment of 16.5 billion yuan. The number of equity and cooperative joint ventures launched with foreign investors had reached 26,000, with a total investment of US$47.3 billion, including US$30.7 billion from foreign investors.

It is predictable that the country's rural economy (including the primary, secondary and tertiary industries) is bound to occupy a very important position in the total value and added value of China's economy, and that the TVEs (mainly in the secondary and tertiary industries) are bound to occupy a major position in China's rural economy. The country's agriculture and TVEs are expected to shoulder an arduous task as China's economy reaches out to the rest of the world.

China's accession to the WTO has presented both opportunities and challenges to TVEs. It is necessary for TVEs to start anew by integrating their development with the national economy and keeping in step with the development of agriculture.

1. China's accession to the WTO has put TVEs in an unfavorable position. As the development of TVEs directly affects the migration of surplus rural labor and the scale of agricultural operations and the level of agricultural modernization, China's WTO membership has put China's agriculture in an even worse position, as here agriculture itself is small in operational scale, low in labor productivity and technical content, and inferior in product quality. These, plus the poor ecological environment, have deprived agriculture of its competitiveness. Plus the technical barriers imposed by some other countries, these factors will inevitably have an adverse impact on the development of China's agriculture and the rural economy as a whole. If we fail to adopt effective measures to eliminate these unfavorable factors, China's accession to the WTO will turn out to be more harmful than good.

2. There is no choice but to face up to the difficulties and take up challenges, trying to reverse the disadvantages. One the one hand, China should, together with other developing countries, strive to formulate rules in favor of developing countries and adjusting the existing ones according to the principle of reciprocity in rights and obligations. Then, the country should make full use of the WTO "green box policies" to protect agriculture and the interests of grain growers. On the other hand, China should persist in the principle of fairness in bilateral and multilateral negotiations, and fight against discriminatory treatment. In this sense, China and other developing countries should wage a common struggle against "economic colonialism," oppose the dumping of their surplus products and their policies of using "technical barriers" to restrict China's exports. At home, it is necessary to persist in the principle of making agriculture the foundation of the economy, and put in first place the task of developing agriculture and increasing the income of peasants. This two-pronged approach should be the fundamental principle to be adhered to following China's accession to the WTO.

3. Overhauling the policies toward agriculture and the rural economy, and adjusting the structure of the distribution of national income. Governments at all levels should remain firm in making agriculture the foundation of the national economy. This requires the adoption of the following measures:

(1) Make greater efforts to develop TVEs in the course of implementing the strategic adjustment of agriculture and the rural economic structure, and take further steps toward rural industrialization, urbanization and agricultural modernization. It is necessary to develop the

secondary and tertiary industries to absorb surplus rural labor, so as to prepare conditions for an appropriate scale of agricultural operation and accelerate the pace of agricultural modernization.

(2) Promote the industrialized operation of agriculture while developing TVEs. It is necessary to raise the rate of processed agricultural products, increase the amount of labor in the processing businesses, and streamline production, processing and marketing. It is also necessary to shift the focus of production from primary products to end products, and from meeting the domestic market demand to meeting the demand of both the domestic and international markets.

(3) Increase the concentration of TVEs by building small new-type towns (including county towns, townships and central villages) to stimulate the development of tertiary industry that serves the production and well-being of the rural population. At present, the proportion of tertiary industry is too small, as is that of the processing sector. Therefore, TVE development should focus on agricultural processing, including food processing, fiber processing and the pharmaceuticals industry.

(4) Realize the reorganization and optimal reallocation of the factors of production under the condition of clearly defined property rights through the conversion of TVEs into joint stock cooperatives or joint stock companies. This is aimed at expanding their operational scale and raising the cluster and scale effect. At the same time, it is necessary to properly handle the relations among owners, managers and workers, and protect the interests of managers, strengthen the internal governance structure and improve the operational mechanism, so as to raise the general qualities of enterprises.

(5) Solve the household registration problems for rural people looking for jobs in cities. After rural migrants become city residents, they should be treated the same as regular city residents in social security and other areas, and all discriminatory regulations in this regard should be scrapped. Whether or not rural people working in cities and small towns give up the land they have contracted should be left up to them.

(6) Encourage rural migrants working in cities to transfer land

they have contracted to others. That means the secondary separation of management right from land-use right and ownership, with the rents on the land-use rights to be turned into stock capital.

(7) Display regional resources advantages, and promote TVE development in the central and western parts of the country. The ratios of added value of TVEs in the eastern, central and western parts of the country in 1995 were 66.8%, 29.5% and 3.7%, respectively. But they rose to 67.9%, 28.5% and 3.6%, respectively, in 1999, which reveals the disparities in TVE scale, market environment, resources conditions and business management level. That means that the central and western parts of the country need more government support, especially policy support. In the great drive to develop the western region, it is necessary to persist in the foundation status of agriculture while developing TVEs.

(8) Strengthen government support for TVEs in fiscal, loan and taxation policies, and in reducing their burdens. The government should treat TVEs and State-owned enterprises equally regarding policy-based loans, and should implement an equitable policy toward private businesses in the areas of public finance, national treatment and market access. The government should shed their functions of managing enterprises, and exempt TVEs from all kinds of fees in addition to tax breaks, in order to really reduce the burdens on them. This calls for positive efforts to push political reforms, including that of the administration of towns and townships.

(9) Implement in earnest the strategy of reinvigorating the nation by relying on the development of education and science and technology, and bring the development of agriculture and TVEs onto the path of technical progress and improving the general qualities of workers. On the one hand, TVEs should strengthen alliance and cooperation with universities, colleges and research institutions in raising the rate of application of appropriate research achievements and the technical contents of products to enhance market competitiveness. On the other hand, they should establish and develop technology innovation systems to introduce, absorb, digest and develop new and high technologies, including biotechnology and information technology, to catch up with advanced international levels.

(10) Implement in a down-to-earth way the strategy of sustainable development, strengthen the construction of the basic facilities for agriculture, and improve the ecological environment and production conditions to enhance the ability to resist natural adversities. For this purpose, it is necessary to promote in a big way eco-agriculture, build ecological towns and villages to integrate the quintessence of traditional agriculture with modern science and technology. It is also necessary to develop hazard-free products, green products and organic products to increase their market shares. At the same time, great efforts are needed to control and eliminate pollution caused by secondary and tertiary industries, and strictly ban the practice of building polluting projects first and introducing control measures later, so as to realize the benign circulation of the economy and ecology, and achieve unity of economic, social and ecological efficiency.

4. TVEs should follow the "going-out" strategy to secure a standing in the international market. All TVEs should develop competitive specialty products in the light of their respective geographical areas and resources, including natural, cultural and human resources. First of all, they should establish their presence in neighboring countries; then they should put their products on the markets in other Asian as well as African and Latin American countries. Finally, they should secure niches in the markets of Europe, and the United States and Japan, and other developed countries. The outward-going strategy should include trade, technology transfer and labor export. All these require a development program, together with corresponding policies and measures.

People and people alone are the motive force in creating history. The past two decades and more have witnessed TVEs rising and creating miracles. Looking further ahead into the 21st century, we expect to see TVEs "flying higher" in restarting their pioneering development and creating even more splendid feats in the course of reinvigorating the Chinese nation.

Chapter XII

Review of TVE Development from the Theoretical Perspective

The rapid development of China's economy over the past 20 years or so has attracted extensive attention, and so has the country's rural industrialization led by TVEs. The rise of China's rural industrialization and rapid development constitute the core of China's economic miracle, and is a great challenge to the theories about traditional structural transition and property rights. It has provided new materials, data and logical support for the advancement of economics.

Section 1 General Theories of Industrialization

Industrialization is an inevitable road in the transition from traditional economy to modern economy and an objective developing countries long to achieve.[1] Correspondingly, theories about indus-

[1] There are many definitions of industrialization. The most representative are:

(1) Industrialization is the increase of the proportion of manufacturing (especially heavy industry) in the national economy. Until the end of the 1970s, almost all Western development economists still construed industrialization as pure development of manufacturing, and made such industrialization the objective of economic development. See Zhang Peigang, ed. *New Development Economics* (additional edition), Henan People's Publishing House, Aug. 1999, pp. 35, 54 and 55.

trialization have become central to development economics. Such literature once occupied an important position in the study of economies. But from the 1980s, when development economics was in disfavor,[2] the basic theories and views on industrialization have till today had a strong interpretative power.

The most famous work of all the classic literature on the theories of industrialization is an article written by W. A. Lewis (1954), titled, "Economic Development with Unlimited Supplies of Labor," in *The Manchester School.* The article touched off great disputes and follow-up studies. For this, W. A. Lewis shared the Nobel Memorial Prize in Economic Science in 1979 with T. W. Schultz. After Lewis, G. Ranis and J. Fei revised and expanded Lewis' model to form the theory of the dual economy, which is, in fact, a fairly systematic theory of industrialization.

---

(2) From the aspect of tools of production, some economists hold that industrialization is the development process of modern industry that replaces hand operation with machine operation. German economist Rudolf Lübbert, in his *History of Industrialization*, says, " ... only at the dawn of the machinery era, with the mechanization of the textiles industry and the steam engine as a new source of energy, and the transition from piece production to serial production and to large-scale production, human society began to undergo tremendous changes, changes that we call industrialization." See Rudolf Lübbert: *History of Industrialization*, Chinese edition, Shanghai Translation Publishing House, 1983, P. 1.

(3) Industrialization is defined as "a process of continuous changes of strategic production function," and such changes of strategic production function are best illustrated by such industrialized departments as transportation, power, and the machinery and iron and steel industries. The concept of industrialization is very extensive, including the modernization and mechanization of both agriculture and industry. This definition was given by noted Chinese economist Prof. Zhang Peigang in the 1940s. See Zhang Peigang, *General Theories of Development Economics*, Vol. 1, *Industrialization of Agricultural Countries*, Hunan Publishing House, 1991, pp. 190-192.

(4) From the aspect of the transition of the structure of resources allocation, industrialization is defined as a process of the transfer of resources from agriculture to industry. Simon Kuznetz calls the process of industrialization the "transfer of product sources and resources from agricultural activities to non-agricultural activities." See Simon Kuznetz, *Modern Economic Growth.*

[2] Deepak Lal, *The Poverty of Development Economics*, Shanghai People's Publishing House, 1992; Albert Hirschman (1981), *The Rise and Decline of Development Economics, 1981*

W. A. Lewis was once widely quoted in China, because his accurate description of the dual economy exactly reflected the realities in China.

In his article, Lewis assumes that developing economies are made up of two departments of different natures: One is subsistence agriculture, and the other is highly productive modern industry. He holds that the wage level of modern industries in cities is obviously higher than that in agriculture. Without interference, it would be natural for agricultural laborers to move toward cities, while the expansion of industries would obtain ceaseless supplies of labor from agriculture. The availability of surplus rural labor and the low income level determine the low income level of modern industry, that is, "the wage which the expanding capitalist sector has to pay is determined by what people can earn outside that sector." So long as the surplus agricultural labor is not absorbed, the wage level of industries will remain unchanged. To expand production, industries tend to ceaselessly employ labor at the current wage level.

The migration of surplus labor from agriculture with low marginal productivity to industries with high marginal productivity stimulates the growth of profits and capital of industries, thus pushing up the demand for surplus rural labor. As long as there is surplus labor in agriculture, the migration of labor and industrial expansion will continue until all the surplus rural labor has moved into industries. When all the surplus rural labor has been absorbed by industries, the dual economy will become a single economy, and traditional agriculture will have completed its historical mission of development.

In Lewis' dual economy model, an important presumption is that traditional agriculture has a large amount of surplus labor whose marginal productivity is close to or equal to zero. Studies of resources allocation in traditional agriculture show that this presumption holds water. In fact, this proposition is entirely identical with that of "overdue increase."

In the resources allocation of traditional agriculture, labor has strong supply elasticity, while land and funds are rigid. This determines that the rational option of rural households is to use the maximum labor input to replace land and funds until the marginal products of labor are zero or close to zero.

As the following diagram shows, peasant households reach production equilibrium at point L', but at the same time, their labor allocation has exceeded the progressive increase in their gains and the stable areas in the decelerating stage so much that the marginal products of labor are not enough to meet the basic consumption demand of unit labor. That is to say, peasant households reach the maximization of efficiency at point L' (marginal quantity=average quantity) and realize the optimal combination of factors. But due to the continued presence of survival pressure, what peasant households pursue is the maximization of physical quantity but not the maximization of efficiency (output/input ratio), and so they continue to input labor until it reaches point L, where the total quantity is maximal and consumption pressure is minimal. But the maximization of quantity is in fact realized at the expense of the maximization of efficiency.[1]

Figure 12-1 Over-Intensive Growth

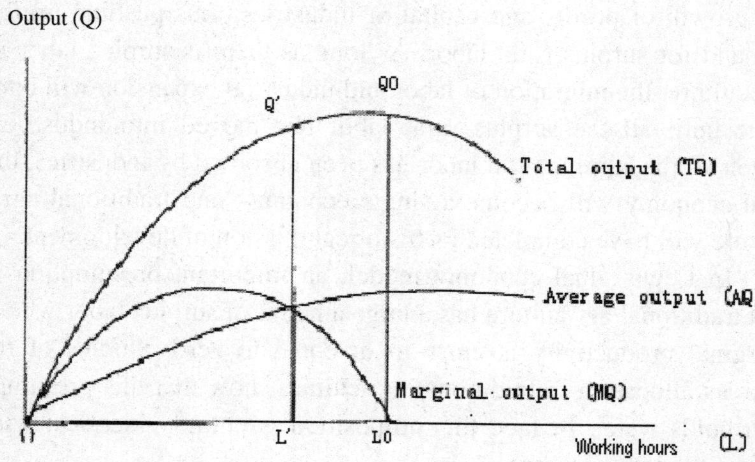

[1] The concept "over-intensive growth" put forward by Mr. Huang Zongzhi a few years ago should refer to the part of L' L_0Q_0Q', which is more accurate. See Li Chenggui, "Analysis of Allocation of Resources and Efficiency Level of China's Traditional Agriculture," *History of Chinese Agriculture*, Issue No. 2, 1997.

After making clear the important proposition of Lewis clear, we may further interpret his dual economy theory by using the diagram in Figure 12-2. Here, the horizontal axis denotes labor quantity, while the vertical axis represents real wage, which is equal to the marginal product of labor. OS is the mean real income for maintaining subsistence living in traditional agriculture, while OW represents the wage of modern industry, and WN_1Q_1 represents the surplus in the initial stage. As part of the surplus is used as reinvestment, fixed capital increases, and so does marginal labor productivity, which reaches N_2Q_2 level.

Figure 12-2 Labor Movement under the Dual Economy

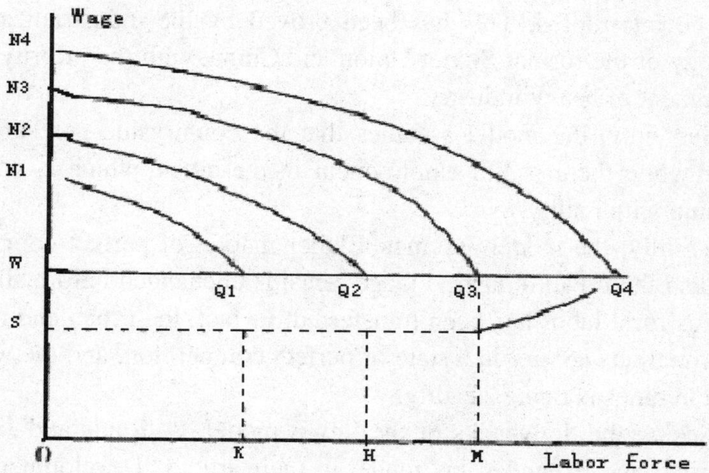

At this point, labor employment rises from OK to OH. Continued investment raises marginal productivity to N_3Q_3, when OM, in which marginal productivity of surplus labor is zero, is moved into modern industry. As the agricultural wage is still lower than modern departments, labor in agriculture where the marginal productivity is still lower than industrial wage continues to migrate into industries until N_4Q_4, when labor migration stops as the average agricultural wage is equal to the wage provided by industry. At this point, the movement of labor between agriculture and industry is determined by market forces.

Lewis came to firm grips with the core issue of labor migration in developing economies, and made a dynamic analysis. But there are also some obvious drawbacks in his theory. For instance, in his model he ignores the option and tendency of agricultural development and industrialized technologies, population growth and urban employment, and other factors.

First of all, the model assumes a positive ratio between capital accumulation and labor movement and employment. In fact, even if capital accumulation is fairly high in modern industrial departments, employment would not grow significantly if the capitalists invest in capital-intensive products, and the movement of surplus rural labor will be interrupted. This has been proved by the industrialization strategy of the former Soviet Union and China, with the priority development of heavy industry.

Secondly, the model assumes that the countryside has surplus labor while there is full employment in the cities, which is not in keeping with reality.

Thirdly, the model assumes a labor market of perfect competition and the urban industrial wage remains unchanged before all the surplus rural labor has been transferred. In fact, the urban and rural labor markets are not in a state of perfect competition, and the wage level in cities is rising steadily.

Seeing the drawbacks of the Lewis model, G. Ranis and J. Fei modified and expanded his model in their article "Development of Labor Surplus Economy: Theory and Policy," published in 1964. They point out that the transfer of labor from agriculture to non-agriculture should be pre-conditioned by the rise of agricultural productivity, and surplus rural labor is of decisive significance for industrial expansion. The amount of agricultural surplus affects the wage level of industries.

In the process of the flow of redundant laborers whose marginal productivity is zero to industries, when the total output of agriculture is not reduced and the average agricultural surplus, that is, the per capita agricultural surplus of outflow of labor is the mean output of agriculture, it will not cause grain shortages in industrial departments, and therefore does not affect the current industrial wage level. The labor supply curve in this stage is horizontal. When the outflow of agricultural labor breaks the limit of surplus labor, the total agricultural output is reduced. Then the average agricultural surplus is less than the constant institutional wage, and the grain supplied to industrial departments is not enough to satisfy the demand of workers according to the constant institutional wage. So when the grain price rises, the industrial wage level has to be raised.

In this stage, the labor supply curve will turn upward. In the Ranis-Fei model, agricultural surplus is in fact the wage foundation of industries. They also point out that the demand for labor by industries is determined not only by capital accumulation but also by technical innovation, especially the labor-intensive propensity of technical innovation. These factors directly affect the labor demand of industries.

After Lewis, Ranis and Fei, development economist H. Chenery carried out an empirical study of structural change and industrialization.[1] In 1975, he and M. Syrquin published *Patterns of Development: 1950-1970*. The book processes the historical data of 101 countries in the period 1950-1970, reveals the relationship between output structures and employment structures, and develops the standard pattern of structural change in the process of economic growth (See Table 12-1). By using the related structural data, they come to the conclusion that when a country's economic development level is low, agriculture is the main economic activity and the population is concentrated in rural areas; but with economic development, industries move toward manufacturing and services, and population moves from the rural areas to the cities.

---

[1] Before Chenery, Kuznetz made a pioneering study of economic growth and structural transfer. The purpose of his comparative statistical studies and comprehensive analysis is to find the common features of modern economic growth, and determine the universal characteristics of structural change. Chenery and others carried forward the economic metering methods using time-series and cross-section analysis, and carried out fruitful theoretical testing and expansion.

Table 12-1 Urbanization and Industrialization of Multi-National Models

Per capita GDP	% of urban population	% of manufacturing in GDP	Share of industrial labor
<$100	22.0	12.5	7.8
$200	36.2	14.9	16.4
$300	43.9	25.1	20.6
$400	49.0	27.6	23.5
$500	52.7	29.4	25.8
$800	60.1	33.1	30.3
$1,000	63.4	34.7	32.5
>$1,000	65.8	37.9	36.8

Note: Per capita GDP is calculated based on the 1964 US dollar.

Source: H. Chenery and M. Syrquin, 1975

In 1986, Chenery published another book, *Industrialization and Growth: A Comparative Study*. By using output/input analysis, general equilibrium analysis and an economic metering model, he studied the industrialization of developing economies after World War II, and analyzed the general relationship between structural change and economic growth and the factors affecting industrialization and economic growth during different stages of development (see Table 12-2). The book is representative of "neo-classic structuralism" and has become an important reference for Chinese scholars in their study of development programs and strategies.

Table 12-2 Per Capita Economic Aggregate and Economic Development Stages

Per capita GDP (1970 US dollar)	Per capita GDP (1980 US dollar)	Period	Development stages	
140-280	300-600	1	stage of primary product production	
280-560	600-1,200	2	primary stage	industrialized stage
560-1,120	1,200-2,400	3	middle stage	
1,120-2,100	2,400-4,500	4	higher stage	
2,100-3,300	4,500-7,200	5	primary stage	developed stage
3,300-5,040	7,200-10,800	6	higher stage	

Source: H. Chenery, 1986

Section 2 TVEs and Structural Transformation

In studying economic development, the term "structural transformation" is widely used. It has, in fact, become the core of development economics. In his book, *Structural Change and Development Policy*, H. Chenery tried to give a definition to the term, when he writes, "Structural transformation is a series of changes in the economic and mechanism structure caused inevitably by the continued growth in GNP, including human capital accumulation and demand, production, trade and employment structure. These are widely regarded as the economic contents of transformation. Social and economic processes such as urbanization, population growth and income distribution associated with these contents are regarded as phenomena other than the main changes in the structure transformation."[1] In order to find the universal law guiding structural transformation, H. Chenery analyzed a large amount of data, and put forward "standard structure" theory (prototype model) for the economic structural change that is inevitable with economic development.[2]

The classic study by Chenery has provided a more accurate understanding of structural transformation. But we hold that it should not become a "universally applicable standard" and the yardstick for all countries. Even in the classic cases, what is observed in the cross-section multinational estimates and time series estimates is not simple identity but obvious differences, changes and diversities. Such differences seem to have gone far beyond Chenery's "slight difference."

---

[1] H. Chenery, 1979, *Structural Change and Development Policy*

[2] Both Kuznetz and H. Chenery sought a universal model for economic growth and structure transformation, because they believed that human nature would respond in the same way to the rise in per capita real income, and therefore there should be convergent factors in industrial systems worldwide. Such a metaphysical assumption is the prerequisite for their research, which is called by Chenery the "core assumption" in the research procedure.

But Kuznetz seemed more candid on this point when he said (1966): "I have made some necessary contributions to this broad assumption." One of the important reasons for his saying so was that his analysis did not include the communist countries. He said, "The differences in both social and political structures between communist countries and our sample countries are so big that we have to exclude them in order to find the common features of modern economic growth."[1] This leads to the question: Are there common features if the communist countries are excluded?

Indeed, we hold that both Kuznetz and Chenery hold to an obvious structuralist tendency in the study of structural transformation and industrialization. They stress the structural factor in the process of industrialization, and fail to pay sufficient attention to institutional factors. That is why their theories are inadequate for interpreting the realities of countries with unique systems. In fact, industrialization and structural transformation, as an inevitable phenomena in economic growth, are significantly affected by social systems in their direction and features. (See Figure 12-3)

Figure 12-3 Comprehensive Factors in Economic Growth

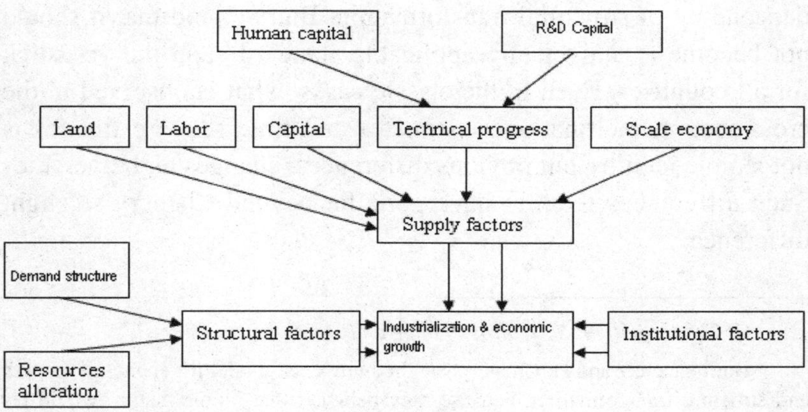

[1] Simon Kuznetz, 1966: *Modern Economic Growth*

China is a large developing country, with very special institutional factors and conditions for initiating industrialization. For instance:

(1) China has a large population. In Chenery's large country models, the starting point for population was 15 million in 1960 and 20 million in 1970. But in China, the population of an average province would be far higher than these figures. To China, a country with 15 million is a small country. There is of course something in common, such as the demand changes covered in Engel's law. Here, however, differences are probably principal, such as in production, employment, and the direction and features of changes of trade.

(2) China started industrialization with heavy industry, and State investment was biased toward this. The development of capital goods was given priority. This presented a sharp contrast to the industrialization process of most other countries. The government adopted this policy in order to swiftly change the situation of accumulating poverty and weaknesses. This strategy was reflected in the First Five-Year Plan (1953-1958) and the ensuing five-year plans.

The capital-intensiveness of heavy industry came into conflict with shortages of resources. Heavy industrial enterprises are incapable of self-generation in an environment of perfect competition. In order to ensure priority development of heavy industry, the government had to create a distorted macroeconomic policy environment featuring low interest rate, exchange rate, prices of energy and raw materials and wages and prices of daily necessities, and allocation of resources in a planned way and by administrative means. However, heavy industry is a capital-intensive industry. The size of investment was big but it did not create more jobs. The result of the strategy was the weakening of the ability of economic growth to absorb labor in non-agricultural sectors, thus obstructing the structural transformation in employment that should have moved out of primary industry along with economic development.

(3) China's political structure and social control are different from those of other countries. China is one of a few countries that introduced the household registration system that artificially split the unified urban and rural factors market, thus leading to a dual economy, and making the urban and rural areas two different closed

economic systems. That deprived the rural people of opportunities of normal entry into the urban economic system, thus institutionally excluding them from the industrialization process. So, in the period 1950s-1970s China's industrial expansion went on in an entirely self-sealed environment. The Chinese peasants did not get any direct employment opportunities from industrial expansion. They only contributed cheap products and sacrificed their employment opportunities in the cities.

China's structural transformation is naturally far from the so-called universal model. It differs in the following areas:

(1) Employment structural transformation lags far behind output value structural transformation. While the cities amassed and developed modern productivity, the movement of surplus rural labor into them was banned. In the period 1952-1978, the proportion of agricultural output value dropped by 24.9 percentage points from 57.7% to 32.8%, while the shares of labor in agriculture dropped by only 10.2 percentage points from 83.5% to 73.3%.

(2) Urbanization level is significantly lower than the level of industrialization. In 1952-1978, China's urbanization level rose by 0.2 percentage points a year from 12.6% to 17.92%. The urbanization level rose by only 0.59 percentage points, from 17.33% to 17.92% in the period 1962-1978. If calculated on the basis of the 1964 US dollar, the per capita GNP in 1980 was about US$154, and the urbanization level in that year was only 19.4%, not only far lower than the urbanization level at the US$200 point but also lower than that at the US$100 point in the standard structure presented by Chenery. When China shifted its focus of economic development to the cities and to industry, a huge part of its population remained in the rural areas, which is rare in the history of the industrialization process worldwide.

Since China introduced economic reform, relaxed social control and introduced the market mechanism, the country's structural transformation has been accelerated, changing completely the situation in which employment structural transformation lagged behind output value structural transformation. In the period 1980-1999, the share of agriculture output value in the national economy dropped

12.5 percentage points from 30.1% to 17.6%, while the share of employment in agriculture dropped 18.6 percentage points from 68.7% to 50.1%. The speed of employment structural transformation was obviously higher than the output value structural change (table 12-3). This is identical with Chenery's "standard structure."

Table 12-3 China's Economic Structural Changes 1980-1999

	% of agricultural output value	% of employment in agriculture	% of rural non-agricultural labor in total labor force	% of TVE added value in GDP	Urbanization rate
1980	30.1	68.7	4.7	--	19.4
1985	28.4	62.4	13.8	8.6	23.7
1990	27.0	60.1	15.7	13.5	26.4
1995	20.5	52.2	18.4	25.0	29.0
1999	17.6	50.1	19.8	30.3	30.9

Source: *China Statistical Yearbook 2000*, China Statistics Publishing House, 2000

The table shows that in the period 1980-1999 the percentage of employment in agriculture dropped greatly while that in non-agricultural activities rose by 18.6 percentage points from 31.3% to 49.9%, and the urbanization rate in the period rose by11.5 percentage points from 19.4% to 30.9%. This indicates that China's urbanization picked up speed after the introduction of reform, but it was still slower than the industrialization rate, which is quite different from Chenery's model. As shown in Table 12-1, in the low-income area, the urbanization rate is higher than that of industrialization, but the difference is not big. When the per capita GDP is bigger than US$300, the urbanization rate is obviously higher than that of industrialization. But the very opposite is true in China.

According to the World Bank 2000/2001World Development Report, China reached the level of lower-middle-income countries in 1999, ranking 140th among 206 countries worldwide, calculated according to per capita GNP using the PPP method. China's urban population made up 30.9% of the total, while in Honduras, which ranks 141st, the urban population makes up 52%. The proportion of China's urban population was also far lower than that in lower-middle-income countries, which averaged 43%.

While China's industrialization has picked up speed, the urbanization process is very slow. This is mainly because China's industrialization has taken place in a considerable part in the rural areas since the reform and opening-up policies were introduced, and the vigorous development of rural industrialization gave a significant push to the industrialization level of the whole country. But it has not brought about a corresponding urbanization effect. Although a large number of peasants have moved to non-agricultural activities, due to the highly dispersed nature of TVEs, this has failed to promote urbanization when most of them remain in their native land.

The Ministry of Agriculture claims that 80% of the TVEs are scattered in natural villages.[1] In the wake of the reform, rural people have been eager to seek a road to prosperity, but lack funds and technical forces. This, plus the shortage economy and the restrictions of the household registration system, has confined TVEs to the development model featuring dispersed, low-level and quantity expansion. After 20 years of rapid development, the situation has not changed much. In 1999, each TVE employed an average of 6.1 persons, had average fixed assets of 116,000 yuan and an average annual output value of only 120,000 yuan.[2] Such a pattern of scattered allocation of resources naturally stands in the way of rural urbanization.

Table 12-4 shows that since reform the speed of the movement of agricultural labor to non-agricultural activities has been so fast that it has changed the employment structure greatly. In the period 1980-1999, a total of 119.57 million agricultural laborers moved to non-agricultural activities, averaging 6.29 million a year. If they, plus their family members, had moved to cities it would have raised the urbanization level by 20 percentage points.

---

[1] Ministry of Agriculture: *Tenth Five-Year Plan for the Development of TVEs*, 1999

[2] *China Agricultural Development Report*, China Agricultural Publishing House, 2000

Table 12-4 Rural Employment

	Rural labor force (million)	Labor in farming (million)	% in total rural labor	Non-agricultural labor (million)	%	Industry (million)	Construction (million)	Transportation (million)	Commerce & catering (million)
1985	370.65	303.515	81.9	67.14	18.1	27.41	11.30	4.34	4.62
1986	379.90	304.68	80.2	75.22	19.8	31.39	13.09	5.06	5.32
1987	390.00	308.70	79.2	81.30	20.8	32.97	14.31	5.63	6.07
1988	400.67	314.56	78.5	86.11	21.5	34.13	15.26	6.07	6.57
1989	409.39	324.41	79.2	84.98	20.8	32.56	15.02	6.14	6.52
1990	420.10	333.36	79.4	86.73	20.6	32.29	15.23	6.35	6.93
1991	430.93	341.86	79.3	89.06	20.7	32.68	15.34	6.55	7.23
1992	438.02	340.37	77.7	97.65	22.3	34.68	16.59	7.06	8.14
1993	442.56	332.58	75.2	109.98	24.8	36.59	18.87	8.00	9.49
1994	446.54	326.90	73.2	119.64	26.8	38.49	20.57	9.08	10.84
1995	450.42	323.35	71.8	127.07	28.2	39.71	22.04	9.83	11.70
1996	452.88	322.60	71.2	130.28	28.8	40.19	23.04	10.28	12.62
1997	459.62	324.35	70.6	135.27	29.4	40.31	23.73	10.58	13.82
1998	464.32	326.26	70.3	138.06	29.7	39.29	23.94	10.88	14.62
1999	468.97	329.12	70.2	139.85	29.8	39.53	25.32	11.16	15.85
2000	479.62	329.98	68.4	151.65	31.6	41.09	26.92	11.71	17.52
2001	482.29	324.51	67.3	157.78	32.7	42.96	27.97	12.05	18.65
2002	485.27	319.91	65.9	165.36	34.1	45.06	29.59	12.59	19.97
2003	489.71	312.60	63.8	177.11	36.2	49.37	32.01	13.28	20.59

Source: *China Agricultural Development Report 2004*, China Agricultural Publishing House, 2004

Due to special initial conditions and restricting factors, China's structural transformation is quite different from what Chenery imagined, and is also entirely different from Lewis' path and model for the transition from a dual economy to a single economy. By Lewis' theory, surplus rural labor should move to modern industries in cities, and bring about average profitability of industries. But in China, while surplus rural laborers move to cities as guest workers in the secondary and tertiary industries, the larger part of them participate in rural industrialization in their localities.

Besides, the dispersed nature of TVEs has had little impact on the development of services. This situation has changed a little in recent years, but until 1999, the added value of township and town industries still made up 69.8% of the total added value of TVEs, presenting a sharp contrast to the situation in most other countries. In his *Industrialization and Growth: A Comparative Study*, Chenery found that in the process of industrialization, with the rise of per capita GNP, elasticity coefficient of employment in the service industry is not only bigger than one but assumes a continuous progressive increase as compared with the manufacturing sector, and it can absorb more labor than other industrial sectors. China's rural industrialization is obviously different from the experience and laws as outlined by Syrquin.

The participation in rural industrialization by peasants resulted in an urban/rural dual pattern of industrialization, thus making the features of industrialization in China quite different from those of other countries. This is the unique experience of China in its industrialization process.

Section 3 TVE Property Rights — Theoretical Perspective

Township enterprises are the carriers of rural industrialization in China. This is a kind of enterprise unique to China. To study industrialization in rural China, it is necessary to have a profound understanding of the TVEs, their inception, nature and path of development.

TVEs in China are unique because they feature property rights structures outside the scope of orthodox economics and pose a challenge to prevailing theories. We know that modern economics has successfully interpreted the inception of enterprises and the boundary between enterprises and the market, as well as a whole series of issues related to the internal distribution of rights and interests in enterprises.

However, the theory of enterprises has evolved assuming a perfect market mechanism, the background of which is: private ownership of property rights, free transactions, respect for contracts and developed factor market. These conditions are obviously unavailable to underdeveloped economies and economies in transformation. Therefore, when applying modern enterprise theory to the analysis of enterprises under imperfect market mechanism conditions, we should not confine ourselves just to the objects and forms of transactions and other generalities, we should go further to study the institutional background and the transaction costs of the market influenced thereby. Why did TVEs in China achieve such tremendous successes in their early days? Why did they become the most lively and vigorous department and the leading driver of the country's rapid economic growth in the 1980s and early 1990s? Why did they run into difficulties, and then take up the road of reform in the mid- and late-1990s? All these questions are closely related to the unique property rights structure of TVEs and the relevant institutional environment, which finds no direct answer in the prevailing enterprise theory or property right theory. This problem has aroused extensive interest among Chinese and foreign scholars.[1]

---

[1] The development of TVEs involves many factors such as political and economic systems and even history and culture during the transitional period. It reflects a changing society and this has made the research achievements of some sociologists (Nee, Walder) important documents in this area. Weitzman and Xu Chenggang analyzed TVEs as organizations of public ownership with obscure property rights from the angle of traditional Chinese culture and discussed why they have the same

Reviewing the history of the reform of TVEs, we can also see that "market development leads to changes in the internal property rights structure of TVEs."[1]

In the 1980s, TVEs experienced the reform of the contract system and joint stock conversion. The contract system involves short-term contracts reached between township governments and managers on the right of control and residual claim right. It does not touch the nature of property right structure. Although the joint stock cooperative system divided the stock capital and allocated parts of it to individuals, the proportion of collective shares was so high that the township government remained the absolute owner controlling collective enterprises.

---

efficiency as private enterprises (1994). From the repeated games theories, they held that property right is important in an environment when the tendency toward cooperation is low and the importance of property rights decreases in the context of a higher tendency of cooperation. They attributed the high efficiency of TVEs to oriental community and cooperative culture. This is a denial of the traditional theory that clear definition of property right is the necessary condition for high efficiency of enterprises. We hold that their analysis lacks the support of empirical, positive and statistical analysis. There is no real proof for the assumption that oriental culture entails a cooperative spirit.

[1] The key steps determining the reform of collective enterprises were: (a) in 1984, the State allowed the setting up of rural private enterprises, and community governments began to lose their power to control resources. From then on, collective TVEs began to compete with private enterprises in their own communities for materials, financial capital and human capital. (b) In the same year, the State began an overall reform of the planned economic system, lifting control over the product and factor markets, and encouraging the development of private, joint-venture and wholly foreign owned enterprises, and delegate powers and yields to State-owned enterprises. At the same time, it also recognized the economic interests of managers and workers. All these steps brought about fiercer competition with TVEs. Meanwhile, policy-based rents resulting from State control, which used to be an important source of profit for TVEs, evaporated. (c) In the late 1990s, after the start of the financial system reform, banks and credit cooperatives were no longer policy-based organizations controlled by the government. They began to be aware of their own interests and to have greater autonomy in their operations. They provided loans not according to the capacity of ownership but according to their profitability and debt-repayment prospects. The community government once again lost its advantage of organizing resources. (d) After the taxation reform of 1994, the State unified tax rates, and TVEs gained their equal economic status. (Tan Qiucheng, 1999)

Radical reform of TVEs did not take place until after 1992. Although joint stock cooperatives were the main form of collective enterprises, as compared with the 1980s, the community government no longer controlled enterprises in the name of collectives. Assets of enterprises were more and more owned by individuals, and more and more so by the managers. In Zhoucun, Shandong Province, the ratio of collective shares dropped to 10-30% after two rounds of reform. In Zhucheng, joint stock cooperative enterprises scrapped collective shares altogether, and community governments gave up their claims to the ownership of enterprises. Even in Wuxi, Jiangsu Province, where the collective economy is the most developed, individuals are encouraged to hold shares. After joint stock conversion, collective shares make up 28.8%. All this, together with the auctions of a large number of small enterprises with thin profits or running in the red, is evidence that community governments have begun to take a back seat in the ownership of collective TVEs.

Information from the Ministry of Agriculture in 1999 shows that after more than 10 years of reform of the property right system, more than 50% of TVEs had carried out reforms by the end of 1998. Over 80% of the collective TVEs had changed their property right system. Some large- and medium-sized TVEs had been formed into enterprise groups; some had been converted into joint stock companies; and some had become limited liability companies. Medium-sized and small TVEs had either adopted the joint stock cooperative system or been sold, auctioned, leased out, contracted out or gone bankrupt. As a result of the reform of the property right system that has broken through the boundaries between different types of ownership, regions and trades, the property owners of TVEs have changed from being mostly rural collectives to also include solely private owners, ownership shares, corporate persons, employees and foreign businessmen shareholders, with collectives holding shares as the core. All these have given rise to a situation described as "multi-wheel driven and multi-track operation." Private enterprises have developed the fastest, to become a major force behind the growth of TVE economies. Since 1997, the added value of private enterprises in the total of TVEs has accounted for over 50%. It reached 1,221.5 billion yuan in 1998, up 25.2% over the previous year and accounting for 55.1% of the total TVE added value of 2218.6 billion yuan of the year.

Theoretical and empirical experience shows that for a considerably long period of time community governments exercised the ownership right over TVEs as they had the advantages in the control and allocation of resources. But the development of the market has weakened the control of community governments, and given more trading opportunities and freedom to individuals, thus changing the internal structure of property rights. Community governments lost their power and capital to control collective enterprises, and in the end yielded ownership. When the market is moving from disorderly development to orderly development, the negative effect of government interference becomes bigger, and capable managers will gradually replace community governments to become owners of enterprises. The reform of the property right structure of TVEs has sounded the death knell of local state corporatism.[1]

In practice, there have emerged two major models of property right among Chinese TVEs, namely the Southern Jiangsu type and the Wenzhou type.[2] The Wenzhou Model is characterized mainly by private property right with a strong feature of self-organized economy, whereas the Southern Jiangsu Model is characterized mainly by collective property right, with TVE development under the guidance of community governments. This amply proves that the nature of property right and its structure have a fundamental

[1] This is the most obvious in the reform of the Southern Jiangsu Model. There are many treatises on the subject. This book will not go into detail due to limited space.

[2] The term "economic model" began to appear in writings on socialist economy in the 1950s, and there are numerous definitions. But in general they all try to probe the laws governing socialist economic activities. The study of economic models in China began in the early days of the economic restructuring, focusing on "models of economic structure." Rural economy studies later focused mainly on "models of economic operations," with emphasis on practical experience. Fei Xiaotong gave it this definition: "Economic model refers to the path of economic development of unique features in a region under specific historical circumstances." (Jiang Yongtao, 1999)

effect on the growth of enterprises and sustained economic development.

Southern Jiangsu has long been known as a "land of fish and rice" for its economic prosperity with brisk business and developed transportation around the Taihu Lake area. In the 1920s and 1930s, Suzhou, Changzhou and Zhenjiang were already important centers of national industry and commerce. During the people's commune period in the late 1950s and early 1960s, the enterprises run by communes and production brigades were front-runners in the country. For instance, by the end of 1958 there were 20,000 commune-run enterprises in southern Jiangsu, which employed more than 300,000 workers and produced a gross output of 300 million yuan. Wuxi County ranked first among Chinese counties in the gross output of its commune- and production brigade-run enterprises in 1970. Under the slogan of "running industry centered on agriculture and making industry promote agriculture," communes and production brigades energetically set up small workshops and factories to produce simple farm implements and machinery, hardware, chemicals, cotton yarn and cloth, and cement. And they soon became an important force in the local rural economy. They were the embryonic forms of the Southern Jiangsu Model of TVE property rights because their road of development determined the ownership form to be mainly that of the collective ownership under the traditional community government administration as a result of the blurred delineation of property rights, and in the meantime the local community governments played a leading role in developing TVEs. Specifically, the community governments organized the land, fund, labor power and other means of production, and invested in setting up enterprises. They also put capable personnel in charge of the enterprises. This form of organizing capable persons (entrepreneurs) and surplus social labor power into capital entities grew rapidly under conditions of economic scarcity, and enabled the southern Jiangsu region to take the lead in developing TVEs by transcending the stage of primitive accumulation.

Wenzhou has some similarities with southern Jiangsu in that both are densely populated but short of farmland, and both have a tradition of business activities.[1] Wenzhou had even less farmland and more businessmen than southern Jiangsu. But enterprises run by communes and brigades were underdeveloped in Wenzhou during the time of the people's communes.[2] During the economic restructuring, the collectives were short of public accumulation, and this, plus the backward transportation conditions, made the area slow in receiving industrial radiation[3] from other regions of the country. However, Wenzhou had no lack of adventurous and experienced businessmen, who managed to develop family workshops and small commodity market places for developing non-farming industry. With this form of developing rural enterprises through family workshops and small factories, they went to all parts of the country to market their products and accomplished primitive accumulation. The only thing the local governments were in a position to command was labor resources, particularly people experienced in running businesses. So at the very beginning, TVEs in the Wenzhou area grew on the basis of investment by labor rather than by capital, and the primitive accumulation of capital was a process of accumulation of returns from labor capital, which gave rise to a large number of small business owners and private entrepreneurs. Private business was lively. It is safe to say that the primitive accumulation

[1] Wenzhou has been a city known for its handicraft and small industry since the Tang and song dynasties (618-1279). It is noted for its own cultural tradition that promotes material utility and commerce and respects practical entrepreneurship. The Wenzhou School, represented by Ye Shi of the Song Dynasty, advocated the simultaneous development of agriculture and commerce as against the school represented by Zhu Xi, who advocated agriculture ahead of commerce.

[2] Both Southern Jiangsu and Wenzhou areas have a tradition of commerce, but they have different TVE property right mechanisms. An important reason is that enterprises run by communes and production brigades developed well in Southern Jiangsu during the commune period, whereas that was not the case for the Wenzhou area.

[3] Southern Jiangsu shows its advantage in this respect. In the 1980s, the so-called "Sunday engineers" were very popular there. These were engineers and technicians from research institutes or State-owned enterprises invited, with high salaries, by TVEs in southern Jiangsu from nearby Shanghai to give technical guidance on Sundays.

of capital in rural Wenzhou repeated the process of the development of the classic market economy of Western Europe in the 18th century. The result was the formation of a market economic model that integrates family industry, specialized markets, small towns and sales agents.

A comparison of the two models shows that the Southern Jiangsu Model is virtually one with government intervention, or a type of "local state corporatism." In the early period of the transition from a planned economy to a market economy, the market order needed to be improved, and TVEs themselves found it necessary to seek government and community protection for the sake of cutting back expenses on market expansion. On the other hand, the community governments generally were original organizers and investors of TVEs, and the profits of collective TVEs constituted a major source of revenue for local governments, and, to a certain extent, the economic basis for the town and village administrations to exercise their functions. This state of affairs explains why the community governments serve as both patrons and extorters of TVEs. This so-called Southern Jiangsu Model of vague property rights did play an important role in the growth of TVEs and the rural economy, but the super-powerful intervention by community governments, the spillover of the power of the local governments and party organizations in the economic field and the covered-up private ownership of collective property in the hands of community cadres inevitably led to a deterioration of the operational mechanism of TVEs, overburdened them and hampered their development as subjects in the market. This has also led to the self-seclusion of some communities in the TVE and small-town trade development, making them more dependent on the local governments in a self-sealed environment, and resulting in the insufficient development of private economy. One result of government intervention, despite its early positive role, was arrangement of collective property rights based on a blurred delineation of the power of government and enterprises, and ultimately forced the Southern Jiangsu Model onto the road of property right reform in face of the changes in the external macro environment and competition environment (the emergence of a buyer's market, for example).[1] In other words, the maturing of the market and growth of competition ultimately led to a change within the structure of property rights. The assets of enterprises were gradually turned over to private ownership with the emergence of a trend of the concentration of business operators, as more and more capable business operators become enterprise owners while the proportion of collective shares decreased.[2]

The Wenzhou Model has been developing in line with the law of the market economy, and therefore continues to show its vitality along with the maturation of the market. It has been moving with the times, and is still evolving. For example, (1) organizationally, it is developing from family workshops, to private business, to joint-stock cooperative enterprises, and finally to companies and enterprise groups; (2) in market operation, the commodity market is undergoing a change from that of tangible specialized markets to intangible markets; (3) markets of factors of production, such as the information market, technology market and property right trading market are growing rapidly in the wake of the growth of the capital and labor markets; (4) the local governments are beginning to exercise their proper functions instead of non-function. Since 1992, they have

---

[1] In the early days of their development, TVEs in Southern Jiangsu fulfiled multiple tasks under the slogan of "developing industry centered on agriculture and promoting agriculture by developing industry," such as making rural industry aid farming, making peasants' income from industry subsidize income from farming and developing rural industry as a means of consolidating collective ownership. Those tasks were too heavy for TVEs. Wu Dongcai, Chairman of the Board of Directors of the Jiangsu Yonggang Group, said, "The Southern Jiangsu Model wasted the energy of a generation of entrepreneurs in the area, and pampered a generation of peasants."

[2] Data from the Suzhou Rural Economic Research Society show that there used to be 8,811village-run collective enterprises in Suzhou. A reform of the property right mechanism began in 1996, and was virtually completed in 1999. By then, 87.9% of the TVEs had become private businesses or joint-stock enterprises, 7.4% had become enterprises with collectives holding shares, and 4.7% had become enterprises solely owned by the collective or holding companies belonging to the village collective. Meanwhile, the net assets and income at the disposal of the villages grew as compared with the pre-reform period (*Suzhou Rural Reports*, 1st Issue, 2003).

been playing a positive role in guiding the transition of the economic structure, innovation of enterprise organizations, and in infrastructure construction, environment protection, etc.

In a nutshell, a comparison may lead to a basic conclusion that the evolution process of the Southern Jiangsu Model and the Wenzhou Model shows that TVEs, with the rural people as the subject, must follow the law governing the market economy, persist in separating government functions from enterprise management, and set up a clear mechanism of property rights, as TVEs cannot display their vitality as independent businesses unless the subject of the enterprises have independent property rights.

References

1. Chang, Chun, and Wang, Yijing. (1994). "The Nature of the Township-Village Enterprise," *Journal of Comparative Economics*, pp. 434-452

2. Chenery, H. and Syrquin, M. *Patterns of Development, 1950-1970*

3. Chenery, H. *Industrialization and Growth: A Comparative Study*

4. Chenery, H. (1981). *Structural Change and Development Policy*

5. Feng Qu. "Progressive Transition of Rural Industries in China," *China Rural Observer*, May 2000

6. Grossman, S. and Hart, O. (1986). "The Costs and Benefits of Ownership: A Theory of Vertical and Lateral Integration," *Journal of Political Economy*

7. Hirshman, Albert. O. (1981) "The Rise and Fall of Development Economics in Essays," in *Essays in Trespassing: Economics to Politics and Beyond*, edited by Albert O. Hirshman, New York: Cambridge University Press, pp. 1-24

8. Kuznetz, Simon. *Modern Economic Growth*

9. Lal, Deepak. *The Poverty of Development Economics*

10. Lewis, A. (1954). "Economic Development with Unlimited

Supplies of Labor," *The Manchester School*, (May), pp. 139-191

11. Li Chenggui. "Analysis of the Allocation of Resources and Efficiency Level of China's Traditional Agriculture," *History of Chinese Agriculture*, Feb. 1997

12. Li Daokui. "Theories of Vague Property Rights in Transitional Economies," *Economic Studies*, April 1995

13. Luebbert, Rudolf. *History of Industrialization*

14. Ministry of Agriculture. *China Agricultural Development Report 2000,* China Agricultural Publishing House

15. Ranis, G., and Fei, J. (1964) *Development of the Labor Surplus Economy: Theory and Policy*, Homewood IL, R.D Irwin

16. Tan Qiucheng. (1999). *Features and Reform of the Property Right Structure of Collective Township and Village Enterprises*, Hunan People's Publishing House

17. Tian Guoqiang. "Property Right Structure and Reform of China's TVEs," *Economic Studies*, March 1995

18. World Bank: *World Development Report 2000/2001*

19. Zhang Peigang. (1991). *General Theories of Development Economics*, Vol. 1: "Industrialization in Agricultural Countries," Hunan Publishing House

20. Zhang Peigang. (1999). *New Development Economics*, Supplementary Edition, Henan People's Publishing House

21. Zhang Shouzheng, Zhu Ming, Xu Jianjun. (1997). "Pay Attention to the Study of the Movement of Production Factors and the Adjustment Trend of the Relations of Production"

22. Zheng Yongjun, Chen Panwu. "Institutional Analysis of the Evolution of the Property Right Structure of Collective TVEs in China," *Zhejiang Academic Journal*, April 2000

23. Zhoucun Rural Reform Experimental Zone Office. "Breakthrough in the Reform of the Property Right Regime of TVEs," *China Rural Economy*, May 1995

24. Zhucheng City People's Government. "Property Right Reform of TVEs," 1995

Profiles of TVE Entrepreneures

The TVE Success Stories

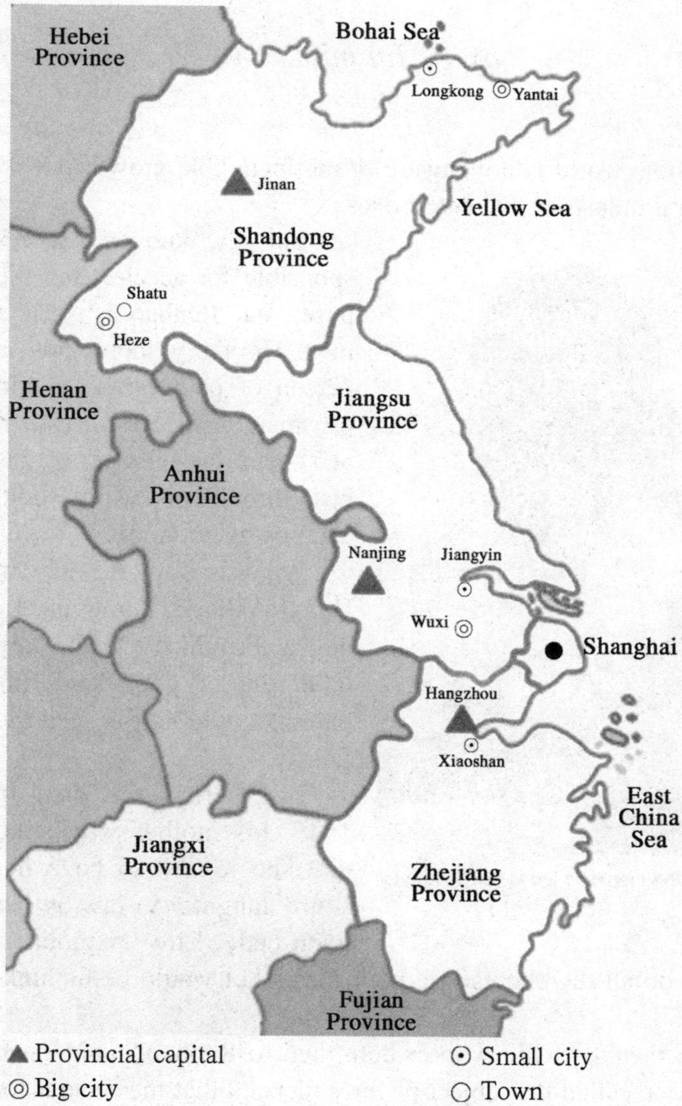

Wu Leads His Village to Prosperity

by Yu Junmin

The whole world is now aware of the incredible growth rate of China's rural industries and enterprises.

Wu Renbao, the man who led Huaxi Village to prosperity

But few know those responsible for accelerating the pace. Wu Renbao is such a man. His story shows how a person of poor farmer origin can make a successful career, and help the village of his birth through his own wisdom and positive outlook.

Wu was born in 1928 in Huaxi Village, Jiangyin, Jiangsu Province. With only 0.086 ha of poor land, his parents could hardly feed the family.

Just before she died in 1949, his mother whispered that she longed to have her future daughter-in-law by her death-bed. Life without a woman to do all the chores in a poor man's hut would be unthinkable she said.

"I was then a textile worker betrothed to Renbao," said Zhao Gendi, who recalled that abject poverty dictated that the funeral for Renbao's mother ended with their wedding, to save money.

For the 20 years before 1949 Wu Renbao worked as a child cowherd, then as a farm laborer toiling on the small family plot or doing household chores plus farm work for landlords, and then as a peddler, haunted by hunger or cheated by gangsters.

But, by a bit of luck, his illiterate parents managed to send him to a teacher to learn to read and write. Wu's formal education lasted, off and on, for three years, ending before he was 11. Those few years, however, did broaden his horizons, and since then, his quest for knowledge has never ceased.

The 21-year-old Wu was happy when New China was founded in 1949, and more so when land was given equally to all tillers.

A Dreamer

Wu has always been considered a most clever, reliable and diligent person, and so he has been elected or appointed to a variety of posts of responsibility. He has acted as head of different farming teams or brigades, as village head of the Communist Party branch and, at one time, even Party secretary, the number one man in Jiangyin County. But he convinced his superiors that his lifelong wish was to make Huaxi prosperous, and he finally returned to that village.

Today, he is still Huaxi's Party secretary. Among the 1,500 villagers in 350 households, 157 are Party members in 10 Party branches. Working with the majority non-party board members, managers and engineers, the Party members have turned old and poor Huaxi into a small modern industrial town with thriving commercial, cultural, educational, tourism and recreational facilities.

Farming is done only by a few villagers, for the great majority have become workers, technicians, administrators or service industry employees. Nearly 90 percent of the villagers have completed more than nine years of education, more than 400 have completed high school and about 250 have college diplomas.

No one in pre-1949 Huaxi knew how to operate a diesel engine or make a sickle," said Wu. "Now we're using computers in production."

One strategy for success has been to get experts to help. Before

1949, the only work the entire population of Huaxi knew was tilling the land. Terms like "science and technology," "modernization" and "industrialization" were missing from their language.

But the limited knowledge Wu had acquired since childhood plus the socialist theory he'd learned after 1949 made this soft-hearted and modest man a dreamer. His strong desire to shake off poverty and his brotherly feelings towards his neighbors who shared the same rural roots made Wu a stern man of action.

Alternating between "dreaming" and "acting," Wu and his fellow villagers developed a new farming-industry-commerce conglomerate on Huaxi's 0.96 sq km.

Huaxi's output was worth four billion yuan (about US$480 million) in 2001.

"Our collectivism ensures wealth and welfare for all, as well as job security, and avoids polarization," said Wu. "However, we don't favor egalitarianism."

The individual bank savings accounts of villagers vary from 80,000 yuan to over 900,000 yuan, and investment from villagers in the Huaxi conglomerate now exceeds 80 million yuan (about US$9.6 million).

The Golden Tower — symbol of the Huaxi Group — amid villagers' houses

"With our own system of reinvestment in production, welfare and the payroll, socialism and collectivism work well here," Wu Xuedong, Wu Renbao's son, said.

When China began to open up in the late 1970s, reform started first in the rural areas with the abolition of the people's communes, which had stifled farmers' initiative. Families were then allowed to manage small plots of land under the responsibility system. Production increased.

Today, this system still predominates, but here and there, are villages where citizens voted to pool their land, and level it for mechanized farming.

Led by Wu Renbao, Huaxi chose collective farming, and seized the opportunity to develop rural industries. Its villagers are free to stay or quit the collective in favor of running their own businesses. Both the family contract system and collective ownership are now working in China to suit different conditions and purposes.

Realism and Ethics Bring Wealth

When the catastrophic "cultural revolution" (1966-1976) ended, China was nearing economic collapse. Production everywhere stopped or was neglected.

One of the recreational areas in Huaxi Village

But in Huaxi, although Wu, as village head, was also intimidated and persecuted by the Red Guards, the villagers still had faith in him.

Never a bureaucratic leader, he was a skilled rice planter and could repair farm machinery.

Even when he was Party Secretary in Jiangyin, now and then he returned to Huaxi to work in the fields or at construction sites. And so during the 10 years of the "cultural revolution," openly or secretly, he was still guiding farming in Huaxi. This was why, when Deng Xiaoping initiated the reform and opening-up policies in the late 1970s, Huaxi's villagers had the strength to increase farming and develop rural industries ahead of others.

Market-Oriented Farmers

Unlike State-owned industries in the long years of the planned economy, budding rural industries even in the people's commune days were market-oriented. The farmers learned from experience that without industries and markets they would remain forever poor; unless they took the initiative, the State would never fund and teach them how to run industries.

But in spite of vigorous growth rates in the 1980s, rural industries encountered skepticism from non-sympathizers.

Yet, sharp of mind and sensitive to political events, Wu guided Huaxi to a climatic success close on the heels of Deng Xiaoping's talks given during his early 1992 inspection tour of South China.

By then this "chief architect of China's reform" had been retired for two years. But Wu sensed from his talks that an economic boom period was imminent. And so, without waiting for the Central Committee of the CPC to meet and endorse Deng's talks, Wu called an emergency meeting one midnight. He knew the value of opportunity, and convinced Huaxi's leading body to act immediately — borrowing large sums and buying plenty of raw material before prices shot up.

Now Huaxi has begun to aim at large-scale new projects, top products and international markets.

The villagers decided to improve management, employ highly qualified people, and invest more in education and training.

They said that by 2010, young villagers would all have a college education, and 20 percent of them would be sent abroad for advanced study or work.

To let board members, managers and villagers see the world, in 1993 to 1994 Wu organized several tours of 400 people each to visit Singapore, Malaysia, Thailand, the US, France, Israel and Japan, as well as Hong Kong, all paid for by the collective.

Today, Huaxi has steel, copper and aluminum, chemistry, textile, garments and building materials industries. The village turns out more than 1,000 different products.

There are 10 joint ventures funded by overseas capital there. About management, Wu said, "The more you use your brain, the more sensible and helpful it can be."

Honest answers to knotty problems are sought from facts and philosophy, his favorite subject. But he has his own flexible method of applying theory. One basic creed never changes: whatever is done must be in the interests of the villagers.

Realism and Ethics

In the 1960s, when top-level bureaucrats showed ignorance of the world below them but loved to issue orders Wu would flatly say "No."

Seeing that this made things worse, he changed tactics: "Thanks for your advice," he would say, and then forget it as soon as the bureaucrats were safely out of sight.

He was strict with his own people: No lies, no fake products and no unfair prices. For Wu, "socialism means our people are happy," he explained, and "communism means the world's people are happy."

When a villager in Huaxi reaches the age of 90, his or her children receive a 10,000-yuan (about $1,200) bonus for the loving care they have given to their parent.

Now Huaxi boasts no crime, no gambling and no superstitious practices. Leading members must work hard, usually 12 hours a day.

James Madison, an engineer at Huaxi's joint venture paper mill, said, "These are hard-working, trustworthy guys."

No one so far has been charged with graft or corruption.

Huaxi has offered money and helped five neighboring villages to develop. They've decided to help 100,000 people in the poor regions of the Ningxia Hui Autonomous Region and Heilongjiang Province to escape poverty, and 10,000 people there to lead a comfortably well-off life by the year 2000.

Already 333 ha of waste land have been cultivated in these areas, twice Huaxi's own area. Because farming accounts for less and less of Huaxi's net profit, to help poor inland people develop farmland is one way of compensating for the loss of farmland in Huaxi. Indeed, for China as a whole how to maintain existing farming acreage is a pressing problem in the drive toward industrialization and urbanization.

During the past few years, nearly one million people from other parts of China, as well as from abroad, have visited Huaxi annually. One group of 500 foreign tourists stayed separately with Huaxi families. They saw that 80 percent of the families live in two-story villas, and nearly 20 percent in three-story ones. Many have air-conditioning, running water, gas and electricity.

Pleasure boats await tourists on a lake.

Scene in a Huaxi Village garment workshop

Huaxi's forested recreational parks contribute to the boom in tourism. The goal is to make Huaxi "look like a garden."

To help the former farmers feel closer to the outside world, local builders have erected copies of famous monuments. One is the Arch of Triumph in Paris. On top of a reproduction of the US Capitol building in Washington DC stands a miniature Statue of Liberty!

Huaxi is to invest 700 million yuan to 800 million yuan (about US$84 million to US$96million) to build a new steel plant, a joint venture with investors from Taiwan Province.

How is it that Wu enjoys unfailing prestige?

He has always refused the top pay and the best house. In fact, he always refuses to accept the bonuses to which he is entitled.

To those who criticize him for allowing his relatives to occupy senior positions, Wu says, "They are a small minority among the managerial personnel. And if they show themselves unworthy, they can easily be voted out."

One result of Huaxi's success is that there are bound to be dinner parties going on most evenings.

But Wu doesn't waste time. He usually goes to one or two parties with just a toast for the guests, and then hurries back home to tune in to radio or TV news.

[Abridged from a profile in *China Daily*, June 4, 1997]

Writer's Notes:

Wu Renbao's fourth son Wu Xue'en is now Communist Party Secretary of Huaxi Village and Chairman of the Board of Directors of Huaxi Group that manages all eight companies in the Village.

Wu Renbao, now 78, as deputy Party secretary and vice-chairman of the Group's Board, still helps to guide village work. He says that he'll never be too old to work.

The gap between the old Huaxi and the village today is illustrated by the following facts and figures:

- In the 1980s, Huaxi was the first rural village in China in which each family owned at least one telephone and one color TV, and some houses were also equipped with air conditioning;
- In the 1990s, it was the first rural village in China in which each family had at least one sedan car (some had two or three) and one computer;
- In 2003, the combined sales of Huaxi Group's eight companies (involved in heavy and light industries, and the service sector) amounted to 10,500 million *yuan* (about US$1,280 million). Village land: 18 square km. Population: 17,000. Huaxi's products were exported to more than 40 countries.
- Tax paid in 2003: more than 300 million *yuan* (about US$36.5 million)
- In 2004, estimated sales were 20,000 million *yuan* (about US$2.43 million). Estimated net income of Huaxi Travel Service: 200 million *yuan* ($24.3 million). Roughly one million people visit Huaxi every year. The village has, besides farming, industrial and residential areas, and commercial sections. It also has forested land, parks, a botanical garden, recreational facilities, hills, lakes and ponds. Hotels and registered families can accommodate 3,500 visitors overnight at a time.
- From June 2001 till mid-2004, 14 poor neighboring villages asking to be merged with rich Huaxi, and were accepted. The total land by then was 23.36 sq km, and the total population reached 25,830.
- By mid-2004, the tourism-farming acreage was more than 3,000 mu (200 ha). Estimated bank savings per household, were

500,000 yuan to five million yuan (about US$60,000 to US$610,000).

Living space per household: 450-600 sq m

Collectively owned fixed assets: more than 4,000 million yuan (about US$487 million)

Individually owned fixed assets: 800 million yuan (about US$97 million).

Income of villagers: a. wage and bonuses b. welfare paid by the village collective c. share dividends

Educational fees from kindergarten to college are all paid by the village collective.

Those who earn postgraduate qualifications are awarded prizes by the village collective.

All villagers enjoy either medical care or medical insurance benefits

All seniors (males over 65 and females over 50) enjoy pensions.

- Principles for Merging with Neighboring Villages:

  1. Independent Management: The merged villages maintain their right to run their own industries and enterprises independently.

  2. Unified Management: a. solving economical and financial problems b. appointment of staff c. labor force employment d. welfare benefits e. master plan for the development and usage of the whole land and water areas

- The Three Goals of Huaxi Village:

  1. Agriculture is to be modernized
  2. Farmers are to be well educated
  3. The whole village is to be urbanized

September 28, 2004

Lu Guanqiu from Home Soil to the World

by Yu Junmin

On Jan. 29, 1945 was born a baby boy in a shabby thatched hut in Ningwei, Xiaoshan County of Zhejiang Province. In 1984 his name, Lu Guanqiu, made both Chinese and Western headlines. And on May 6, 1991, he appeared on the cover of *Newsweek* magazine.

The crux of it was that the first made-in-China auto parts sold on US markets in 1984 were not from big State-owned factories but from a small, so-called Township & Village Enterprise (TVE) founded by Lu and his local friends. From 1997 onwards, their auto parts and accessories, at first mainly universal joints, were the first China products to enter regular assembly lines of giant auto makers like Ford and General Motors. Officials, foreign journalists, diplomats and their wives found Lu's workshops clean and tidy. In Aug. 1997 observers from GM remarked that Wanxiang factories were "first rate" and their employees were "very devoted to their work."

Lu Guanqiu has built up a modern corporate group on the basis of a rural smithy.

Lu's multi-national Wanxiang

Group — developed from a rural blacksmith shop and set up in 1969, today boasts of nearly 40 companies and corporations all over China as well as 25 subsidiary ones overseas, including four listed on stock exchanges. Their sales network covers more than 60 countries and areas.

A Dream Shattered

His first cries were echoed by tears of his mother who, during pregnancy had only wild herbs or beans added to cereal gruel for meals. Breast-feeding wasn't possible so rice soup was the main substitute.

Red China was founded before little Lu turned six. During the Land Reform, the Lu family, designated as "Poor Peasants," were allocated 0.5 ha of land to till. Still it was hard for a family of 5 to 6 to lead a decent life. Father tried to learn and practise traditional medicine using herbs and later even use a corner of his hut as a "shop" selling cheap daily necessities. All these never made life easier. Yet Mother often told her children to observe the Confucian doctrine of "*ren*" — benevolence — and the Buddhist faith of mercy. Even as a boy, Guanqiu talked about when growing up, to help people get rid of poverty.

As a junior two (8th grade) student, Guanqiu had to drop out because Father, already old, felt too tired to support the family. He would like the son to learn and help him practise traditional medicine. "No," said Guanqiu, "I want to go to town and be a worker." Not like the rustics, industrial workers could just work and wages would safely be paid!

It was the late 1950s, the crazy "Great Leap Forward" and people's commune days. ultra-leftist tendencies were rampant. Tens of millions of people neglected their regular work to build indigenous "furnaces" to produce iron and steel! These were supposed to speed up productivity and hasten the pace for building, not just socialism, but communism! So, People's Communes were quickly set up everywhere — a crazy age that ridiculed rationale and laws of economics and sciences were blatantly ignored!

For the 15-year-old Guanqiu, however, it was a golden chance to be accepted by an ironware workshop run by the Xiaoshan County. More than two years' training had made him a technically strong hand. Nevertheless, policies could change any time. A government decision said that a certain proportion of workers, like intellectuals, should also leave cities or towns and be sent to live and work in rural areas.

Was it groundless? No. The nation had suffered badly from both natural disasters — floods and drought — and the wrong, ultra-leftist economic policies. One remedial measure, even if for not too long a period, was to smooth down burdens on urban areas.

But why a model young apprentice like Lu should be sent away first?

To begin with, old China didn't leave strong modern industries to its successors. To the policy makers, both the international and domestic situations seemed to claim that China could only follow the Soviet Union's pattern of highly centralized planned economy and priority for building heavy industries. But where to get the original capital to begin with? Borrowing money from abroad? No way. It seemed to collect taxes from the more than 800 million peasants and get funds from the differences between State-controlled prices of agricultural and industrial products — scissors' differential — were among the major measures.

To cope with the above economic demand, New China adopted a strict household registration system which dictated those born or living in rural areas — with rural household registration — could not change into urban household registration to live in cities and get the rice and cloth coupons for urban citizens. Also they couldn't enjoy the welfare or chances for education, medical care etc. there. This dualism blatantly separated urban and rural economic life. So young Lu was bound to be trapped there.

Tears dazzling in his eyes, he had to pack up and headed for his native soil, which he would never leave again. Since that day onward, the question of why the peasants should remain poor would never leave him in peace. The desire to lead a better life spurred him to begin his pilgrimage to success.

Self Reliance

Back home and by the end of the 1960s, the per capita cultivated land at Ningwei still remained at 0.8 mu (one-fifth of a ha) and per capita income was 300 yuan (about $37). Determined to blaze a new trail, Lu noticed the villagers had to send wheat kernels, a staple food, to town for processing. Within a month, he gathered some 4,000 yuan ($500) from relatives and other villagers to buy machinery. He thought he was doing it not only for himself but others. Yet he ignored one basic fact: it was still the era of the ultra-leftist people's communes. Individually or jointly owned businesses, however small, were still "following the capitalist road" and untitled to get a business license. To make it worse, an accident occurred and some one had a narrow escape. Thus, superstition plus political pressure threw him in debt. Lu was forced to go back tilling the land like his forefathers.

From Seven-Member Smithy to Farm Machinery Factory

But the flame of his entrepreneurial spirit was never quenched and in July 1969 Lu and wife Zhang Jinmei and five others opened a 7-member smithy. It consisted of three small shacks with a total area of 84 sq. m. When in Dec. 1973, the smithy with capital of only 4,000 yuan or $500 became attached to the local people's commune, it was re-named Ningwei Commune Farm Machinery Factory, although they produced only spare parts and poverty still lingered.

Nevertheless, the 24-year-old Lu was now addressed as "Director." With his wife and family of 6, he lived in the space partitioned off from the forge. This was also his "office." Situations like this were typical of the early TVEs. "Even as Director, I too, had to forge iron, using a heavy, big hammer in the day. In the evenings, while others could rest, I had to think about how to get raw materials or run about selling our products," Lu recalled.

During the so-called "cultural revolution (1966-76)," young ultra-leftist Red Guards took over power nationwide. Director Lu was told to "stand aside." Things were in great chaos. Finally Lu was allowed to take over again. Here one key person was the factory's Communist Party secretary Zhu Bingshan, sent by the Commune to the smithy.

One incident illustrated well Lu's boldness and Zhu's support. In those days still during the "cultural revolution," "eating from the same big rice pot — equalitarianism" was still the rule. People got equal pay for unequal work. As early as Aug. 1971, to stimulate enthusiasm and raise efficiency, Lu had the guts to give more pay to those having done more and better work, and the director, Party secretary, accountant and cashier each got six more yuan (less than $1) per month. The Red Guards charged Lu as "money bonus in command" meaning not politics in command and worse, "counter-revolutionary!" Zhu stood out and said: "Our Party group made that decision. If it's wrong, I should be the first to be punished."

The season for ploughing was ahead. Lu carried samples of plough blades for tractors on his back to ask the Farm Machine Company to place an order. To his surprise, the State-owned company's people coldly said "no" and turned back to reading newspapers. "They had the big iron rice bowl, so why should they be serious with their work," Lu thought angrily. Instantly, he decided to produce 10,000 blades and manage selling themselves. (Years later when he was in full charge of the factory, reforming the distribution system was among the first things he did.)

Soon the plough blades were out of stock, the said company men hurriedly came saying "we'll be your sole agent..."

"O.K. But you must provide 40 tons raw materials — fine quality manganese steel for exchange!" Lu smartly grabbed this heaven-sent opportunity. Under the then highly centralized economic system, TVEs' needs for raw materials and energy had no way to be listed in State plans. Lu's men sometimes even had to go to big cinder dumping grounds of giant State-owned factories to get something. But from that day on, Lu's name began to be known. "Like a small fish hooked to a big boat," his biographers wrote:

"Lu's business began to swim into the big domestic market!"

Lu's factory began producing universal joints in 1974, when they were out of stock.. He had learned from the Hangzhou Municipal Machinery Bureau that a plan for producing these was given to the State-owned Hangzhou Motor Car Fitting Company previously, but nothing seemed to have happened. Lu approached the bureau and persuaded the officials there to give the contract to his company. His sample products were soon approved by both the city and provincial authorities.

Passion for Study

To explain Lu's unbroken series of successes after winning the universal joint contract, it is necessary to glance at his passion for study.

Lu has never given up reading and self study since finishing his 8-year schooling. He wrote: "I don't have any other hobby at all besides work and study." "Work is always my greatest enjoyment… Without work, I feel as if I am ill, and my life loses its vitality." He also said, "My thirst for work may have originated in the fact that the early TVEs could exist only in crevices of the national economic life and there were no safety belts for us while struggling against the adverse currents for survival…." Lu repeatedly warned his staff and workers that the differences between people originate largely in how they spend their spare time. When on business trips, he must have books and notebooks with him. He regularly keeps large amounts of clippings taken from newspapers and periodicals.

Lu Guanqiu's home in Xiaoshan, Hangzhou
Sketch by Yu Junmin, writer of the text

In 1984 Lu began auditing classes at Zhejiang University in Hangzhou, while still intensely engaged in work. Later in 2000, he was invited by the University to guide doctoral students. Also he once attended a short term class for managers or directors in Norway organized by the UN. His many visits abroad were also chances to learn. Today he holds an honorary doctoral degree from the Hong Kong Polytechnology University, the professional title of Senior Economist conferred by the State and more than 20 titles of honor for his achievements. The Wanxiang Group, too, has earned more than 20 honorific titles bestowed by the State.

In June 1999, a collection of his own articles was published, and some theses won awards. Lauded as a "theoretician from the soil," Lu's writings are known for convincing facts, clarity of logic, to the point arguments and no redundancy, cliches or jargons that are familiar to Chinese readers.

One important information from reading newspapers: freight transport on highways would reach 540 million tons by 1980. Experts said to ease the pressure on railroads, highway transport should be stepped up. Instantly after reading the news he decided on specializing one key-product — universal joints! But a marketing research showed there were already 56 factories producing these in China. Not willing to yield, he visited Beijing's China Motor Industry Co. and was told that only those for imported cars were in demand.

Lu instantly said: "Allow us six months...We TVEs have to avoid hot spots and reach for those not yet heeded... whatever brand or model, as long as they run on our highways I'll produce..."!

Yet when he led his salesmen attending a national fair in Shandong Province, they were met with cold shoulders. Not being allowed to show their products inside the building, the angry Lu and his men put them in the open air just near the entrance. In the first three days, there were few transactions between buying and selling parties. People were waiting for cheaper prices. After consulting his salesmen, Lu decided quickly to cut 20% prices down than those designated by State authorities. When purchasing agents flocked to Lu's ground stand, it was too late for big State-owned factories men to lower theirs, because they had to go through slow bureaucratic procedures to get permission from senior officials. The total purchasing orders Lu got was more than two-thirds of his planned yearly output value. Then and there, this small Ningwei TVE factory enjoyed a higher fame. "Market is the only way for TVE existence," he later wrote, "We circle around in the markets, and grasp chances through the narrow crevices in the planned economy, and find our way for existence."

When one success succeeded another, Lu held to some tenets testifying to his philosophy on career, as well as faith on life. He said:

"A man without any ideals is spiritually as poor as a beggar. And ideals have to be created by oneself. No one else can really help."

"Entrepreneurs...are bound to create, offer and sacrifice. His whole life is one that creates and offers. If one believes so, then he'll never...cheat people. Of course...one that doesn't known how to earn money is not an entrepreneur at all, but...he shouldn't turn out a slave to money..."

"We rely on credibility, on laws and on contracts."

Throughout the years of 1970s and early 1980s, even though his company had only crude equipment, Lu still demanded meticulous precision and workmanship. In 1979, Lu decided to specialize in making universal joints and renamed his factory the Xiaoshan (name of county) Universal Joint Factory. In 1984, it was again renamed, this time as Hangzhou (city name!) Universal Joint Factory.

Since the early 1990s, all Lu's employees have had to pass the national TQC (total quality control) tests. Bu 2000, the factory won the country's Certificate of Confirmation for Measurement Level.

Contract for Independence

Over the years, even with greater and greater successes crowning him, Lu felt in his inner most self a subtle desire for something much more valuable — independence in creative work. His faithful partner Party Secretary Zhu Binshan too, subtly sensed it even before Lu told him so.

To step up reform for better economic results, the Communist

Party's Central Committee in Beijing issued its No.1 Document for the year 1983, allowing directors or managers of factories to sign contracts to run factories on their own.

On March 20, 1983 a meeting chaired and audited by county, district and *xiang* (Ningwei) leaders was held. It stipulated that the output value of 1983 should reach 6,330,000 yuan (about $760,000) and annual increase of 10% should be added for 1984 and 1985. If the annual output exceeded the target, then 10% of the excess profit should be awarded to the contractor, who should let outstanding staff and workers share half of it.

But Lu refused to accept the bonuses he earned. In 1986, his bonus was 250,000 yuan ($30,480). In exasperation, Lu wrote an article for the nation's leading *People's Daily,* "Why I Don't Want to Accept a Huge Amount of Bonus." Also he explained at a Xiaoshan County meeting: "I could have taken all those bonuses stipulated in the Contracts... But my aim in signing a contract was not for the bonus money but to declare that we peasants are all capable of mastering our own fate, and capable of managing a modern factory... I'll put all the 250,000 yuan bonus money under the factory' gross income."

In 1984, Lu built 10 branch workshops or factories in Ningwei to make semi-finished products. The new plants offered 600 jobs and more than 1 million yuan ($120,000) a year in increased income for the local people.

Export

After Wanxiang universal joints were displayed at the Canton Export Commodities Fair, representatives from the Doyle Pacific Industries. Ltd and Zelle Doyle Co. of the US offered Lu a contract to manufacture 30,000 universal joints for them. The difficult part was that the customers didn't provide any written technical specifications and these US ones were quite different from Wanxiang's own. To ensure quality and timely delivery, Lu's staff worked out a schedule of more than 100 technical procedures.

The next year, the same companies asked Lu to produce 10 more kinds of universal joints, again with no specifications. To their surprise, it took Lu's factory only one month to turn out the trial products. Since then, good quality and low prices have guaranteed export markets for Wanxiang. In 2000, Lu's Wanxiang American Corporation took even one of the aforesaid American companies.

Management

Beginning in November 1988, his enterprise consolidated its strength by merging with eight TVEs and other enterprises. In Oct. 1990, it became the first modern corporate group in Zhejiang Province, the Wanxiang Group. Since then, it has steadily invested in or entered into partnerships with other enterprises in various trades, both in and outside China.

A view of the Wanxiang Group's American company in Chicago, USA

In 1993 the Third Plenary Session of the 14th CPC Central Committee passed a resolution to set up a socialist market economy, signaling the end of the more than 40 years of the highly centralized planned economy. Also at the end of 1993, the "Company Law" went into effect. In January 1994, Wanxiang Qianchao's stock was listed on the stock exchange in Guangdong Province' Shenzhen Special Economic Zone. Prior to this only State-owned companies had been allowed to be listed. In July 1994, Wanxiang Group's Board of Directors was set up, with Lu Guanqiu as Chairman, and his only son Weiding as CEO. All subordinate corporations or companies have full operational rights. Also in 1994, the Group opened its first company overseas — the Wanxiang American Company. Today, the Group embraces undertakings in agriculture, industries, export & import, insurance broking, stocks and futures, real estate, investment banking and high-tech undertakings both at home and abroad, and even a golf course with 18 holes in the USA. All the Group's subsidiaries overseas adhere to local practices and laws.

Lu insists that the differences between wages shouldn't be too small. Efficiency and contribution are major determining factors. Workers now fall into 4 categories: regular, on contract, on probation and short-term. Beginning from 1992, the Group recruits roughly 500 people yearly and fires about 100 who don't meet the requirements.

Human Resources

Lu believes that in the last analysis competition is essentially competition in intellect or human resources. Hence education should be placed ahead of scientific research and production. Beginning from 1980, Wanxiang recruited more than 300 senior high graduates, and set up technical, vocational education classes for them. Also 49 staff and workers were sent to colleges at the enterprise's expense.

Beginning in 1981, Wanxiang has organized 33 training sessions of various standards and subjects and set up a vocational school for all employees. Professors, engineers, researchers, and college graduates were invited to teach there. Wage increases accompany improvements in qualifications.

In 1993, Wanxiang sent 16 staff members abroad to be trained in the US, Germany and Spain. In 1994 alone, more than 150, and in recent years, roughly 200 college graduates have joined Wanxiang every year.

Today of Wanxiang's 13,800 staff and workers, 1% hold master's, doctor's or post-doctor's degrees, 7% have bachelor degrees, and the rest are junior college or senior high graduates. In Wanxiang's companies abroad, there are nearly 580 foreign employees. The Group boasts a State-level technical center, an auto parts and accessories laboratory, a post-doctoral workstation, a high tech incubator center, the Wanxiang Research Institute (co-founded with Zhejiang Uni.) and an R&D center in the U.S. The Group has even had two academicians of the Chinese Academy of Engineering working for it. Now designated as China's auto parts & systems export base, Wanxiang supplies six categories of products — universal joints, transmissions, brakes, shock absorbers, bearings and also rolling and rubber products.

Epilogue

Right after the people's communes collapsed in the early 1980s, the TVE Bureau was set up in the Ministry of Agriculture to take care of and guide the TVEs. When the China Association of TVEs was set up in 1990, in view of the still present prejudices and restrictions against them, the then Minister of Agriculture had to assume the role of its president to signal firm support. By 2000, when TVEs had already become an important force in the national economy, Lu Guanqiu was elected President of the Association.

Lu's aim is to become one of the 30-50 largest groups in China that have international competitive strength.

August 21, 2005

A Small Town Does Big Business

— Profile of Zhang Xiuji, Chairman of the Board of Conglin Enterprise Group

by Zhang Qingnian

July 1, 2002. A small town in East China's Shandong Province made front-page headlines in major newspapers across China. It had become the birthplace of the world's first and largest 10,000-ton oil press capable of producing extra-long and extra-wide aluminum alloy profiles urgently needed in the aerospace and high-speed railway industries.

This giant machine was independently designed and built in China with a total investment of 250 million yuan (about US$30 million). In the 1960s, the State-owned Shanghai Heavy Machinery Plant had succeeded in building China's first 10,000-ton hydraulic press, a feat which aroused cheers across the country. "This 10,000-ton oil press is much more advanced technologically," remarked Shi Changxu, a prominent member of the Chinese Academy of Sciences, after inspecting the giant press in operation. The machine can press a ton of aluminum profiles in one minute. An inspection team made up of specialists and government officials concluded that the product quality had reached the international advanced level, while the cost of production was only one third that of similar products made abroad with machines of lesser size.

What really excited Academician Shi and his colleagues, however, was the fact that the prime mover of this project was not a large State-owned enterprise as one would have expected from past

President Hu Jintao (then Vice-President) chats with Zhang Xiuji during an inspection of the Conglin Enterprise Group

experience for a project of this proportion, but rather a non-public township enterprise in the small city of Longkou, or more specifically, in a small town nearby named Zhuyouguan. Furthermore, this Conglin Enterprise Group, as it is called today, is headed by a local entrepreneur named Zhang Xiuji. And it was further noted that while the initiative and investment came solely from Conglin, a privately owned enterprise, it was the product of joint efforts by Conglin and two well known State-owned public institutions — the Xi'an Heavy Machinery Research Institute, which designed the giant press, and the Shanghai Heavy Machinery Plant, which built it. Such a combination of effort by one non-public and two public enterprises was previously unheard of in China. Furthermore, it was done entirely on their own initiative and at their own risk, without government planning, supervision or intervention.

The oil press is now housed in a huge workshop 252 m long and 30 m wide. The machine itself weighs 1,630 tons and is taller than a three-story building. It has a capacity of 10,000-tons of aluminum profiles annually, including seamless aluminum tubes 30 m in maximal length, 600mm in diameter and 970mm in section breadth. Orders came immediately from both around the country and abroad. As an Intellectual Property Right (IP) owner, within a year Conglin recorded US$8 million-worth of sales thanks to this press alone. Its prized products include a 1,300mm (the world's largest) aluminum alloy shading panel for the International Convention and Exhibition Center in Shenzhen, China's first special economic zone in the southern province of Guangdong. Previously, 60% of China's fixed assets investment in machinery and equipment had gone on purchasing imported products, a drain on the country's foreign currency reserves. Conglin's success in building the 10,000-ton oil press represented a major breakthrough in reducing the country's reliance on imported machinery in major developmental projects.

How did all this come about? How was it possible for a small town like Zhuyouguan to do such big business? To answer these questions, it is necessary to start from the beginning.

Some 20 years ago, with the introduction of the government's policy of reform and opening up to the outside world, Zhuyouguan decided to build a cement factory. But no one in the town had any experience at building such a project. Besides, where was the money to come from? A local man named Zhang Xiuji rose to the challenge.

Zhang comes from a former landlord family, and, being the son of a former exploiter, he was ostracized in many ways in the newly liberated countryside. However, he was determined to prove his mettle in whatever he did. As he had a brilliant mind, strong willpower and a pair of very skillful hands, he was gradually accepted by the new society.

In the early 1980s, the central government introduced the reform and opening-up policies, which greatly invigorated the country's economy. The local government of Zhuyouguan decided to build a 600,000 ton cement factory, and Zhang Xiuji offered to undertake the task. The town was not short of raw materials, but where was the money going to come from to buy the machinery and pay the workers? Zhang negotiated a bank loan of two million yuan, and set the project in motion. Before long, Zhuyouguan's first-ever factory was in operation, churning out cement to support other projects mushrooming in the area.

Zhang rallied around him a group of energetic young and middle-aged men determined to change the face of their land and the life of the local people. Zhang himself studied with great gusto in order to acquire the knowledge he needed not only of industrial technology, but of management and entrepreneurship too. Over the years, he managed to finish the country's college curriculum through self-study, and was accredited with the professional title of senior economic administrator. Under Zhang's guidance, Conglin Cement increased its output from 800,000 to 1,800,000 tons, and won international recognition for the reliability of its product. Conglin cement has, for years now, enjoyed "inspection-free" status around the world.

After the initial success of the cement factory, Zhang saw that with the growing competition in that industry, Conglin would not be able to hold on to its leading position for long if it stuck to a single product. "We can't walk on only one leg" is the way he put it. "We would fall!" He thought of using the gains from cement production to develop other branches of industry.

During a visit to Singapore in 1994, Zhang reached an agreement with a sizeable enterprise group there to jointly invest 240 million yuan in building a 100,000-ton nodular cast iron pipes and fittings factory in Conglin. This was no small sum for Conglin at that time. After consulting with his high-level staff, Zhang took a brave move: he decided to turn a significant portion of Conglin Cement's fixed assets into shares, 50% of which would be for sale. In this way, the enterprise was able to attract 92.4 million yuan's worth of foreign capital. Zhang took 50 million out of that sum and invested it in the nodular cast iron pipe project. This factory began operation 16 months ahead of schedule.

Today the Conglin Enterprise Group has under its umbrella 18 enterprises, including Conglin Rubber Belts, Conglin Pipes and Pipe Fittings, Conglin Aluminum, Conglin Electrolytic, Conglin Car Body Systems Engineering (a joint venture between Conglin and Germany's MIW), Conglin Automobile, and Conglin Sewing

Equipment. The Group has total fixed assets of 2.5 billion yuan (about US$300 million), and a cash flow of 550 million yuan. All its backbone subsidiary companies have gained the ISO9000 quality system certification. Its aggregate domestic and international sales volume has reached 1.7 billion yuan, making it one of the top 500 industrial enterprises in China and one of the biggest providers of tax revenue in Longkou City. For his part in Conglin's remarkable success story, Zhang Xiuji has been honored as a National Outstanding Entrepreneur and a May 1st National Labor Medallist.

Zhang Xiuji is a man of vision. His concern goes far beyond the interests of his enterprise group. He feels strongly his responsibility in the nation's drive for modernization and for a better life for the people. In the late 1990s, Zhang paid a visit to the Changchun Railway Carriage Factory in Northeast China's Jilin Province. The factory had begun research on high-speed railway technology in 1994, and had trial-produced China's first aluminum alloy carriage. However, because it had to rely totally on imported aluminum profiles, the cost would have been much too high if it were to go into serial production. The whole project was thus aborted, leaving only a sample carriage. But with Conglin's experience in aluminum alloy profile production, it didn't take long for the factory to turn out the profiles badly needed by the Changchun factory. When the first magnetic levitation train rolled off the assembly line on August 4, 2001, the news brought cheers from the entire staff of Conglin as they knew that all the aluminum alloy profiles used in building the carriage bodies had come from their workshop.

Zhang now fully realized how important it was for China to be able to produce its own large-size aluminum alloy profiles for industrial use and the key machinery needed for processing such profiles was a ten-thousand ton oil press. With the support and cooperation of two prestigious State-owned institutions — the Xi'an Heavy Machinery Research Institute, which agreed to do the designing, and the Shanghai Heavy Machinery Plant, which would produce the parts — Conglin constructed the biggest press in China, and perhaps in the world. The cost was 250 million yuan (US$30 million). The final product performed superbly right from the start.

Very soon, large orders came from big container factories around the country. Conglin's large-section aluminum alloy profiles have been sold to the US, Canada, Japan, Britain, the Netherlands, Denmark and Spain. In one year, sales of products from this machine alone brought in 8 million US dollars for Conglin.

This further boosted Conglin's contribution to Longkou City. Its aggregate annual tax revenue topped 60 million yuan. It has also provided a solution to the township's employment problem, as two-thirds of its 5,000 workers are recruited from the locality. Moreover, the corporation's rapid expansion has stimulated the development of the local transportation and mining industries. Today, the per capita GDP of Longkou, thanks to Conglin, is 4,000 yuan, about three times as high as that for the entire province of Shandong. Longkou now ranks 27th among China's 2,863 counties and county-level cities, while Conglin is listed among China's top 500 enterprises.

There are many things worth noting in Zhang's management style. He studies management skills that have proved successful both in China and abroad. Moreover, he invites representatives from other enterprises to attend the lectures and demonstrations he arranges for

German specialists examine Conglin's products

his employees, with the idea of benefiting the whole community and not just Conglin.

Attached to the walls of the workshops at Conglin are slogans such as "Never feel contented, and never succumb to failure," and "Either do a first-class job or don't do it at all." Zhang's favorites are "Quality is the life of the enterprise" and "First-class technology plus first-class management equals first-class quality and first-class results."

Zhang does not hesitate to import the most advanced equipment and technology from abroad, and he makes sure that along with these he also imports advanced management and technical skills. One of Conglin's latest procurements is a welding robot imported from Germany. Zhang, ever ready to employ skilled technicians and pay them well, invited two German technicians to install it and train Conglin's staff to operate it.

Meanwhile, Zhang and his partners have worked out a new standardized and modernized mode of management, stressing honesty and ability as the criteria for promotion as against any sort of favoritism. Promotions and demotions, rewards and punishments are based on strict and fair rules. This system has greatly boosted the morale of all Conglin's employees.

All this is part of "Conglin Enterprise Group Culture," which Zhang Xiuji and his colleagues are creating.

Despite the after-effects of a serious stroke, Zhang still goes to the office every day, even though his son Peiliang has taken over as president of the Group while he remains Chairman of the Board. "The enterprise is his life," said his wife, "He hardly thinks of anything else. It makes him happy to see things running so well."

A Woman Entrepreneur's Dream of Silk

by Yu Junmin

For six generations Shen Aiqin's ancestors had raised silkworms, which secrete natural silk fibers. She's sung this rhyme from childhood:

Peasant maidens,
Having shouldered bamboo baskets and picked mulberry leaves,
Listen to the soft sizzling of treasured silkworms,
Enjoying their s-w-e-e-t, f-r-e-s-h, l-e-a-v-e-s!

Shen Aiqin at the Mogao Grottoes, located along the ancient Silk Road. Chinese silk was transported to the West along this trade route for 10 centuries.

Shen's homestead was in Jianqiao, a farming suburb of Hangzhou, a tourism city in Zhejiang Province famed for its West Lake. The Italian traveler Marco Polo was there more than 700 years ago. While strolling in the city, he was surprised by the tumult of spinning and weaving sounds or noises from dye houses. In his travelogue, the gorgeous silks and garments he saw in Hangzhou and elsewhere in China were repeatedly mentioned. But by then not even a Chinese could have been aware that, with its favorable soil and climate, Zhejiang Province, had

Feeding silkworms with mulberry leaves the old-fashioned way

been a homeland for silkworms for at least 7,000 years! Two archaeological excavations (in 1973 and 1977) at Hemudu revealed weaving and silkworm patterns on bone wares dating back 5,000 years. Other findings proved that wild silkworms were domesticated in Zhejiang at that time. While some of our heroine's forefathers were quite learned and had left precious woodblock printed books to their descendents, Shen Aiqin's grandfather and father were just plain small landholders and later were but poor peasants. When New China was born in 1949, Aiqin was only five years old. While growing up, she was, said her friend Li Dexin, but a very ordinary "silkworm-and-mulberry leaf maiden." Yet today her name is inseparable from China's leading brand for innovatively designed women's silk garments — Wensli, sold in 21 countries and regions, including those with leading fashion markets. In 2001 *Forbes* magazine put her 85th in China's 100 richest people. Her response was: "Wensli doesn't belong to me alone!"

Youthful Days

In feudal China farming was a family affair. Until the emergence of New China, the great majority of poor farming families rented land from landlords, and farming was essentially on a very small scale. Reform was carried out in 1950 to distribute land to poor peasants, and landlords as a social class were no more. Peasants who got very small plots of land soon joined mutual-aid teams, and then farming co-ops. Agriculture was later more and more collectivized, and government policies became more and more "Leftist." Aiqin, innocent and warm-hearted, and also an avid learner of all Party policies that sounded then so fresh and great to her and the average peasant, became a Communist Youth League member.at age 16 and then a Party member at 18. She had never finished junior middle school (ninth grade), because of her political and social work loads and interests besides financial difficulties.

The year 1958 was significant. Party and State authorities decided to promote the people's commune system nationwide in rural areas. The production team, identical with the scale of the natural village, was the grassroots unit of the commune's three-level ownership system. Several such teams formed a production brigade, and several brigades formed the top-level people's commune. Thus a people's commune acquired not only the economic potential of an agricultural production entity, but also — unbelievable as it sounds today — the function of a government body! Following the "cultural revolution" (1966-1976), the age of reform and opening up began, and, beginning in the early 1980s, the people's communes were gradually dissolved. Household farming regained its role, and there was a definite upsurge of market activities.

During the "cultural revolution," Shen Aiqin became a "bare-foot doctor" at the age of 16, and then at 18 head of Women's Work Section of the production brigade her family belonged to. Since generally proper doctors did not care to work in poor farming areas, Chairman Mao Zedong had the idea of giving short periods of medical training to urban youth, and assigning them to work in the countryside. Female "bare-foot doctors" had the additional duties of joining collective farming efforts, helping solve family disputes and conflicts between families, wiping out illiteracy, and helping females to meet specific difficulties, such as family planning and birth control. Her hard work won her the role of deputy head of her brigade.

Before a new page of history was turned, this young woman, largely self-taught, had acquired qualities often lacking in rustic females: She was strong-willed, with a broader mental horizon, a critical eye and an enterprising yet still equable temperament.

Trying Something New

In the afore-said period, subsistent farming was still the identity of most of China's peasantry, some better and others worse or much worse. Aiqin noticed that the local people still gathered mulberry leaves to feed to silkworms, as they had done since time immemorial, and then sold the cocoons or the reeled raw silk to the cities, where urban dwellers weaved the silk threads, and got better paid than the peasants. Why shouldn't the villagers weave as well, she wondered. Just one year before the Cultural Revolution ended in 1976, the local brigade leaders finally agreed to set up a small weaving workshop. It was just a row of small rooms in a thatched cottage, with 17 old looms. Shen was entrusted with only 3,600 yuan (about US$440) and 22 farmhands (only four males), who for the first time in their lives put aside their hoes. The excited womenfolk, led by Aiqin, quickly cleaned and whitewashed the place. Local people with expertise in silk weaving were invited to teach the workers their skills. There were also people who argued: "With so many old silk factories inside the city competing, can a bunch of rustic women get their things sold out? Then gossipers said: "Shen Aiqin has the gut to eat thorny crabs!"

In the old days, peasants in Jianqiao, Shen Aiqing's native place, carried cocoons and raw silk on boats like this to factories in cities.

Shortly after they went into production, officials of relevant offices above the township level came and said that their "factory" had not been ratified by the State, therefore not entitled to go into production. Since those were still the planned and highly centralized economy days in China, and market economy generally was nowhere to be seen, enterprises set up by peasants couldn't have their demands for raw materials, credits and energy etc got listed in State planning. Of course when Shen went to the relevant government bureaus, refusal was definite on account of scale and size of production too limited or small.

Shortly after they went into production, officials of relevant offices above the township level came and said that their "factory" had not been ratified by the State, therefore not entitled to go into production. Since those were still the planned and highly centralized economy days in China, and market economy generally was nowhere to be seen, enterprises set up by peasants couldn't have their demands for raw materials, credits and energy etc got listed in State planning. Of course when Shen went to the relevant government bureaus, refusal was definite on account of scale and size of production too limited or small.

However, it was only when State leader Deng Xiaoping openly supported the growth of TVEs (township and village enterprises) that the workshop got the official go-ahead, and adopted the proud title of Jianqiao Silk Factory.

Learning that satin quilt covers were in short supply all over China, Aiqin got her work team to learn how to make them, and personally took the products to sell in Beijing, the nation's capital. The workshop's profit at the end of the year was 60,000 *yuan* (about US$7,317).

Initiating Reforms

Aiqin raised eyebrows when she stuck to her Communist principles and insisted that female workers receive the same pay as male workers. Moreover, she arranged spare-time classes to train the workers. Her far-sighted stubbornness paid off when in 1993 she was awarded the title of Senior Economic Administrator.

On a trip to the US for a market survey, she found that not only raw Chinese silk but also dyed and printed silk articles were re-processed and sold for much higher prices. This convinced

Aiqing that the way forward was to equip her workshop with more advanced machinery. To get the funds to upgrade the outdated facilities, Aiqin personally approached the head of the All-China Textile Association in Beijing, and, after much persuading, was granted a total of 100 million yuan (about US$10 million) in bank loans. With this money, she bought the most advanced looms and other automatic machinery and equipment from Japan, South Korea, Italy, Germany, Switzerland and the US.

By March 1993, the Wensli Group had extended its operations from textiles, dyeing and garments to other industrial, agricultural, service and high-tech production, thanks to the newly formulated Corporation Law. Aiqing herself became CEO and President of the Group's Board of Directors. Prior to this, during the nationwide ownership reform wave beginning in the mid-1980s, she had severed her enterprise from the local government's control (dating back to the people's commune days) by letting the latter hold a percentage of shares. With a free hand in management, she and her team boldly introduced the system of basic wage plus bonus, something unheard of in the old days. Besides qualified Chinese experts, foreigners too, have been invited to visit, work, or for consultation in Wensli's factories or research institutes. The Group also has connections with joint ventures on the mainland, and in Hong Kong and abroad. Moreover, the Group now has its own export-import corporation selling not only silk items but also seafood and hi-tech products.

The strictest attention is paid to management and quality control, following closely the demands of the international ISO 9000 series and other standards. For garments alone, there are at least 12 checking procedures. The Group's silk products are exempt from Customs inspection because of their established fame and quality. Once, Aiqing learned that one button in a batch of 80,000 garments for export had not been properly sewed. She immediately ordered all the staff to check all the buttons on the garments due for delivery — a mammoth task. Nowadays, Wensli scarves, garments, etc., are used as gifts for visiting heads of state and delegates to international conventions in China. Wensli's products are also popular with tourists, and can even be found in the China Silk Museum in Hangzhou.

The name Wensli is an echo of the name of the leading Italian garment brand name Viensli, for which company Aiqing's group processed orders for nearly a decade, starting in the early 1980s. It was in this period that the group started to sound out the export market.

The Group now has over 3,000 employees (70% female and over 35% with higher education), who, for the first time in their lives, are shareholders, either individually or collectively. The Group's assets were estimated at 800 million yuan (about US$10 million) in 2003.

The Hangzhou Culture Arcade, built by the Wensli Group

In 2003, Aiqing realized that customers abroad generally were only aware of three kinds of silk fabrics: plain-woven silk, crepe and satin. But 14 kinds of silk in some 30 varieties have been known in China for centuries, such as spun silk, noil poplins and tussores. In fact, many don't even have equivalent foreign names. To revive and refine ancient techniques needs advanced scientific research, and Wensli's technicians hope to successfully accomplish this. They also solved the problem of wrinkling, which bedevils silk garments, and made the surface textures of their new materials suit the human body perfectly, while reviving ancient techniques of painting and embroidering on silk. In addition, Wensli's dyestuffs are environmentally friendly.

In October 2002, the Wensli Group opened the Hangzhou Culture Arcade. The five-story building covers 50,000 sq m and cost over 100 million yuan (about US$12 million). It is the biggest building in China for the sale of books and other publications. It also contains various facilities for cultural exchanges and tourism promotion.

From Wasteland to Oasis

— Li Fancong, Chairman of the Board, Shandong Yulu Industrial Enterprise Group

by Zhang Qingnian

We were driving down the road to Shatu, a township tucked away in the heartland of East China's Shandong Province. Once perennially flooded by the Yellow River, its land deteriorated year by year until practically nothing was left but yellow sandy soil, which is what the name of the town — Shatu — stands for. The peasants here were miserably poor. When life became intolerable, many left their homes to seek a living elsewhere, notably to the north of the Great Wall; others turned bandits or outlaws. In fact, this area provided the very setting for the well-known Chinese classic, *Outlaws of the Marsh*. And yet, on this trip, what met the eye when we looked beyond the tall trees lining the highway were large stretches of luscious green fields reaching far into the distance. I had heard about the dramatic changes that had taken place here in recent years, but still could hardly believe what I saw. In reply to my query, I was told that 30 years ago, the yield of wheat in this area was at the most 750 kg per ha. In those days, the per capita annual cash income was only 38 yuan, or less than five US dollars. The peasants relied on government relief grain to survive. Today, they told me, not without pride, that figure has shot up to 4,000 yuan, or nearly US$500.

I was eager to find out what it was that had brought about this tremendous change. I searched for the answer, and it was not hard to find. It came with the introduction of the government's reform and opening-up policy some 30 years ago, and a key figure in making the change a reality is a man named Li Fancong.

Eminent Chinese sociologist Fei Xiaotong (front row, right) was delighted by what he saw of the remarkable changes taking place in Shatu when he visited the township, accompanied by Li Fancong (front row, left). Fei is known for his deep interest and involvement in the cause of bringing prosperity to the impoverished parts of China's vast countryside.

Li was born and raised on this piece of what people regarded as a "land of no hope." But his life as a youth was better than that of most of his peers, as his father was a landlord and merchant, and so was able to send him to school. A good student in middle school, upon graduation Li was admitted to the Chemistry Department of the University of Hunan. Later he took up graduate studies at the University of Taiwan. After more than 20 years of trials and tribulations away from home, Li Fancong returned to Shatu in 1973. He was shocked and saddened by what he saw. Nothing had changed much — the land still smothered by yellow sand; everywhere, the same desolation, the same poverty. From that day on, Li Fancong decided he would use the knowledge he had acquired to help his fellow villagers shake off poverty, and to be able to do that he must first help them free themselves from apathy.

But where was he going to start? He had no funds, and nor did the local government. There was no factory, and no workable equipment to speak of. After much thought, he came to the conclusion that the only way to start was to utilize whatever local resources there were and produce something that required the minimum investment but would reap the fastest results, something that entailed no risk and would have a good market. He counted on his fingers the crops that grew on this land — grain, cotton, peanuts, soybeans, water melons, mushrooms, and some fruit and pawlonia trees. He chose to start with the local soy bean and make soy sauce. With the local authorities' agreement, he moved into a small deserted temple on the outskirts of town. With his grounding in chemistry, he was able to produce soy sauce with a fast fermenting method, and made a profit of 10,000 yuan for the locality within six months. To the local peasants, this bonanza was no less than, as they put it, "giving birth to a child of gold." Soon, Li was recruited to be the technician for the commune-run "Chemical Plant."

The "Plant" did not have even the semblance of a factory. The building was dilapidated, what machinery there was left was rusty, the factory's name plate swayed in the wind. There were only three workers left, the rest having deserted when the factory had no money to pay them. Again, the question — where to start? Li called to mind several attempts by scientists in the past to improve the land by turning over the soil and covering the sand with the upturned mud sediment. All their efforts had been in vain. But Li knew the soil here. He realized that to fundamentally transform the soil of Shatu, the one thing that was needed was NPK (nitrogen-phosphorous-potassium) compound fertilizer. But where and how was he going to get it? Buy it? Where was the money to come from? He told himself he would figure out a way to produce it.

A key ingredient for making this type of compound fertilizer was sulphate. Li himself designed the sulphate tower, hunted for the materials needed and which the factory could afford, and personally organized and directed the building of the project. Despite being allergic to lacquer, an indispensable element in the process, he never left his post. Moved by his determination and devotion, the workers rallied around him, and finally succeeded in turning out the new fertilizer which, when applied to their experimental plot, brought the wheat yield per ha to 3,750 kg. The word went around: The Chemical Plant has come alive.

Two years later, when it came to Li's knowledge that there was a great shortage of ferric oxide pigment (dyestuff) on the market, he saw immediately a new prospect opening for the plant. He went to every nook and corner in search of left-over pieces of iron as well as iron from abandoned machinery and equipment. These he collected as raw material for the experimental making of ferric oxide pigment. The plant finally succeeded in turning out the quality product. The red pigment brought them profits in the very first year. It was officially included in the provincial government's production plan, and was rated No. One four years running in that trade.

In 1979, Li was promoted director of the chemical plant, and simultaneously head of the newly established Shatu Brewery. In the course of conducting market research for new product ideas, Li heard that the sesame oil produced by a certain well-known factory in China had been rejected by their client in Japan, and the factory had been fined for its sesame oil's not being up to standard. He applied to the authorities for the right to produce sesame oil for export. He knew Shatu's sesame seed was of good quality, and that there were not a few experienced sesame oil makers in his hometown. He was certain that by combining modern technology with traditional skills, they would be able to come up with a product of international standard.

He called on dozens of traditional sesame oil makers in four counties, hoping to learn from their experience. He worked out a whole set of technical procedures after repeated experiments, carefully checking every quality index, and personally carrying out every sample analysis. When the product was shipped to Japan, orders came in from all over. One of the reasons Li gave me when I asked him how he managed to succeed was his strict rules regarding the quality of the sesame seeds bought from the farmers. Simple as it seems, it was not easy to adhere to, as a good many of the workers and staff of the factory were farmers themselves to begin with, and therefore had innumerable ties with the farming population. Not to be swayed by personal ties when purchasing the seeds, such as lowering the standards required, demanded a stamina which not all could maintain. To guarantee quality, Li would not hesitate to discharge those who violated the rules, not even his own relative or the son of a higher-ranking official. Throughout those days, he set an example of hard work and frugal living. In fact, for many years his monthly salary was still a meager 41.50 yuan. His example won him many followers. Shatu Brewery became known for its "Twelve Staunch Trail-Blazers."

In 1982, Li Fancong and his fellow workers set out to produce a special brand of soy sauce that brought Shatu international fame. Again, they were prompted by a report about how a major Chinese soy sauce brand had been squeezed out of the international market for being unable to compete with such world-famous brands as Switzerland's Maggi Seasoning and Japan's Kikkoman. Li and his colleagues loved challenges. With support from the provincial foreign trade department in the form of favorable loans, they did a great deal of research, and plunged into countless experiments, analyzing the contents of high-quality soy sauce produced abroad, and even drawing inspiration from the 16th century Chinese classic on pharmacology the *Compendium of Materia Medica*. They finally discovered an ingredient in the soy starch which had a uniquely strong and long-lasting flavor. Used in making soy sauce, it produced an extraordinarily good result. The new brand contained 18 kinds of amino-acid, its total content exceeding that of Japan's Kikkoman by 1.25% and the Swiss Maggi by 0.70%. Furthermore, the sauce is free of any kind of harmful chemical element. That very first year, the product found a ready market in 22 countries. The firmness of the quality of the Sunflower Brand Te Xian Soy Sauce was further testified to in 1994, when, during a nationwide quality check, a few bottles of the brand made in 1988 were found in the storage of a retail store which had earlier closed down. Laboratory tests showed that all of the 13 indices met the original standards, proving that the quality of the sauce had not deteriorated in any way. The news created such a stir that, in no time, more than 40 factories had requested technical cooperation with Shatu's brewery, or technological transfer. Shatu's own production scale expanded rapidly. Li Fancong's name became familiar to many as "The King of Soy Sauce."

This success brought in its wake unprecedented changes to Shatu's traditional mode of production. It greatly boosted the production of soybeans, sesame seeds and other high-profit industrial crops, which in turn doubled and redoubled the local farmers' income. All of a sudden, Shatu became the focus of the news media. One newspaper carried a report under the title, "A Golden Phoenix Emerges from the Sand Dunes!" In its peak years 1986-1988, the factory's annual output value hit the 100-million-yuan mark. In 1989, the township's per capita annual income had risen to 620 yuan, and the net profit from exports had reached 24.71 million US dollars.

Meanwhile, a comprehensive modern management system gradually took shape at the Shatu Brewery under Li's leadership. His remark that the quality of a product reflects the entrepreneur's conscience has become the motto for the whole factory. "Isn't it true," Li said during our interview, "that when one mentions a product of a township enterprise, some people shake their heads and query its quality. Or if a product's quality has defects, it's not rare for people to respond with, 'It must have been made by a township enterprise.' That poses a serious question for all township enterprises. If we don't improve our products, it will be the end for us."

Li went on to explain that many of the workers in his factory used to be small individual handicraft workers. "You can call them workers, or you can call them farmers. They may be relatives, friends or neighbors. That can sometimes create problems. For instance, it might be hard to reject the sesame seeds sold by a relative or friend even though they are not up to standard. My principle is, if you can't make 21 kg of sesame oil from 50 kg of sesame seeds, you pay for the loss. And if you produce more than the quota, you are paid 50% of the extra profit from that surplus. But, whatever the case, quality must be guaranteed. We are very strict about carrying out the system of rewards and penalties. It is an iron rule." The factory has also set up a Quality Check Group composed of the heads of the various departments, technical staff and workers to lead the work at every level. "They see to it that sub-standard raw materials do not enter the factory, sub-standard semi-finished products are not passed down the production line, and sub-standard finished products do not leave the factory." Li Fancong set a good example when, despite attempts at persuasion, bribery and pressure from above, he firmly rejected a consignment of sesame seeds because some were found to be moldy. "How can you make good sesame oil when the seeds are bad?" Li said, still agitated when he recalled that incident. "If we had accepted those seeds, our exports would have been affected. We would have brought harm to the country, besides smearing our own name. I told them to ask themselves whether they had any conscience left."

This was only one aspect of Li Fancong's efforts to improve management and raise the quality of his workers and staff. He has invested a considerable amount of funds in education and training programs in collaboration with universities and colleges in Shandong and elsewhere and with research institutions in Shanghai and Beijing. At the same time, the factory has set up a vocational school of its own to offer short-term training in such areas as management, accounting, fermentation, food canning, and electrical and mechanical engineering. These people, Li said, who grew up on farms and have inherited the down-to-earth and hard-working principles of their elders, can do wonders once they are equipped with modern management ideas and modern technology as well as public spirit.

By the end of the 1980s, Shatu Brewery had collected a number of gold and silver medals for its outstanding products. But Li Fancong set out to make the "cake" still larger. He had three strategic plans in mind, which he put into practice one by one:

First, in 1988, in cooperation with a Taiwan enterprise, he established the Yulu Food Company, Ltd. This gradually grew into an enterprise group embracing 29 subsidiary companies, with Li Fancong as Chairman of the Board and the Taiwan partner, the manager. These turn out more than 280 kinds of products in ten series, such as canned food, seasonings, dehydrated vegetables, frozen vegetables, vegetable and fruit juices, etc.

Second, Li set out to industrialize agriculture. By coordinating agriculture with industry and commerce, he hoped to give a bigger boost to the economy. Li introduced from abroad more than 50 high-quality vegetable and fruit seeds, taught the local farmers the techniques of growing them, and signed contracts with them guaranteeing purchase of their produce at prices favorable to the farmers while all risks were to be borne by the Corporation. In this way, the vegetable farmers were able to gain 5,000 to 10,000 yuan from each *mu* (one-fifteenth of a ha) of land. In 2000, the local population's per capita income shot up to 4,280 yuan, 12 times that of 1980. Soon, the practice was picked up by 38 townships in five neighboring counties.

In his third strategic move, Li Fancong began to invest in other Chinese provinces, to help the locals develop agro-product processing as a means of enlivening the mountainous and grassland areas. While seeking markets abroad, including in the US, Japan, Canada and Germany, Yulu has also strengthened its commercial and technical cooperation with European countries, including Germany, Britain and Spain.

However, Li said, the road has not been without twists and turns and bumps and falls. For instance, the Taiwan entrepreneur alone was in charge of the enterprise group's finance and international business. In December 1997, when a financial storm hit East Asia, Yulu's Taiwan partner, for fear of personal loss, abruptly withdrew all his funding from Yulu, causing tremendous difficulties to the entire Group. His withdrawal left behind a debt of eight million yuan to the vegetable farmers and another of nearly a hundred million yuan to the bank. That was a dark day for Li Fancong, as it was for the local farmers. Li decided to draw on the Group's assets to pay the farmers first. He was able to pay the total sum within two years, as well as part of the debt to the bank.

In 2001, with the deepening of the economic reform in China, Yulu Corporation became a totally private entity. With no more government intervention, Li Fancong could now go ahead and reorganize the enterprise. All the companies under the Group's umbrella introduced the shares system. Each has its own board of trustees. The employees are at the same time the share-holders, and all accounts are open for scrutiny.

Li said, "We are realigning to attract foreign investment. We are also recruiting talented people familiar with the profession, and experienced in marketing, management and legal affairs. They will be given power as well as responsibility." Thanks to all these measures, Li is revitalizing the enterprise group and reactivating the enterprise spirit.

The Minister of Agriculture of the Netherlands (third from left) on a visit to Yulu Industrial Group in 1999

For all these achievements, Li Fancong has been honored with many titles and awards. He is a member of the Shandong People's Political Consultative Conference, the top advisory body at the provincial level, a provincial Labor Model and a National Outstanding Township Entrepreneur.

Who would have thought that 53 years ago, at the age of 23, this same man had been convicted as a counter-revolutionary and sentenced to death?

Li Fancong was born in Shatu on April 6, 1928, into a landlord family. After finishing secondary school, he enrolled at the University of Hunan in 1945, majoring in chemistry. It was right after the end of World War II and Japan's surrender. While the nation hoped for peace and democracy to rebuild the country on the rubble left by Japan's eight-year war of aggression against China, the Chiang Kai-shek government resolved to start a civil war in an attempt to wipe out the people's forces led by the Communist Party of China. While at university, Li was a student activist in the nationwide popular movement against the civil war and was on a government blacklist. In 1948, when the Kuomintang was preparing to retreat to Taiwan and trying to coerce students of some universities in southern China to do the same, Li Fancong was one of the student leaders firmly opposed to the move. As fate would have it, however, in an attempt to escape arrest, Li, by mistake, got on a Kuomintang air force transport plane. By the time he realized it, the plane had landed in Taiwan. There, caught in a situation with no other way out, he entered the University of Taiwan as a graduate student, using an assumed name.

Meanwhile, the mainland of China had been completely liberated from Kuomintang rule, and the People's Republic was founded. Li was eager to return and help build New China. In 1951, when the Kuomintang in Taiwan launched another crackdown on progressives, Li was helped by a friend of his father's to leave the island for the mainland in a boat heading for the Zhoushan Archipelago, which is off the mainland's coast but at that time was still under Kuomintang control, not realizing that two of his companions were special agents being sent to the mainland by the Kuomintang for subversive activities. It turned out to be a most adventurous and hazardous voyage, as they battled storms and pirates along the way. When they arrived at the mainland, the three each went his own way. Alone, Li headed straight for home. He was welcomed as a returned university graduate, and was given the job of teacher in a local secondary school.

The next year, China launched a drive to uncover subversive elements who were out to undermine the newly-founded People's Republic. In that campaign, Li's two fellow-passengers on the boat were captured. In their confessions, they revealed there was a third traveler whom they believed to be a KMT special agent, too. It did not take long for the security department to locate Li Fancong. Despite his efforts to explain and clear himself, he was sentenced to death. However, since no wrongdoing had been found on his part, his sentence was commuted to 22 years in prison. Li was then only 23 years old.

"I felt it was the end for me," Li said. "I felt my life was finished. The only thing that kept me going was reading and studying. That's how I spent the evenings in the prison cell. Chemistry was still my greatest interest. I couldn't give that up. Fortunately, while in prison, I became acquainted with Prof. Cao Zhenghua, a prominent chemist, formerly chair of the Chemistry Department of Wuhan University, now an inmate as well. One thing he said lifted my heart: 'The future may not look so bright to you, but that doesn't mean you need to lose hope and remain passive and idle.' I decided to grasp the opportunity and learn more chemistry from him. Surely it would be useful some day, I thought."

When the two learned that the Chinese textile industry was then very short of dyes that keep the colors fast, they threw themselves into research to produce such a dye. They spent night after night in the prison laboratory, experimenting, with only a coal stove to keep off the bitter cold of winter. "Once," Li recalled, "someone reported to the prison authorities that we were spending the nights planning to escape. The prison warden decided to find out the truth for himself. He and another senior officer quietly entered the laboratory, and watched and listened to what we were doing and saying. We did not realize they were there until about 20 minutes later. At a meeting of the entire prison staff the next day, the warden complimented us on our work. Our product, known as AC.AS — D6011, eventually won a national first prize."

Li told me that at one point he contracted blood poisoning, and was on the verge of death. The prison staff went all out to save his life, including a blood donation by the warden himself. The warden said to Li: "You are still young. You've had a good education. Do a good job of remolding yourself, and you will have a great future."

Those words injected new hope in Li Fancong. During his years in prison, Li Fancong was commended sixteen times for his achievements in chemical research, and had his sentence reduced three times. He would have been released in 1966 if not for the outbreak in that year of the tumultuous "cultural revolution," which delayed his release by five years. Throughout this period, Li never stopped appealing for a re-examination of his case and a clearing of his name, but with relations across the Taiwan Straits as they were, it was not possible to prove his innocence.

In 1971, Li Fancong was released and returned to his hometown,

Shatu. His parents had passed away in 1959. His wife, and his son, born shortly after he left home, lived in a ramshackle hut which served both as the bedroom and kitchen. A broken wash basin, which also served as a feed bowl for the only goat they had, a broken iron wok, three broken bowls and two pairs of makeshift chopsticks of sorghum stalk were just about their only possessions. After Li was sentenced and imprisoned as a counter-revolutionary, life became even harder for his wife, as she was ostracized by her neighbors. "I owe her too much," Li said several times, as his eyes moistened.

Asked what kept him going through all the trials and tribulations, he said, "I grew up in a country torn by war and poverty, and humiliated by foreign invaders. From a very early age, I had a vision to learn something useful, so that I could help the country become strong, so that China would no longer be bullied. That always remained at the back of my mind, whatever happened. Then, of course, I love chemistry. It has always fascinated me what chemistry can do to change the world around us. Of course, what my teacher Professor Cao taught me and the prison warden's encouraging words also gave me the courage to push ahead despite all difficulties to do something useful for my people."

Appendixes

Law of the People's Republic of China on Township and Village Enterprises

(Adopted at the 22nd Meeting of the Standing Committee of the Eighth National People's Congress on October 29, 1996, promulgated by Order No. 76 of the President of the People's Republic of China on October 29, 1996, and effective as of January 1, 1997)

Article 1 This Law is enacted for the purpose of facilitating and guiding the sound and sustained development of township and village enterprises (TVEs), protecting their legitimate rights and interests, standardizing their operations, bringing about a prosperous rural economy and promoting the socialist modernization drive.

Article 2 The term TVEs as used in this Law refers to the different types of enterprises that are established in townships (including the villages under their jurisdiction) with the bulk of their capital being invested by rural economic collectives or farmers and that undertake the obligations to support agriculture.

The words "the bulk of their capital" as used in the preceding paragraph mean that the capital invested by the rural economic collectives or farmers exceeds 50 percent of the total, or is less than 50 percent but enough to play a holding or dominating role.

A TVE that meets the qualifications for an enterprise legal person shall obtain the status of a legal person as an enterprise.

Article 3 TVEs provide the mainstay of the rural economy and constitute an important component of the national economy.

The main tasks of TVEs are to develop production of commodities in light of market demands, provide service to the public, increase the supply of marketable products, absorb surplus rural labor, help raise the income of farmers, support agriculture, advance agricultural and rural modernization and promote the development of the national economy and social undertakings.

Article 4 In developing TVEs, the principle of taking the rural collective economy as the leading force and promoting the simultaneous development of the diversified economic sectors shall be adhered to.

Article 5 The State gives active support to TVEs, makes rational planning for their development, provides different guidance to different types of them and administer their affairs pursuant to law.

Article 6 The State encourages and mainly helps the economically underdeveloped areas and areas inhabited by ethnic minorities to develop TVEs, and encourages TVEs and other economic organizations in economically developed areas to support, by different means, the economically underdeveloped areas and areas inhabited by ethnic minorities in their efforts to run TVEs.

Article 7 The administrative department for TVEs under the State Council and other relevant departments shall, in accordance with their respective functions and responsibilities, make plans for and arrange coordination among, exercise supervision over and provide service to TVEs nationwide; the administrative departments for TVEs and other relevant departments of the local people's governments at or above the county level shall, in accordance with their respective functions and responsibilities, do the same with regard to TVEs within their respective administrative regions.

Article 8 The TVEs established through registration pursuant to law shall go through the procedure of registration for the record with the local administrative department for TVEs.

Where a TVE wishes to change its name or domicile, or to divide itself or merger with another, to suspend operation or close down, it shall, after making the registration of alteration, establishment or cancellation according to law, report to the administrative department for TVEs for the record.

Article 9 The branches established in cities by TVEs and the enterprises set up by rural economic collectives in cities to undertake the obligations in support of agriculture shall be treated as TVEs.

Article 10 Where a TVE is established with the investment of a rural economic collective, its property rights shall be owned collectively by all the farmers who help establish such enterprise.

Where a TVE is established with the joint investment of rural economic collectives and other enterprises, organizations or individuals, its property rights shall be owned by the investors in proportion to the amount of their shares.

Where a TVE is established with the investment of farmers in partnership or of a farmer alone, its property rights shall be owned by the investor(s).

Article 11 TVEs shall, in accordance with law, practice independent accounting and independent management and take full responsibility for its own profits and losses.

A TVE that has acquired the status of an enterprise legal person shall enjoy the right to the property of the legal person.

Article 12 The State protects the lawful rights and interests of TVEs; the legitimate property of TVEs shall be inviolable.

No organizations or individuals may, in violation of laws, administrative rules and regulations, intervene in the production and operation of TVEs, remove or replace the leading members of the enterprises; and they may not illegally take into their own possession or use without compensation the property of TVEs.

Article 13 TVEs shall be established in the forms provided by laws, administrative rules and regulations. The investors shall, in accordance with relevant laws, administrative rules and regulations, decide on major issues of the enterprises, institute operation and management systems, and enjoy the rights and undertake the obligations according to law.

Article 14 TVEs shall practice democratic management in accordance with law. The investors shall, before instituting the operation and management systems of the enterprise, deciding on the leading members of the enterprise, making decisions concerning major issues such as operation, the employees' wages and welfare, their occupational protection and safety, listen to the opinions of the trade union and the employees of such enterprise, regularly make public the implementation of the above-mentioned decisions and accept supervision by the employees.

Article 15 The State encourages the institution of a sound social insurance system for the employees of TVEs in areas where conditions permit.

Article 16 If a TVE suspends operation or closes down, where the social insurance system has been instituted, it shall make arrangements for the employees in accordance with relevant regulations; where a labor contract has been concluded, it shall handle the matter as agreed in the contract. Those employees who came from rural economic collectives shall have the right to return to their original rural economic collectives to engage in production or they may try to seek jobs themselves.

Article 17 TVEs shall draw a certain proportion of their after-tax profits to support agriculture and to spend on rural social undertakings. The proportion of such profits and measures for its use and management shall be prescribed by the people's governments of provinces, autonomous regions and municipalities directly under the Central Government.

Unless otherwise provided by laws, administrative rules and regulations, no State organs, organizations or individuals may, in whatever form, impose charges on or apportion expenses among TVEs.

Article 18 The State reduces a certain proportion of the tax to be collected from TVEs for a certain period of time, depending on the level of their development. The types of tax to be reduced, the period of time for and the proportion of such reduction shall be prescribed by the State Council.

Article 19 The State applies a preferential policy of taxation, for a certain period of time and in light of different circumstances, towards the small and medium-sized TVEs that meet one of the following conditions:

(1) Being a collectively owned township enterprise that truly has difficulties in operation in the incipient stage after its establishment;

(2) Being established in an area inhabited by ethnic minorities or in an outlying and poverty-stricken area;

(3) Being engaged in processing, storage, transport or marketing of grain, feed or meat; or

(4) Being in need of special assistance according to the industrial policy of the State.

The specific measures for executing the preferential policy of taxation mentioned in the preceding paragraph shall be prescribed by the State Council.

Article 20 The State encourages and facilitates the development of TVEs by means of credit and loan. With regard to the TVEs that meet one of the conditions provided in the preceding article and the qualifications for loan, the relevant financial institutions of the State may grant them priority loan or provide concessional loan to the ones that lack funds for production but have a promising future.

The specific measures for granting priority loan and concessional loan mentioned in the preceding paragraph shall be prescribed by the State Council.

Article 21 The people's governments at or above the county level may, in accordance with the relevant regulations of the State, set up development funds for TVEs. The funds shall consist of the following:

(1) The working funds allocated by the government for the development of TVEs;

(2) A certain proportion of the increased taxes annually turned over to the local people's governments by the TVEs;

(3) The profits derived from use of the funds; and

(4) The funds provided of their own free will by the rural economic collectives, TVEs and farmers.

Article 22 The development funds for TVEs shall specially be used for supporting the development of such enterprises in the following ways:

(1) To support the development of TVEs in areas inhabited by ethnic minorities, in outlying areas and poverty-stricken areas;

(2) To support economic and technological cooperation between TVEs in economically developed areas and such enterprises in economically underdeveloped areas and areas inhabited by ethnic minorities and support their efforts in undertaking jointly-invested projects;

(3) To support TVEs in their efforts to readjust the structure of

production and the mix of their products in accordance with the industrial policy of the State;

(4) To support TVEs in their efforts to update technology, to develop famous-brand, special, excellent and new products and to produce traditional handicrafts;

(5) To develop such TVEs as manufacture means of production for agriculture or directly serve the needs of agricultural production;

(6) To develop such TVEs as are engaged in processing, storage, transport and marketing of grain, feed and meat;

(7) To support vocational education and technical training for employees of TVEs; and

(8) Other projects that need support.

The specific measures for establishment, use and management of the development funds for TVEs shall be formulated by the State Council.

Article 23 The State helps train skilled people for TVEs and encourages scientists, technicians, managers and administrators and graduates of universities, junior colleges and specialized secondary schools to work in such enterprises and serve them in various ways.

TVEs shall, through various channels and forms, train their own technicians, managers, administrators and producers and adopt preferential measures to recruit skilled people.

Article 24 The State adopts preferential measures to encourage all forms of economic and technological cooperation between TVEs on the one hand and scientific research institutions, institutions of higher learning, State-owned enterprises and other enterprises and organizations on the other.

Article 25 The State encourages TVEs to carry out economic and technological cooperation and exchange with other countries, build export-oriented commodity production bases and increase foreign exchange earnings from exports.

TVEs that meet the requirements may, after approval in accordance with law, be authorized to engage in foreign trade.

Article 26 Local people's governments at all levels shall, under the principle of unified planning and rational geographical distribution, combine the development of TVEs with the construction of small towns, guide and promote the properly concentrated development of TVEs and gradually increase the building of infrastructure and service facilities to accelerate the construction of small towns.

Article 27 TVEs shall, in accordance with market demand and the industrial policy of the State, appropriately readjust the structure of production and the mix of products, promote technical updating, constantly adopt advanced technology, production techniques and equipment and improve the standard of management and administration.

Article 28 The land used for construction of TVEs shall be in line with the general plan for the use of land, and it shall be kept under strict control and used rationally and economically; where it is possible to use wasteland or land of inferior quality, no cultivated land or land of good quality shall be used.

Where land owned by rural collectives is used for construction of a TVE, relevant procedures shall have to be gone through to obtain approval and to register for the use of the land in accordance with laws and regulations.

If the land owned by rural collectives to be used for construction of a TVE has been left unused for two successive years or more, or left unused for one year or more because its construction has been called off, the right to use of the land shall be taken over by the original owner, which shall make new arrangement for its use.

Article 29 TVEs shall rationally develop and use natural resources in accordance with law.

In order to extract mineral resources, a TVE must, in accordance with relevant laws, obtain approval of the relevant department, a mining permit and a production permit, operate in line with relevant rules and guard against waste of resources, and destruction of resources is strictly prohibited.

Article 30 TVEs shall, in accordance with relevant regulations of the State, set up a financial and accounting system to tighten financial control and keep account books according to law to record financial activities truthfully.

Article 31 TVEs must, according to the statistical regulations of the State, submit reports of truthful statistical data. They shall have the right to refuse to fill in statistical survey forms prepared and issued in violation of State regulations.

Article 32 TVEs shall go through the formalities for tax registration according to law, submit tax returns regularly and pay taxes in full.

The people's governments at all levels shall strengthen the administration of tax collection in relation to TVEs in accordance with law and the relevant administrative department shall not reduce the taxes of TVEs or exempt them from taxation beyond the limit of its authority for administration.

Article 33 TVEs shall pay close attention to the quality control of their products and make efforts to improve the quality; the products they manufacture and market must meet both the national standards and the trade standards for safeguarding human health and safety of the person and property; no products that have ceased to be effective, that have gone bad or that have been eliminated by formal State orders shall be manufactured or marketed; and it is forbidden to mix impurities or imitations into products, or pass a fake or defective product off as a genuine or good one.

Article 34 TVEs shall use trademarks in accordance with law and cherish their own reputation; they shall print trademarks for the commodities they produce in accordance with State regulations, and they shall not forge the place of origin or forge or falsely use the name and address of a factory of another producer, as well as authentication marks and famous-and-excellent product marks of another producer.

Article 35 TVEs must abide by laws and regulations regarding environmental protection and, in adherence to the industrial policy of the State and under the unified guidance of the local people's governments, take measures to make themselves enterprises that discharge little or no pollution and consume less resources, in order to prevent and control environmental pollution and ecological disruption and to protect and improve the environment.

Local people's governments shall formulate and implement the plans of TVEs for protecting the environment, thus increasing their ability to prevent and control pollution.

Article 36 If a TVE undertakes a construction project that will have an impact on the environment, it must strictly apply the evaluation system governing impact on the environment.

Installations for preventing or controlling pollution embraced in the construction project that is undertaken by a TVE must be designed, constructed and put into operation or use simultaneously with the main part of the project. The project shall not be put into operation or use until the installations for preventing or controlling pollution have been examined and accepted by the administrative department for environmental protection.

No TVEs may adopt or make use of production techniques and equipment formally prohibited by the State for they cause serious environmental pollution; and they may not manufacture or market products formally prohibited by the State for they seriously pollute the environment. Those TVEs that discharge pollutants in excess of the standard set by the State or local authorities and thus seriously pollute the environment shall bring the pollution under control within a time limit; those that fail to do so within the time limit shall close down, suspend production or change the line of production.

Article 37 TVEs must abide by laws and regulations regarding occupational protection and safety, conscientiously carrying out the principle of putting safety and prevention first, adopting effective technical and managerial measures for occupational health and preventing the occurrence of casualties in production and occupational diseases; and they shall remove the hidden elements of accidents that may endanger the safety of employees within a time limit or suspend production for rectification. Managers are strictly forbidden to give instructions against rules and regulations or compel employees to work at risk. Once casualties occur, they shall take emergency rescue measures, make proper arrangements for the victims according to law, and report the matter to the departments concerned.

Article 38 Whoever, in violation of this Law, commits any of the following acts shall be ordered to put it right by the administrative department of the people's government at or above the county level that is in charge of TVEs:

(1) Altering ownership of a TVE in violation of law;

(2) Taking into his/her possession or using without compensation the property of a TVE in violation of law;

(3) Removing or replacing the leading members of a TVE in violation of law; or

(4) Encroaching on the right of a TVE to independent management.

If any of the said acts causes economic losses to a TVE, compensation shall be made in accordance with law.

Article 39 TVEs shall have the right to accuse or report against any units or individuals that collect charges from, apportion expenses among or impose fines on them in violation of law to the administrative departments for audit, supervision, finance, price control and TVEs. The department concerned and the organ at higher levels shall order the persons who are responsible for the violation to desist and return the money within a time limit. The departments concerned may, in light of seriousness of the violation, impose appropriate sanctions on the persons who are directly responsible for the violation.

Article 40 Before they put it right, TVEs that violate laws or regulations of the State regarding product quality, environmental protection, land administration, development of natural resources, occupational safety, taxation, etc. shall, in light of seriousness of the violation, be deprived of part or all of the preferential treatment they have enjoyed in accordance with this Law, in addition to sanctions imposed pursuant to relevant laws and regulations.

Article 41 TVEs that, in violation of this Law, refuse to undertake the obligations in support of agriculture, shall be ordered to put it right by the administrative department for TVEs and may, before they put it right, be deprived of part or all of the preferential treatment that they have enjoyed according to this Law.

Article 42 If a party is not satisfied with the handling done or sanctions imposed according to the provisions from Article 38 through Article 41 of this Law, it may apply for administrative reconsideration or bring a lawsuit in accordance with law.

Article 43 This Law shall be put into force as of January 1, 1997.

Table 1 Total Number of TVEs (1978-2004)

(Unit: enterprise)

	Total	Agriculture	Industry	Construction	Transport	Trade	Tourism and catering	Others
1978	1 524 268	494 638	793 977	46 707	65 112	60 328	61 988	1 518
1979	1 480 416	443 947	767 098	49 651	82 142	66 134	69 960	1 484
1980	1 424 661	378 342	757 806	50 772	89 387	70 836	76 055	1 463
1981	1 337 563	319 042	725 355	48 340	88871	76125	78 405	1425
1982	1 361 771	292 896	749 290	53 724	95 767	82 136	86 271	1 687
1983	1346 407	269 838	743 971	56 976	91 574	89 072	91 180	3 796
1934	1 649 641	248 420	900 981	80 425	129 563	137 855	111 824	40 573
1985	12 225 000	224 194	3 985 350	592 912	2 743 694	3 004 025	1 344 750	330 075
1986	15 153 065	239 723	6 354 977	692 513	2 819 815	2 568 645	1 570 134	907 258
1987	17 502 540	231 267	7 082 831	902 595	3 252 411	3 251 116	1 950 575	831 745
1988	18 881 644	232 846	7 735 213	955 810	3 725 541	3 420 959	2 022 976	788 299
1989	18 686 282	226 829	7 364 664	925 512	3 798 800	3 609 564	2 123 674	637 239
1990	18 734 397	223 643	7 320 357	904 665	3 893 725	3 633 870	2 063 528	694 609
1991	19 087 422	230 974	7 426 691	888 436	4 008 610	3 863 209	2 049 881	619 621
1992	20 919 581	249 233	7 938 214	984 855	4 369 503	4 277 487	2 393 744	706 545
1993	24 529 272	279 084	9 184 409	1 216 948	4 863 989	5 205 490	2 844 632	934 720
1994	24 944 663	246 438	6 985 839	829 865	3 691 073	6 212 977	4 312 659	2 665 812
1995	22 026 681	277 721	7 181 621	1 067 483	4 951 694	5 486 997	2 435 196	625 969

1996	23 363 285	289 444	7 564 336	1 045 824	5 464 886	5 948 610	2 504 036	546 149
1997	20 148 598	214 575	6 655 712	825 821	4 170 764	5 484 426	2 222 898	574 402
1998	20 039 353	189 197	6 619 625	821 344	4 148 150	5 454 690	2 210 846	595 501
1999	20 708 863	165 138	6 735 126	825 466	4 126 601	5 831 200	2 414 064	611 268
2000	20 846 637	151 192	6 740 109	795 215	4 125 160	5 912 993	2 491 859	630 109
2001	21 155 389	127 412	6 721 707	762 601	4 128 603	6 141 689	2 627 013	646 364
2002	21 326 857	321 686	6 276 813	697 496	3 801 280	6 271 174	3 173 074	785 334
2003	21 850 797	414 327	6 431 297	680 633	3 834 459	6 478 492	3 394 145	637 444
2004	22 132 161	414 401	6 402 750	654 086	3 774 969	6 773 498	3 451 984	660 473

Table 2 Total Employment of TVEs (1978-2004)

(Unit: person)

	Total	Agriculture	Industry	Construction	Transportation	Trade	Tourism & catering	Others
1978	28 265 566	6 084 227	17 343 595	2 356 133	1 038 297	544 289	588 289	310 736
1979	29 093 382	5 330 010	18 143 805	2 984 520	1 168 960	568 934	589 508	307 645
1980	29 996 774	4 560 722	19 423 033	3 346 690	1 135 565	617 346	623 248	290 170
1981	29 695 646	3 799 413	19 808 024	3 488 258	1 073 823	603 723	631 148	291 257
1982	31 129 107	3 439 973	20 728 083	4 212 932	1 129 397	632 865	661 615	324 242
1983	32 346 356	3 092 224	21 681 301	4 827 200	1 097 080	711 375	684 784	252 392

1984	38 480 993	2 839 337	25 489 125	6 834 888	1 293 020	697 163	831 074	496 386
1985	69 790 000	2 523 836	41 036 520	10 468 500	5 164 460	5 878 880	3 670 954	1 046 850
1986	79 371 390	2 407 966	47 619 559	12 703 666	5 412 587	4 864 727	3 650 008	2 712 877
1987	88 051 829	2 441 836	52 666 905	13 739 769	6 231 432	6 014 308	4 500 868	2 456 711
1988	95 454 636	2 499 876	57 033 912	14 848 142	6 841 553	6 717 071	5 120 780	2 393 302
1989	93 667 793	2 392 996	56 241 046	14 037 287	6 993 660	6 923 355	5 143 258	1 936 191
1990	92 647 539	2 360 648	55 716 921	13 468 447	7 112 152	7 029 472	4 906 367	2 053 532
1991	96 136 273	2 431 697	58 149 265	13 853 649	7 331 569	7 415 503	5 063 039	1 891 551
1992	106 247 146	2 618 203	63 363 961	15 524 240	7 997 384	8 667 901	5 799 732	2 275 725
1993	123 453 082	2 853 606	72 595 609	18 269 309	9 314 494	10 572 614	6 996 925	2 850 525
1994	120 174 691	2 604 586	69 615 092	16 220 441	7 255 935	12 578 297	7 748 727	4 151 613
1995	128 620 586	3 135 221	75 647 153	19 325 217	9 520 275	12 261 104	6 765 349	1 966 267
1996	135 082 851	3 359 955	78 601 383	19 488 380	10 623 245	13 845 798	7 400 485	1 763 605
1997	130 504 229	2 769 642	76 348 656	17 007 132	9 226 668	14 770 588	7 990 939	2 390 604
1998	125 365 458	2 739 147	73 342 330	16 337 455	8 863 356	14 188 978	7 676 286	2 217 906
1999	127 040 877	2 473 796	73 953 221	16 134 539	8 857 215	15 140 193	8 349 011	2 132 902
2000	128 195 720	2 220 415	74 667 299	15 810 917	8 984 854	15 569 348	8 640 388	2 302 499
2001	130 855 754	2 000 282	76 151 065	15 644 119	9 026 864	16 437 365	9 245 355	2 350 704
2002	132 877 100	2 053 744	76 676 121	14 603 632	8 616 179	16 912 665	11 327 193	2 687 566
2003	135 729 324	2 904 247	78 562 347	14 084 440	8 479 454	16 733 612	12 101 355	2 863 869
2004	138 661 740	2 847 173	81 605 448	13 759 756	8 444 657	16 993 032	12 438 503	2 573 171

Table 3 Total Added Value of TVEs (1978-2004)

(Unit: 1 million yuan)

	Total	Agriculture	Industry	Construction	Transportation	Trade	Tourism & catering	Others
1978	20 832.24	1 537.20	15 954.92	1 257.07	903.61	431.95	487.10	260.39
1979	22 834.75	1 688.50	17 521.76	1 626.90	1 069.29	375.35	437.34	115.61
1980	28 531.46	1 741.28	20 917.69	2 449.88	1 274.35	909.70	963.41	275.15
1981	32 14 6.52	1 671.61	24 548.34	2 532.45	1 321.35	916.54	969.76	186.47
1982	37 441.36	1 946.94	27 232.58	2 979.56	1 588.98	1 087.50	1.169.48	1 436.32
1983	4 0 841.57	2 123.75	30 233.20	3 252.15	1 732.28	1 280.50	1 188.62	1 031.07
1984	63 321.06	2 353.16	41 790.18	8 391.87	2 905.36	2 425.03	2 089.12	3 366.34
1985	77 231.00	1 862.00	51 808.00	9 592.00	4 520.00	4 024.00	3 035.00	2 390.00
1986	87 316.27	1 711.80	59 583.48	11 573.36	5 059.60	4 572.45	2 927.48	1 888.10
1987	141 642.73	2 077.89	106 521.06	14 356.90	6 941.62	5 994.31	3 753.53	1 997.42
1988	174 204.65	2 231.82	130 563.30	18 595.74	8 285.70	8 209.66	4 157.00	2 161.43
1989	208 316.25	2 439.28	156 217.32	20 566.52	10 873.62	10 546.12	5 075.93	2 597.46
1990	250 431.88	3 672.18	185 540.12	24 053.20	16 608.48	12 021.23	7 118.07	1 418.60
1991	297 214.56	4 458.22	222 714.97	27 343.74	18 130.09	13 266.30	9 808.08	1 493.16
1992	448 534.20	5 648.48	335 013.82	43 017.75	27 231.74	23 374.65	12 645.86	1 601.90
1993	800 683.32	10 302.14	593 573.55	78 690.82	48 053.71	44 611.99	22 080.52	3 370.59

1994	1 092 803.36	20 763.26	808 674.49	96 166.70	60 104.18	72 125.02	29 505.69	5 464.02
1995	1 459 522.68	27 982.32	1 080 404.23	128 135.39	80 416.87	96 007.30	39 125.95	7 450.62
1996	1 765 929.64	34 468.53	1 262 765.80	143 710.80	114 598.96	142 880.43	56 934.17	10 570.95
1997	2 074 032.09	32 180.57	1 451 799.40	166 493.52	127 267.20	184 143.10	85 619.37	26 528.93
1998	2 218 645.61	34 615.66	1 553 027.25	178 102.42	136 141.01	196 982.62	91 589.25	28 187.40
1999	2 488 255.71	33 865.12	1 737 410.98	194 461.57	150 945.15	231 184.82	110 299.36	30 088.71
2000	2 715 622.88	31 385.43	1 881 241.15	210 078.90	165 765.01	262 561.38	128 845.12	35 745.89
2001	2935 638. 86	28 662.27	2 031 466.21	219 352.28	182 190.79	295 574.04	137 524.66	40 868.61
2002	3 238 579.88	34 177 10	2 277 302 94	228 778.32	180 945.86	303 644.07	163 711.76	50 019.83
2003	3 668 632.54	51 903.78	2 574 533.24	241 149.95	196 517.32	342 044.48	201 600.12	60 883.65
2004	4 187 536.25	56 439.23	2 935 856.60	266 601 60	218 868.01	390 919.22	224 761.88	88 089.71

Table 4 Total Output Value of TVEs (1978-2004)

(Unit: 1 million yuan)

	Total	Agriculture	Industry	Construction	Transportation	Trade	Tourism & catering	Others
1978	51 437.62	4 314.07	38 876.34	3 103.87	2 231.13	1 066.54	1 202.71	642.96
1979	56 073.46	4 391.89	42 494.86	3 995.06	2 625.78	921.73	1 073.95	570.19
1980	67 832.56	4 481.04	51 907.82	5 111.28	2 791.98	1 449.54	1 577.23	513.67

1981	76 725.70	4 868.52	58 517.36	5 781.39	3 158.02	1 639.58	1 884.01	876.82
1982	89 232.65	5 662.13	64 941.06	6 723.80	3 672.80	1 906.85	2 191.12	4 134.89
1983	101 931.12	6 167.89	75 421.78	7 680.65	4 095.47	2 502.93	2 278.20	3 784.20
1984	142 084.25	5 325.07	102 100.96	21 729.69	4 763.42	3 687.58	2 247.78	2 229.75
1985	272 840.00	5 728.08	182 720.00	24 773.80	16 097.50	17 734.60	8 076.00	17 710.02
1986	371 704.74	7 287.14	244 348.87	52 673.30	25 795.78	22 019.13	12 462.27	7 118.25
1987	505 497.82	9 197.65	341 240.09	65 534.93	36 220.08	32 076.56	13 402.77	7 825.74
1988	750 243.93	12 382.17	499 290.43	84 883.95	48 451.01	81 924.56	14 843.49	8 468.32
1989	840 181.82	13 468.01	610 054.85	91 015.36	55 348.17	44 530.60	17 345.77	8 419.06
1990	978 034.59	15 125.69	709 704.98	97 381.36	65 885.19	50 682.19	32 467.12	6 788.06
1991	1 181 057.87	17 929.02	869 958.46	114 100.42	76 715.41	56 763.58	38 786.23	6 804.75
1992	1 787 995.64	26 509.09	1 319 337.43	179 127.72	110 749.77	93 498.60	51 197.83	7 575.20
1993	3 213 232.32	41 346.06	2 355 858.03	325 825.10	200 068.57	185 187.23	91 420.76	13 526.57
1994	4 612 404.24	59 638.74	3 468 800.26	417 965.24	230 191.60	280 797.39	135 094.28	19 916.73
1995	6 956 866.68	101 807.57	5 125 917.01	633 596.81	411 668.38	454 813.95	199 631.60	29 431.36
1996	7 677 764.37	123 929.27	5 623 902.08	596 874.40	417 511.85	591 094.17	266 713.94	57 738.66
1997	8 990 059.78	134 950.66	6 585 148.16	698 893.10	488 873.62	692 124.90	312 301.10	77 768.24
1998	9 669 365.61	145 147.79	6 912 753.19	804 010.67	562 418.20	796 224.98	359 300.91	89 509.87
1999	10 842 606.87	139 198.78	7 673 622.88	873 860.40	621 045.43	972 835.28	43 904.87	123 002.23
2000	11 615 027.45	126 897.48	8 245 641.20	899 747.60	672 891.21	1 033 188.91	491 761.18	144 899.87

2001	12 604 687.93	116 210.96	8 984 544.09	930 996.91	700 360.58	1 161 347.64	542 607.92	168 619.83
2002	14 043 450.16	183 089.18	10 035 782.67	969 335.24	706 002.26	1 209 540.46	671 970.62	267 729.73
2003	15 236 071.59	190 969.99	1 108 7870.00	996 346.55	735 208.15	1 416 186.99	735 826.25	219 861.66
2004	17 251 673.36	204 834.30	12 554 710.79	1 078 356.80	789 432.30	1 269 988.99	826 695.04	381 457.14

Table 5 Total Operational Income of TVEs (1978-2004)

(Unit: 1 million yuan)

	Total	Agriculture	Industry	Construction	Transportation	Trade	Tourism & catering	Others
1978	43 146.05	3 618.66	32 609.61	2 603.54	1 871.48	892.96	1 006.96	542.84
1979	49 109.89	3 846.48	37 217.57	3 498.93	2 299.69	807.26	940.58	499.38
1980	59 612.52	3 938.02	45 555.72	4 491.89	2 453.65	1 273.88	1 386.10	513.26
1981	67 036.09	3 896.81	51 099.13	5 257.65	2 497.54	1 752.34	1 956.90	575.72
1982	77 177.90	4 005.88	57 690.49	7 509.32	2 918.42	2 017.45	2 252.96	783.38
1983	92 869.86	4 371.82	68 675.41	10 188.19	3 262.84	2 712.74	2 440.10	1 218.76
1984	126 815.13	5 171.90	89 794.93	16 199.16	4 716.11	6 449.48	2 730.15	1 753.40
1985	256 560.00	5 728.08	131 155.03	23 295.65	15 137.00	16 676.40	7 594.20	56 973.64
1986	336 426.63	6 813.04	212 253.99	39 812.01	25 391.33	32 451.39	12 586.62	7 118.25

1987	459 772.03	8 367.85	310 392.10	59 586.45	32 919.67	29 195.54	12 183.96	7 126.46
1988	661 970.02	11 921.08	450 872.03	77 000.00	48 028.50	47 421.31	17 656.00	9 071.10
1989	776 267.77	12 674.78	508 664.23	70 241.90	58 364.55	86 385.34	31 517.91	8 419.06
1990	861 360.66	14 084.65	567 998.29	74 639.96	66 475.18	79 272.58	49 039.23	9 850.77
1991	1 058 279.49	16 578.05	723 195.11	91 215.52	90 842.16	73 800.04	48 541.27	14 107.34
1992	1 638 955.82	24 475.88	1 199 416.91	141 265.34	109 429 74	88 900.56	58 473.50	16 993.89
1993	2 895 351.04	35 314.10	2 133 335.28	263 693.65	174 279.49	189 285.75	83 084.77	16 358.00
1994	3 927 431.86	47 902.21	2 893 786.92	357 690.25	236 403.40	256 758.81	112 701.28	22 188.99
1995	5 729 931.84	83 852.47	4 221 894.20	521 853.69	339 065.25	374 601.53	164 423.94	24 240.76
1996	6 834 314.96	102 591.75	5 006 139.12	531 310.22	371 649.89	526 164.92	237 416.51	59 042.55
1997	8 182 658.08	122 832.09	5 993 801.85	636 132.50	444 972.76	629 972.08	284 256.46	70 690.34
1998	8 935 101.40	134 125.68	6 387 798.71	742 954.10	519 708.16	735 759.65	332 015.60	82 739.50
1999	10 093 216.15	129 577.36	7 143 222.07	813 459.16	578 118.77	905 592.89	408 695.30	114 550.60
2000	10 783 433.10	117 539.42	7 655 159.15	835 716.06	624 360.78	959 186.37	456 139.22	135 332.10
2001	11 658 546.85	116 210.96	8 038 399.41	930 996.91	700 360.58	1161 347.64	542 607.92	168 623.43
2002	12 975 962.64	165 343.83	8 768 600.11	846 244.46	680 602.58	1612 651.34	673 243.07	229 277.25
2003	14 678 343.72	179 921.55	10 274 526.98	889 151.92	705 271.56	1683 192.59	729 837.18	216 441.94
2004	16 636 848.33	188 991.38	10 652 448.57	949 664.11	748 776.60	1875 303.86	820 364.73	401 299.08

Table 6 Total Value of Goods Delivered for Export by TVEs (1978-2004)

(Unit: 1 million yuan)

	Total	Direct export	Chemical products	Mechanical products	Minerals	Light industrial goods	Foodstuffs
1986	9 948.70	7 099.44	547.18	305.13	557.21	1 716.44	952.11
1987	16 915.77	11 902.67	817.23	219.59	778.02	1 572.73	1 485.01
1988	26 870.70	19 537.67	1 504.68	1 122.88	1 357.77	2 871.86	2 712.88
1989	37 144.33	27 162.35	2 075.56	1 781.93	1 915.24	3 845.98	3 492.05
1990	48 563.31	36 440.95	2 469.74	2 639.47	2 449.96	6 351.58	4 186.19
1991	78 912.17	59 175.24	3 461.33	4 055.81	2 844.34	14 273.10	5 393.71
1992	119 279.40	90 471.41	6 693.21	7 281.57	4 063.75	18 600.69	7 944.73
1993	219 300.14	141 679.75	10 958.94	14 556.85	6 867.16	44 619.92	12 872.24
1994	339 830.80	228 391.61	18 652.05	24 217.32	14 876.12	68 234.58	23 198.85
1995	539 454.72	347 185.39	29 624.54	38 443.10	23 614.92	108 320.22	36 825.88
1996	600 787.92	423 855.06	32 992.68	42 813.93	26 299.88	120 635.67	41 012.91
1997	682 647.96	543 079.94	36 614.73	50 645.05	27 303.43	146 225.38	43 991.51
1998	685 364.53	530 042.01	34 626.27	51 808.02	28 612.37	147 667.44	42 531.76
1999	774 358.27	612 150.66	38 549.09	63 538.23	27 895.47	187 877.58	46 937.87
2000	886 944.59	694 881.65	44 029.68	74 362.33	33 204.71	222 357.98	52 855.06

2001	959 881.05	785 472.11	47 418.12	78 998.22	38 107.28	241 506.07	54 521.24
2002	1 156 341.94	922 526.02	55 805.38	122 213.75	42 573.06	268 699.13	65 346.29
2003	1 419 661.31	1148 931.90	63 346.08	142 668.04	56 098.39	349 071.25	76 612.68
2004	1 693 247.39	1390 409.34	75 103.66	192 856.69	71 266.36	458 594.67	95 328.26

Table 7 Comprehensive Indices of TVEs (1978-2002) (1)

(Unit: 1 million yuan)

Year	Total payroll		Total profit		Net profit		Tax paid	
	Total	Collective enterprises	Total	Collective enterprises	Total	Collective enterprises	Total	Collective enterprises
1978	8 664.31	8 664.31	9 551.09	9 551.09	8 808.88	8 808.88	2 196.04	2 196.04
1979	10 382.11	10 382.11	11 156.45	11 156.45	10 450.75	10 450.75	2 255.96	2 255.96
1980	11 941.99	11 941.99	12 626.17	12 626.17	11 837.92	11 837.92	2 565.63	2 565.63
1981	13 063.67	13 063.67	12 231.00	12 231.00	11 279.37	11 279.37	3 428.17	3 428.17
1982	15 333.74	15 333.74	12 806.26	12 806.26	11 551.77	11 551.77	4 473.34	4 473.34
1983	17 580.54	17 580.54	13 668.56	13 668.56	11 781.59	11 781.59	5 888.10	5 888.10
1984	23 928.96	23 928.96	15 501.83	15 501.83	12 871.75	12 871.75	7 912.83	7 912.83

1985	47 210.00	30 142.79	24 705.00	20 400.48	21 740.00	17 133.89	13 700.00	10 860.00
1986	58 565.33	35 551.48	32 891.13	21 114.77	30 238.38	16 103.43	17 714.85	12 183.25
1987	73 615.21	42 768.16	38 110.42	24 944.88	34 526.62	18 775.13	22 183.80	13 072.70
1988	96 347.69	54 116.78	64 971.91	34 977.39	55 001.82	25 918.15	25 030.39	17 652.53
1989	10 549.85	58 067.09	67 508.76	33 391.97	56 977.86	24 014.87	28 823.73	19 608.81
1990	11 296.53	60 675.12	68 345.58	31 847.00	58 242.75	22 970.83	31 283.68	20 323.47
1991	13 050.55	70 653.01	81 478.61	39 899.33	68 762.11	28 465.86	36 510.51	24 431.33
1992	17 467.07	96 535.70	111 934.81	53 483.08	104 788.38	48 130.80	49 432.66	33 619.78
1993	256 317.71	132 390.34	216 157.64	109 305.04	195 927.25	92 526.72	94 781.78	64 853.47
1994	300 331.45	165 124.32	257 231.03	135 208.16	228 617.32	114 741.08	103 530.54	65 424.11
1995	438 132.16	219 240.72	369 724.58	177 531.06	325 087.21	149 610.47	127 971.33	80 868.85
1996	524 400.83	251 140.12	435 079.61	203 558.25	388 556.02	173 093.07	130 661.86	82 650.76
1997	582 707.61	252 925.54	486 506.86	203 409.69	435 546.86	173 451.51	152 633.12	85 942.51
1998	625 186.22	248 299.81	511 236.31	196 931.41	463 530.52	169 778.13	158 297.93	86 618.65
1999	659 669.27	239 903.57	598 453.46	201 278.54	539 176.90	172 309.59	178 947.35	91 733.59
2000	706 048.31	231 986.67	648 181.14	200 934.00	588 255.03	173 353.97	199 649.82	93 142.53
2001	773 206.32	224 565.21	670 945.99	195 040.01	600 150.02	166 428.39	230 808.56	97 317.65
2002	852 846.57	207 052.75	755 779.12	274 183.75	696 265.93	183 595.91	269 353.58	142 357.03

Table 8 Comprehensive Indices of TVEs (1978-2002) (2)

(Unit: 1 million yuan)

	Floating assets		Original value of fixed assets		Bank loans		Grants to agriculture and other social spending
	Total	Collective enterprise	Total	Collective enterprise	Total	Collective enterprise	
1978	9 498.97	9 498.97	22 958.49	22 958.49	2 200.81	2 200.81	3 034.15
1979	13 269.86	13 269.86	28 016.12	28 016.12	3 534.27	3 534.27	3 183.44
1980	17 724.14	17 724.14	32 632.06	32 632.06	5 610.37	5 610.37	2 947.52
1981	20 099.55	20 099.55	37 544.09	37 544.09	7 033.62	7 033.62	2 365.91
1982	23 048.58	23 048.58	42 928.03	42 92 8.03	8 153.71	8 153.71	2 377.48
1983	26 250.42	26 250.42	47 564.55	47 564.55	9 770.47	9 770.47	2 494.98
1984	39 868.72	39 868.72	57 499.72	57 499.72	19 795.90	19 795.90	4 573.40
1985	64 708.00	59 013.87	82 300.00	75 038.60	28 800.00	27 779.62	6 900.00
1986	92 838.99	76 980.84	121 173.84	94 674.64	53 833.92	51 993.36	7 800.00
1987	134 163.24	113 464.45	160 355.30	122 96 4.57	59 755.87	57 712.84	8 900.00
1988	182 449.16	154 057.85	209 870.16	158 43 1.58	78 503.00	73 238.01	10 400.00
1989	222 359.71	189 011.03	249 956.07	192 06 7.16	96 013.25	86 521.83	11 587.62
1990	263 190.30	224 465.16	285 706.99	220 20 0.13	112 826.89	105 605.97	13 821.22
1991	337 611.68	292 502.48	338 520.46	262 63 1.45	144 408.50	135 182.70	15 481.36

1992	469 872.77	409 528.94	454 023.34	349 07 9.55	207 091.56	184 932.77	17 163.16
1993	765 769.07	633 963.65	695 819.91	516 09 4.85	310 721.42	279 027.64	19 501.35
1994	1 056 641.18	809 483.72	886 833.52	631 56 8.55	305 840.18	267 227.56	21 972.50
1995	1 449 304.16	1 096 583.32	1 284 123.38	912 33 1.05	444 101.76	379 321.06	24 810.56
1996	1 579 939.79	1 142 075.53	1 492 426.07	1 002 23 6.69	531 65 1.07	445 253.28	26 831.42
1997	1 796 706.40	1 349 181.30	1 942 706.21	1 253 93 3.89	551 07 4.04	457 174.48	22 575.05
1998	2 070 589.05	1 385 793.02	2 156 648.12	1 344 30 7.98	579 60 7.54	456 816.13	18 592.28
1999	2 248 405.31	1 402 396.13	2 397 783.11	1 391 58 4.20	628 85 0.13	453 744.89	18 535.26
2000	2 395 313.32	1 367 303.20	2 622 356.72	1 368 52 7.77	628 20 6.50	410 876.60	16 719.33
2001	2 610 982.15	1 329 590.14	2 905 159.45	1 351.44 9.50	650 25 7.49	376 820.57	14 700.40
2002	2 964 541.18	1 334 953.12	3 569 810.58	1 774.66 6.57	690 53 3.40	327 845.83	31 201.01

Table 9 Number of TVEs by Province in 2004

(Unit: enterprise)

Area	Total	Agriculture	Industry	Construction	Transport & warehousing	Commerce	Hostel & catering	Social service	Others
National	22 132 161	414 401	6 402 750	654 086	3 774 969	6 773 498	2085 836	1 366 148	660 473
Beijing	158 039	4 050	24 541	5 113	49 537	38 951	13 032	21 003	1 812
Tianjin	138 370		41 704	2 697	35 302	35 800	12 598	9 084	1 185

Hebei	1 180 890	19 240	359 209	29 036	205 027	359 415	115 090	80 622	13 251
Shanxi	437 228	7 771	81 938	13 806	135 096	119 800	44 711	25 753	8 353
Inner Mongolia	459 566	10 979	66 477	7 634	65 381	184 768	58 407	53 434	12 486
Liaoning	1 153 051	13 887	293 085	26 005	287 460	349 870	88 375	65 104	29 265
Jilin	550 970	42 230	90 124	15 599	100 509	182 405	59 524	49 548	11 031
Heilongjiang	313 187	833	90 028	8 670	70 358	83 540	38 506	19 153	2 099
Shanghai	29 187		29 187						
Jiangsu	1 103 535	5 164	504 202	26 775	118 591	245 540	64 908	79 723	58 632
Zhejiang	1 082 178	1 514	701 246	6 123	92 773	206 470	36 916	30 073	7 063
Anhui	830 710	21 418	227 495	37 495	145 968	241 809	83 956	53 704	18 865
Fujian	827 413	21 797	220 671	33656	118 632	273 088	71 958	52 504	35 107
Jiangxi	712 014	17 878	203 667	30 419	99 032	233 060	64 494	31 693	31 771
Shandong	2 177 311	43 073	868 531	56 174	257 822	611 248	194 074	98 324	48 065
Henan	1 535 363	25 225	519 094	49 448	201 925	431 970	124 524	81 455	101 722
Hubei	1 041 679	39 211	257 073	45 565	161 544	326 605	124 241	60 989	26 451
Hunan	1 701 325	41 621	430 837	74 946	332 375	511 016	149 398	81 532	79 600
Guangdong	1 308 373	14 255	349 637	48 137	169 223	494 455	116 299	69 484	46 883
Guangxi	880 038	8 182	169 791	16 701	157 179	357 992	87 700	66 323	16 170
Hainan	44 773	2 524	8 763	1 531	5 489	13 811	8 071	3 198	1 386
Chongqing	74 597	1 370	35 495	2 837	5 800	15 569	9 518	2 137	1 871

Sichuan	1 588 624	29 136	312 361	41 264	280 682	560 310	181 807	124 943	58 121
Guizhou	487 845	7 036	101 705	8 102	102 659	178 420	48 022	32 389	9 512
Yunnan	831 768	10 393	125 728	9 449	197 008	315 031	99 741	58 950	15 468
Tibet	1 262	163	233	179	69	296	225	28	69
Shaanxi	871 904	13 738	193 547	42 167	210 241	221 758	105 627	65 111	19 715
Gansu	262 732	2 162	68 498	8 740	57 007	79 909	29 414	14 231	2 771
Qinghai	57 355	644	13 335	734	14 453	17 592	6 120	2 517	1 960
Ningxia	152 138	844	27 541	5 733	51 328	40 866	12 518	12 969	339
Xinjiang	368 553	12 366	53 492	6 143	85 698	112 469	57 721	34 356	6 308
Separately-listed cities in State plan	508 220	18 697	200 754	12 010	73 968	123 072	36 421	33 192	10 106
Dalian	164 966	8 108	38 616	5 336	36 434	49 381	12 912	10 981	3 198
Qingdao	174 770	608	64 228	5 795	23 399	46 539	16 261	14 885	3 055
Ningbo	94 846		93 852	69	41	670	179	21	14
Xiamen	22 021	175	2 655	432	2 816	10 331	2 069	1 060	2 483
Shenzhen									
Xinjiang Production Corps	51 617	9 806	1 403	378	11 278	16 151	5 000	6 245	1 356
Eastern part	9 064 225	121 716	3 357 153	231 314	1 320 653	2 587 964	705 919	500 722	238 784
Central part	9 558 348	237 960	2 416 566	358 493	1 725 612	2 897 752	976 169	589 893	355 903
Western part	3 509 588	54 725	629 031	64 279	728 704	1 287 782	403 748	275 533	65 786

Table 10 Number of TVE Employment by Province in 2004

(Unit: person)

Area	Total	Agriculture	Industry	Construction	Transport & warehousing	Commerce	Hostel & catering	Social service	Others
National	138 661 740	2 847 173	81 605 448	13 759 756	8 444 657	16 993 032	8 179 079	4 259 424	2 573 171
Beijing	1 355 937	27 388	679 661	190 505	102 218	136 093	66 999	131 844	21 229
Tianjin	1 510 628		1 088 875	58 703	110 381	140 774	67 904	37 385	6 606
Hebei	9 145 316	84 566	5 446 982	995 195	579 911	1179 545	512 654	290 476	55 987
Shanxi	3 750 705	58 944	2 185 122	314 344	409 478	415 856	234 248	86 590	46 123
Inner Mongolia	2 243 817	66 752	770 932	212 303	166 021	543 207	253 982	178 800	51 820
Liaoning	5 682 804	124 378	3 025 974	425 101	599 610	840 901	346 379	198 709	121 752
Jilin	1 979 070	133 971	732 665	122 858	214 284	393 390	187 958	132 757	61 187
Heilongjiang	1 656 575	9 063	873 319	136 405	152 706	248 300	156 912	67 107	12 763
Shanghai	1 873 502		1 873 502						
Jiangsu	12 328 820	92 073	9 458 224	792 778	296 623	751 232	344 123	342 092	251 675
Zhejiang	11 767 356	13 565	10 391 538	448 860	174 678	513 927	134 879	70 572	19 337
Anhui	5 227 213	183 618	2 712 466	803 529	408 083	532 363	341 380	169 745	76 029
Fujian	6 380 740	230 226	3 957 789	522 649	303 957	745 888	279 411	167 409	173 411
Jiangxi	3 591 627	106 325	1 933 164	292 645	216 612	557 965	255 141	86 423	143 352
Shandong	16 278 425	315 410	9 800 172	1 602 545	972 421	1 843 688	1 044 591	497 411	202 187

Henan	9 939 412	242 859	5 489 391	1281 492	552 521	1 258 252	553 347	247 676	313 874
Hubei	6 725 319	338 497	3 258 628	875 177	399 047	1 000 566	503 870	220 140	129 394
Hunan	8 233 627	311 685	3 820 466	1239 882	662 151	1 216 551	503 126	218 661	261 105
Guangdong	12 684 162	117 120	9 002 045	620 238	349 944	1 348 742	687 285	281 823	276 965
Guangxi	3 600 960	61 900	1 442 442	245 975	330 902	925 457	324 203	190 183	79 898
Hainan	312 417	33 323	101 034	24 172	19 740	57 660	50 040	17 316	9 132
Chongqing	1 916 309	38 493	1 097 254	473 973	55 919	116 144	70 395	22 220	41 911
Sichuan	6 984 873	121 215	3 164 245	979 978	488 156	1 137 154	583 418	311 977	198 730
Guizhou	2 364 137	63 138	1 108 311	186 888	213 709	446 234	196 725	104 043	45 089
Yunnan	3 318 740	124 027	1 146 761	449 777	299 370	716 098	360 954	159 555	62 198
Tibet	25 500	2 725	16 861	3 231	273	885	750	450	325
Shaanxi	4 048 549	67 243	1 587 195	721 291	495 829	556 846	383 182	176 100	60 863
Gansu	1 905 731	31 069	690 199	506 094	230 756	262 911	125 191	50 445	9 066
Qinghai	243 342	2 434	100 188	25 983	33 992	45 451	19 318	7 153	8 823
Ningxia	599 984	4 061	229 061	119 979	93 715	83 585	39 029	29 275	1 279
Xinjiang	933 473	45 356	275 201	74 305	117 454	196 415	138 437	70 650	15 655
Separately-listed cities in State plan	5 051 122	163 539	3 680 179	360 076	204 271	317 762	167 607	117 864	39 824
Dalian	1 114 208	91 599	579 949	155 029	78 959	114 579	46 301	37 062	10 730
Qingdao	1 636 773	53 528	979 132	162 156	100 951	152 341	99 654	66 449	22 562
Ningbo	2 068 704		2 036 238	21 806	2 128	4 410	3 182	600	340

Xiamen	135 411	2 151	69 447	17 568	8 437	22 709	7 921	3 696	3 482
Shenzhen									
Xinjiang Production Corps	96 026	16 261	15 413	3 517	13 796	23 723	10 549	10 057	2 710
Eastern part	73 719 214	937 473	51 061 693	5 277 946	3 256 153	6 998 715	3 251 004	1 882 662	1 053 568
Central part	50 435 155	1 504 018	25 056 415	6 756 850	3 783 374	6 935 824	3 520 428	1 622 967	1 255 279
Western part	14 507 371	405 682	5 487 340	1 724 960	1 405 130	3 058 493	1 407 647	753 795	264 324

Table 11 Added Value of TVEs by Province in 2004

(Unit: 1 million yuan)

	Total	Agriculture	Industry	Construction	Transport & warehousing	Commerce	Hostel & catering	Social service	Others
National	4 181 536.25	56 439.23	2 935 856.60	266 601.60	218 868.01	390 919.22	152 585.28	72 176.60	88 089.71
Beijing	45 073.96	483.61	22 080.61	5 924.09	3 615.59	5 303.37	1 851.48	3 922.13	1 893.08
Tianjin	68 161.85		44 120.47	2 705.72	7 217.55	7 903.02	3 485.64	1 338.82	1 390.63
Hebei	319 289.48	2 323.25	217 819.62	17 103.75	19 542.46	39 012.20	14 687.06	7 127.88	1 673.26
Shanxi	111 328.90	1 126.97	80 005.13	5 888.11	10 936.02	7 485.31	3 747.87	1 321.20	818.29
Inner Mongolia	74 973.09	1 824.73	35 837.78	5 445.45	5 380.40	15 178.26	5 574.23	4 004.39	1 727.85

Liaoning	281 684.03	4 736.78	172 790.71	15 740.19	25 700.08	37 145.56	12 256.93	6 017.37	7 296.41
Jilin	62 140.72	3 243.47	31 171.31	4 114.09	5 677.91	10 508.99	3 519.48	1 786.10	2 119.37
Heilongjiang	51 034.66	146.89	33 693.25	4 167.08	3 159.98	4 729.41	3 419.26	1 472.36	246.43
Shanghai	124 446.71		124 446.71						
Jiangsu	550 704.66	2 095.44	451 286.76	18 290.79	8 425.04	38 481.12	10 882.17	8 510.46	12 732.88
Zhejiang	531 115.53	529.11	479 662.05	15 374.93	5 941.31	22 874.64	3 999.76	1 663.94	1 069.79
Anhui	97 680.47	2 982.13	54 432.02	11 417.11	8 552.89	11 004.73	5 358.92	2 491.44	1 441.23
Fujian	189 686.28	5 778.69	128 963.22	11 654.98	8 820.05	20 596.07	6 345.13	2 968.38	4 559.76
Jiangxi	68 454.79	1502.15	44 682.96	4 780.95	4 376.75	7 581.13	2 574.24	1 144.78	1 811.83
Shandong	580 034.96	9 433.39	421 628.53	47 242.77	29 461.57	40 054.28	19 860.48	6 219.07	6 134.87
Henan	264 315.07	5 414.27	190 681.94	18 607.25	12 384.64	21 609.49	8377.56	3 267.19	3 972.73
Hubei	165 669.38	6 625.93	100 726.51	15 278.74	9 583.71	18 209.12	8 937.46	3 646.88	2 661.03
Hunan	184 044.45	4 807.88	85 607.52	24 080.27	19 776.87	29 902.66	10 471.77	3 536.41	5 861.07
Guangdong	342 350.26	2 068.28	274701.14	11 343.32	7 474.03	25 635.40	11 483.88	4 487.36	5 156.85
Guangxi	44 687.29	666.79	20 241.47	2 642.74	5 100.90	10 128.48	3 445.97	1 674.57	786.37
Hainan	5 301.98	451.44	2 495.13	340.16	358.10	729.53	567.62	209.19	150.81
Chongqing	55 422.60	685.59	34 930.62	10 071.99	1 685.56	3 881.96	1 886.98	656.63	1 623.27
Sichuan	154 824.03	2 129.38	90 435.14	16 092.96	11 741.77	16 676.44	9 797.06	4 563.41	3 387.87
Guizhou	39 989.78	713.19	21 378.24	2 739.39	4 517.89	6 118.61	2 426.20	1 489.55	606.71
Yunnan	50 569.69	615.51	19 606.24	5 219.96	5 970.36	11 741.39	4 315.63	2 204.74	895.86
Tibet	360.00	17.13	186.77	108.00	7.20	10.90	10.60	7.40	12.00

Shaanxi	61 909.45	574.14	32 598.37	7 395.13	6 989.26	7 511.79	4 241.19	1 700.12	899.45
Gansu	33 449.91	389.63	14 104.06	6 034.93	4 643.21	5 190.94	2155.13	807.24	124.77
Qinghai	3 079.19	27.44	1 893.54	190.45	276.78	323.80	147.36	102.64	117.18
Ningxia	7 825.19	48.78	4 021.28	976.16	1 093.59	1 034.63	399.11	241.20	10.44
Xinjiang	11 535.61	390.84	5 361.58	1 107.87	1 372.62	1 714.11	940.89	491.29	156.41
Separately-listed cities in State plan	252 308.72	4 919.96	196 828.84	15 498.11	11 288.35	11 730.47	5 371.23	2 982.21	3 689.55
Dalian	76 366.32	3 725.38	40 685.54	7 545.17	7 501.93	9 654.07	2 820.37	1 829.80	2 604.06
Qingdao	74 338.95	1 018.31	58 498.87	6 914.39	3 100.15	787.76	2 145.02	882.07	992.38
Ningbo	96 116.20		95 189.36	512.27	49.48	285.84	38.13	25.44	15.68
Xiamen	3 283.19	25.19	1 839.57	465.52	192.96	516.98	161.29	54.16	27.52
Shenzhen									
Xinjiang Production Corps	2 204.06	151.08	615.50	60.76	443.83	485.82	206.42	190.74	49.91
Eastern part	2 768 022.19	25 054.25	2 133 602.50	132 699.17	106 061.90	216 331.94	77 450.95	38 569.52	38 251.96
Central part	1 165 448.64	26 688.33	711 016.60	111 261.04	86 590.37	126 967.41	56 894.66	23 354.64	226 75.59
Western part	248 065.42	4 696.65	91 237.50	22 641.39	26 215.74	47 619.87	18 239.67	10 252.44	27 162.16

Table 12 Total Output Value of TVEs by Province in 2004

(Unit: 1 million yuan)

Area	Total	Agriculture	Industry	Construction	Transport & warehousing	Commerce	Hostel & catering	Social service	Others
National	17 251 673.36	204 834.30	12 554 710.79	1 078 356.80	789 432.30	1 416 186.99	567 552.84	259 142.20	381 457.14
Beijing	202 042.24	2 116.19	103 333.78	27 400.16	12 678.70	26 090.98	7 224.74	13 528.84	9 668.85
Tianjin	290 278.10		233 586.38	9 345.80	17 446.26	13 844.17	8 929.67	4 117.79	3 008.03
Hebei	1 220 057.73	8 918.36	837 070.35	61 695.79	70 880.64	151 110.43	57 090.83	27 452.97	5 838.36
Shanxi	393 991.57	4 240.33	279 459.68	21 865.02	39 147.35	27 978.51	13 225.88	5 228.88	2 845.92
Inner Mongolia	225 765.26	6 001.77	107 124.17	17 387.59	16 941.43	44 404.94	16 994.91	12 085.78	4 824.67
Liaoning	1 113 456.99	14 766.04	766 245.20	55 463.52	84 352.13	111 416.14	38 696.89	19 828.64	22 688.43
Jilin	195 054.35	9 780.80	96 977.51	11 597.39	17 940.14	34 502.14	10 841.86	6 837.07	6 577.44
Heilongjiang	212 007.78	549.06	141 349.57	20 090.66	16 973.36	13 616.33	13 078.88	5 389.98	959.94
Shanghai	601 123.03		601 123.03						
Jiangsu	2 440 109.27	5 164.55	2 110 717.78	76 086.98	25 143.34	136 505.49	28 616.52	23 926.50	33 948.11
Zhejiang	2 641 616.06	2 294.50	2 433 176.08	91 653.46	20 702.15	81 043.28	12 746.59		
Anhui	340 914.68	9 063.39	193 130.43	39 996.01	26 371.66	44 507.32	16 020.42	6 996.88	4 828.57
Fujian	819 095.37	25 635.43	556 619.19	50 908.31	38 947.24	91 353.21	26 243.99	11 865.22	17 522.78
Jiangxi	251 392.86	5 121.25	167 713.75	17 084.21	14 766.25	27 416.56	8 853.67	3 870.01	6 567.16
Shandong	2 435 877.00	34 171.59	1 773 639.89	195 538.44	113 688.55	162 899.62	97 081.35	33 983.94	24 873.62
Henan	1 016 175.59	19 950.30	707 787.51	75 246.76	46 286.83	94 055.22	34 823.33	12 959.59	25 066.05
Hubei	689 255.38	27 003.50	410 792.55	71 178.45	39 610.66	75 313.98	36 776.04	15 785.58	12 794.62
Hunan	608 685.63	14 737.61	292 920.15	81 766.10	60 950.22	93 681.60	32 748.42	11 504.06	20 377.47
Guangdong	1 520 543.08	8 782.74	1 247 651.47	50 586.50	31 709.63	98 217.89	45 320.26	16 246.72	22 027.87

Guangxi	200 095.08	3 741.00	97 422.44	13 490.24	23 156.53	38 174.89	14 692.63	5 777.35	3 640.00
Hainan	19 337.26	1 647.37	9 622.05	1 490.94	1 001.10	2 545.72	1 878.91	683.93	467.24
Chongqing	215 967.26	2 897.19	138 078.27	40 126.69	6 869.68	12 063.99	6 583.86	2 502.40	6 845.18
Sichuan	613 090.93	7 867.79	355 691.99	65 638.03	47 104.85	67 813.72	37 839.30	17 064.61	14 070.64
Guizhou	151 065.91	2 973.87	79 655.70	10 711.67	16915.49	23 887.98	8 854.20	5 448.77	2 618.23
Yunnan	234 216.33	3 518.67	98 051.62	25 494.84	28 699.50	38 627.34	22 428.38	11 299.25	6 096.73
Tibet	1 529.99	126.00	733.07	322.67	30.18	201.10	49.60	11.00	56.37
Shaanxi	234 817.72	2 499.90	129 797.96	27 320.62	25 980.52	23 564.63	16 365.75	6 217.61	3 070.73
Gansu	142 410.95	1 689.38	57 825.20	26 326.65	20 434.35	22 846.65	9 459.18	3 308.96	520.58
Qinghai	14 489.20	105.93	8 276.51	902.13	1 259.73	1 954.44	646.30	523.05	821.11
Ningxia	29 756.94	259.99	16 161.90	3 632.59	3 765.95	3 773.12	1 343.14	768.80	51.45
Xinjiang	45 628.99	1 391.21	22 119.05	4 783.30	5 165.11	6 133.79	3 557.36	1 990.40	488.77
Separately-listed cities in State plan	1 071 430.16	15 165.38	893 694.76	59 520.86	35 340.20	31 935.24	17 558.61	9 729.46	8 485.65
Dalian	264 847.67	10 438.49	166 475.52	25 499.95	21 104.82	23 359.72	7 993.70	5 607.75	4 367.72
Qingdao	302 315.37	4 103.71	238 821.58	28 190.28	12 098.64	3 521.63	8 402.28	3 482.99	3 694.26
Ningbo	480 006.38		474 699.21	3 421.15	313.29	1 333.33	81.99	25.06	132.35
Xiamen	18 131.87	203.07	11 548.80	2 214.97	861.41	2 354.34	586.40	202.57	160.31
Shenzhen									
Xinjiang Production Corps	6 128.87	420.11	2 149.65	194.51	962.04	1 366.22	494.24	411.09	131.01
Eastern part	11 986 217.34	91 897.83	9 621 279.55	558 228.66	374 945.93	787 232.22	290 493.45	136 201.43	125 938.27
Central part	4 305 151.07	93 577.64	2 629 005.65	425 800.24	308 585.00	464 241.52	204 962.16	85 137.20	93 841.66
Western part	960 304.95	19 358.83	304 425.59	94 327.90	105 901.37	164 713.25	72 097.23	37 803.57	161 677.21

Table 13 Operational Income of TVEs by Province in 2004

(Unit: 1 million yuan)

Area	Total	Agriculture	Industry	Construction	Transport & warehousing	Commerce	Hostel & catering	Social service	Others
National	16 636 848.33	188 991.38	1 652 448.57	949 664.11	748 776.60	1 875 303.86	550 921.17	269 443.56	401 299.08
Beijing	210 391.85	2 250.83	98 533.20	26 639.62	13 476.77	35 642.65	9 092.44	14 397.03	10 359.31
Tianjin	287 564.00		217 190.20	6 524.56	17 414.75	29 417.36	9 948.53	3 683.48	3 385.12
Hebei	1 193 232.16	8 738 76	808 136.45	59 922.83	71 225.76	154 765.49	57 057.19	27 366.49	6 019.19
Shanxi	355 453.46	3 132.58	248 261.02	19 254.81	36 471.63	27 302.57	13 148.92	5 125.69	2 756.24
Inner Mongolia	226 241.93	5 929.81	101 662.22	15 766.47	17 035.17	52 415.95	16 679.77	11 934.41	4 818.13
Liaoning	1 017 688.14	13 258.39	673 122.42	47 129.22	75 521.45	133 709.78	36 829.69	18 500.72	19 616.47
Jilin	176 190.64	9 808.60	85 264.78	9 706.79	16 453.45	32 094.32	10 202.11	7 687.29	4 973.30
Heilongjiang	218 768.04	548.77	132 100.09	15 258.72	16 973.36	34 455.07	13 082.07	5 390.02	959.94
Shanghai	590 184.23		590 184.23						
Jiangsu	2 352 877.70	5 343.25	1 996 962.20	69 235.20	24 386.89	171 649.50	29 081.28	26 133.94	30 085.44
Zhejiang	2 629 261.72	2 192.40	2 311 719.12	77 297.17	21 159.00	192 255.04	13 571.82	5 642.58	5 424.59
Anhui	338 303.29	9 051.58	190 760.43	38 733.24	25 263.24	46 648.93	16 020.42	6 996.88	4 828.57
Fujian	779 108.42	23 674.97	518 517.68	47 086.40	36 856.19	98 103.82	26 073.00	11 379.13	17 417.23
Jiangxi	233 528.34	4 484.62	155 308.16	15 769.47	14 676.22	25 440.75	8 137.02	3 483.52	6 228.58
Shandong	2 456 149.51	32 031.60	1 716 579.47	171 654.90	108 115.07	247 856.78	90 969.69	44 731.30	44 210.70
Henan	965 157.30	18 384.42	659 959.66	68 585.02	45 704.47	100 767.19	33 973.47	13 568.53	24 214.54
Hubei	670 463.31	24 176.30	383 648.10	65 304.53	38 492.21	93 591.86	37 022.69	15 287.41	12 940.41
Hunan	584 973.27	13 964.52	277 108.08	75 901.44	57 431.35	101 207.26	31 270.15	11 077.30	17 013.17
Guangdong	1 489 418.62	8 415.91	1 195 328.78	49 083.13	30 763.33	122 111.59	46 123.86	16 486.98	21 105.04

Guangxi	238 137.32	3 968.08	99 753.10	13 418.79	26 240.63	66 153.68	17 566.75	6 912.11	4 124.18
Hainan	19 029.57	1 481.35	8 494.52	1 148.63	1 001.10	3 752.52	2 000.28	683.93	467.24
Chongqing	220 436.26	2 779.81	135 655.39	34 884.78	6 853.05	24 463.43	6 452.22	2 502.40	6 845.18
Sichuan	583 921.70	6 977.22	322 798.60	57 394.34	43 443.48	88 908.60	35 517.31	16 401.88	12 480.27
Guizhou	171 610.40	2 717.10	77 291.31	10 909.30	17 137.34	46 154.24	9 270.33	5 516.67	2 614.11
Yunnan	302 706.98	3 622.86	100 872.38	24 474.00	27 993.75	105 854.98	22 882.16	10 676.97	6 329.88
Tibet	1 200.00	68.20	395.74	347.89	46.57	176.93	69.05	30.21	65.41
Shaanxi	236 484.66	2 692.20	121 899.83	20 467.08	25 877.43	40 869.46	15 126.35	6 101.50	3 450.81
Gansu	122 289.14	1 296.40	47 567.66	20 287.39	18 206.29	23 114.97	8 541.65	2 822.41	452.37
Qinghai	13 721.97	107.22	7 346.81	924.05	1 237.53	2 084.17	637.64	520.67	863.88
Ningxia	29 473.83	255.16	15 113.76	3 425.28	3 815.90	4 759.59	1 283.89	768.80	51.45
Xinjiang	47 578.07	1 774.62	20 950.06	4 410.98	5 129.73	9 071.07	3 647.75	2 044.24	549.62
Separately-listed cities in State plan	989 737.55	13 205.39	808 414.86	47 461.03	27 590.79	59 746.06	162 31.73	9 058.11	8 029.58
Dalian	238 005.97	9 025.84	149 278.70	21 114.41	16 874.93	26 069.87	7 027.99	4 739.75	3 874.48
Qingdao	266 084.82	3 590.98	199 106.14	20 024.85	8 748.28	19 595.96	7 841.36	3 482.99	3 694.26
Ningbo	460 847.20		447 450.09	3 988.80	421.80	8 160.42	395.84	290.27	139.98
Xiamen	19 498.59	207.36	10 964.46	2 140.45	834.91	4 346.08	569.11	215.33	220.89
Shenzhen									
Xinjiang Production Corps	5 300.97	381.21	1 615.47	192.52	710.87	1 573.73	397.43	329.77	99.97
Eastern part	11 532 993.82	85 044.99	8 979 498.92	491 769.04	353 742.62	1 051 255.78	282 650.15	149 259.65	139 772.67
Central part	4 064 590.11	85 128.79	2 405 550.48	373 553.57	290 535.50	546 017.38	195 043.64	83 019.74	85 741.01
Western part	1 039 264.40	18 817.60	267 399.17	84 341.50	104 498.48	278 030.70	73 227.38	37 164.17	175 785.40

Table 14 Total Profit of TVEs by Province in 2004

(Unit: 1 million yuan)

Area	Total	Agriculture	Industry	Construction	Transport & warehousing	Commerce	Hostel & catering	Social service	Others
National	993 217.88	14 803.87	60 345.25	60 345.25	61 643.70	117 308.67	45 995.63	21 503.31	15 954.26
Beijing	14 738.43	345.97	6 136.10	1 808.35	1 529.33	2 088.34	622.50	1 281.81	926.03
Tianjin	25 518.71		16 770.46	833.70	2 554.87	3 080.50	1 299.41	520.00	459.77
Hebei	99 038.28	954.71	58 344.26	5 743.57	8 364.58	16 072.80	6 129.34	2 731.30	697.72
Shanxi	30 759.73	273.18	21 729.68	1 699.39	2 975.03	2 234.17	1 294.22	353.34	200.72
Inner Mongolia	24 028.36	641.76	10 281.30	1 610.19	1 864.10	5 573.28	1 928.59	1 596.51	532.63
Liaoning	67 230.25	1 687.74	41 475.67	3 297.32	5 833.68	8 705.95	3 261.63	1 378.23	1 590.03
Jilin	11 575.58	586.38	5 397.85	616.95	1 215.85	2 133.00	786.93	480.93	357.69
Heilongjiang	10 574.35	30.89	6 499.54	753.36	917.17	1 303.96	695.81	300.34	73.28
Shanghai	31 885.01		31 885.01						
Jiangsu	98 509.29	595.89	78 825.67	3 162.92	1 860.29	7 587.64	3 243.90	1 417.58	1 815.40
Zhejiang	139 926.56	184.61	123 042.21	2 815.98	2 451.86	9 001.36	1 438.18	696.46	295.90
Anhui	29 589.04	896.92	15 447.79	3 122.77	2 663.97	4 570.87	1 756.98	722.73	407.01
Fujian	37 689.14	1 143.76	25 498.95	2 055.51	1 871.44	4 394.58	1 305.42	626.13	793.35
Jiangxi	14 564.69	320.57	9 458.52	1 068.93	865.27	1 519.33	631.98	251.05	449.04
Shandong	127 298.67	2 551.41	80 403.45	12 133.04	7 743.65	13 957.25	6 017.45	2 778.22	1 714.20
Henan	86 284.76	2 009.27	55 688.87	6 660.86	4 855.64	8 971.01	3 916.80	1 555.87	2 626.44
Hubei	34 263.32	1 325.32	18 997.90	3 231.78	2 361.43	4 585.43	2 264.46	861.82	635.18
Hunan	16 872.71	453.51	8 400.18	2 099.49	1 577.62	2 430.74	1 002.01	430.61	478.55

Guangdong	67 380.54	598.01	48 208.22	3 072.58	2 329.40	6 908.02	3 325.04	1 209.69	1 729.58
Guangxi	12 003.40	207.80	5 025.51	669.65	1 537.51	2 953.11	988.36	403.26	218.20
Hainan	1 637.41	135.31	770.39	102.46	96.51	273.65	165.65	54.57	38.87
Chongqing	7 920.48	96.10	4 968.22	1 063.02	297.03	825.22	310.87	120.18	239.84
Sichuan	19 783.61	269.08	11 225.54	1 739.69	1 638.98	2513.27	1 282.46	578.49	536.10
Guizhou	13 797.40	261.39	6 722.52	960.18	1 776.38	2257.30	1 027.74	565.12	226.77
Yunnan	16 768.60	223.29	5 779.00	1 174.63	2 031.21	4 775.21	1 613.01	829.24	343.01
Tibet	160.00	18.26	42.19	31.30	8.79	24.60	13.80	6.03	15.03
Shaanxi	12 996.28	157.97	6 085.83	1 534.01	1 518.33	2 007.15	1 010.10	497.42	185.47
Gansu	7 837.53	101.26	3 126.62	1 359.32	1 107.92	1 382.97	528.38	197.14	33.92
Qinghai	524.44	10.66	286.75	43.20	53.69	62.66	27.55	10.09	29.84
Ningxia	2 155.84	12.16	957.55	279.70	369.38	313.55	139.34	79.33	4.83
Xinjiang	3 311.56	149.87	1 294.87	242.48	461.15	576.43	346.17	170.58	70.01
Separately-listed cities in State plan	62 322.20	1 510.11	49 541.75	3 039.38	2 116.01	3 333.15	1 264.31	886.84	630.65
Dalian	16 410.57	1 218.32	8 808.62	1 613.60	1 381.80	2 042.18	586.64	435.01	324.40
Qingdao	12 653.81	235.16	8 922.27	1 027.98	484.38	898.32	516.89	296.10	272.71
Ningbo	31 725.69		31 191.57	299.91	40.24	96.02	20.92	67.57	9.46
Xiamen	850.04	9.85	505.81	82.79	53.79	112.67	47.65	26.31	11.17
Shenzhen									
Xinjiang Production Corps	682.09	46.78	113.48	15.10	155.80	183.96	92.21	61.85	12.91
Eastern part	679 670.93	7 626.91	481 798.52	33 971.34	35 156.10	72 315.81	26 931.32	12 673.82	9 197.11
Central part	241 413.21	5 631.41	143 785.72	20 695.20	18 323.10	29 032.75	13 117.60	5 397.70	5 429.73
Western part	72 133.74	1 545.55	30 078.95	5 678.71	8 164.50	15 960.11	5 946.71	3 431.79	1 327.42

Table 15 Tax Paid by TVEs by Province in 2004

(Unit: 1 million yuan)

Area	Total	Agriculture	Industry	Construction	Transport & warehousing	Commerce	Hostel & catering	Social service	Others
National	365 833.35	2 308.66	274 530.81	20 995.60	13 210.78	29 942.87	12 550.36	6263.99	6 030.28
Beijing	7 042.08	24.56	3 538.41	908.09	352.95	786.03	235.45	660.26	536.33
Tianjin	11 805.28		8 824.13	560.88	844.69	910.33	347.03	159.86	158.36
Hebei	24 000.67	143.24	15 221.35	1241.75	1 702.02	3 225.59	1 393.24	883.93	189.55
Shanxi	14 323.97	47.22	11 801.49	462.07	730.81	744.60	348.13	128.31	61.34
Inner Mongolia	6 681.80	81.32	3 597.73	472.18	385.89	1 193.97	460.11	298.74	191.86
Liaoning	15 122.27	155.73	9 988.03	1 133.43	866.47	1 528.26	551.56	395.86	502.93
Jilin	3 753.67	91.43	2 306.40	172.42	275.64	450.61	208.95	141.30	106.92
Heilongjiang	3 145.80	2.97	1 992.53	237.10	213.67	349.42	214.58	97.37	38.16
Shanghai	19 965.90		19 965.90						
Jiangsu	67 516.77	153.86	55 803.04	2 138.36	830.28	4 743.40	1674.53	862.19	1 311.11
Zhejiang	79 579.38	41.97	71 999.26	3 151.82	594.73	2 758.03	508.06	263.18	262.33
Anhui	7 949.66	160.14	4 694.31	960.58	586.50	691.67	518.11	163.79	174.56
Fujian	18 170.65	296.20	13 118.21	955.61	650.10	1 872.24	590.97	289.24	398.08
Jiangxi	6 099.42	82.82	4 277.53	394.95	300.30	563.16	253.58	79.51	147.57
Shandong	43 169.91	533.82	30 425.13	3198.90	2 147.18	3 211.75	2107.61	933.03	612.49
Henan	13 209.33	113.71	9 083.41	941.83	516.17	1 337.52	570.06	251.96	394.67
Hubei	8 568.78	233.07	5 020.05	824.16	489.14	1 115.89	534.89	197.54	154.04
Hunan	10 727.32	138.48	6 222.28	1 416.16	743.17	1 311.29	524.79	163.77	207.38
Guangdong	35 268.24	103.45	27 133.39	1 454.20	672.83	2 999.07	1 513.85	499.40	892.05

Guangxi	5 304.69	55.96	2 694.13	301.79	501.03	1 135.54	379.24	147.50	89.50
Hainan	625.38	48.18	314.02	37.75	27.85	97.42	64.31	23.23	12.62
Chongqing	6 577.45	31.79	4 179.22	1 192.56	133.71	602.50	235.44	52.34	149.89
Sichuan	11 766.75	69.86	7 436.32	1 143.15	635.79	1263.77	611.60	267.93	338.33
Guizhou	4 154.07	28.43	2 894.85	195.32	282.46	439.62	178.17	87.77	47.45
Yunnan	6 233.32	38.77	3 007.55	626.92	458.74	1 262.11	434.75	220.47	184.01
Tibet	70.99	7.68	28.75	14.54	2.01	4.80	4.41	3.46	5.34
Shaanxi	3 793.72	29.14	2 043.25	396.90	357.18	562.74	267.53	94.04	42.94
Gansu	2 112.94	15.93	944.12	369.94	236.83	350.27	138.66	47.19	10.00
Qinghai	325.40	2.13	181.93	22.15	30.75	54.91	17.80	9.95	5.78
Ningxia	1 058.94	2.98	507.29	144.75	151.72	160.13	60.35	29.90	1.82
Xinjiang	1 522.45	39.64	678.47	161.59	155.69	257.76	134.87	74.84	19.59
Separately-listed cities in State plan	27 637.33	177.43	22 903.10	1912.54	486.97	1 099.54	383.72	301.97	372.06
Dalian	3 830.18	123.06	1 889.03	627.45	211.31	472.97	104.20	175.76	226.40
Qingdao	7 285.84	44.98	5 186.85	1 009.27	200.16	400.56	227.86	91.99	124.17
Ningbo	15 820.59		15 483.73	190.32	15.67	99.24	10.64	11.61	9.38
Xiamen	526.35	2.35	299.96	82.69	21.44	77.14	24.13	11.24	7.40
Shenzhen									
Xinjiang Production Corps	174.37	7.04	43.53	2.81	38.39	49.63	16.89	11.37	4.71
Eastern part	267 639.86	1 208.91	213 033.42	12 267.79	7 207.09	18 335.23	7 424.31	4116.39	4 046.72
Central part	74 819.64	832.63	49 141.57	6 774.92	4 145.62	7 483.28	3 567.79	1362.87	1 510.96
Western part	23 373.85	267.12	12 355.82	1 952.89	1 858.07	4 124.36	1 558.26	784.73	472.60

Table 16 Original Value of Fixed Assets of TVEs by Province in 2004

(Unit: 1 million yuan)

Area	Total	Agricultural	Industrial	Construction	Transport & warehousing	Commerce	Hostel & catering	Social service	Others
National	4 787 236.59	62 803.84	3 618 828.55	203 919.77	236 480.09	320 076.51	176 485.88	88 504.12	80 137.83
Beijing	80 164.00	1 632.85	44 670.42	5 668.44	7 024.35	6 235.24	4 163.44	8 268.69	2 500.57
Tianjin	88 932.72		62 107.26	3 760.28	6 406.80	7 847.71	5 307.30	1 519.19	1 984.18
Hebei	357 871.14	1 897.07	274 577.75	12 124.71	18 457.39	28 699.24	12 189.29	5 544.49	4 381.20
Shanxi	161 467.85	1 722.54	122 842.33	5 446.55	14 539.24	8 392.07	5 215.63	2 104.03	1 223.46
Inner Mongolia	76 247.41	2 062.69	43 599.17	4 214.89	5 518.79	10 723.49	5 163.73	3 371.87	1 592.78
Liaoning	221 140.86	6 545.34	152 587.58	9 444.77	15 178.14	15 473.95	9 603.33	7 237.69	5 070.06
Jilin	51 726.00	2 976.94	25 849.89	3 002.53	4 984.31	6 587.89	3 762.50	1 712.65	2 849.29
Heilongjiang	43 051.29	190.55	26 466.09	2 971.77	3 213.59	6 980.56	2 118.22	967.90	142.61
Shanghai	273 330.66		273 330.66						
Jiangsu	591 772.14	1 991.59	512 951.26	14 577.93	9 526.82	19 341.72	8 972.47	9 009.66	15 400.69
Zhejiang	617 750.48	748.60	576 340.88	8 327.37	7 901.85	15 913.24	4 573.62	2 841.42	1 103.50
Anhui	121 985.67	3 314.11	74 001.19	9 359.74	11 898.81	12 800.98	6 050.66	2 555.57	2 004.61
Fujian	225 931.31	7 291.83	165 984.28	8 308.47	10 663.10	16 873.10	7 191.60	3 010.16	6 608.77
Jiangxi	78 852.07	1 824.59	52 542.88	4 014.41	6 486.49	6 812.61	4 149.73	1 065.74	1 955.62
Shandong	570 405.23	10 969.48	396 068.84	36 216.91	33 716.47	505 75..05	27 104.65	9 580.74	6 173.09
Henan	264 163.07	5 136.23	185 751.03	12 973.88	12 007.13	21 816.14	10 074.31	7 391.09	9 013.26
Hubei	150 928.08	4 671.00	89 974.93	12 755.61	10 870.48	16 577.65	10 349.56	3 523.54	2 205.31
Hunan	147 870.38	2 972.54	88 960.21	13 044.70	13 943.54	16 010.25	7 562.23	2 376.91	3 000.00
Guangdong	515 059.11	2 374.99	431 062.27	9 810.33	10 709.32	21 589.59	22 775.45	7 265.35	9 471.81

Guangxi	61 816.31	798.98	35 005.36	2 508.52	7 910.99	9 059.46	3 901.28	1 868.27	763.45
Hainan	11 319.22	1 199.18	5 568.28	556.51	588.81	1 195.87	1 402.94	477.74	329.89
Chongqing	63 979.03	769.97	42 866.36	8 189.72	2 806.00	3 633.44	2 040.43	1 082.27	2 590.84
Sichuan	170 510.36	1 605.81	111 948.80	12 357.03	12 332.11	13 275.55	11 314.19	4 362.17	3 314.70
Guizhou	53 112.67	1 072.48	32 947.14	2 362.89	6 024.34	5 416.56	3 059.25	1 372.59	857.42
Yunnan	87 555.70	1 851.04	42 763.03	7 667.12	9 103.83	14 447.40	6 669.40	3 345.17	1 708.71
Tibet	1 363.01	46.13	599.07	420.88	16.74	67.14	112.35	53.34	47.36
Shaanxi	62 179.62	1 114.28	37 351.23	5 595.65	6 881.19	5 425.88	3 809.60	1 373.23	628.56
Gansu	35 278.97	756.47	19 846.99	4 312.08	3 852.98	3 787.72	1 872.89	745.54	104.30
Qinghai	5 918.17	87.08	3 566.82	315.33	665.85	582.56	424.47	131.49	144.57
Ningxia	15 688.81	145.40	8 930.27	1 293.26	2 262.79	1 239.93	692.84	1 096.03	28.29
Xinjiang	22 191.61	836.97	12 153.23	1 159.07	2 837.89	2 268.63	1 165.29	1 427.11	343.42
Separately-listed cities in State plan	215 970.02	5 924.99	175 658.46	8 952.78	6 547.49	7 724.72	4 779.22	4 706.59	1 675.77
Dalian	48 040.73	4 812.35	28 288.42	4 227.84	2 807.88	2 575.84	1 817.23	2 870.70	640.47
Qingdao	58 198.18	666.35	43 058.15	3 871.55	2 501.94	3 846.57	2 271.86	1 207.31	774.45
Ningbo	100 818.03		99 368.09	466.24	244.78	390.77	161.99	149.95	36.21
Xiamen	5 805.88	72.42	3 917.49	342.83	373.09	590.79	304.08	137.14	68.04
Shenzhen									
Xinjiang Production Corps	3 107.20	373.87	1 026.31	44.32	619.80	320.75	224.06	341.49	156.60
Eastern part	3 242 738.31	30 622.34	2 645 266.47	99 084.13	109 469.58	167 108.51	93 263.85	49 686.51	48 236.92
Central part	1 205 343.29	24 074.18	785 920.25	82 123.61	91 507.84	108 305.88	60 826.84	26 103.24	26 481.45
Western part	339 154.99	8 107.32	187 641.83	22 712.03	35 502.67	44 662.12	22 395.19	12 714.37	5 419.46

Table 17 Net Value of Fixed Assets of TVEs by Province in 2004

(Unit: 1 million yuan)

Area	Total	Agriculture	Industry	Construction	Transport & warehousing	Commerce	Hostel & catering	Social service	Others
National	3 681 393.65	51 987.20	2 741 049.95	162 753.67	185 680.49	260 814.19	143 309.35	74 148.04	61 650.76
Beijing	60 652.74	1 283.54	34 086.07	4 015.79	4 862.27	5 049.91	3 241.94	6 106.91	2 006.31
Tianjin	59 815.66		42 174.21	3 301.26	3 283.96	4 731.76	4 022.90	1 046.93	1 254.64
Hebei	265 623.63	1 614.76	191 339.17	10 254.98	17 161.18	25 721.96	11 328.95	4 999.45	3 203.18
Shanxi	123 789.41	1 256.75	95 447.13	3 934.39	10 615.54	6 071.59	3 911.97	1 666.99	885.05
Inner Mongolia	62 800.12	1 764.12	36 655.25	3 370.34	4 399.29	8 744.73	4 120.61	2 524.85	1 220.93
Liaoning	168 643.84	5 086.56	116 372.66	7 236.61	11 198.82	11 587.36	7 241.31	5 901.72	4 018.80
Jilin	41 459.54	2 463.56	20 106.70	2 488.31	3 960.24	5 251.55	3 142.14	1 493.66	2 553.38
Heilongjiang	35 085.69	163.62	21 202.96	2 347.53	2 586.09	6 145.99	1 744.27	763.82	131.41
Shanghai	128 821.15		128 821.15	.					
Jiangsu	433 339.39	1 547.97	375 751.30	10 233.57	7 301.75	14 603.05	6 955.73	6 894.81	10 051.21
Zhejiang	448 211.54	561.78	417 241.90	5 725.30	5 795.56	12 482.33	3 176.52	2 425.06	803.09
Anhui	90 588.76	2 505.19	54 794.24	7 050.72	8 911.04	9 326.83	4 492.55	1 965.00	1 543.19
Fujian	170 230.49	5 548.93	124 858.23	6 139.71	7 905.43	12 878.66	5 422.19	2 322.67	5 154.67
Jiangxi	63 655.55	1 446.99	43 490.62	2 986.84	5 018.70	5 440.12	3 059.40	866.60	1 346.28
Shandong	416 955.86	9 014.80	281 532.58	28 604.97	23 537.70	39 583.14	22 153.53	7 816.82	4 712.32
Henan	212 343.61	4 378.05	149 300.60	10 340.84	9 662.81	17 558.62	8 190.74	6 757.16	6 154.79
Hubei	107 218.69	3 370.50	64 646.62	8 565.39	7 661.35	11 930.73	6 905.86	2 581.48	1 556.76
Hunan	107 931.49	2 162.29	65 545.77	9 291.05	9 583.86	11 836.09	5 514.97	1 765.48	2 231.98
Guangdong	367 408.88	1 533.94	306 188.25	7 215.21	7 943.76	16 123.90	16 058.86	5 461.99	6 882.97

Guangxi	44 128.45	616.44	25 454.19	1 614.80	5 312.52	6 492.22	2 777.50	1 311.63	549.15
Hainan	9 112.70	915.52	4 556.97	388.10	486.81	975.74	1 152.53	367.35	269.68
Chongqing	52 519.56	654.03	35 551.48	6 860.26	2 061.33	2 845.83	1 612.85	948.84	1 984.94
Sichuan	121 261.02	1 196.00	79 345.43	8 725.83	8 608.33	9 544.19	8 272.08	3 219.47	2 349.69
Guizhou	42 130.78	857.25	26 259.43	1 782.99	4 780.47	4 328.87	2 385.07	1 126.02	610.68
Yunnan	65 976.70	1 453.44	32 223.62	5 855.56	6 790.14	10 419.32	5 234.68	2 614.93	1 385.01
Tibet	1 145.04	34.48	507.14	368.75	8.56	60.61	102.73	34.73	28.04
Shaanxi	47 073.80	897.60	28 355.58	4 211.60	5 262.05	4 034.94	2 772.90	1 041.00	498.13
Gansu	28 213.27	647.33	16 061.98	3 431.86	2 979.34	2 914.26	1 511.46	581.02	86.02
Qinghai	4 828.76	62.86	3 022.20	243.01	516.90	463.44	318.64	104.20	97.51
Ningxia	12 732.18	130.98	7 207.93	1 003.92	1 840.18	1 010.98	592.99	918.48	26.72
Xinjiang	17 078.38	645.02	9 283.13	884.18	2 170.27	1 821.82	928.10	1 124.91	220.95
Separately-listed cities in State plan	161 428.44	4 373.87	130 192.03	6 864.73	5 120.75	6 050.21	3 701.55	3 809.64	1 315.66
Dalian	35 867.34	3 625.17	20 697.81	3 202.61	2 064.35	1 884.06	1 426.28	2 475.52	491.54
Qingdao	44 106.43	443.39	31 911.15	3 033.56	2 214.29	3 181.16	1 760.15	926.17	636.56
Ningbo	74 864.95		73 790.28	365.74	175.10	311.15	124.82	68.63	29.23
Xiamen	4 541.08	50.30	3 125.90	235.16	280.96	459.73	234.88	113.25	40.90
Shenzhen									
Xinjiang Production Corps	2 048.64	255.01	666.89	27.66	386.05	214.11	155.42	226.07	117.43
Eastern part	2 434 154.53	25 303.00	1 949 838.21	79 918.65	85 969.04	137 915.03	76 899.29	41 517.23	36 794.08
Central part	968 875.85	19 798.75	635 454.02	64 534.68	71 421.23	86 931.27	47 935.05	22 286.25	20 514.60
Western part	278 363.27	6 885.45	155 757.72	18 300.34	28 290.22	35 967.89	18 475.01	10 344.56	4 342.08

Table 18 Labor Remuneration of TVEs by Province in 2004

(Unit: 1 million yuan)

Area	Total	Agriculture	Industry	Construction	Transport & warehousing	Commerce	Hostel & catering	Social service	Others
National	975 613.62	14 820.74	619 874.67	92 055.71	60 098.21	98 975.33	46 797.21	25 519.05	17 472.70
Beijing	14 335.85	223.87	7 050.54	2 169.96	1 208.21	1 401.47	557.06	1 373.00	351.74
Tianjin	23 769.83		14 569.18	1 133.62	2 877.59	2 636.36	1 419.73	526.55	606.80
Hebei	51 255.81	426.86	32 434.29	4 555.36	3 300.00	6 198.68	2 572.00	1 437.51	331.11
Shanxi	30 172.12	314.21	19 804.23	2 071.42	3 541.83	2 358.86	1 275.95	507.33	298.29
Inner Mongolia	17 489.10	445.65	6 939.90	1 722.13	1 532.99	3 479.63	1 654.56	1 265.06	449.18
Liaoning	39 457.85	1 048.10	22 533.26	3 280.47	3 791.35	4 612.51	1 992.40	1 492.34	707.42
Jilin	10 876.71	643.33	4 252.09	709.69	1 356.97	2 107.69	1 026.93	558.75	221.26
Heilongjiang	9 427.43	25.34	5 240.00	785.96	896.73	1 240.66	848.86	316.09	73.79
Shanghai	25 683.33		25 683.33						
Jiangsu	116 698.41	474.68	89 517.76	7 688.98	3 116.40	7 175.68	3 022.43	3 113.09	2 589.39
Zhejiang	130 285.18	170.86	113 103.22	7 889.33	2 227.35	4 925.92	1 193.00	586.87	188.63
Anhui	36 149.58	1 048.02	19 774.98	5 835.25	3 253.99	2 590.75	2 087.80	1 088.23	470.56
Fujian	50 643.43	1 394.16	33 090.43	4 417.95	2 606.11	5 076.94	1 907.50	1 113.35	1 036.99
Jiangxi	21 260.77	523.17	12 178.39	1 758.53	1 377.53	2 888.89	1 201.85	462.66	869.75
Shandong	107 765.97	1 663.93	65 083.64	11 600.63	6 112.10	11 610.05	6 060.55	3 093.88	2 541.19
Henan	62 692.17	1 249.47	37 076.11	7 471.55	3 583.07	6 800.01	3 293.24	1 496.92	1 721.80
Hubei	43 997.17	1 913.70	22 384.63	5 654.88	2 804.47	6 180.44	3 112.74	1 223.86	722.45
Hunan	58 062.57	1 510.46	27 616.88	9 318.83	5 457.74	8 278.10	2 993.77	1 219.97	1 666.82
Guangdong	105 141.40	724.20	79 425.31	4 416.06	2 770.60	9 065.65	4 847.79	1 927.71	1 964.08

Guangxi	21 494.92	336.43	9 219.01	1 496.20	2 382.50	4 925.75	1 778.34	964.12	392.57
Hainan	1 753.94	154.22	656.26	145.60	134.25	269.68	263.58	78.98	51.37
Chongqing	18 193.00	356.23	10 169.69	4 975.27	466.84	997.88	619.09	202.28	405.72
Sichuan	36 409.81	449.60	18 631.08	5 296.24	2 761.37	4 561.28	2 403.91	1 346.28	960.05
Guizhou	13 802.22	266.79	7 078.40	1 064.85	1 528.21	2 233.24	892.99	527.04	210.70
Yunnan	66 646.15	1 484.31	32 754.07	6 037.24	6 965.36	9 969.84	5 220.67	2 822.89	1 391.77
Tibet	190.36	14.69	62.22	74.15	3.91	12.15	7.76	3.63	11.85
Shaanxi	19 175.74	283.29	8 192.79	3 374.07	2 375.93	2 415.70	1 569.57	704.98	259.41
Gansu	9 239.25	130.85	3 380.14	2 442.40	1 207.12	1 259.06	555.71	225.88	38.09
Qinghai	941.25	8.67	482.65	97.57	109.50	126.04	71.41	26.89	18.52
Ningxia	2 979.25	9.69	1 176.18	527.16	492.50	464.89	201.13	104.78	2.92
Xinjiang	5 365.87	195.70	1 975.55	626.88	681.52	940.52	574.74	305.02	65.94
Seprately-listed cities in State plan	48 305.78	1 348.04	37 658.97	3 317.80	1 555.51	2 109.39	978.68	1 012.71	324.68
Dalian	8 871.43	830.22	4 473.35	1 475.20	563.77	677.58	259.72	474.37	117.22
Qingdao	11 778.28	399.81	7 613.46	1 190.29	625.68	922.03	510.06	371.31	145.64
Ningbo	25 265.70		24 775.51	336.04	25.58	70.18	36.68	13.69	8.02
Xiamen	1 242.09	17.23	615.64	278.36	78.80	154.62	46.12	26.53	24.79
Shenzhen									
Xinjiang Production Corps	1 148.28	100.78	181.01	37.91	261.68	284.98	126.10	126.81	29.01
Eastern part	563 525.92	5 191.49	408 843.63	39 955.03	23 734.31	44 658.64	19 974.36	12 425.94	8 742.52
Central part	293 540.03	7 047.34	157 033.53	40 039.20	23 621.41	34 250.52	17 314.71	7 734.15	6 499.17
Western part	118 547.67	2 581.91	53 997.51	12 061.48	12 742.49	20 066.17	9 508.14	5 358.96	2 231.01

Table 19 Export by TVEs in 2004

Area	Number of TVEs (enterprise)	Year-end employment (person)	Value of goods delivered for export (1 million yuan)			
			Total	Direct export		
					Own export	Earnings
National	154 727	16 123 303	1 693 247.39	1 390 409.34	843 673.72	60 373.95
Beijing	712	140 494	11 129.79	7 865.56	3 277.92	291.40
Tianjin	1 122	228 270	28 842.11	28 842.11	12 691.46	162.70
Hebei	9 444	436 721	33 724.91	23 986.71	17 509.83	205.29
Shanxi	526	155 628	16 067.56	13 839.14	10 228.05	
Inner Mongolia	139	52 503	3 266.52	2 630.67	1 826.78	102.80
Liaoning	7 951	436 411	51 918.72	39 710.79	24 591.26	265.93
Jilin	1 555	27 428	1 586.22	1 131.85	615.42	
Heilongjiang	135	24 122	1 265.87	1 074.98	277.45	2.46
Shanghai	3 513	648 282	218 630.51	191 110.15	49 336.57	4 324.50
Jiangsu	24 368	2 170 666	259 534.76	205 102.56	143 108.84	3 064.17
Zhejiang	38 618	3 139 140	430 045.78	359 978.11	212 458.81	164.03
Anhui	3 371	245 443	12 457.94	7 146.37	4 788.06	727.92
Fujian	9 389	1 193 107	123 361.45	97 994.52	41 698.63	3 360.42
Jiangxi	961	116 926	7 870.69	5 067.40	3 609.89	106.57
Shandong	15 373	2 027 633	195 685.56	149 074.90	106 061.97	5 712.29
Henan	4 807	271 389	14 164.07	9 336.82	6 367.55	124.57
Hubei	760	179 673	11 066.53	8 537.95	6 271.97	376.70
Hunan	1 442	221 520	13 008.66	11 832.25	6 666.34	175.59

Guangdong	26 523	3 885 724	367 629.72	315 850.07	253 443.55	45 982.09
Guangxi	1 422	143 024	5 475.75	4 187.58	2 355.64	65.46
Hainan	15	1 313	172.32	172.32	161.82	6.60
Chongqing	576	124 969	9 015.39	9 015.39		
Sichuan	581	102 145	6 580.80	4 882.95	2 384.01	8.42
Guizhou	159	30 036	3 597.39	1 934.12	750.93	0.10
Yunnan	156	31 774	3 217.63	2 326.36	1 339.64	14.60
Tibet						
Shaanxi	328	26 087	1 440.10	907.37	569.43	44.05
Gansu	616	32 999	1 393.39	1 011.03	484.84	55.04
Qinghai	6	5 472	284.77	284.77	82.40	55.88
Ningxia	143	18 862	1 477.94	1 127.47	823.17	
Xinjiang	16	5 542	297.44	198.70	127.36	0.50
Separately-listed cities in State plan	10 171	1 186 301	166 734.63	145 497.85	84 471.11	262.43
Dalian	1 546	175 190	24 709.99	19 475.86	12 472.34	80.29
Qingdao	2 558	298 104	37 446.42	30 817.70	18 435.48	164.23
Ningbo	5 991	696 976	102 754.01	93 392.22	52 494.44	17.91
Xiamen	74	14 174	1 795.05	1 790.05	1 046.83	
Shenzhen						
Xinjiang Production Corps	2	1 857	29.16	22.02	22.02	
Eastern part	137 013	14 306 448	1 588 279.03	1 310 422.73	797 764.88	58 650.18
Central part	15 042	1 495 330	87 259.48	67 179.74	38 567.44	1 445.90
Western part	2 672	321 525	17 708.88	12 806.87	7 341.40	277.87

Postscript

The preparation of this book lasted for three years, from choosing the subject to the completion of the final version. The authors are all professional workers and researchers involved in the work and study of TVEs for a long time. They are personal witnesses of the process of TVE development from the very beginning. The chapters have been penned by:

Guo Shutian (former Director of the Policy and Law Department of the Ministry of Agriculture) — Section 2 of Chapter 5, Chapter 6, Chapter 11;

Zhang Yi (former Deputy Director of the TVE Bureau of the Ministry of Agriculture, senior economic administrator) — Chapter 1, Chapter 2, Section 3 of Chapter 3, and Chapter 4;

Zhang Tong (senior economic administrator of the Information Center of the Ministry of Agriculture) — Sections 1 and 2 of Chapter 3, and Sections 1 and 3 of Chapter 5;

Chen Fugui (assistant inspector and senior economic administrator, TVE Bureau of the Ministry of Agriculture) — Chapter 7;

Gu Dazhi (assistant inspector and senior economic administrator, TVE Bureau of the Ministry of Agriculture) — Chapter 8;

Zhou Hongda (professor and former Deputy President of the TVE Management Institute of the Ministry of Agriculture) — Chapter 8;

Chen Naixing (researcher of the Institute of Industrial Economy, Chinese Academy of Social Sciences) — Chapter 9;

Zhou Handa (senior economic administrator, TVE Bureau of the Ministry of Agriculture) — Chapter 10; and

Li Chenggui (PhD and Director of Rural Policy Research Center, Research Institute of Rural Development, Chinese Academy of Social Sciences) — Chapter 12.

After the completion of the first draft, those taking part in revising and finalizing the script, in addition to the editors of this book, were Niu Ruofeng (researcher and former Director of the Institute of Agricultural Economy, Chinese Academy of Agricultural Sciences), Hong Wujin (professor of the Department of Economic Management, Chinese University of Agriculture), Xu Renjun (senior economic administrator and former Director of the Institute of Land Reclamation Economy of China), Chen Naixing and Li Chenggui. Huang Peimin checked all the statistics and data in the book.

The TVE Bureau of the Ministry of Agriculture and *China Township Enterprises News* provided the statistics and photographs. The TVE Bureau and the TVE Development Center of the Ministry of Agriculture, and the China Foundation of Science and Education financed the publication of this book. The Chinese Agriculture Press and the Foreign Languages Press did much work for the publication of the book, in both Chinese and English. Xu Xiaoping of the Bureau of Senior Cadres of the Ministry of Agriculture did valuable work in the statistics and data updating and in the coordination of the editing, translation and publication of the book. To all of them, we extend our heart-felt thanks.

The Editors
August 2005

Index

图书在版编目(CIP)数据

中国的乡镇企业 / 何康主编. —北京：外文出版社，2005

ISBN 7-119-04184-3

I. 中... II. 何... III. 乡镇企业—企业经济—中国—英文

IV. F276.3

中国版本图书馆 CIP 数据核字（2005）第 092343 号

摄　　影　乔仲林　郁隽民　王苗等

英文编辑　郁　苓　Paul White

封面设计　蔡　荣

电子排版　李　耀

印刷监制　张国祥

中国的乡镇企业

主　编　何　康

副主编　郭书田　马杰三

撰　稿　郭书田　张　毅　张　桐　张庆年

陈福桂　顾大智　周宏大　郁隽民

陈乃醒　周涵达　李成贵

翻　译　刘炳文　金绍卿

外文出版社出版

（中国北京百万庄路 24 号　邮编　100037）

外文出版社网址：http://www.flp.com.cn

外文出版社电子信箱：info@flp.com.cn

sales@flp.com.cn

三河市汇鑫印务有限公司印刷

中国国际图书贸易总公司发行

（中国北京车公庄西路 35 号）

北京邮政信箱第 399 号　邮政编码 100044

2006 年（小 16 开）第 1 版第 1 次印刷

（英）

ISBN 7-119-04184-3（外）

07000（精）

4-E-3686S